Children's
Literature
Review

Guide to Gale Literary Criticism Series

For criticism on	Consult these Gale series
Authors now living or who died after December 31, 1999	*CONTEMPORARY LITERARY CRITICISM (CLC)*
Authors who died between 1900 and 1999	*TWENTIETH-CENTURY LITERARY CRITICISM (TCLC)*
Authors who died between 1800 and 1899	*NINETEENTH-CENTURY LITERATURE CRITICISM (NCLC)*
Authors who died between 1400 and 1799	*LITERATURE CRITICISM FROM 1400 TO 1800 (LC)* *SHAKESPEAREAN CRITICISM (SC)*
Authors who died before 1400	*CLASSICAL AND MEDIEVAL LITERATURE CRITICISM (CMLC)*
Authors of books for children and young adults	*CHILDREN'S LITERATURE REVIEW (CLR)*
Dramatists	*DRAMA CRITICISM (DC)*
Poets	*POETRY CRITICISM (PC)*
Short story writers	*SHORT STORY CRITICISM (SSC)*
Black writers of the past two hundred years	*BLACK LITERATURE CRITICISM (BLC)* *BLACK LITERATURE CRITICISM SUPPLEMENT (BLCS)*
Hispanic writers of the late nineteenth and twentieth centuries	*HISPANIC LITERATURE CRITICISM (HLC)* *HISPANIC LITERATURE CRITICISM SUPPLEMENT (HLCS)*
Native North American writers and orators of the eighteenth, nineteenth, and twentieth centuries	*NATIVE NORTH AMERICAN LITERATURE (NNAL)*
Major authors from the Renaissance to the present	*WORLD LITERATURE CRITICISM, 1500 TO THE PRESENT (WLC)* *WORLD LITERATURE CRITICISM SUPPLEMENT (WLCS)*

ISSN 0362-4145

volume 69

Children's Literature Review

Excerpts from Reviews,
Criticism, and Commentary
on Books for Children
and Young People

Jennifer Baise
Editor

Thomas Ligotti
Associate Editor

Detroit
New York
San Francisco
London
Boston
Woodbridge, CT

STAFF

Lynn M. Spampinato, Janet Witalec, *Managing Editors, Literature Product*
Kathy D. Darrow, Ellen McGeagh, *Product Liaisons*
Jennifer Baise, *Editor*
Mark W. Scott, *Publisher, Literature Product*

Rebecca J. Blanchard, Motoko F. Huthwaite, Thomas Ligotti, *Associate Editors*
Jenny Cromie, Mary Ruby, *Technical Training Specialists*
Deborah J. Morad, Joyce Nakamura, Kathleen Lopez Nolan, *Managing Editors*
Susan M. Trosky, *Director, Literature Content*

Maria L. Franklin, *Permissions Manager*
Margaret Chamberlain, *Permissions Specialist*

Victoria B. Cariappa, *Research Manager*
Tracie A. Richardson, *Project Coordinator*
Sarah Genik, Ron Morelli, Tamara C. Nott, *Research Associates*
Nicodemus Ford, *Research Assistant*

Dorothy Maki, *Manufacturing Manager*
Stacy L. Melson, *Buyer*

Mary Beth Trimper, *Manager, Composition and Electronic Prepress*
Carolyn Roney, *Composition Specialist*

Theresa Rocklin, *Manager, Technical Support Services*
Ryan Cartmill, *Programmer/Analyst*

Michael Logusz, *Graphic Artist*
Randy Bassett, *Imaging Supervisor*
Robert Duncan, Dan Newell, *Imaging Specialists*
Pamela A. Reed, *Imaging Coordinator*
Kelly A. Quin, *Editor, Image and Multimedia Content*

Library of Congress Catalog Card Number 76-643301
ISBN 0-7876-4575-3
ISSN 0362-4145
Printed in the United States of America

10 9 8 7 6 5 4 3 2 1

Contents

Preface vii

Acknowledgments xi

Preface

Literature for children and young adults has evolved into both a respected branch of creative writing and a successful industry. Currently, books for young readers are considered among the most popular segments of publishing. Criticism of juvenile literature is instrumental in recording the literary or artistic development of the creators of children's books as well as the trends and controversies that result from changing values or attitudes about young people and their literature. Designed to provide a permanent, accessible record of this ongoing scholarship, *Children's Literature Review* (*CLR*) presents parents, teachers, and librarians—those responsible for bringing children and books together—with the opportunity to make informed choices when selecting reading materials for the young. In addition, *CLR* provides researchers of children's literature with easy access to a wide variety of critical information from English-language sources in the field. Users will find balanced overviews of the careers of the authors and illustrators of the books that children and young adults are reading; these entries, which contain excerpts from published criticism in books and periodicals, assist users by sparking ideas for papers and assignments and suggesting supplementary and classroom reading. Ann L. Kalkhoff, president and editor of *Children's Book Review Service Inc.,* writes that "*CLR* has filled a gap in the field of children's books, and it is one series that will never lose its validity or importance."

Scope of the Series

Each volume of *CLR* profiles the careers of a selection of authors and illustrators of books for children and young adults from preschool through high school. Author lists in each volume reflect:

- an international scope

- representation of authors of all eras

- the variety of genres covered by children's and/or YA literature: picture books, fiction, nonfiction, poetry, folklore, and drama

Although the focus of the series is on authors new to *CLR,* entries will be updated as the need arises.

Organization of the Book

A *CLR* entry consists of the following elements:

- The **Author Heading** consists of the author's name followed by birth and death dates. The portion of the name outside the parentheses denotes the form under which the author is most frequently published. If the author wrote consistently under a pseudonym, the pseudonym will be listed in the author heading and the author's actual name given in parentheses on the first line of the biographical and critical information. Also located here are any name variations under which an author wrote, including transliterated forms for authors whose native languages use non-roman alphabets. Uncertain birth or death dates are indicated by question marks.

- A **Portrait of the Author** is included when available.

- The **Author Introduction** contains information designed to introduce an author to *CLR* users by presenting an overview of the author's themes and styles, biographical facts that relate to the author's literary career or critical responses to the author's works, and information about major awards and prizes the author has received. The introduction begins by identifying the nationality of the author and by listing genres in which s/he has written for children and young adults. Introductions also list a group of representative titles for which the author or illustrator being profiled is best known; this section, which begins with the words "major works include," follows the genre line of the introduction. For seminal figures, a listing of major works about the author follows when appropriate, high-lighting important biographies about the author or illustrator that are not excerpted in the entry. The centered head-ing "Introduction" announces the body of the text.

■ **Criticism** is located in three sections: **Author Commentary** (when available) **General Commentary** (when avail-able), and **Title Commentary** (commentary on specific titles).

The **Author Commentary** presents background material written by the author or by an interviewer. This commentary may cover a specific work or several works. Author commentary on more than one work appears after the author intro-duction, while commentary on an individual book follows the title entry heading.

The **General Commentary** consists of critical excerpts that consider more than one work by the author or illustrator being profiled. General commentary is preceded by the critic's name in boldface type or, in the case of unsigned criti-cism, by the title of the journal. *CLR* also features entries that emphasize general criticism on the oeuvre of an author or illustrator. When appropriate, a selection of reviews is included to supplement the general commentary.

The **Title Commentary** begins with the title entry headings, which precede the criticism on a title and cite publication information on the work being reviewed. Title headings list the title of the work as it appeared in its first English-language edition. The first English-language publication date of each work (unless otherwise noted) is listed in paren-theses following the title. Differing U.S. and British titles follow the publication date within parentheses. When a work is written by an individual other than the one being profiled, as is the case when illustrators are featured, the parentheti-cal material following the title cites the author of the work before listing its publication date.

Entries in each title commentary section consist of critical excerpts on the author's individual works, arranged chronologi-cally by publication date. The entries generally contain two to seven reviews per title, depending on the stature of the book and the amount of criticism it has generated. The editors select titles that reflect the entire scope of the author's literary contribution, covering each genre and subject. An effort is made to reprint criticism that represents the full range of each title's reception, from the year of its initial publication to current assessments. Thus, the reader is provided with a record of the author's critical history. Publication information (such as publisher names and book prices) and parenthetical numerical references (such as footnotes or page and line references to specific editions of works) have been deleted at the discretion of the editors to provide smoother reading of the text.

■ A complete **Bibliographical Citation** of the original essay or book precedes each piece of criticism.

■ Selected excerpts are preceded by brief **Annotations,** which provide information on the critic or work of criticism to enhance the reader's understanding of the excerpt.

■ Numerous **Illustrations** are featured in *CLR*. For entries on illustrators, an effort has been made to include illustra-tions that reflect the characteristics discussed in the criticism. Entries on authors who do not illustrate their own works my include photographs and other illustrative material pertinent to their careers.

Special Features: Entries on Illustrators

Entries on authors who are also illustrators will occasionally feature commentary on selected works illustrated but not writ-ten by the author being profiled. These works are strongly associated with the illustrator and have received critical acclaim for their art. By including critical comment on works of this type, the editors wish to provide a more complete representa-tion of the artist's career. Criticism on these works has been chosen to stress artistic, rather than literary, contributions. Title entry headings for works illustrated by the author being profiled are arranged chronologically within the entry by date of publication and include notes identifying the author of the illustrated work. In order to provide easier access for users, all titles illustrated by the subject of the entry are boldfaced.

CLR also includes entries on prominent illustrators who have contributed to the field of children's literature. These entries are designed to represent the development of the illustrator as an artist rather than as a literary stylist. The illustrator's sec-tion is organized like that of an author, with two exceptions: the introduction presents an overview of the illustrator's styles and techniques rather than outlining his or her literary background, and the commentary written by the illustrator on his or her works is called "Illustrator's Commentary" rather than "Author's Commentary." All titles of books containing illustrations by the artist being profiled are highlighted in boldface type.

Indexes

A **Cumulative Author Index** lists all of the authors who have appeared in *CLR* with cross-references to the biographical, autobiographical, and literary criticism series published by the Gale Group. A complete list of these sources is found facing the first page of the Author Index. The index also includes birth and death dates and cross-references between pseudonyms and actual names.

A **Cumulative Nationality Index** lists all authors featured in *CLR* by nationality, followed by the number of the *CLR* volume in which their entry appears.

A **Cumulative Title Index** lists all author titles covered in *CLR*. Each title is followed by the author's name and corresponding volume and page numbers where commentary on the work is located.

Citing *Children's Literature Review*

When writing papers, students who quote directly from any volume in the Literary Criticism Series may use the following general format to footnote reprinted criticism. The first example pertains to material drawn from periodicals, the second to material reprinted from books.

Cynthia Zarin, "It's Easy Being Green," *The New York Times Book Review* (November 14, 1993): 48; excerpted and reprinted in *Children's Literature Review,* vol. 58, ed. Deborah J. Morad (Farmington Hills, Mich: The Gale Group, 2000), 57.

Paul Walker, *Speaking of Science Fiction: The Paul Walker Interviews,* (Luna Publications, 1978), 108-20; excerpted and reprinted in *Children's Literature Review,* vol. 58, ed. Deborah J. Morad (Farmington Hills, Mich: The Gale Group, 2000), 3-8.

Suggestions are Welcome

In response to various suggestions, several features have been added to *CLR* since the beginning of the series, including author entries on retellers of traditional literature as well as those who have been the first to record oral tales and other folklore; entries on prominent illustrators featuring commentary on their styles and techniques; entries on authors whose works are considered controversial; occasional entries devoted to criticism on a single work or a series of works; sections in author introductions that list major works by and about the author or illustrator being profiled; explanatory notes that provide information on the critic or work of criticism to enhance the usefulness of the excerpt; more extensive illustrative material, such as holographs of manuscript pages and photographs of people and places pertinent to the careers of the authors and artists; a cumulative nationality index for easy access to authors by nationality; and occasional guest essays written specifically for *CLR* by prominent critics on subjects of their choice.

Readers who wish to suggest new features, topics, or authors to appear in future volumes, or who have other suggestions or comments are cordially invited to call, write, or fax the Managing Editor:

Managing Editor, Literary Criticism Series
The Gale Group
27500 Drake Road
Farmington Hills, MI 48331-3535
1-800-347-4253 (GALE)
Fax: 248-699-8054

Acknowledgments

The editors wish to thank the copyright holders of the excerpted criticism included in this volume and the permissions managers of many book and magazine publishing companies for assisting us in securing reproduction rights. We are also grateful to the staffs of the Detroit Public Library, the Library of Congress, the University of Detroit Mercy Library, Wayne State University Purdy/Kresge Library Complex, and the University of Michigan Libraries for making their resources available to us. Following is a list of the copyright holders who have granted us permission to reproduce material in this volume of *CLR*. Every effort has been made to trace copyright, but if omissions have been made, please let us know.

COPYRIGHTED EXCERPTS IN *CLR*, VOLUME 69, WERE REPRODUCED FROM THE FOLLOWING PERIODICALS:

The ALAN Review, v. 25, Spring, 1998. Reproduced by permission.—*American Book Review,* v. 10, May-June, 1988. Reproduced by permission.—*Book Report,* v. 5, no. 2, September-October, 1986; v. 12, no. 4, January-February, 1994. Copyright © 1986, 1994 by Linworth Publishing, Inc., Worthington, Ohio. Both reproduced by permission.—*Book World—The Washington Post,* v. 17, November 8, 1987. © 1987, *The Washington Post.* Reproduced by permission./v. 16, April 27, 1986; v. 17, November 8, 1987. © 1986, 1987, Washington Post Book World Service/Washington Post Writers Group. Reproduced by permission of the authors.—*Booklist,* v. 64, January 15, 1968; v. 77, May 15, 1981; v. 82, February 1, 1986; v. 83, August, 1987; v. 84, October 1, 1987; v. 84, December 1, 1987; v. 84, February 15, 1988; v. 85, June 1, 1989; v. 86, September 1, 1989; v. 86, March 1, 1990; v. 87, October 15, 1990; v. 87, August, 1991; v. 88, September 1, 1991; v. 88, November 15, 1991; v. 89, May 1, 1993; v. 89, June 1, 1993; v. 90, May 1, 1994; v. 91, April 15, 1995; v. 92, September 1, 1995; v. 92, March 15, 1996; v. 93, April 1, 1997; v. 94, November 15, 1997; v. 94, February 1, 1998; v. 95, January 1, 1999; v. 95, July, 1999; v. 96, November 15, 1999; v. 96, January 1 & 15, 2000. Copyright © 1968, 1981, 1986, 1987, 1988, 1989, 1990, 1991, 1993, 1994, 1995, 1996, 1997, 1998, 1999, 2000 by the American Library Association. All reproduced by permission.—*Books for Keeps,* n. 54, January, 1989; n. 83, November, 1993. © School Bookshop Association 1989, 1993. Both reproduced by permission.—*Books Magazine,* v. 12, Summer, 1998. Reproduced by permission.—*Bulletin of the Center for Children's Books,* v. 21, May, 1968; v. 38, April, 1985; v. 39, January, 1986; v. 39, March, 1986; v. 40, November, 1986; v. 40, July, 1987; v. 41, October, 1987; v. 41, February, 1988; v. 42, September, 1988; v. 42, March, 1989; v. 44, September, 1990; v. 44, November, 1990; v. 45, November, 1991; v. 46, December, 1992; v. 47, November, 1993; v. 48, June, 1995; v. 49, November, 1995; v. 50, September, 1996; v. 50, March, 1997; v. 50, June, 1997; v. 52, February, 1999. Copyright © 1968, 1985, 1986, 1987, 1988, 1989, 1990, 1991, 1992, 1993, 1995, 1996, 1997, 1999 by The Board of Trustees of the University of Illinois. All reproduced by permission.—*Children's Book Review Service,* v. 19, November, 1990. Copyright 1990 Children's Book Review Service, Inc. Reproduced by permission.—*Children's Literature,* v. 8, 1979; v. 21, 1993. © 1979, 1993 The Children's Literature Foundation, Inc. Both reproduced by permission.—*Children's Literature Association Quarterly,* v. 11, 1986. Reproduced by permission.—*Children's Literature in Education,* v. 20, 1976; v. 19, 1988. © 1976, 1988 Agathon Press, Inc. Both reproduced by permission of the publisher and the authors./v. 22, 1991. © 1991 Human Sciences Press, Inc. Reproduced by permission of the publisher and the author.—*Critique,* v. 26, Fall, 1984; v. 28, Fall, 1986; v. 29, Spring, 1988; v. 31, Fall, 1989. Copyright © 1984, 1986, 1988, 1989 Helen Dwight Reid Educational Foundation. All reproduced with permission of the Helen Dwight Reid Educational Foundation, published by Heldref Publications, 1319 18th Street, NW, Washington, DC 20036-1802.—*The Five Owls,* v. 5, November-December, 1990; v. 8, November, 1993; v. 10, November-December, 1995; v. 10, January-February, 1996. Copyright © 1990, 1993, 1995, 1996 by the Trustees of Hamline University. All reproduced by permission.—*The Horn Book Magazine,* v. LVI, December, 1980; v. LXI, July, 1985; v. LXIII, March, 1987; v. LXIII, May, 1987; v. LXIV, January-February, 1988; v. LXV, May-June, 1989; v. LXVI, January-February, 1990; v. LXVI, March-April, 1990; v. LXVI, May-June, 1990; v. LXVII, May-June, 1991; v. LXVII, November-December, 1991; v. LXIX, January-February, 1993; v. LXIX, September-October, 1993; v. LXIX, November-December, 1993; v. LXXI, November-December, 1995; v. LXXII, March-April, 1996; v. LXXVI, January, 2000. Copyright, 1980, 1985, 1987, 1988, 1989, 1990, 1991, 1993, 1995, 1996, 2000, by The Horn Book, Inc., 11 Beacon St., Suite 1000, Boston, MA 02108. All rights reserved. All reproduced by permission.—*Journal of Youth Services in Libraries,* v. 10, Winter, 1997. Reproduced by permission.—*Kirkus Reviews,* v. XXXV, September 15, 1967; v. LV, September 1, 1987; v. LVI, July 1, 1988; v. LVII, March 1, 1989; v. LVIII, September 15, 1990; v. LIX, August 15, 1991; v. LXVI, June 15, 1994; v. LXIII, October 15, 1995; v. LXIV, August 1, 1996; v. LXV, March 15, 1997; v. LXVI, January 1, 1998. Copyright © 1967, 1987, 1988, 1989, 1990, 1991, 1994, 1995, 1996, 1997, 1998 The Kirkus Service, Inc. All rights reserved. All reproduced by permission of the publisher, Kirkus Reviews and Kirkus Associates, L.P.—*Kliatt Young Adult Paperback Book Guide,* v. 17, January, 1983; v. 18, September, 1984. Copy-

COPYRIGHTED EXCERPTS IN *CLR*, VOLUME 69, WERE REPRODUCED FROM THE FOLLOWING BOOKS:

Judy Blume
1938-

American novelist.

Major works include *Are You There, God? It's Me, Margaret* (1970), *Tales of a Fourth-Grade Nothing* (1972), *Forever* (1975), *Superfudge* (1980), *Tiger Eyes* (1981), *Just as Long as We're Together* (1987), *Summer Sisters* (1998).

Major works about the author include *Judy Blume's Story* (Betsey Lee, 1981), *Presenting Judy Blume* (Maryann N. Weidt, 1989), *Judy Blume* (Jill C. Wheeler, 1996).

For further information on Blume's life and works, see *CLR,* Volumes 2 and 15.

INTRODUCTION

Perhaps the most popular contemporary author of works for upper elementary to junior high school readers, Blume is the creator of frank, often humorous stories which focus on the emotional and social concerns of suburban adolescents. Recognized as a pioneer for her candid treatment of such topics as menstruation, masturbation, and premarital sex, she is also considered a controversial and provocative figure by those critics and librarians who object to her works as overly explicit and harmful, and denounce her for not taking a moral stand on the actions of her protagonists. However, Blume has won the devotion of an extensive and loyal youthful following, as evidenced by the record sales of her books and the thousands of letters she receives regularly from children; as critic Naomi Decter observes, "there is, indeed, scarcely a literate girl of novel-reading age who has not read one or more Blume books." Blume deals with issues that are significant to the young, such as friction between parents and children, friendship, peer group approval, divorce, social ostracism, religion, and death, as well as sexuality. Combining intimate first-person narratives with amusing dialogue supplemented by familiar everyday details, her books reveal Blume's East Coast upper-middle-class Jewish background while describing the anxieties of her protagonists, characteristically female preteens and teenagers who encounter problematic situations and survive them. Despite the

fact that she often ends her works on a note of uncertainty, Blume consistently underscores her books with optimism about the successful adaptability of her characters.

BIOGRAPHICAL INFORMATION

The daughter of Rudolph, a dentist, and Esther (Rosenfeld) Sussman, Blume was born February 12, 1938, in Elizabeth, New Jersey. A good student and an avid reader, Blume was educated in public schools and graduated from New York University with a bachelor's degree in 1961. She married attorney John M. Blume in August 1959, and they had two children. The Blumes divorced in 1975. She has since remarried and lives on the East Coast with her husband, the nonfiction writer George Cooper.

Blume began writing when her own two children were preschoolers and continued submitting works in response to numerous rejections from publishers. Her perseverance paid off with the publication of *The One in the Middle Is the Green Kangaroo* in 1969, and she continued working without the benefit of a literary agent through two additional works. Throughout her career Blume as been the focus of strong opinions, as young readers praised her works while some adults attempted to censor them. In interviews Blume has related that she was inspired to write *Forever*, one of her most controversial stories for adolescents during a period when her own daughter was reading books about teenagers whose sexual activity invariably led to negative consequences. Blume believed that there ought to be more sensitive portrayals of the difficult decisions facing young people. Many readers have agreed with her, for, according to Blume's official web page, more than seventy million copies of her books have been sold, and her work has been translated into more than twenty languages.

MAJOR WORKS

Although Blume is best known for her fiction for adolescents, she began her career by writing books for younger children, an audience she still continues to address; *Tales of a Fourth-Grade Nothing* and *Superfudge*, two entertaining tales about ten-year-old Peter and his incorrigible baby brother, Fudge, are especially popular with readers. *Are You There, God? It's Me, Margaret* depicts eleven-year-old Margaret's apprehensions about starting her period and choosing her own religion. At the time of the book's publication, Blume was praised for her warm and funny re-creation of childhood feelings and conversation but was criticized for her forthright references to the human body and its processes. *Margaret* is now considered a groundbreaking work due to the candor with which Blume presents previously taboo subjects. *Forever*, in which Blume relates the particulars of her eighteen-year-old heroine's initial sexual experience, created an even greater furor. Despite the fact that it was published as an adult book, protestors pointed out that Blume's name and characteristically uncomplicated prose style attracted a vulnerable preteen audience who could be influenced by the intimate details of the novel. In *Tiger Eyes*, Blume relates the story of how fifteen-year-old Davey adjusts to her father's murder. Hailed by many critics as Blume's finest work for her successful handling of a complex plot, *Tiger Eyes* includes such issues as alcoholism, suicide, anti-intellectualism, and violence. *Letters to Judy* (1986) was promoted as a response to the voluminous amount of mail that Blume receives from her readers. Selecting a number of representative letters to reprint anonymously with accompanying com-

ments, she created the book for a dual purpose: to enable children to see that they are not alone and to make parents more aware of their children's needs.

Reviewers commend Blume for her honesty, warmth, compassion, and wit, praising her lack of condescension, superior observation of childhood, and strong appeal to children. Critics are strongly divided as to the success of Blume's plots, characterization, writing style, and nonjudgmental approach; they object to her uninhibited language and permissive attitude toward sexuality, and complain that her cavalier treatment of love, death, pain, and religion trivializes young people and the literature written for them. However, most commentators agree that Blume accurately captures the speech, emotions, and private thoughts of children, for whom she has made reading both easy and enjoyable.

AWARDS

Blume has won more than ninety national and international child-selected awards for her various works. Among them are: *New York Times* best books for children list, 1970, Nene Award, 1975, Young Hoosier Book Award, 1976, and North Dakota Children's Choice Award, 1979, all for *Are You There God? It's Me, Margaret*; Charlie May Swann Children's Book Award, 1972, Young Readers Choice Award, Pacific Northwest Library Association, and Sequoyah Children's Book Award of Oklahoma, both 1975, Massachusetts Children's Book Award, Georgia Children's Book Award, and South Carolina Children's Book Award, all 1977, Rhode Island Library Association Award, 1978, North Dakota Children's Choice Award, and West Australian Young Readers' Book Award, both 1980, United States Army in Europe Kinderbuch Award, and Great Stone Face Award, New Hampshire Library Council, both 1981, Young Teens Award, 1991, all for *Tales of a Fourth Grade Nothing*; Arizona Young Readers Award, and Young Readers Choice Award, Pacific Northwest Library Association, both 1977, and North Dakota Children's Choice Award, 1983, all for *Blubber*; South Carolina Children's Book Award, 1978, for *Otherwise Known as Sheila the Great*; Texas Bluebonnet List, 1980, Michigan Young Reader's Award, and International Reading Association Children's Choice Award, both 1981, First Buckeye Children's Book Award, Nene Award, Sue Hefley Book Award, Louisiana Association of School Libraries, United States Army in Europe Kinderbuch Award, West Australian Young Readers' Book Award, North Dakota Children's Choice Award, Colorado Children's Book Award,

Georgia Children's Book Award, Tennessee Children's Choice Book Award, and Utah Children's Book Award, all 1982, Northern Territory Young Readers' Book Award, Young Readers Choice Award, Pacific Northwest Library Association, Garden State Children's Book Award, Iowa Children's Choice Award, Arizona Young Readers' Award, California Young Readers' Medal, and Young Hoosier Book Award, all 1983, all for *Superfudge,* which also won a Young Teens honor in 1990; American Book Award nomination, Dorothy Canfield Fisher Children's Book Award, Buckeye Children's Book Award, and California Young Readers Medal, all 1983, all for *Tiger Eyes.*

Golden Archer Award, 1974; Texas Children's Choice Awards, First Place, 1979, 1980, 1981, 1982, 1983, 1984, 1985, 1986, 1987, 1988, 1989, 1990, 1991; Today's Woman Award, 1981; Eleanor Roosevelt Humanitarian Award, Milner Award, and Jeremiah Ludington Memorial Award, all 1983; Carl Sandburg Freedom to Read Award, Chicago Public Library, 1984; Civil Liberties Award, Atlanta American Civil Liberties Union, and John Rock Award, Center for Population Options, Los Angeles, both 1986; D.H.L., Kean College, 1987; South Australian Youth Media Award for Best Author, South Australian Association for Media Education, 1988. In 1996 Blume was named a Distinguished Alumna of New York University and was awarded the Margaret A. Edwards Award for Lifetime Achievement from the ALA.

AUTHOR COMMENTARY

Judy Blume and Roger Sutton

SOURCE: An interview in *School Library Journal,* Vol. 42, No. 6, June, 1996, pp. 25-7.

[Blume]: As I tell the kids, you can ask me anything.

[Sutton]: *Well, I was told I had to ask you whether you married the man on the motorcycle* [*in* **Wifey**].

No way. That came from a little story I heard from a friend of my husband's who was picked up by the police just after he got out of the army. A sheet was found with his military ID on it and they brought him in for questioning. A woman had seen some guy drive up on a motorcycle, throw off a bedsheet, masturbate, and then drive away. It was 20 years later that I used that [incident as a catalyst for sexual awakening] in **Wifey.**

I was working in a public library when **Wifey** *came out, and the kids were coming in looking for "Judy Blume's new book." We had 10-year-olds asking for it.*

Oh, well, I hope they stopped reading soon. It's like **Forever.** I've had letters from kids as young as 10 who said, "I have read this book and I understood everything in it and everything about it." When kids at a book signing ask me, "How old do I have to be before I read **Forever**?," I say, "I think you should be at least 12 and then you should have somebody to talk to about it." I think you get more out of a book when you are closer to the protagonist's age. I've also had letters from kids that said, "I started **Forever** and I don't think I'm ready. So I'm going to wait."

Would you keep younger kids away from **Forever,** *if you could?*

No, but I was bothered when I saw it—more than once—on a bookstore shelf right next to **Tales of a Fourth Grade Nothing.** I said to the manager, "This makes me uncomfortable. This book doesn't really belong here. It's a whole other group of readers, and I would feel much better if you had it with the mass market paperbacks." She said, "Oh, we did, but it just wasn't moving, and as soon as we put it in the children's section it flew off the shelf."

The hardcover edition of **Forever** *states very prominently on both jacket flaps that the book is "Judy Blume's first novel for adults."*

It wasn't. Bradbury Press did that to protect themselves. It was a shock to me when I saw on the inside flap, "her first book for adults," because it wasn't. I never said it was. I didn't want anybody to be told that it was. But Bradbury was young then. [Bradbury's founders] Dick Jackson, [the late] Bob Verrone, and I were all young. I think that they just wanted to say that so they could say to angry parents or teachers or whomever, "But look, this says clearly. . . ." When **Wifey** was published, I insisted it say right on the cover *An Adult Novel* because it is. **Forever** isn't. There really weren't any YA books at that time.

Well . . .

There were no YA books. This was 1975. When did YA books happen?

Well, there was The Outsiders *in '67,* The Pigman *in '68.*

But they weren't called YA books. We were writting for "young people." *Forever* was for an older audience than the younger kids I had written for. I wrote it because my daughter Randy was then 14. It's the only book of mine that came that way. She was reading what a librarian friend called the "pregnant books." They were books about teenaged girls pregnant. And the girls had sex because there was something terribly wrong in their lives. They did this terrible thing with a guy not because it felt good, not because they were turned on, not because they loved him, but because something bad was happening in their family. And when they inevitably got pregnant, the pregnancy was linked with punishment. Always, If you had sex you were going to be punished. Now the guys, they were never punished, only the girls.

Randy was reading a lot of these, and she said to me, "Couldn't there ever be a book about two really nice kids in high school who love each other and they do it and nothing bad happens?" That's how I got the idea for *Forever.* I wrote it because it really bothered me that the message being sent to kids—and primarily to young women—was that sex was being linked with punishment, rather than with pleasure and responsibility. It's the only book I've written because somebody asked me to, and I'm not sure that's how the best books are written. I had a letter last week from the director of a national Down Syndrome organization, and she asked me to write a book for kids who may meet Down Syndrome kids in their classes. I wrote back the letter that I always do, saying that the best books come from someplace deep inside.

A good writer doesn't write what somebody else needs to read.

Sometimes it turns out to be what somebody else needs to read, but you don't write it for that reason. When Marilee Foglesong, chair of the Edwards Award committee, called to tell me I had won, she said "We're giving you this award for *Forever.*" I said, "Really? That's not my best book. For the same age group, I think *Tiger Eyes* (S. & S., 1982) is a much better book." And she said, "Oh." So then I said, "But, you know, that's very nice if you want to do this."

You know this was a very controversial award.

I'm sure it was. It's been 26 years since I published *Are You There God? It's Me, Margaret,* and I've never had an award from the library world. I've enjoyed that. I never felt accepted and that was ok. The kids like the books and I don't even remember how *SLJ* reviewed *Forever.*

They hated it, but noted—presciently—that it would be very popular.

Did they?

I also had a student in a YA lit class who felt that **Forever** *should be pulled from the shelves because Katherine and Michael don't practice safe sex.*

In all the new reprints of the book there is a letter from me about sexual responsibility, which has a different meaning in 1996 than it did in 1975.

The student said that **Forever** *should be removed from libraries—although she liked the book a lot—because it is presented as contemporary fiction yet does not address AIDS, not to mention the more complicated understanding we have of the Pill's benefits and drawbacks. Can you expect fiction to fulfill the need for nonfiction information about sex?*

No. My very dear friend Leanne Katz, who heads the National Coalition Against Censorship, has had this very discussion with me. Sometimes I feel, Oh dear, is it responsible, is it okay to have *Forever* in the library? She really yells at me. *Forever* is about people. It is about feelings. It is not a sex manual. Does it mean we shouldn't be allowed to read [John O'Hara's] *A Rage to Live* or [Saul Bellow's] *The Adventures of Augie March*—two of the "forbiddens" from my youth—because they don't address AIDS? Just because the rules have changed? You can't do that.

I wonder how today's kids read **Forever.**

I think they read it as an absolutely contemporary novel.

Do they wonder why the characters don't practice safe sex?

You know, there are still so many kids who are not practicing safe sex at all, who feel invulnerable. And so many girls who still say, "He doesn't like condoms, and he says if I won't do it without one then he'll find someone who will." I say to them, "Good, tell him to find somebody else. You tell him that if he's not willing to use a condom, you're not willing to have sex." Of course I couldn't write the same book today. I'm different. The times are different. *Forever* was published in 1975, and obviously I have to look at where I was, too. I was on the brink of divorce. I had never rebelled as a teenager. I was a very good girl, married very young, and felt that at 35, 36, which was the age I was when writing *For-*

ever, that I had missed out on a lot. And yet, while writing the book, I didn't identify so much with Katherine as I did with her mother.

She's a really good mother.

She's a nice mother—she's a librarian.

I don't think **Forever** *is so much a sex manual as it is an introduction to what having sex "is like."*

If you're lucky. When that book came out 20 years ago, I really got it for allowing a young woman to enjoy her first sexual experiences. I can remember an angry letter from a librarian who said, "How dare you? Women don't enjoy their first sexual experiences. It takes years and years." Well, not always. Granted, this girl has a very gentle and loving boyfriend, and not everyone is so lucky.

You know, people said you broke a taboo in **Forever** *and changed the rules for YA literature, doing for adolescent sex what Robert Cormier did for down-beat endings in* The Chocolate War. *Yet YA books, by and large, still have optimistic conclusions, and I think I could count on one hand those that feature on-the-page sex the way* **Forever** *does.*

I don't think you'd call *Forever* erotic.

If I were 16, I might. What about those ellipses, starting right in the title? I think that has something to do with it.

That's just the way I write. That's just me.

There's hardly a sentence in there that comes to a full stop.

That's how people talk. Maybe I do it too much. Even when I write letters, it's always dot, dot, dot. People rarely talk in full sentences.

I think it gives an atmosphere of expectancy to the book. There's more to come, there's something left out, there's something not on the page. It sort of heats the book up because you keep thinking. What would happen if that sentence got finished?

It would be nice if I could tell you I did it on purpose, but I didn't. When I read things that other people have written about my books, I'm always surprised. I wonder, Is that what I meant? Or, oh, *that's* what I meant. I never analyze. Norma Klein, a wonderful friend and writer, once decided that book by book, she was going to analyze what I wrote. She started with *Forever* and sent me pages on it. It was

a very generous and loving analysis, and I wrote back and said, "Don't ever do this to me again. If you want to analyze my books, fine, but don't send the results to me." I don't want to know. It's too scary. We're all scared enough, those of us who write: will it ever happen again? Will I get another idea? How did I do this? When I pick up a book of mine that I wrote even a few years ago, I wonder, How did I do this? I think the more you understand something the worse off you are. It's taken me 20 years to figure this out. I suppose everybody else already knows this, but it's been news to me. When you're writing, you're operating out of some different part of the brain. When it's happening, you're not aware of it, you don't know where what you write is coming from. And when you read it later, you think, Wow. I did that? It's like a surprise.

Judy Blume

SOURCE: Margaret A. Edwards Award Acceptance Speech, in *Journal of Youth Services in Libraries,* Vol. 10, No. 2, Winter, 1997, pp. 148-56.

I'm as surprised by this honor as many of you. In fact, I was so totally flabbergasted when Marilee reached me in January at my mother-in-law's apartment in Baltimore, I didn't get it at first. I thought she was asking me to serve on a committee to choose a YA author for an award. And what went through my mind was, *funny she should ask me, because I'm not a YA author.*

When it finally sank in that I was being honored and that the book being cited was **Forever,** I blurted out, "But **Forever's** not my best book for that age group!"

There was a deadly silence on he other end of the phone. Finally, Marilee asked, "What is?"

"Tiger Eyes," I told her.

Another silence. Then, "Oh."

That's when it hit me. You don't argue with someone who's trying to give you an award. You accept it graciously And so, Marilee, I'm here today to tell you that I am truly honored and grateful—because the next day, on that long train trip to Florida, when I finally digested what you were trying to say, I sat up in my tiny berth, nudged my sleeping husband, and said, "Oh my god! What a gutsy decision they've made—giving me this award in today's fearful climate, with the far right breathing down their necks, demanding family friendly libraries."

As if libraries haven't always been family friendly. I can't think of a family friendlier place. I can still see myself at four sitting on the floor of the public library in Elizabeth, New Jersey, sniffing the books and choosing *Madeline* to take home with me. I loved that book so much I hid it from my mother, so she couldn't return it.

And then the thrill of taking my own small children to the public library—and now, my almost five-year-old grandson, who chooses books for me to read to him. He negotiates at bedtime.

"Seven books, Nonie."

"How about four?"

"How about six?"

"We'll see how tired you are."

"I'm never tired."

And so, on that train, I wanted to stand up and cheer, not for myself, but because this committee is sending those would-be censors a powerful message—a message that *you* are out there protecting our young people's right to read and to choose books freely; a message that you recognize and respect my need and every writer's need to create in an atmosphere free from fear; a message that no one individual or group is going to frighten you or intimidate you—and if that's not what you're saying, don't tell me, okay?

As Carolyn Caywood wrote in *SLJ* [*School Library Journal*], she'd rather have heard what went on in that committee meeting than what I have to say today. I think we all would, Carolyn.

When I began to write in the late sixties and publish in the early seventies, I had never heard of a category called YA books, which is probably why I've never thought of myself as a YA writer. So I did some research in preparation for this talk. It was Dorothy Broderick who put me in touch with Betty Carter, who told me YA has a revisionist history. There are those who will argue that *Little Women* was the first YA novel, an idea that really appeals to me.

Betty also told me a wonderful *Forever* story about her daughter and her first summer at sleepaway camp following fifth grade. And how, when Betty asked what was the best thing about camp, her daughter said, "I read *Forever,* Mom! Each of us chipped in 25 cents to buy it but then we made the boys pay 50

cents apiece if they wanted to read it." For this, Betty spent a hefty amount to give her young daughter a summer experience she'd never forget. There are a lot of *Forever* stories.

Until I wrote *Forever* in 1975, I had never written about older teenagers. My characters were the tens, elevens, and twelves, the kids on the brink—full of secret thoughts and active imaginations. Sometimes they had older siblings, but I wasn't as interested in their points of view. Maybe because my own teenage years were a fifties mix of the bland and the boring, when every feeling and concern was kept tightly under wraps, when we all pretended to be so happy, so fine. *What . . . problems? Not us!*

Then, in '75, Randy, my fourteen-year-old daughter, a voracious reader, was racing through a group of books a librarian friend of mine referred to as "the pregnant books"——you know the ones—if a girl succumbs, if she gives in, she faces pregnancy, abandonment, a gruesome illegal abortion, even death or, at best, a long train trip to another place. Sexuality linked with punishment.

In those books, girls never do it because they want to. They're passive, not active participants. They're never sexually turned on. And in those books, boys have no feelings, boys never have their hearts broken. So when Randy asked, "Couldn't there be a book where two nice kids from nice families do it and nobody has to die?" I began to think about sexuality linked with responsibility. About young people making decisions and living with the consequences of those decisions.

Now, I've always believed that the best books come from some place deep inside and that a good writer doesn't write to order, doesn't write what somebody else needs to read, although sometimes it turns out to be what somebody else needs to read. And maybe the reason I told Marilee *Forever* isn't my best book is because of the way it was conceived. I'm reconsidering now, Marilee. Maybe it doesn't matter where the idea originates, maybe the only thing that matters is how deeply it's felt.

But writing *Forever* was one thing. Publishing it was something else. My first thought, after the first few drafts was, *Oh oh . . . how am I going to work with Dick Jackson on this one?* Then I reminded myself, Dick and I had been through menstruation and breast development with Margaret, and we'd been through wet dreams with Tony and masturbation with Deenie. We'd been through puberty together! And somehow, some way, given Dick's humor and delicacy in working with his authors, we'd get through this too.

I remember sitting in Dick's office, at his desk, feeling awkward and shy, with such a dry mouth that I could hardly speak. I'd taken some kind of pill to calm my stomach, and it ate up all my saliva. Every time I coughed Dick would jump up, leave the room, and bring me back something to drink. I remember a discussion about whether or not Michael would dab aftershave on his (you should pardon the expression) balls. "Impossible!" Dick cried. "It would burn like hell!"

"But I know someone who did that," I argued. We went back and forth, back and forth, and finally compromised, yet until I reread the book for today's event, I couldn't remember how we'd resolved it.

Of course, there is no other editor like Dick Jackson. I know all his writers feel the same warmth toward him as I do, but when I think of the books we've done together, when I think of how he's nurtured me as a writer, encouraged me to tell whatever stories I needed to tell, to write as honestly as I could, as naturally as I could—well, this is his award as much as mine.

The seventies was a good time for writers and a good time for young readers. "Be glad you wrote those books when you did," Dick said recently. That's such a sad comment on where we are today.

I don't remember being concerned about how *Forever* would be published. I don't think I knew enough then to be concerned. I just assumed Dick and Bob Verrone at Bradbury Press would know what to do, and they'd do it.

I finally asked Dick about that, and he told me he and Bob didn't have a clue. They knew *Forever* wasn't for the eleven-year-olds who were reading my other books. And they didn't publish anything else like it, nothing in that new category called YA. So they dodged the issue by labeling it my first book for adults, which they knew it wasn't—and when I saw that line on the dust jacket, I was *not* happy, to say the least. No one had discussed it with me. I'm sure if Dick and Bob knew how that label would play to the censors years later, they'd never have used it.

So *Forever* was launched. The only review that's stayed with me was written by Margaret Drabble for the *Times* in London, where I was then living. She wrote about how fascinated the English have always been by how American teens managed to do all those things to one another in their cars, whereas English teens, if they were lucky, had only minis. Although I enjoyed and admired Margaret Drabble's novels, I never understood her point since in *Forever* Katherine and Michael don't use his car for anything but transportation.

When I returned from London in the summer of '76, to move to New Mexico, Pocketbooks was about to publish the paperback edition of *Forever*. I have to thank my agent Claire Smith for sending the book to Phyllis Grann, then the editor of Pocketbooks, who bought it as a mass-market title.

I spoke to Phyllis yesterday and asked if she remembered anything about that decision. She told me it was because her daughter, Allison, a young teenager, had read the book in galleys and had proudly told her friends that *her* mom wasn't afraid to talk to her about sex and wasn't afraid to give her books about it either. Allison Grann is a physician today, with a baby daughter, in case any of you are wondering how the first readers of *Forever* turned out. And Phyllis' decision to publish the book on a mass-market list helped it reach a much wider audience than it might have otherwise.

Whenever I go into bookstores, I check to see where *Forever* is shelved. And more than once, I've found it mixed in with the children's books. In Santa Fe, I once grabbed it off the shelf, where it was sitting next to *Tales of a Fourth Grade Nothing*. "Look," I told the manager of the store, "this book doesn't belong in the children's section. It's not meant for my younger readers."

"Oh, I know," the manager said, "and we tried shelving it with adult fiction, but it just wasn't moving—and since we put it with the children's books, it's been flying out of the store!"

What's an author to do? It's a real dilemma because I enjoy writing for different age groups. I think it helps to keep my writing fresh, and I know it helps to keep me excited about writing.

I have a wonderful collection of letters from my readers about *Forever*. My favorite is from the mother who wrote to tell me about her ten-year-old daughter who was determined to read the book. The mother had already read it and felt ten was too young. But she also knew her daughter was going to read it one way or another, so rather than forbid it, she said, "All right, but I want to answer all your questions after you've read it . . . okay?" The daughter agreed.

And then the mother waited nervously, and she waited, wondering if she'd be able to answer those questions when the time came. She rehearsed what she might say, until she felt comfortable. And finally her ten-year-old handed her the book. "I'm done," she said. The mother looked at her and said, "Do you have any questions?"

"Yes, Mom . . . what's fondue?"

The mother laughed hysterically until she cried.

And another letter:

> Dear Ms. Blume,
>
> On behalf of all boys named Ralph . . . how could you do this to us?

And just one more:

> Dear Ms. Blume,
>
> I have read *Forever* twenty-one times. The only thing wrong with it is the ending. Kath and Michael belong together. The only thing I am requesting is that you write a sequel. Because it makes me cry whenever I think about it. I write tons of stories, so I hope you don't mind, but I rewrote the ending of your book, so I wouldn't be so sad.

Most of the letters are about the love story, and they would break your hearts; but this is July Fourth weekend, and I've promised myself I will *not* cry during this talk, so I'll save them for another time.

And then there are the inevitable *Forever* questions whenever I talk to kids:

"Where'd you get the idea?" Usually asked by a thirteen- or fourteen-year-old girl whose friends are egging her on.

"Did you . . . ah . . . have experiences like Katherine's?" Lots of giggling. Major disappointment when I tell them I didn't.

"Wasn't your mother embarassed when she read the book?" My mother was so shy, so afraid to talk to me about anything, we never really discussed it, anymore than we discussed *Wifey*. Actually, my mother went to high school with Philip Roth's mother in Elizabeth, New Jersey, and when *Wifey* was published they ran into each other. Mrs. Roth said to my mother, "Listen, Essie . . . when they ask you how she knows all those things you say, 'I don't know, but not from me!'"

Recently I was interviewed by a graduate student at NYU, for a magazine on the Net. She asked if I had deliberately set out to create female characters who

are sexual beings, rather than sexual objects. Until she asked the question I had never thought about it. *Sexual beings rather than sexual objects.* Yes, that made sense to me. Female sexuality. Isn't that what frightens so many adults about the book? The idea that Katherine enjoys her sexuality? Or that Deenie does? Or Margaret or any of my characters?

I thanked that young woman for making her point. I love those wonderful twenty-and-thirty-somethings who grew up reading my books. They seem to be intelligent, thoughtful, decent human beings. I'm proud they remember my characters so well.

In the book I'm trying to finish this summer, a book about two friends whose lives are woven together from ages twelve to thirty, a book that doesn't fit neatly into any category, there's a lot of talk about sex.

There's experimental sex between girlfriends at twelve, there's self-sex (the safest kind, after all), there's falling madly in love at seventeen sex, there's confused sex, and there's *Last Night Never Happened* sex (the title of the book). None of it is as explicit as the scenes in *Forever,* yet it's a much more sophisticated book.

I lost three months of writing time over the winter because I couldn't figure out who the audience would be for this book. I'd ask myself the same question over and over, although by then I was deeply involved in my characters' lives, and there was no way I was going to give up on them. Finally I thought, maybe it's for all those readers who grew up reading *Forever.*

George, my husband, grew so tired of my dilemma that one morning when I turned on my computer, dancing across my screen in purple letters was a message: It's *Forever,* stupid . . . It's *Forever* . . .

I can't talk about *Forever* without talking about responsibility. I've had endless discussions with Leanne Katz, director of the National Coalition Against Censorship. (And today's generous cash award will be contributed to NCAC.) The question I always ask Leanne is: Is it responsible in the age of AIDS for young people to read a story like *Forever?* And every time Leanne reminds me it's *fiction.* It's a *love* story. "What are you going to do?" she says. "Remove every love story that takes place before AIDS? Better to let the kids read it and talk with them about it."

Still, because the book is read as a contemporary love story, I felt the need to add a note to my readers. (It appears in all the newer editions of the book.)

I tell them when I wrote *Forever* in 1975, sexual responsiblity meant emotional readiness, plus preventing unplanned pregnancy. Today it means much more. I tell them where to go for help. I also tell them I'm glad that some things, like feelings, never change.

We all want today's kids to be aware, to be intelligent, to practice safe sex. They don't, you know. The *safest* sex is reading about it. Norma Klein used to say, reading about it satisfied her curiosity and kept her a virgin. Me, too. But it's probably not going to keep today's teens virgins. So we'd better try to prepare them for the decisions they're going to have to make, not by hiding from the issues but by facing them. *Forever* can be used to foster discussion. Katherine and Michael can help adults talk to young people without personalizing, patronizing, or preaching.

I can't begin to count the number of times *Forever* has been challenged in schools and libraries since its publication. I know how many of you have bravely defended not just *Forever* but my other books, and the books of other authors. You've stood up for your students and your beliefs, sometimes risking your jobs, and there's no way any of us can thank you enough.

If it happens in your community, if it happens to you, don't keep it a secret! Censors work quietly through intimidation. They *hate* publicity. So pick up the phone, call the National Coalition Against Censorship at (212) 807-NCAC. Call ALA's Office of Intellectual Freedom. Send a fax to me via my publisher, and I'll send you a *Forever* packet. Involve the students, their parents, the community. And remember, you're not alone!

Of course, it's easy for me to stand here and tell you what to do. Ultimately you have to make your own decisions. But every time a book is removed from the library, it's the kids who are the real losers. It's the kids who get a negative message about books and reading, and too often, about their own sexuality, as well.

I've been blessed with the most loyal and loving group of readers any writer could ask for. I've been blessed with loyal and supportive publishers and editors, some of whom are here today, and I thank all of them for keeping my books in print and available, even when they've come under fire. Most of all, thanks to every one of you for being here today and for sharing this moment with me. Where would I be without you?

GENERAL COMMENTARY

John Gough

SOURCE: "Growth, Survival and Style in the Novels of Judy Blume," in *The School Librarian,* Vol. 25, No. 2, May, 1987, pp. 100-06.

Judy Blume is commonly regarded as that trivially popular writer of simple children's books on taboo problem topics such as puberty and sex. Her style is considered feeble, her characterisation shallow, her plots boring and didactic; and, anyway, those sorts of topics are just unacceptable. I do not believe this. Judy Blume's enormous commercial success, her prolific output and her easy-to-read stories distort and conceal her real achievement. She is an under-rated writer, critically abused or neglected, who deserves close attention and stands up to critical scrutiny very well.

Setting and Action

Let's begin with setting. Judy Blume writes about what she knows. This happens to be middle-class East Coast children and teenagers, usually from a Jewish background, living in city apartments or well-appointed suburban villas. Her characters are not particularly clever or intellectual, not highly articulate or desperately sensitive, not talented or eccentric. They are pretty ordinary people. Most of the famous modern teenage characters in children's books are not ordinary. They *are* extremely bright or talented or difficult or sensitive or tough or eccentric. Consider the characters of Alan Garner, Paul Zindel, Jane Gardam, S. E. Hinton, Betsy Byars, Ursula Le Guin. These characters are very easy to be interested in; but we should not rush to dismiss more ordinary characters, such as Blume's. They are human, too, and probably more like most readers than their more extreme and critically acceptable counterparts. Give yourself a chance to know Blume's characters: give yourself a hard look in a mirror.

What about the action? Well, not much happens. No ancient stone axes are discovered, there are no crazy parties, no secret machine guns, no plotting by secret police, no ghosts, murder or incest, no crippling psychopathic trauma. Judy Blume's novels are filled with everyday events. Is this necessarily grounds for criticism?

A Plausible Defence

It is ironic that David Rees, who is such a fierce critic of Judy Blume, once offered a defence of Jill Chaney, as a simple writer of ordinary life, in exactly the way I am defending Blume:

There are no unwanted pregnancies in her [Chaney's] books, no pot-smoking, no abortions, no V.D. . . . There are no exciting plots in her novels. The prose style is not particularly exciting, but it is a perfectly satisfactory instrument for her purposes. Not a great deal happens other than the usual routines of the suburban middle class (where she seems most at home) . . . There are, it is true, a few oddities . . . But, on the whole, the even, monotonous pace of everyday life ticks in the foreground, and behind it we are constantly aware of what [the main characters] think and feel. For most of the time we are inside their heads and hearts, exploring, muddling, analysing, and almost always compromising.

If Rees can make a plausible defence of an apparently ordinary writer, such as Chaney, let me try a defence of Blume, whose ordinariness is very similar, once we take a cool look behind her sensational reputation.

Style in the Novels

Nicholas Tucker (1983) and David Rees 1980 claim that Judy Blume's writing style is 'slack', with the 'soggy consistency' and 'built-in throw-away quality' of the 'used tissues that play such an important part in Kath's and Michael's post-amatory techniques' in *Forever*. . . . (I have a theory that British critics, such as Tucker and Rees, have a bit of a hang-up about these used tissues because the kind of heavy petting that Blume describes is not usually part of British teenage relationships. In nearly all the British books I have read about such relationships there is no intermediate stage of intimacy between kissing and intercourse. B. S. Johnson (1975) gives a sample of twenty *true* British deflorations, for example.) But what is Blume's style really like?

Two of Blume's novels are fairly plain third-person past-tense narratives: *Iggie's house* (1970) and *Starring Sally J. Freeman as herself* (1977). But this is deceptive. *Iggie's house* is her first full-length novel, written chapter by chapter, week by week, in a university course on 'how to write for children' to satisfy the course teacher. But even there Blume introduces a stylistic subtlety. As Winnie tries to cope with her best friend, Iggie, having moved away, and with the tensions that result from a black family moving into Iggie's house, Winnie writes letters to Iggie. At least she tries to write letters about the situation. But each letter, except the very last one, remains incomplete and unsent. Letter by letter we see Winnie's *own* incomplete view of the situation presented within the impartial third-person narrative. An ironic dialogue is set up in the reader's mind between the

letters, or Winnie's self, and the narrative. Nothing startling as a literary device, but satisfying.

Blume uses letters in a similar way in most of her books. (She does not do this in the strong way that Paul Zindel, for example, uses facsimile handwritten letters, and typewritten papers, and printed invitations in *My darling, my hamburger* (1969). You can't copy someone else's literary device.) She also uses Margaret's direct remarks to God (*Are you there God? It's me, Margaret*), Karen's diary entries (*It's not the end of the world*), foreshadowing chapter headings (*Blubber*), and Sally's imaginary films (*Starring Sally J. Freeman as herself*) as a way of commenting on the action and thoughts of the main character.

Apart from these two books and *Tiger Eyes,* all of Blume's novels are written in a fairly simple first-person past tense. But even here there are subtleties. For example, at moments of crisis the straightforward retelling of what happened breaks into a vivid, here-and-now present tense, as when Tony wakes up after his first wet dream, panic-stricken (*Then again, maybe I won't*). Sometimes the dominant past tense gives way to a present tense, as the main character reflects on what has been happening. It is what the character is thinking at the time, rather than after the events of the book. For instance, in *It's not the end of the world,* Karen tells us the aftermath of her attempt to get her parents back together:

> I got back into bed . . . all set to cry . . . I must have been a crazy person to think that my silly diorama could work magic. Now I know the truth . . . Well, I'm through fooling myself . . . I rolled over.

Again, this gives the reader a sense of immediacy and involvement; but it also allows Blume, as author behind the character's telling, to establish an ironic view of the action. We all know the pitfalls that lie ahead of someone who thinks she is through with fooling herself.

Such concealed irony occurs in *Are you there God? It's me, Margaret* (Chapter 9), when Margaret, in her search for religious allegiance, has gone to synagogue, and done nothing more than count different coloured hats. Her father, an unbeliever raised as a Jew, married to a lapsed Christian, and estranged from his intolerant Christian parents-in-law, remarks that he too used to count hats. Despite this, and here is Blume's irony, Margaret remarks to God: 'I'm really on my way. By the end of the school year I'll know all there is to know about religion.'

The same kind of irony happens in *Forever*. . . . For example, Kath's parents talk about themselves having once gone steady with other boyfriends and girlfriends, clearly implying that Kath and Michael may be in the same situation. But Kath thinks to herself, 'It's not just some fifties fad, like going steady . . . with us it is love—real, true honest-to-god love'. The reader realises that love is not always what people, such as Kath, think it is. Blume's irony clearly shows us this.

Tiger Eyes (1981) is written in first-person *present* tense. The opening sentence plunges the reader into what is happening: 'It is the morning of the funeral and I am tearing my room apart, trying to find the right kind of shoes to wear.' The present tense heightens suspense as the facts of and feelings about the death are slowly revealed and gradually coped with. As the blurb on the paperback edition claims, this is Blume's best book so far, strongly written, strongly plotted, and full of character and dramatic clashes. *Tiger Eyes,* however, is unusual in that its driving force comes from the father's death. He was casually murdered in an armed hold-up. This is not quite Blume's usual ordinary everyday topic, though violent crime is increasingly 'everyday', and murder is as American as apple pie. This is not a book for young children but for young people: the main character is nearly sixteen.

More Than One Aspect

Tiger Eyes, like Blume's other books, does not deal with only one aspect of one problem situation. Several situations, including alcoholism, suicide, racism, childlessness, peer-group pressures, and jealous guilt are introduced and shown from different points of view. Davey's, the main character's, grief is paralleled by her mother's grief, as well as by her aunt's. Later the aunt suffers again when Davey's family relinquishes her comforting to resume their own life. The murder is mirrored by Davey's uncle being a weapons researcher at Los Alamos. Davey begins to come to terms with her father's death only when she nurses a terminally ill old man. As the seasons move through a year, from a claustrophobic summer to the spring when the lizards run again, the many threads of the novel form a dense texture of image and feeling.

All of Blume's books are about coping with difficult situations. In seven of them families move home, forcing the main characters to make new friends and redefine themselves. Other difficult situations include changes in parents' lifestyles, separation and divorce, changes in allegiance to and from friends, peer-group pressures, the beginnings of puberty and sexual awareness, sibling rivalry, phobias, the death of relatives, and the tensions of family relationships. Again and again Blume's characters find that something as simple as waking up in the morning and getting on, however unwillingly or unhappily, with the day's tasks, can help adjust to a new and unpleasant situation. Survival can be a matter of just hanging on. Karen, in *It's not the end of the world,* changes her mind about divorce. At first she says in her diary, with much feeling and childish misunderstanding: 'Divorce . . . it's the end of the world'. Later she understands that none of her schemes, nor even her brother running away, can repair her parents' relationship. Eventually she finds she can accept that her parents are better apart, and she can have B-plus days again.

Consider *Then again, maybe I won't* (1971), notorious for its, thirteen-year-old hero who begins to have wet dreams and who secretly watches his neighbours' sixteen-year-old daughter undressing at night. In fact, only a few pages mention wet dreams, spying or related sexual matters, and these things *are* only mentioned, not described in detail. Far more attention is given to thirteen-year-old Tony's family: his older brother killed some years before in Vietnam; his father whose invention has made them newly rich; his sister-in-law who gets pregnant, then has a baby girl; his grandmother who is left mute after a larynx operation and is forced out of the family kitchen by the new maid; his status-seeking mother who buys a grand piano, though no one in the family plays. And Tony himself, seeing through the phoney values of wealth, agonising over his grandmother's unhappiness, jealous of the sixteen-year-old and her youth group leader boyfriend, suffering stomach pains of anxiety when he sees his friend Joel shoplifting. There's a lot more going on in this book than a little bit of anxious puberty.

At the end, though his family have not changed, Tony has survived. He knows himself better. He is beginning to come to terms with his developing sexuality, enjoying his dreams, and finding that the skinny girl his own age who likes him is also likeable. There are no easy solutions or happy endings. Tony's grandmother still locks herself away from the rest of the family in protest at being banished from the kitchen. The family's new wealth tempts his school-teacher brother into a pointless job in the firm. Tony bursts into tears, seeking comfort from his grandmother, realising they both 'have a lot in common', being 'outsiders in [their] own home'. Joel is not sent to the Juvenile Detention Centre, but to a military school to get the discipline his family do not have and cannot teach him. And Tony realises, 'it was funny. Funny and sad both'.

Typical Heroes and Heroines

Tony is typical of Blume's heroes and heroines: human, confused, not arriving at clear-cut conclusions, but persisting, trying to understand, trying to be honest with himself. Kath, in **Forever** . . . , is another archetypal Blume main character. Behind the few honest pages that describe Kath's developing sexual relationship with Michael, plainly written, and roundly damned by the critics, is a story of a girl trying to come to terms with independence and adulthood. Kath struggles to redefine her friendship with her schoolfriend Erica, as she grows closer to Michael. Kath and her parents muddle their way towards recognising and accepting Kath's coming independence, at a new stage in their parent-daughter relationship. Kath comes to rely on her up-to-date grandmother, and grieves when her grandfather dies. She realises that love and sex are only part of her friendship with Michael: 'besides everything else he is really my best friend now'. But she learns that love and friendship are not necessarily 'forever', that she is not always in control of situations, and not always blameless. She knows that the end of the relationship, and Michael's pain, is her fault, even if she could not help it. The reality she is growing into is adult, complex, and not easy. Blume does not trivialise her characters or subject-matter.

Explicit Sex

It might be objected that Judy Blume puts sex in her books in an exploitative, almost pornographic, way. Certainly **Wifey** (1978), her adult novel, spares no four-letter words or intimate details. But **Wifey** is no more pornographic than, say, books by Philip Roth or Norman Mailer, who give a male point of view. Such explicit discussion of sex may offend the taste of some readers, but the anguish and subtle delineation of the characters, and the reality of their predicament, are unmistakable. What about the children's novels? Maybe she puts the sex in to titillate and make the books sell? I do not think so. She herself says:

> **Margaret** came right out of my own sixth-grade life, except for the family situation. Her feelings, her actions, her friends, her concerns—they were all the things we were interested in in sixth grade. I never wrote it thinking it would be widely accepted as the way kids think today, but apparently they do.

This seems to be a clear statement of the honesty of Judy Blume's intentions. There is a consistency of characterisation, theme and treatment in all her novels (including **Wifey**) that leads me to conclude that she is seeking honest discussion of ordinary lives in her books.

It is interesting to compare Blume's novels with the true-life story of Anne Frank (1947). None of Blume's characters experience the terrible imprisonment that Anne Frank and her family and friends suffered; but Anne Frank, like Blume, speaks honestly about love, physical attraction (to girls, as well as boys), parental tensions, a mother's jealousy and disapproval, and the whole messy business of adolescence. I believe that Anne Frank's *Diary* is a touchstone by which we can measure the truth of Judy Blume's fiction, and its non-pornographic nature.

There is an honesty in Anne Frank's *Diary* that is astonishing in a fourteen- or fifteen-year-old: 'Once, when we spoke about sex, Daddy told me that I couldn't possibly understand the longing yet; I always knew that I did understand it and now I understand it fully' (7th January, 1944). 'Sometimes, when I lie in bed at night, I have a terrible desire to feel my breasts . . . I remember that once when I slept with a girlfriend I had a strong desire to kiss her, and that I did so. I could not help being terribly inquisitive about her body, for she had always kept it hidden from me' (5th January, 1944), Call this sad, tender story pornographic, who dares!

Like Anne Frank, Judy Blume is concerned to describe characters surviving, finding themselves, growing in understanding, coming to terms with life. This is apparent in the endings of Blume's novels. There are no grand resolutions, no happy tying-up of loose ends, no miraculous solutions to problems. Some insight is achieved, and then new problems await to be confronted. Margaret realises that religious belief cannot simply be chosen. Tony's last words are typically equivocal, 'Then again, maybe I won't.' Kath wants to tell Michael:

> I will never be sorry for loving him. That in a way I still do. . . . Maybe if we were ten years older it would have worked out differently. Maybe. I think it's just that I'm not ready for forever . . . all I could manage to say was, 'See you around . . . ' (**Forever**).

Davey, coming to terms with her father's murder, realises that, 'you can't go back. Not ever. You have to pick up the pieces and keep moving ahead. (**Tiger Eyes,**)

Such conclusions may not be original or profound; but neither are they trivial. The high sales of Blume's books are testimony to the fact that what she has to say is said well and is well worth saying.

Robin F. Brancato

SOURCE: "In Defense of: *Are You There, God? It's Me, Margaret, Deenie,* and *Blubber*—Three Novels by Judy Blume," in *Censored Books: Critical Viewpoints,* Nicholas J. Karolides, Lee Burress, and John M. Kean, eds., The Scarecrow Press, Inc., 1993, pp. 87-97.

> "My mother says God is a nice idea . . . "
>
> "I don't even believe in God!" (from *Are You There God, It's Me, Margaret*)
>
> "I turned away from the kitchen door and ran back to my room. As soon as I got into bed I started touching myself. I have this special place and when I rub it I get a very nice feeling." (from *Deenie*)
>
> "Caroline and Wendy started another game of Tic Tac Toe while Bruce went to work on his nose. He has a very interesting way of picking it." (from *Blubber*)

These are some of the lines, obviously taken out of context, that are most likely to raise the hackles, the blood pressure, and the eyebrows of Judy Blume's critics. Those who are disturbed by America's most popular author of books for young readers include religious conservatives, parents worried about sexual precocity in their children, and certain academics who say Blume lacks taste and/or literary merit. These critics range from rabid censors who would love to see all Blume's books banned, to middle-of-the-roaders who object primarily to her book *Forever,* to mild-mannered skeptics who merely wonder if certain Blume titles might trouble children who read them at too young an age. Judy Blume's critics are numerous, but the number is negligible when compared to the hordes of kids who buy and devour her books as if they were Big Macs (over 50 million Blume books sold!), or even when compared to the number of kids who write to Blume without a parent ever suggesting, or a teacher assigning, such an active response. To find out what Judy Blume is up to, especially in *Are You There God? It's Me, Margaret* (1970), *Deenie* (1973), and *Blubber* (1974), what it is that her critics fear, and what can be said to calm those fears . . . read on.

Are You There God? It's Me, Margaret, is about twelve-year-old Margaret Simon's attempts at coming to terms with her interreligious background and her entrance into puberty. The candor with which Judy Blume describes Margaret's feelings and experiences shocked some people back in 1970 and continues to unsettle certain readers even now, when Margaret, if real, would be a thirty-something yuppie. The novel deals with such universal concerns as dislocation (moving and readjusting), family tensions (grandma interferes), and preoccupation with physical maturation, boys, and sex (Margaret practices kissing her pillow; Margaret exercises to increase her bust and pretends she has gotten her menstrual period before she actually gets it). After seeking, by way of a school project, to learn about comparative religion, Margaret doesn't come to any easy decision about her own religious identity. The novel, which concludes with Margaret's resuming her talks with God and thanking him that she had finally gotten her first menstrual period, is not primarily about physical changes in puberty but about an adolescent's personal relationship with God.

Deenie has to do with complications in the life of beautiful Wilmadeene Fenner, seventh grader, when she discovers that she has scoliosis. This trial is intensified by the fact that Deenie's mother has had her heart set on Deenie's becoming a successful model. In addition to the theme of learning to cope with a physical handicap, *Deenie* deals with additional adolescent concerns, such as sibling rivalry, peer acceptance and sexuality. (The references that have created the greatest stir have to do with masturbation. The first-person narrator tells the reader that she sometimes touches a "special place," and then later, in a sex-education class in school, Deenie's gym teacher assures the students, as part of a question-and-answer session, that " . . . it's normal and harmless to masturbate.")

At the end of the novel, which is mainly about the discomforts, physical and emotional, that Deenie suffers as a result of scoliosis, she is still confined most of the time to her restricting body brace but is on her way to accepting her temporary disability. She is also on her way to becoming sensitized to others who have to live with handicaps or disfigurement.

Blubber gives us a picture of a typical fifth grade, where Jill Brenner and her classmates have taken to tormenting an easy victim, overweight Linda Fischer. Jill participates in the teasing, not knowing that her classmates will soon turn the tables and pick on her instead. As a sufferer Jill comes to realize, though not through any great epiphany or with any great remorse, that kids are cruel and fickle and that today's Miss Popularity can be tomorrow's outcast.

Before examining why each of these three books has had censorship attempts made against it, let's consider what it is in general about Blume's works that her critics object to. First, some fear that her frankness about sex and her nonjudgmental position will "give kids ideas," or that this frankness will cause hangups where none existed previously. Some critics are primarily concerned with the marketing of certain Blume books—the fact that *Forever* (about the pre-marital sexual relationship of a senior girl, who is seventeen at the outset) and Blume's adult novels, *Wifey* and *Smart Women,* have sometimes attracted the same pre-teen readers who know Blume through her much less controversial *Tales of a Fourth Grade Nothing* or *Superfudge.* These two objections will be rebutted by kids, by sympathetic adults, and by Judy Blume herself in the pages ahead.

In addition to these complaints about references to sexuality and about marketing methods, some critics are offended, as well, by what they perceive as Blume's general permissiveness, by her so-called simplistic resolutions, by her so-called stereotyped characters, and by her language (a sprinkling of words such as "damn," and "ass"). Others deplore the so-called nastiness of some of her main characters, such as Jill in *Blubber;* or the unwillingness of many of her adult characters to stand up to children; or the everybody-speaks-in-the-same-voice quality of her protagonists, regardless of their age or sex. Still others say that Blume doesn't challenge young readers enough and that she creates a narrow view of the world in her focus on the affluent suburbs. One such opinion comes from John Garvey, writing in *Commonweal* (in July, 1980):

> There is something dismal about teaching children to cope, where in previous generations books for children encouraged a larger imagining, a thrill at the size of the universe they might encounter.

Let's take a look at these criticisms and come back with a defense for each:

Permissiveness—Is Blume really so permissive, or is she merely inviting kids to think for themselves? According to Robert Lipsyte in *The Nation* (1981), Blume "asks more questions than she answers, gently nudging her readers toward a healthy skepticism."

Easy resolutions—Each of Blume's heroines confronts a critical experience, and it's true that each comes to tolerate, accept, or embrace his or her life, but so do Alcott's Little Women, so does Laura Ingalls Wilder's Laura, so does Anne Frank in her diary. Jack Forman in *The Horn Book Magazine*

(January-February 1985) reflects on this point in the following statement that agrees with the criticism but still praises Blume:

> Her characters almost always survive heavy personal, family, and school problems by turning to their own internal resources, absorbing any temporary discomfort or hurt, and getting on with their lives. They learn from their mistakes, and become more self-reliant. Very little attention, however, is given to how others are affected by the resolution of problems, and rarely does Blume confront the lingering pain and hurt which characters might feel after resolving the problems. . . . Unquestionably, children and teenagers need to believe in themselves and carve a niche for themselves in their society; they need the reassurance of a life after problems. Judy Blume gives them this. But they also need to know that there are consequences to their actions affecting other people and that there is a price paid for their mistakes—even if they learn the right lessons.

Stereotyped characters—Blume characters, admittedly, are pretty ordinary people, says John Gough (*The School Librarian,* May 1985).

> Most of the famous modern teenage characters in children's books are not ordinary. They are extremely bright or talented or difficult or sensitive or tough or eccentric. . . . These characters are very easy to be interested in; but we should not rush to dismiss more ordinary characters, such as Blume's. They are human, too, and probably more like most readers than their more extreme and critically acceptable counterparts.

Everybody-speaks-the-same, limited focus, and wimpy adults—First of all, it's not true that Judy Blume's adult characters are always weak. Margaret's grandmother, for instance, is strong-willed, caring, and feisty. Second, if the characters often speak alike and if the focus is "limited," then consider the fact that all Blume's books are about twentieth century, middle class, mostly suburban life, which she's showing more honestly than most other writers of books for children. Is it possible that if there is a sameness among the characters and a limited focus, that this says more about middle-class America than about Judy Blume's limitations?

Language—In an age when, sad as it is to admit, harsh, unseemly, abusive language is often the lazy norm, rather than the refined, original, truly expressive language that most of us would prefer, in an age when a President of the United States was widely quoted as threatening to "kick ass" in the Middle East, Judy Blume is a model of discretion. She's simply trying to suggest how kids really speak. Although standards differ from one community to another, surely the sprinkling of "bad words" used by her characters puts them in the conservative camp almost anywhere in this country today. If Blume's characters don't think and talk like real kids, why should readers put any stock in their feelings, hopes, and dreams?

No literary merit? Let's wrap up these allegations with two summary statements. Though Blume's style is simple, according to Jack Forman, it's "an attractive simplicity and a very natural sense of humor." "She's an underrated writer," says John Gough "critically abused or neglected, who deserves close attention and stands up to scrutiny very well."

This is the nature, then, of the literary criticism of Blume's books. As for the meaner critics, the ones who yearn to censor her, who are they, and where do they come from? Some are reviewers or educators, but most, let's assume, are parents, alarmed at the thought of their children nibbling at the apple on the Tree of Knowledge. These parents are vocal and geographically diverse. In Leesburg, Florida, in 1981 (according to an Associated Press story in the *St. Petersburg Times*) a Baptist minister led "a movement to purge school libraries of novels by Judy Blume, saying some of the stories amount to a sexual "how-to" lesson for young students." Other censors tried to ban *Margaret* and *Blubber* in Xenia, Ohio in 1983. *Margaret* was accused of being anti-Christian and against parental and school authority, and *Blubber* was pulled off the shelves for containing the word "bitch" in connection with a teacher.

In Peoria, Illinois, in 1984 the ACLU urged school officials to rescind a ban on three Blume novels, but the officials subsequently found three others to be unsuitable. Objections were to language and to descriptions of sexual coming of age. A director of elementary education in Daviess County, Kentucky instructed elementary librarians in 1990 to avoid purchase of additional Blume titles. Although attempts at banning Blume have often been resolved, eventually, in favor of the author, her books are sometimes assigned to a shelf where they may be read only by children who bring a note from home. Here's a sampling of additional places where censorship attempts were made against Judy Blume during the 1980's: Brigham City, Utah; Gilbert, Arizona; Dedham, Massachusetts; Tuscaloosa, Alabama; Fond du Lac, Wisconsin; and Des Moines, Iowa. There are undoubtedly many unreported cases, as well, of Blume books not being purchased in the first place, or being quietly removed from library shelves, or being kept in libraries under wraps.

Why is this censorship of Blume so inappropriate, so misguided, so unfair? Let's look at statements for the defense, first from Blume's staunchest supporters—kids; then from adults sympathetic to what she is doing; and finally from Judy Blume herself. This is what kids say (according to Barbara Ann Porte in *The Advocate,* University of Georgia)—and, by the way, *kids should know,* because unlike many would-be censors who have read only selected passages thought to be provocative, young defenders have read the books from cover to cover:

"She writes about people I would like to know."

"She knows what I am like."

"Her books are funny."

"Her books are sad."

"Your books help me not to be afraid."

A typical reader comment begins like this one, from *Letters to Judy,* a collection of some of the nearly 2,000-a-month pieces of mail received by Blume and published by Putnam's and by Pocket Books in 1987, royalties from which go to Kids Fund, a foundation that finances projects intended to enhance the lives of kids:

Dear Judy,

Whenever I have a fight with somebody I sit right down and write a letter to you. I don't always send it but it makes me feel better just to write it.

Jennifer, age 11

The volume of an author's fan mail and the willingness of young readers to bare their souls to a famous stranger may not be the measure of that writer's literary merit, but surely in an age when most adolescents look at the world and feel confusion, anxiety, or even terror, Judy Blume should be regarded as a national treasure. She provides comfort ("I thought I was weird for doing and thinking some things but your books make me feel okay."); she fills a need ("My mom never talks about the things young girls think most about."); she offers hope ("The main reason I am writing is I want your advice."). Emily Dickinson wrote: "If I can stop one heart from breaking, I shall not live in vain. . . . " Judy Blume's candid novels may not be exactly what Emily Dickinson had in mind, but let the censors consider for a minute the thousands of appreciative responses from Blume's readers, and let those censors weigh all the hearts stopped from breaking, the lives saved from aching, and the pains cooled by Blume, against the unlikely possibility of a child's being damaged by a so-called unpleasant word, an unholy thought, or a grim truth in one of her books.

Adult supporters of Blume admire in her books the same things that kids admire—her authentic contemporaneity and, mainly, her honestly. As a supplement to the decorous fiction of the past, from *Little Women* to Nancy Drew, as an alternative to fantasy and science fiction, as a giant step up from the sanitized fluff of Sweet Dreams and The Babysitter's Club, let there be Judy Blume, whose realism, it's true, brings with it some "unpleasant details," says Faith McNulty in a 1983 assessment of Blume in the *New Yorker,* some "things we all notice but usually don't mention," in books of "mesmerizing intimacy," that give us a "feeling of reading a secret diary." Let librarians spend the bulk of their shrinking budgets, if they must, on the challenging, ennobling classics, on books that, according to Garvey in *Commonweal,* encourage a larger imagining, so long as they save a few dollars for Judy Blume books, books that show young people who are, according to critic John Gough, "surviving, finding themselves, growing in understanding. . . . "

Here are some testimonials from mothers, as reported by Barbara Ann Porte:

1) "My gynecologist recommended Margaret to me for my daughter."

2) "I wish I'd had books like that when I was thirteen."

3) "They (Blume's books) help me talk with my children about subjects I could otherwise not bring up."

This last comment is a recurring one, and is probably the basis of the strongest argument in favor of Blume's works. How many parents, through the ages, have languished in uneasy silence, waiting for a child to take the initiative in asking the big question? How many other parents have, in embarrassment, thrust a sex-ed book at their offspring and then hurried out of the room, or else bumbled into an artificial monologue about "Now that you're growing up . . . "? Even John Garvey of the "larger imagining" school, writes " . . . if parents and schools won't tell their children about sex, better they should learn from Judy Blume than not learn at all."

But what better recommendation can there be for a book, any book, than that it served as a catalyst for fruitful discussion, especially discussion between parent and child? Whether the parent gives the child the Blume book as a present or catches him or her reading it under the bedcovers, the odds are much more favorable for a natural exchange of ideas and opinions than in the "Here, read this article" ap-

proach. How relatively easy to talk about fictitious characters: "Do you know anybody like Margaret?" "I understand that some people are embarrassed by certain references in *Deenie.* . . . " "Whose fault do you think it is that Blubber gets picked on?" Teachers can ask these questions, too, of course, but ideally it is parents who will do the asking. There may be parents who will still shy away from such discussions, even under the protective cloak of fiction. And there will be parents who don't have the time or interest to read the books, let alone to initiate a friendly book talk. So be it. Let them have their selfish silence. Just don't let them deny their own children, and other people's children, access to books that may inform, or comfort, or sensitize. As Judith Goldberger says in the *Newsletter on Intellectual Freedom* of May 1981,

> . . . an adult's agony over discussing these matters with children is nothing when compared to the personal agony the young experience when faced with the actual situations. And that is one reason why young people devour Judy Blume's books. They deal with matters of primary concern to their readers, with which many of those readers' parents can't or won't help them. Often, rather than talking *with* their children about touchy subjects, parents talk *at* them. Or they don't talk at all.

Let's look for a moment now at the three specific Blume titles and see what each has to recommend it.

Are You There God? It's Me, Margaret—According to Judith Goldberger, "*Margaret* is not about a girl who wants a bra any more than *Hamlet* is about a man who is in love with a woman who goes crazy. . . . " In addition to Margaret's concern with her first menstrual period, with playing a kissing game called "Two minutes in the Closet," and with looking at her friend's father's anatomy book, she is also concerned with exploring the nature of religious faith, with trying to get along with friends, parents, and grandparents, and with worrying, as most young people do, whether she is normal. Says Faith McNulty, "Except perhaps in *Forever,* Blume imparts no illicit knowledge but merely fills in an area of adolescent experience usually left blank in print."

Deenie—In addition to being a book often recommended by orthopedic surgeons to patients who have scoliosis, *Deenie* is the story of a down-to-earth teenager, who deals surprisingly well with her mother's pushiness and insensitivity. By the end of the book Deenie arrives at a better understanding with her older sister; she realizes that the people she cares about most accept her, body-brace and all, and she convinces the reader that a condition such as scoliosis doesn't have to stand in the way of normal psychological and sexual development. The two or three brief references to masturbation are an understated, realistic minor motif in a novel that is about an adolescent's wish to be accepted.

Blubber—Blubber is a book that is sometimes used by teachers in the upper elementary grades to sensitize students to the cruelty of scapegoating. In New Zealand the book is used in teacher training. Although some critics object to Blume's nonjudgmental stance, this gives the book the ring of truth. Bullying is a given in the world Blume has created. Whereas in other books, and often in the real world, adults step in, in a crisis, and absolve children of responsibility, in ***Blubber*** the adults are too preoccupied, or unsuspecting, or ineffectual, just as they sometimes are in life. This leaves the young people to take charge themselves, and to learn, the hard way, that allegiances shift quickly among kids, and that (without a word about religion) the Golden Rule is a worthwhile principle to uphold.

In addition to the sympathetic critics already cited, Judy Blume, in her own defense, makes the following points about her books (in a speech sponsored by the National Coalition Against Censorship, May 17, 1990, and elsewhere):

> 1) She purposely takes no moral stand, because there are usually no purely "right" answers to difficult questions and to act as though there were is unrealistic.
>
> 2) The cause she aligns herself with is the child's right to know. "If children ask," she says, "they're entitled to an answer. These people (censors) want to go back to not being honest with children, but you can't go back, and you can't make the rest of the world go back with you."
>
> 3) Communication is everything. When children and parents talk, fear is diminished.
>
> 4) "Kids are their own best censors," she says. "Children don't read books, including mine, until they're ready." Bookstores support Blume in this claim.

In an age when we have serious reason to wonder whether books and reading will continue to attract young people who have grown up with television, we clearly need Judy Blume. Thousands of young readers who are hungry for understanding and affirmation particularly need her. "More than any other author, before or now," says Dorothy Broderick of *Voice of*

Youth Advocates, "(Blume) knows that our real lives are first and foremost internal; only when we get ourselves together can we begin to share life with another person." Can anyone be against books that help us understand ourselves and each other?

Herbert N. Foerstel

SOURCE: "Voices of Banned Authors," in *Banned in the U.S.A.: A Reference Guide to Book Censorship in Schools and Public Libraries,* Greenwood Press, 1994, pp. 101-33.

Several years ago, the head librarian of the New York Public Library's Children's Room said she had never seen a children's author as popular as Judy Blume. Indeed, Blume's novels became so popular with adolescents that one critic observed that "there is, indeed, scarcely a literate girl of novel-reading age who has not read one or more of Blume's books."

Judy Blume has written more than twenty books, including ***Are You There God? It's Me, Margaret; Deenie; Blubber;*** and her most recent, ***Here's to You, Rachel Robinson.*** Among her books for younger readers is the popular "Fudge" series: ***Tales of a Fourth Grade Nothing; Otherwise Known as Sheila the Great; Superfudge;*** and ***Fudge-a-mania.*** She has also written books for young adults (e.g. ***Forever*** and ***Tiger Eyes***) and for adults (e.g. ***Wifey*** and ***Smart Women***). With this broad readership it is not surprising that over 50 million copies of her books are in print, and her work has been translated into fourteen languages.

Blume has received numerous awards for her books, including Children's Choice Awards in thirty states, Australia, England, and Germany. She is a board member of the Society of Children's Book Writers and a member of PEN American Center, and she serves on the Council of the Authors Guild, Planned Parenthood Advocates, and the Council of Advisors of the National Coalition Against Censorship. She has been the recipient of the Carl Sandburg Freedom to Read Award, the Civil Liberties Award, and the John Rock Award, and has been chosen as a "Hero of Young America" for eight of the past nine years in the annual World Almanac poll award. Nonetheless, her candid treatment of mature issues, including adolescent sexuality, and her frank use of language has caused some schools and libraries to ban her books.

Blume thinks she writes about sexuality today because it was uppermost in her mind when she was a child. There was the need to know but no easy way to find out. Like most kids, she *never* asked her parents. Blume told the *New York Times* magazine: "I don't believe that sex is why kids like my books. The impression I get from letter after letter, is that a great many kids don't communicate with their parents. They feel alone in the world. Sometimes, reading books that deal with other kids who feel the same things they do . . . makes them feel less alone."

When I asked if her parents had attempted to control or censor her reading habits, Blume quickly answered, "No, they didn't. I was very lucky. My father had a fairly extensive library, and no one ever told me what I could read or what I could not read. Not that my mother discussed the subjects in those books, but I never felt that I couldn't read them. My mother was very shy, but she was a reader, and reading was always considered a good thing in my house."

When Judy Blume began writing, she had traditional models among the children's and young adult authors: Elaine Konigsburg, Beverly Cleary, Louise Fitzhugh. Indeed, Blume's first two books bore little resemblance to the controversial works that followed. When she wrote **The One in the Middle is the Green Kangaroo** and **Iggie's House,** she was learning her trade, but after they were done, she said to herself, "Now that I've figured out how to write books, I'm going to write what I know to be true." At that point, she began **Are You There God? It's Me, Margaret.** During this period, she was taking a writing course with Lee Wyndham, a children's writer during the late 1940s and 1950s, who gave Blume her first professional encouragement. Wyndham had absolute rules and regulations for writing children's books, and Blume says many students in the class may have felt that they couldn't get anything published if they didn't follow the rules. Blume recalls saying to herself, "Never mind these rules. This isn't what it's really like." She says she was not breaking rules in a hostile or rebellious way. She was simply determined to write about what she remembered. When Wyndham saw the manuscript to **Margaret,** she wrote Blume a long letter about it, questioning some of the sensitive or intimate subjects. But Wyndham was also the first to write to congratulate her when the *New York Times* gave **Margaret** a good review.

While Blume was writing **Iggie's House,** she came across an announcement in a magazine that a new publishing company was interested in realistic books about childhood and adolescence. Through this ad, she contacted Bradbury Press and met Dick Jackson and Bob Verrone. They took a big chance on her

when they agreed to publish **Iggie's House** and, after that, **Margaret.** Blume says she always had the happiest publishing experiences with Bradbury Press, where Dick Jackson taught her how to revise and rewrite her books on her own.

Did it take courage for Blume to write candidly about topics like menstruation, not previously covered in young adult books? She says, "It was not courage. It was naivete. I had absolutely no idea I was writing a controversial book. There was nothing in it that wasn't a part of my sixth grade experience." She recalls that she and her friends talked endlessly about menstruation and breast development, just as Margaret and her friends do in the book.

Blume was shocked when I told her that public libraries were increasingly banning her books. She had assumed bookbanning was primarily confined to school libraries. She added, "It's difficult keeping track of these events, because the authors don't find out unless someone else notifies them. More recently, thanks to the National Coalition against Censorship, we are hearing more promptly about when and where our books are being banned. I don't think any school board or school library or teacher has ever tried to contact me directly. In the past, that information has usually been communicated to me through the newspapers, but today it is more effectively documented in publications by the American Library Association, People for the American Way, and the organization I'm most involved with, the National Coalition against Censorship. As soon as they hear of any book that's been challenged, they will contact the author and try to work with everyone involved. They're a small but wonderfully effective organization, located in New York. Their executive director, Leanne Katz, is up to date on everything. ALA is terrific on censorship issues, and People for the American Way is, too, but they are involved in many other activities. The National Coalition deals only with censorship."

When Blume talked to the National Council of Teachers at their 1991 annual meeting in Seattle, she discovered that the classroom teachers and school librarians knew surprisingly little about how to respond to censorship, how to prepare for it, and the need to have policies in place. She says, "When I gave them the names and phone numbers of the organizations available to help them, most of them didn't seem to know how to proceed, how to get help. I told them that the National Coalition against Censorship was just a phone call or fax away, and the sooner they were informed of a challenged book, the better they would be able to help. I'm not aware of what may be going on in public libraries, but the school librarians, teachers, and principals who are under fire should know that they are not alone, that there is a support group. That is very important. A lot of the censors out there claim that a challenged book can be harmlessly removed from a classroom or school library, because a reader can always go to a public library to find it. That's one way the censor is able to get a book out of a school."

The first act of censorship that Judy Blume recalls against one of her books was initiated by her children's elementary school principal. Blume had given the school some copies of **Margaret** when it first came out, but the principal refused to allow the books in the school's library. Blume thought the principal was "a nut," and it never occurred to her that this sort of thing would happen again. In the beginning, her publishers tried to protect her from controversy, and as a result, she never saw the letters or heard about the phone calls. Today she realizes that was wrong.

When I asked Blume if she was offended or angered when one of her books was banned, she responded: "Years ago a woman called me on the phone and asked me if I had written *Are You There God? It's Me, Margaret*. When I said yes, she called me a communist and hung up. But this was a long time ago, perhaps twenty years ago. I was bewildered and perplexed in the beginning, and I was personally hurt. Now I understand that this is something much bigger than any kind of personal attack on any one of us. It's like a grieving process. One goes through different stages. Of course, all of those angry feelings cross your mind. What is wrong with these people? How can they possibly think this is something to be afraid of? But I don't feel that way anymore, because I'm too familiar with it. I'm glad I'm beyond that.

"This kind of bookbanning has been going on for a long time, but in 1980, after the election of Ronald Reagan, it really took off. I was very lucky because I wrote all of these books that are now under fire before any of the broader controversy arose. Aside from the phone call I mentioned, I really had no early contact with any of the bookbanners. They weren't yet organized the way they are now. The major censorship groups that now exist didn't exist then. There were the occasional frightened parents who came into the library, waving a book that they didn't want their children to read, but today it is organized in a way that is much more dangerous. I feel badly for the children because it sends a message to them that there is something wrong with reading, that we don't want them to read this book because there's something in it that we don't want them to know."

Like most writers for young people, Judy Blume receives a good deal of mail from her readers. She says: "About 99.9 percent of the letters I receive from children are positive. The negative ones will list the curse words and the pages where they appeared. Such letters are curiously similar, though they come from different parts of the country. I have no doubt that they are written by children, but one can't be sure whether an adult requests that they be written. You never know how some of these censorship groups operate. I had my secretary subscribe to the newsletter of one of these organizations, and they were advertising a pamphlet titled *How to Rid Your Library of Books by Judy Blume*."

The most painful letter she ever received from a child was addressed to "Jewdy Blume." It was from a nine-year-old child who referred to her as "Jewdy" throughout the letter, underlining the letters *JEW* in crayon. The letter attacked the book *Starring Sally J. Freedman as Herself*, complaining of its reference to Jewish angels. Blume says that although she is used to objections about sex and language in her books, that kind of hate from a young child was particularly disturbing.

Judy Blume believes that because many adults are uncomfortable with their own sexuality, they can't begin to deal with their children's. They are embarrassed and uneasy when their children ask them questions about sex, and they are often unable to answer those questions. She says the letters she receives indicate that most parents grew up without ever talking about sex. The message they got from their parents was that sex was neither good nor enjoyable, and that pattern may continue generation after generation. Blume notes that adults are suspicious of any books that kids like, and even some children's librarians tend to tell kids which books they *should* read, rather than encouraging them to read what they enjoy.

Blume says parents find it much harder to listen to their children than to impose rules. She believes censorship grows out of fear, and there is a tremendous amount of fear on the part of parents who wish to control their young children and shield them from the world. She points out that children are inexperienced, but not innocent, and their pain and unhappiness do not come from books. They come from *life*.

Blume says parents should ask themselves what harm is likely to occur if their child browses through the books at the library and happens to pick up a book for older children or even adults. The child may ask the parents a question, and if the child does, the parents should answer it. Blume says children have problems not just with sex but with death, with money, with feelings and emotions—everything that is most important in life. Like all age-groups, children simply want people to be honest with them. Blume says children learn from adults, yet many adults do not know how to talk to kids about anything personal. She grew up hating secrets, and she still hates secrets.

I asked Blume what it was that the censors found so objectionable in her books. She said, "I think in the old days the complaints concerned language and sexuality, but perhaps the censors have become more sophisticated. With respect to *Blubber,* which I think may be my best book for younger kids, the complaints focused on something called 'lack of moral tone,' which I now understand to mean that the bad guys go unpunished or, as the bookbanners put it, evil goes unpunished. In other words, I don't beat the kids over the head with the 'message.' When I lecture and refer to 'lack of moral tone,' I always add, 'whatever that means,' and the audience always laughs. But I have read enough of the forms filled out challenging school library books to know that 'lack of moral tone' is used as a justification for banning books. There is also the claim that my books do not show sufficient respect for authority. But the letters of complaint that I have received are much more specific about offensive language, often specifying a particular curse word."

A school librarian once told Blume that the male principal of her school would not allow Blume's book *Deenie* to be put in the library because Deenie masturbated. He said it would be different if the character were a boy. Interestingly, the only time Blume's editors tried to soften her work, the sensitive passages involved masturbation. "I have a story that I tell on my favorite editor," she said. "It pains me to tell it, and it pains him to hear it. But it happened. When *Tiger Eyes* was published about eleven or twelve years ago, it was shortly after the 1980 elections. The censors were all over the place, and my editor said to me, 'We want this book to be read by as many young people as possible, don't we?' And I said yes. He said, 'Well, then, we don't want to make this a target for the censors, do we? Is it really necessary to include this one passage?' He agreed that the passage was psychologically appropriate to the character but asked whether it was necessary.

"I took it out, and I have regretted it ever since. Was the passage essential to the book? Well, every appropriate passage helps you to know the character. This character was a girl who turned herself off, didn't allow herself to feel emotion after her father was killed. She was beginning to get her feelings back as she explored her body. She masturbated. That's the passage that I was asked to take out, because masturbation is far more threatening than intercourse in a book about young people. I'm sorry that I took it out, and I have done nothing of the sort since then. The last time that I was asked to delete material from one of my books, the publisher's concern was with specific language rather than sexuality. There were just three words involved, but the publisher felt that their inclusion would reduce the paperback book club sales. I thought about it long and hard, but I concluded that the characters would not be real with sanitized speech. The book was eventually published without change."

Blume, like some of the other authors interviewed for this book, is uncomfortable with the attempts to narrowly define her audience: "I hate to categorize books. . . . I wish that older readers would read my books about young people, and I hope that younger readers will grow up to read what I have to say about adult life." She is concerned that, increasingly, children's books that deal realistically with life are being published as adult books or young adult books. She is still angry with Bradbury Press for advertising *Forever* as her first book for adults. She says *Forever* was not intended for adults, but the publishers hoped to protect themselves and her from controversy by suggesting that younger people were not the primary audience.

Blume says some teachers have told their students that if they use her books for a book report, they will automatically have points taken off their grade. She says, "When I began writing, I never thought of my books as classroom materials. I've always hoped that my books would be read the way I read books, which is to become involved in a story that I can't put down, to be swept away by a character, to be entertained and shown how other people live and solve their problems. All the reasons that I read fiction are the very reasons that I write fiction and hope what I write will be read. None of that involves the classroom. Over time, I've become used to the fact that teachers read my books aloud. But in the beginning, it bothered me because I thought of reading as a personal experience between the reader and the book, the kind of thing that you go away in the corner to do. You don't have to talk about it, you don't have to do a book report on it, you're never going to be graded on it, and you don't have to share it if you don't want to. On the other hand, if handled sensitively, my books can be useful classroom tools. I know of one teacher who begins his course each year by reading *Blubber* aloud. He then proceeds to a careful, often intense, discussion of the book and the issues it addresses. Of course, my 'Fudge' books are probably the most commonly used in class because they are fun."

The controversy surrounding her books has also discouraged their inclusion in textbooks and anthologies. She notes, "I've turned down a lot of book club editions, and the like, because they asked me to remove this, this, and this. Some of my material for younger kids has been excerpted, for example, *Tales of a Fourth Grade Nothing,* but not much of my work has been included in anthologies. Frankly, I would prefer that a child read an entire book rather than excerpts. Most schools today are moving away from traditional anthologies and texts, toward the creation of genuine classroom libraries. That's very positive." When asked to analyze the First Amendment implications of school and library censorship, Blume commented: "Obviously, school officials, teachers, and librarians engage in a selection process. But do they select under fear and intimidation or under professional guidelines? Do they select books that the students really want to read and need to read? There is a good deal of censorship by selection, by 'avoidance/selection,' one might say. But once the book has been selected for sound reasons, once it's there, then there are First Amendment rights to protect its availability. Children have rights, too, and in some places, children are beginning to understand that they have a right to choose what they want to read. I think it's very positive that they become involved in these struggles within their community. I encourage young people to become involved."

Judy Blume says her books have been defended by teachers, librarians, concerned citizens, and the kids themselves, the people she believes must be encouraged to take a stand to protect the books that they want to read. She told me: "I frankly feel that my job is to write the books, not to defend them. It is always the reader's job to defend the books, to ensure that they are available. What I try to do now is offer all the support I can to those who are under fire by the bookbanners, whether it is the teachers, librarians, or parents, or students. I feel that I should help by making available any information I can, so I send them letters from readers, letters from teachers, letters from parents. In the case of *Forever,* I send my personal letter describing how I came to write the book and why it is dedicated to my daughter. But I don't travel to the scene of the conflict in an attempt to defend my books."

Like Robert Cormier, Judy Blume feels that the more time she spends defending her books, the less time she has to write. "Cormier and I are of an age where suddenly we realize there isn't all that much time remaining. I don't really see the point of entering the fray, interceding in conflicts over my books. I think that should be done without the author present. I don't believe the issue should be personalized. It's not about the author—it's about the book. I cannot defend my books. I wouldn't even know how to do it. How do you explain why you wrote what you wrote when you wrote it? I just don't think that's part of the job. I love to read letters from kids, because it always seems to me that they make the point so much better than I could. I remember when *Deenie* was under fire, and a seventh-grade girl went before the school board and read a letter she had prepared, explaining why the book was important to her and how it had helped her and her friends to talk about scoliosis [curvature of the spine]. She said that if there was something bad in this book, she didn't know what it was—and maybe they could explain it to her. Such comments are far more persuasive and more important than anything Judy Blume or Robert Cormier could say before a school board.

"I'm not saying that no writer should go before a school board and put himself or herself on the line. I just don't feel it's right for me. I once put myself in the position of having to debate the Moral Majority on television, and I came away saying I'm never going to do that again. It's not what I want to do. On the other hand, I can think of many wonderful experiences, like the group of people in Gwinnett County, Georgia, who came together when a group of my books was banned.

They came together without me, because they cared about reading and about choosing. Even people who had no children in the school became involved because they were readers. They became strong, and even though they lost their case and *Deenie* was banned, it will never happen there again. Not to those people. I came to talk to them after the event, and, even now it makes me cry because it was so moving an experience to meet them and talk with them.

"The point I would like to make is that it is the kids who are the losers in all these battles. We're really talking about what they have a right to know, what they have a right to read. The adults' fears prevent them from talking to their children about subjects that all kids have a right to discuss and learn about. You know, puberty is not a dirty subject, but the censors seem to feel that it is, and that message is sent to the kids. When books are taken away from them because the natural events of puberty are discussed, the message is that these biological processes must not be anticipated or discussed, even though they are going to occur. This is bowing to fear. This is giving the censors power. That bothers me more than anything."

TITLE COMMENTARY

ARE YOU THERE GOD? IT'S ME, MARGARET (1971)

Dorothy M. Broderick

SOURCE: A review of *Are You There God? It's Me, Margaret,* in *Voice of Youth Advocates,* Vol. 31, No. 6, February, 1991, p. 346.

In the summer and early fall of 1970, I was on a ten thousand mile travel trailer trip to see America before they finished paving it over. Besides making the final corrections on my doctoral dissertation, the other non-tourist task was reviewing books for *The New York Times.* In a small town in Washington state, I picked up from General Delivery a package from George Woods, Children's Book Editor at the *Times.* Among the titles inside was a first novel by someone named Judy Blume and, while I have many wonderful memories of the grandeurs of our great and beautiful nation, I will also always cherish that first reading of *Are You There God? It's Me, Margaret.* I loved Margaret then, I still love her now. Bradbury Press, to celebrate Margaret's 20th birthday, has reissued the title with a new cover.

I'm 20 years farther away from that time in my life when childhood was ending, but rereading the novel makes it all seem like yesterday. Before Blume, youth literature jumped from *The Moffats* to titles by Du-Jardin, Cavanna, and Emery. No one helped readers make the transition; somehow it was as if you went to bed a child and woke up a full fledged adolescent. But life isn't like that. Before we reach the point where we worry about dates and proms and going steady, there is a time when *we* are our major focus. Hair begins growing in strange places; breasts begin to develop; and then comes the (for my era) totally unexpected trauma of menstruation. Status was measured by who got what first. That's how it was then; that's how it is now.

There are many within our profession who enjoy putting Judy Blume down as a writer, while buying all her books in more multiples than any other author they stock. To cast darts at the hand that feeds us strikes me as mean-spirited. Judy Blume opened up the world of young adult literature and made it possible for the literature to grow and change to meet the needs of modern young readers. More than any other author, before or now, she knows that our real lives are first and foremost internal; only when we get ourselves together can we begin to share life with another person. With *Are You There God? It's Me, Margaret,* Blume's first small novel turned out to be one giant step for young adult literature.

Happy birthday, Margaret. You'll live longer than this writer and almost everyone reading this. It's nice to know you're there to help make that passage from childhood to adolescence easier for those lucky enough to come to know you.

THEN AGAIN MAYBE I WON'T (1971)

Mel Krutz

SOURCE: "Censoring Judy Blume and *Then Again Maybe I Won't,*" in *Censored Books: Critical Viewpoints,* Nicholas J. Karolides, Lee Burress, and John M. Kean, eds., The Scarecrow Press, Inc., 1993, pp. 471-75.

1. Who is the most popular children's author in America today?

2. Who is the most censured?

3. Which of her books are most frequently in question?

Numbers one and two are obviously rhetorical. In order of frequency in a list of the top fourteen of the "most frequently censored titles" between 1985 and 1990, the answer to number three is: *Deenie, Forever, Blubber,* and *Then Again Maybe I Won't. Are You There God? It's Me, Margaret* cannot be far behind.

The answers to these questions open the proverbial Pandoric box. Out of the box comes a cacophony of rackety controversy. People for the American Way identify three of her books in the *top ten* most censored between 1982 and 1989. These are: *Deenie,* number seven; *Then Again Maybe I Won't,* number eight; and *Forever,* number nine. These same books reappear in other People for the American Way surveys, and always in the top numbers. In their list of the top fourteen books challenged between 1982 and 1987, *Blubber* is added as well. A list of forty-eight books most frequently challenged in 1982, reported by Karolides and Burress in *Celebrating Censored Books,* includes *Forever* and *Then Again Maybe I Won't* as challenged and censored. Blume censoring is extensive. Some schools have even blanket-censored all of her books.

Clashing with these censorings is a plethora of accolades for Judy Blume books. Some are: She received the first Golden Archer Award presented by the University of Wisconsin—Oshkosh, "a selection made without a pre-selected list, by the students themselves." In 1982, *Booklist,* the magazine of the American Library Association, in their poll of thousands of children, found that four of the top five of the "fifty most popular children's books in the country . . . were Blume titles." In 1982 The Assembly for Adolescent Literature asked "nearly 3,500 students in grades four through twelve to list up to three of the best books they had read on their own in the previous two years." Her works topped the list in *every* grade. The conductor of that poll, Dr. Donald Gallo, past president of the Assembly on Literature for Adolescents, stated, "There probably hasn't been any writer in history who has been that popular."

Sales figures of her books accentuate their acceptance and value to young readers. While juvenile books generally "sell only ten to fifteen thousand copies in four or five years," by 1983 more than a million copies of her books had sold in hardcover and around twenty-seven million in paperback. By 1987 paperback sales reached thirty-five million. *Superfudge* alone "sold over a million copies in hardcover within four months, and over a million and a half in paperback in six months.

The reasons for these statistics and the censoring are the same. Gallo stated it succinctly, "She is popular because what she writes about and how she writes it make her characters and their actions more real than anything anyone else writes—or perhaps has ever written for preteenage and younger adolescents." The authors of *Literature for Today's Young Adults,* Kenneth L. Donelson and Alleen Pace Nilsen state that Blume's books are popular because of "their refreshing candor about worries that young people have," and "that physical development is not treated separately from emotional and social development," making "Blume's books more fun to read (and more controversial) than are factual books about the development of the human body." Children can face their

realisms "through a character when it would be too painful to laugh at themselves directly," says Barbara Oliver of the Santa Fe, New Mexico Public Library, who points to Blume's ability to mix humor with issues. It is this candor, realism and levity which raise the ire of the censors.

Blume is her own best defense. Rather than moralize and dictate solutions to the realities of reader's lives she stimulates their thinking and problem solving, which leads to the development of mental growth and to emotional and social confidence and security—to stability in response to life. While this is a major goal of education in a democratic society, it is anathema to many conservatives, fundamentalists, and general followers of the ProFamily Forum, Citizens for Excellence in Education (an irony), the Moral Majority, the Eagle Forum et.al.

Blume says, "Censors think that by burying the issue they can control their child's thought. If I don't expose my child to this, they think, then my child is not going to think about this. That is not the way it works. . . . Every idea is insulting to someone. Certain books make me cringe, too . . . but I would never forbid my child or anyone else to read them. I would just make them aware of what else is available. Children are their own best censors. What matters is that they have a choice. It is up to us to provide them with a balanced diet. But if reality is removed from that diet, if they are not encouraged to face it as children, how can we expect them to cope as adults?"

Her readers verify the value of her books by sending her some 2000 letters a month. They say things like: "I like Judy Blume because every book she writes about a kid with problems concerns a little bit of me. . . . It's like she knows me and is writing about me." "She brings out more of me when she writes." "She knows what I am like." "Her books are about life the way it really is." This is not to say that the experiences of her characters are the experiences of every reader. I find a touch of "east coast" specificity in her stories, but nonetheless there is also constant universality, and, as one reader wrote, "She writes about people I would like to know." She shares with us that which is human.

Tony, in *Then Again Maybe I Won't,* typifies these characteristics. He personifies some of all of us, and Blume puts us into his head to see ourselves. Many of Blume's books are written through the eyes of the protagonist, as this is. Like Joyce and Faulkner, she uses a type of stream of consciousness. The thoughts of Tony (Anthony Miglione) flow through sequences of sensitive and generally sensible logic, topics and ideas which develop and unravel the plot. It is more than a first person point of view. It is a merging of reader / character minds.

Tony is initially a seventh grade paperboy in Jersey City who finds solutions to: how to respond to a cranky customer; how to be himself in the shadow of an impressive older brother, Ralph; how to live up to the image of another older brother, Vinnie, killed in Vietnam; how to be at ease with the situation his grandmother faces because of throat surgery leaving her unable to speak; how to understand a father who seems to him to be working on a secret project; how to adjust to a different social situation in the family move to Long Island; how to resolve his infatuation with an "older" neighbor girl, whom he fantasizes about and ogles from his bedroom window—all of these, and more, instances of his reality in the process of growing up.

His major concerns are how to adjust to and survive his father's major career change and resulting rise in social status, in the move to Long Island, and how to handle friendship with a rich, superficial, kleptomaniac neighbor, Joel Hoober. Tony isn't at ease with this new "rich" role and is embarrassed by his mother's eagerness to climb. He misses his good friend Frankie from the old neighborhood, and life as it was. Sensitive, honest, and genuine, Tony is caught in the middle of Joel's transgressions, and takes it out on himself.

Tony strives to avoid superficiality, as does Blume whose writing is not shallow, but moves beyond the surface to express what many seventh grade boys deal with in the climb toward adolescence, including "it" going up and having wet dreams, which are realistically though briefly and tastefully included, giving credence to the realities of maturation and life.

In real ways *Maybe I Won't* is the metaphoric state of mind of insecurity in youth, but usually Tony "will" when the doing is rational, and he is in inner conflict when it is not. He represents and brings out the best of the reader while struggling with human issues real to all. [Maryann] Weidt says of Blume's characters that "they appear to be simple, one-sided; but their simplicity is that of childhood: honest and complex. Tony is a well-rounded character who changes, develops, matures and rises to challenges, realizations and truths. Not narcissistic, he cares so much about others that his health is at stake. It is a story about confronting reality, breaking through simplicity and superficiality and maturing in the process.

It is a story of a boy's epiphany, like John Updike's Sammy in "A & P," or Jackie's in Frank O'Connor's "First Confession," or the boy's in James Joyce's "Araby." It is a story of holding onto one's values.

Weidt recognizes in it the need to belong, seeing it as also the story of isolation. Youth often feel outside of things; Tony and his grandmother both personify separation. Neither is part of the family's major decision making, nor does Tony easily feel a part of his new environment at school or in the neighborhood. Powerlessness goes hand-in-hand with isolation as does transplanting and the clash of societal class levels. But Tony does have the strength of family ties to withstand his disequilibrium, and that theme also matters. In his epiphany he becomes more sure of who and what he is regardless of the world around him. As Margaret prays in *Are You There God? It's Me, Margaret,* "Oh, please, God. I just want to be normal." Fortunately Tony finds his normalcy. His readers will be secure in theirs because of it.

📖 SUPERFUDGE (1980)

Perry Nodelman

SOURCE: "Cultural Arrogance and Realism in Judy Blume's *Superfudge,*" in *Children's Literature in Education,* Vol. 19, No. 4, 1988, pp. 230-41.

In the Newbery award winner for 1933, Elizabeth Foreman Lewis's *Yung Fu of the Upper Yangtse,* the main character is admirable because he is intuitively wise enough to see through the clearly silly, rigidly illiberal, and just plain old-fashioned values of his Chinese ancestors; he has been born with the freedom-loving, supersition-hating, and innately capitalistic soul of an American. The cultural arrogance of *Yung Fu* is relatively obvious; our values have changed enough since 1933 so that what once must have seemed like tolerant pleading for the universal brotherhood of man now baldly announces its embarrassing prejudice. But a less obvious sort of cultural imperialism is still at work in children's fiction.

In one of the stories in Paul Yee's *Teach Me to Fly, Skyfighter,* for instance, a young Canadian girl despises the Chinese heritage that makes her different from others; and not surprisingly, the events of the story teach her that Chinese culture is not merely silly and dismissable. But underlying this plea for acceptance of cultural difference is an apparently unconscious assumption of the absolute rightness of values that are decidedly alien to traditional Chinese culture. Sharon Fong accepts a kite of traditional design from an old Chinese man, who tells her how he made such kites as a lonely young immigrant to Canada, separated from his wife, who was still in China:

> once the kite was up I was a different man. My bones stopped aching, my muscles loosened. I thought I was a seagull flying free, lighter than air. . . . And somewhere over the horizon I could see my wife's beautiful face, waiting for me.

The kite loses whatever traditional significance it might have had when it comes to represent familiar North American values: the need to feel free, optimistic aspirations, the healthiness of faith in an impossible dream, a romantically powerful love. Sharon then decides that "the kite and its story were finally Chinese things that made sense to her," and feels more comfortable about her heritage; ironically, she can accept "being Chinese" only because it means being North American. Not surprisingly, furthermore, the story makes it clear that her doing so leads Sharon to self-acceptance and a more positive self-image; both the Canadian author of this book and its characters simply take the rightness of these mainstream North American values for granted.

By definition, our culture defines the world for us, tells us what reality is; so it is exceedingly hard for writers *not* to take their own culture and its values for granted. When I taught a collection called *Best-Loved Folk Tales of the World* last year, the typical North Americans who were students in my children's literature course happily agreed with the editor's comment that these tales from many different countries "deal with universal human dilemmas that span differences of age, culture, and geography." My students shared the high-minded but ingenuous faith of many North Americans, including many who work professionally with children's literature: the fact that they could equally enjoy and equally approve the moral thrust of stories from around the world showed that, despite our different colored skins and various costumes, we human beings are all basically the same. My attempts to persuade these students that they could so easily enjoy these stories exactly because the original versions of them had been rewritten and reshaped to suit North American ideas about what a story consists of, about how it should be told, and perhaps above all, about what it should mean, were met with disbelief—and more significantly, with outrage. Some students took my conviction that people might actually be different from each other as evidence of my intolerance, and were infuriated when I suggested that accepting different people only because you refuse to acknowledge the differences is hardly an act of tolerance.

But then a student freshly arrived from Singapore began to discuss one particular story in the book, which, he said, he remembered from his own childhood. The story centers on a woman's conviction that she is meant to marry one specific man, who asks for her hand too late and then dies of remorse; on the day of her wedding to another man, she stops the procession, falls on the grave of her true love, and says, "If we were intended to be man and wife, open your grave three feet wide." The grave opens and the woman leaps into it; finally, she and her true intended become rainbows. But, said my student, the title that the tale has been given in *Best-loved Folktales*, "Faithful Even in Death," is not true to the original, and reveals a cultural bias; the story is not at all about faithfulness, but rather, about fate working out properly. The title distorts the story in order to accommodate non-Oriental cultural assumptions: it implies that the woman's faithfulness is a matter of choice on her part, and therefore, a virtue that is being rewarded, whereas the story itself makes it clear that the woman had no choice but to love he whom she was meant to love, and that the situation has nothing to do with virtue or reward. Only someone whose conception of story derived from European fairy tales could have distorted this tale by making the moral health of the characters the driving force behind the events of the plot.

This student from Singapore taught some of the North Americans in the class a valuable lesson: if we are not conscious that other cultures offer different and, for those who live within them, equally satisfactory definitions of meaning and value, and that consequently, these cultures postulate quite different but equally satisfactory realities, then we are doomed to a dangerous solitude, a blindness that amounts to an unconscious form of arrogance. Like Sharon Fong and like many of my students, many of us live inside such a solitude—do simply assume without even consciously doing so that what we value ourselves is universally valued by people around the world. In *Mythologies*, Roland Barthes defines the bourgeoisie of his native France as

> *the social class which does not want to be named.* . . . Politically, the haemorrhage of the name "bourgeois" is effected through the idea of *nation*. This was once a progressive idea, which has served to get rid of the aristocracy; today, the bourgeoisie merges into the nation, even if it has, in order to do so, to exclude from it the elements which it decides are allogenous (the Communists).

(Italics his; "allogenous" is a geologic term for rock found away from its rightful place.)

Indeed, many of us refuse to accept the idea that there *is* such a thing as a bourgeoisie; we say that nowadays we are all members of what we usually call the middle class—that there is no other class. Such ideas can be held only by those who either ignore the differences in the existence of those with different values and ways of living, such as the very rich and the numerous poor, or else define those others as insignificant, as ignorable outsiders; as Barthes goes on to say, "practiced on a national scale, bourgeois norms are experienced as the evident laws of a natural order. . . . " This is a sort of cultural arrogance that emerges from high-minded liberalism, a democratic faith in human equality, rather than from narrow-minded prejudice; but it is arrogant nevertheless.

The less thoughtful of the university students I teach reveal such a bias most clearly when they study books that most closely appear to represent their own class and culture; their primary assumption is always that the best books are the ones that depict a world they can best recognize, and that such books are worthwhile exactly because they are realistic enough to be universally recognizable. Judy Blume's *Superfudge* is one such book; many of my students responded to a test question on this book by almost unanimously telling me that this tale of an eleven-year-old boy confronted with a move from New York to Princeton, New Jersey and the various domestic problems caused by parents, friends, and younger siblings, is so realistic that it could be understood and enjoyed by everyone. One student wrote, "It's so realistic—all eleven year olds go through that." Another wrote, "This book is so real because anyone can relate to it—I have a younger brother myself, and I know just how Peter feels about Fudge."

We can make such statements only by forgetting about the existence of the millions of eleven-year-olds in this world who are too hungry or too poor to face problems as relatively frivolous as those facing Peter, and by assuming that all human beings of all cultural backgrounds respond to experience in much the same way. One can understand Peter's feelings about Fudge *because* one also has a younger brother only if one believes that all cultures countenance exactly the same attitudes toward siblings, and that consequently, all human beings feel the same way about younger brothers. In an earlier article called "How Typical Children Read Typical books," I discussed the dangerous implications of the idea of readers "relating to" or "identifying with" characters, a

sort of reading that I believe we deliberately teach to children: "In training children to identify, to read only about themselves, we sentence them to the solitude of their own consciousness." But such reading not only enforces a dangerous solipsism; it also fosters the confusion of one's limited personal reality with universal truth—the sort of cultural arrogance I have been discussing.

I have suggested that my students' insistence on the universal truth of *Superfudge* ignored the quite different reality of eleven-year-olds in places like Singapore, who do not in fact live like Peter, who not only often look different, but who also live in different physical circumstances influenced by different traditions, and who therefore feel differently about themselves and their world. But one Singaporean in this year's children's literature class told me that he enjoyed *Superfudge* exactly because it reminded him of his own childhood back home—not, however, of his actual life, but of the American television shows he once watched. For him, such shows had been wonderful fantasies, depicting an exotic world quite different from his own: the characters lived not in apartments but in large houses surrounded by lawns, and unlike himself and the other children he knew, the TV children not only got away with defying their parents and teachers but were even praised for the adorable ways in which they did it. He had recognized *Superfudge* as the same sort of fantasy.

That student had now come to North America, had seen houses like the one *Superfudge* describes, had met North American children of the sort who "relate" to Peter and Fudge. Yet he still read *Superfudge* as a fantasy; it did not in fact accurately represent North American reality as he had come to see it. What is interesting is that this book, which strikes insiders as such an accurate rendering of their world, should seem so inaccurate as to be a delightful fantasy to an outsider.

In fact, readers with any degree of literary sophistication would have to admit that *Superfudge* is *not* a very realistic novel. We call a novel realistic when it evokes the details of a specific place and time so accurately that we have no choice but to be convinced by their rightness. But *Superfudge* is the sort of book I described in my earlier article, in which typicality replaces reality: in order to be identified with, the characters must be devoid of any distinguishing characteristic that might separate them from their readers; they must be purely and exclusively "typical" in a way that people never actually are in reality. Thus, Peter at eleven does exactly what eleven-year-olds are supposed to do. He claims to dislike (but actually loves) his younger brother, finds modern art to be an example of the ridiculous pretensions of adults, believes his own parents are insufferably stupid, and is embarrassed by but beginning to be interested in girls; and Peter is the most individual character in the novel. The setting are equally vague. As a result, as I said of a different book, "we cannot possibly understand the story unless we fill in its exceedingly vague outlines with knowledge from our own experience." In part, it was lack of such knowledge that prevented my student from Singapore from seeing the truth of *Superfudge.*

But in fact, *Superfudge* depicts a reality quite different from the ones Singaporeans, North American children's literature students, or even North American children actually experience. Each of its episodes begins and quickly concludes an action in a way that denies the randomness of experience. Furthermore, Peter is supposed to be telling his own story, but he often sounds less like a child than like a middle-aged woman with a keen eye for the cute silliness of kids—including himself, as when he notices his own disregard for towels: "I ran my hands under the faucet and dried them on my jeans." Typical children might perform the action, but only one with a curiously distanced attitude towards his own behavior would be likely to take note of it. Peter also indulges in a sort of sentimentality that seems to be at odds with the rest of his character, as when he speaks of his baby sister: "the little sighs are my favorites, because then I know she's content. And she feels so warm and soft, lying in my arms that way, that I feel good all over." Since this determinedly conventional eleven-year-old male constantly gets infuriated with others for acting in unconventional ways, it is hard to imagine to whom he might be confessing these maternal feelings.

Nor is that uncertainty of audience the only uncertainty in the way the novel expresses itself. Peter also wavers inconsistently between past and present. At times he seems to know the eventual outcome of events, but at other times he is blithely ignorant of them; and he mixes a narrative past, implied by phrases like "The next afternoon when I got home from school" with phrases that imply an ongoing present: "I keep telling my mother that it's not a good idea to let Tootsie grow up with her feet in her mouth. But Mom says she'll grow out of it." The difficulty in determining if Peter tells of these events as they happen or in retrospect further increases the distance between the novel's reality and our own.

Given these oddities, we cannot actually find reality in *Superfudge* by filling in its outlines with our own

knowledge of actual experience; indeed, we must ignore the oddities in order to find the book convincing. The obvious question is, why did so many of my students, and why do so many other child and adult readers of Judy Blume, so easily assume that this book accurately represents reality? In one particular sense, *Superfudge* does accurately mirror the reality that my students and many other adults and children claim to believe in: it confuses egocentric solipsism with universal truth. For people who have read a certain amount of serious literature, the greatest oddity of Judy Blume's writing is that the stories are told by a first person narrator whose view of the events described is assumed to be accurate. When Henry James or Flannery O'Connor allows a character to tell a story he or she is involved in, we immediately detect the irony: the character has not seen the whole truth, and the pleasure in the story is that careful readers can discover a broader truth hidden by the distortions.

But a reading of *Superfudge* that takes note of apparent inconsistencies in Peter's character or of oddities in the reality he describes is clearly acting against the assumptions of the text itself: when Peter Hatcher tells his own story, we must understand that his apparently egocentric and often shallow view of the events he describes is indeed meant to be understood as the whole truth. Peter is right to believe that he is smarter than his parents, he almost always has a perfect understanding of the motivations of the other characters, and his view of experience as a series of discrete episodes is not qualified; apparently, his personal and highly solipsistic vision is directly in accordance with universal reality. So perhaps it is not surprising that so many readers confuse that solipsistic vision with actual reality and presume it to be universal.

But there are other and even more revealing reasons for them to do so: for, while it may not be realistic in any usual sense of that term, the world *Superfudge* describes is exceedingly familiar. As my student from Singapore rightly suggested, it is the world as depicted in numerous television situation comedies. There too the situations are discrete, and unconnected, and quickly resolved, and there too the children speak like cynical adult wiseacres. Indeed, *Superfudge* could easily be transformed into such a television show—a show like many over the past four decades, or like the current show *Family Ties.* The Hatcher family seem to be an ordinary, typical family living an ordinary life; but, like the characters in most TV sitcoms, they clearly have an upper middle class income. Father has a relatively glamorous job, mother has a traditionally feminine revulsion for worms, and they live in a comfortable old house, in a community which seems to have magically maintained some of the amenities of life in the days before the automobile made communities less complete: there is a local movie theater, a local art gallery, good neighborhoods of roomy old houses, and so on. The family's situation is equally nostalgic, and in that way different from the families depicted in most current sitcoms: mom and dad are happy with each other after many years of marriage, the family is complete, mom is happy to stay home and raise children. Most current sitcoms recognize the disruption of North American family life by centering around odd family groupings; but that these groups of single daughter/single mother/single grandmother, or of three unrelated older women living together, or of single father/son/house-keeper act as a family and undergo the typical family disputes of older sitcoms suggests how very much the family of *Superfudge* represents the essence of a nostalgic convention.

But while the Hatchers represent a nostalgic, or at the very least, utopian, idea of what a typical American family might be like, they also express the sort of significant abnormalities that define the "situation" as comic. Family sitcoms need a "concept"—a child who is actually a robot, a house guest from another planet, a conservative son who rebels against his parents' liberalism. In *Superfudge,* Fudge is an adorable brat who is always getting into trouble and never realizing it, and there is a new baby in the house; both these are numbingly familiar "concepts" to viewers of TV sitcoms.

Equally familiar is the peculiar sort of characterization Blume provides. Her characters express the same paradoxical doubleness as that of many TV sitcom characters. On the one hand, they are rigid stereotypes, humorous because they can always be counted on to act out of their few clearly defined traits. Fudge will always be cute, Peter will always be offended by the unconventional. But on the other hand, the rigidity of the stereotype almost always hides a soft heart; Peter, who makes snide remarks when his mother worries about Fudge's disappearance, admits to a lump in his throat when Fudge is found. The comic rigidity almost always yields to an underlying softhearted sentiment, just as it does so often on television; we can laugh at the rigidity without worrying that we are undemocratically looking down on those we laugh at, for they turn out to be only superficially rigid, and in need of the scorn of laughter in order to reveal their true humanity.

The thematic content of both *Superfudge* and many TV sitcoms expresses a similarly shrewd doubleness that also relates to the idea of rigidity. The situations

are all about change—about the flexibility required to face life responsibly, and about the immaturity of a rigid resistance to change. We are allowed to laugh at the rigid characters in sitcoms because their resistance to new ideas and possibilities defines them as dangerously limited beings; the theoretically liberal bias of most popular television tends to equate change with growth, and to see any rigidity or conservatism as stagnant and stultifying. Consequently, many episodes of sitcoms describe how a rigid character first humorously resists and then seriously learns to accept change—the birth of a new baby, the immigrant who moves in next door, a father's first date.

Nevertheless, the beginning of each new episode takes us right back to the beginning: in order to be laughable, the rigid character must go on being rigid, and thus, seems each week to have forgotten the lesson he or she learned last week; and in order to be instructive of properly liberal North American values, the character must learn once more each week to transcend rigidity. The audience then is allowed two contradictory pleasures at once: both the comedy of static egocentricity and the philosophic satisfaction of "growth." Furthermore, the contradiction implies the pleasing truth that "growth" is not real or dangerous—that to grow is merely to repeat the same old comfortable pattern, not the unsettling act of actually transcending it and moving on; the apparent focus on change disguises an intense conservatism, an absolute faith in the rightness of things as they are.

Superfudge seems to be about accepting change. The plot centers on conflicts surrounding having a new baby, moving to a new place, making new friends, and so on. And much is said about change: Peter's angry statement at the beginning of the second chapter that "Life at our house had definitely changed" is a clear signal that readers will soon get to laugh at his rigidity; and of course he is unable to understand when his father says he wants to try living somewhere else or when his mother says she wants to go back to college because "I'm ready for a change." Peter's father sums up what seems to be a central message when he says, "Changes take some getting used to . . . but in the long run they're healthy."

But as in TV sitcoms, the change in *Superfudge* is deceptive. Peter resists and accepts change after change as the book goes on, but he remains enough the same rigid character so that he can continue to resist the changes and thus create comic situations. Similarly, Fudge grows older but no less prone to comic disaster. Furthermore, the ending of the book undercuts its own apparent acceptance of the value of change. When his father says he moved to Princeton "for a change," Fudge wisely suggests that "Daddy ran away when he didn't want to work anymore"; and father, mother, and everyone else happily acknowledge a basic resistance to growth when they decide to move back to the life they always lived before. As in sitcoms, the lip service paid to flexibility disguises an underlying conservatism, a bland acceptance of things as they are. But *Superfudge* ingeniously always manages to have it both ways: the "change" that Hatchers reject is a theoretically conventional family life in a small town, and they conservatively return to a more glamorous urban lifestyle, so that their refusal to change sounds like courageous individualism rather than conservative conformity—while at the same time, father gives up art for business, and mother gives up school for homemaking.

My students can "relate" to all this because they watch TV; they are familiar enough with the patterns of popular culture to recognize them. Yet until it is pointed out to them, the divergence of this novel from the specific conditions of the world they actually live in is not terribly obvious to them—no more obvious than the arrogance of saying that *every* eleven-year-old is like Peter. I'm happy to report that, when I question their assumption that *Superfudge* represents reality, my students quickly acknowledge its inadequacy, and wonder how they could have been so easily deceived by it.

Once again, Barthes offers an explanation, as he discusses the ways in which the artifacts and conventions of culture permeate and define reality for us:

> our press, our films, our theater, our pulp literature, our rituals, our justice, our diplomacy, our conversations, our remarks about the weather, a murder trial, a touching wedding, the cooking we dream of, the garments we wear, everything, in everyday life, is dependent on the representation which the bourgeoisie has and makes us have of the relations between man and the world. . . . practiced on a national scale, bourgeois norms are experienced as the evident laws of the natural order—the further the bourgeois class propagates its representations, the more naturalized they become.

Barthes' argument here would suggest that, by constantly reinforcing the same images and conceptions of reality, TV sitcoms and novels like *Superfudge* come to permeate our conception of the world—*become,* in fact, the world we believe we live in.

Unfortunately, however, the images and conceptions such TV shows and novels offer are untruthful ones that work to replace consciousness of the truth. The world they ask us to believe in is a cleaner, richer, and less distressing one than the one we actually live in; like much popular entertainment, *Superfudge* describes a comfortable and stable upper middle class life as if it were the norm. It also tends to leave out and thus imply the nonexistence of many of the unsettling confusions of actual reality, and it divests the problems it does describe of their real difficulty: each situation focuses only on one problem and quickly solves it, the same problem never recurs again, and the overall pattern of growth and reversion pays a sort of lip service to change that works to create a dangerous complacency. Finally, then, the novel tells a story that cleverly confuses truth with wish-fulfillment. While Peter may be like many real children in believing that he knows better than his parents, the fact that he obviously is right and that he does in fact know better is a clever confusion of truth with desire.

Barthes describes how the big weddings of the "bourgeoisie" are so much assumed to be the universal norm in media representations of marriage that poorer people scrimp and save to be "normal" in this expensive way; and as a result, "the bourgeoisie is constantly absorbing into its ideology a whole section of humanity which does not have its basic status and cannot live up to it except in imagination, that is, at the cost of an immobilization and an impoverishment of consciousness." I believe that my students' faith in the reality of *Superfudge* represents such an impoverishment. They can see this novel as "real" only if they recognize the world it describes from the repetitive depictions of such a world on television and elsewhere. In letting such depictions play their manipulative game of forcing us to suspend our actual knowledge of reality and believe in their truth, we allow ourselves to be captivated by a doubly satisfying solipsism: the belief that our own perceptions of the ways things ought to be is in fact the way they actually are, and the equally comforting belief that our own perception of the way things are is the only possible way of viewing reality. These are comfortable but dangerous delusions.

Clearly, then, a book like *Superfudge* helps to foster personal and cultural blindness—an unconscious but nevertheless dangerous form of arrogance. Furthermore, the ways in which it does so offer a particularly significant challenge for those interested in introducing literature both to children and adults. The simple fact that my students and so many children and other adults find the novel so recognizable suggests how thoroughly the attitudes and patterns of popular culture permeate their lives. The novel is loose, episodic, fragmented in tone and content; in fact, it is constructed less like a conventional novel with a cohesive overall narrative thrust than like a series of episodes of a sitcom, so that a moral parable is followed by a slapstick joke. This is the narrative structure of most TV series; and because the narrative structures of TV are *not* the ones basic to most written fiction, those whose narrative experience is derived mainly from TV and books like *Superfudge* are likely to have trouble comprehending more conventional literary narratives.

The lack of continuity between the weekly episodes of a TV show teaches viewers to focus purely on what is happening in each particular episode and to disregard the overall narrative thrust of a series as a whole; and what Raymond Williams calls TV "flow," the characteristic intermingling of parts of stories, commercials telling different stories, newsbreaks and so on, in a continuous flow of separate events that have no significant relationship to each other, means that even our attentiveness to any one episode of a TV show will be intermittent. Anyone expecting to be able to browse casually through a serious novel in the same way as one watches TV, paying attention to some episodes, ignoring others, and ignoring the overall thrust of the plot or the consistency of the characters or the language will miss much of significance.

People who read in this way—and many children and adults do—need to broaden their conceptions of the possibilities of narrative structure as well as their images of reality; yet the deliberate fostering of complacency implicit in the narrative forms they know is likely to make them unreceptive to different modes of narrative structuring that do actively promote genuine growth and self-awareness. It is the responsibility of parents and educators to teach those brought up on TV narrative how to respond to more demanding narrative structures, so that they may transcend their solip conceptions of the world.

📖 *LETTERS TO JUDY: WHAT YOUR KIDS WISH THEY COULD TELL YOU* (1986)

Phyllis Theroux

SOURCE: A review of *Letters to Judy: What Your Kids Wish They Could Tell You,* in *Book World—The Washington Post,* Vol. 16, No. 17, April 27, 1986, pp. 3-4.

It is almost impossible to be a parent in this country without eventually knowing about Judy Blume. She is the phenomenally successful author of over a dozen books that have found their way into the hands of a readership which, until Blume more or less preempted the field, had gone without a spokesman—your children. Over 30 million of them have taken comfort from her words.

The characters in her stories are too fat, too unpopular, or too meanly treated by their best friends. They want to know about sex, with specifics, but are too embarrassed to ask. They live with parents who are getting divorced, favor their younger brother, or don't understand anything. Judy Blume does. She is one of those adults who forgot to forget what childhood is all about.

Now comes Blume with a book that flowed right out of her mailbox. Based upon the nearly 2,000 letters she receives every month from her mostly young readers, *Letters to Judy: What Your Kids Wish They Could Tell You* is an attempt, heartrendingly successful, to give parents a keyhole glimpse into the world their children inhabit. It is not a pretty place.

Take Molly, age 11. She comes to school one day and finds out that all her friends are ostentatiously crossing her name off their notebook covers. "It's Donna," (confides Molly to Blume) who has turned the class against her. They proceed to call her "Brace Face," "Tinsel Teeth," and "The Ratty Redhead." Molly's mother, sounding eerily like Everymother, tells her that "she's sick of this 'ganging up' thing, and would I please try to find some new friends."

Molly, attempting to confide in a teacher, is told to ignore the situation; it doesn't work. Weeks of social ostracism ensue. . . . "Then I thought of you and I knew you would understand. Please, please help me!"

We don't know what happened to Molly. As she does with all her correspondents, Blume answered her letter but none of her replies are included in the book. In fact, if there is any flaw in *Letters to Judy,* it is the fact that so many children are left floating in our minds, somewhere "out there" as they deal with situations, many of which are far worse than Molly's.

Blume hears from children whose stepfathers have sexually abused them, who are handicapped, have brothers in jail, are being torn by bloody divorces, and are struggling with the ramifications of living with retarded siblings. "Thank you for reading my note," writes Abigail, age 14. "I just hope this note won't bring you down."

Reading *Letters to Judy* with a slightly commercial eye, it is clear that Blume has a gold mine of new plots arriving in her mail on a daily basis. But far clearer is the urgent need of children to articulate their fears, anxieties and real problems. It is Blume's intention in this book to give parents a few hints as to how to ease their children's minds and hearts, based upon her own experience. Interspersed between the letters (divided into various categories) are snatches of autobiographical commentary from Blume's life as a child and parent which address various issues, such as divorce.

Twice-married and divorced, Blume admits that between marriages she was not honest. "At the time my children needed me most, I was least able to give to them. Even though I wanted the divorce it was a time of shock, hurt, anger, sadness and depression." She married almost immediately again "because I was terrified at the idea of being alone." Throughout *Letters,* Blume inserts her own trials and errors where appropriate, giving form and overview to what might otherwise have been a book too full of "cries and whispers" from anonymous children to endure.

It is not all woe. "Dear Judy," writes Melanie, age 11, "How does a girl kiss a boy—arms around the neck or waist? Also, do you squeeze the lips real hard and are the girl's lips placed exactly on the boy's or is the girl's upper lip above the boy's upper lip or what?"

Whether the advice Blume gives to parents is advice you have already taken is a question only you can answer after reading the book. That reason for buying *Letters* is sufficient in itself. But the children Blume introduces are such radiantly candid and innocent human beings that we cannot help but look at our own children with a deeper understanding and compassion. Blume's correspondents quite effortlessly outshine the author which I rather suspect she is happy to allow. Letting them have center stage gives credit to the director. This is a generous book.

Cathi Edgerton

SOURCE: A review of *Letters to Judy,* in *Voice of Youth Advocates,* Vol. 9, Nos. 3 & 4, August & October, 1986, pp. 171-72.

In 1971, Judy Blume received her first letter from a reader saying she felt just like Margaret in Blume's now classic book *Are You There, God? It's Me, Margaret.* Now the popular author's mail brings 2,000 letters each month from her young readers. Kids write to her, Blume says, because as they identify with her fictional characters, they trust her to understand them. They write for the therapeutic release of feelings. They write to ask her to write another book about someone in their exact situation; they outline their lives as suggested plots. When a ten-year-old child wrote to ask her to "write a book for adults about our problems to open their eyes," Blume realized that underlying many letters was the plea: "Help me tell my parents." Believing strongly in her responsibility to those who see her as confidante, Blume wrote *Letters to Judy* to share kids' letters with other kids to let them know they are not alone, and to let their parents know what kids cannot seem to tell them directly.

As she addresses the whole family, Blume is remarkably successful in her dual purpose. Chapters are arranged by subject, covering family relationships, friendship, disability and illness, coping with divorce or death and new family structures resulting, the facts of life, runaways, rape, incest, child abuse, drug and alcohol abuse, depression and suicide. Actual letters appear in the text with Blume's comments, sometimes specifically addressed to "kids" or "Parents", often tying in anecdotes from her own and her children's lives. Her tone is one of warm support and encouragement, without specific advice beyond urging young people to communicate with their families or other adults nearby, seeking professional help when necessary. Stating that she is not a psychologist, Blume acts instead as a facilitator or mediator in family communications. The letters themselves, from children as young as nine all the way through the teens (and some from adults) give clear, sometimes heartbreaking testament to the urgent need for better exchange within families. "What's the difference between right and wrong?" asks 14-year-old Laura, feeling alone in her struggle with drug addiction. "I've tried explaining my side but (my parents) don't understand," says 12-year-old Kimberly, feeling overwhelmed with too much household responsibility.

Readers of all ages will benefit from Blume's insight and concern, for by listening and caring, she inspires others to do so. An extensive resource list by subject incorporates agency referrals and book annotations, helping readers put new understanding into practice. Included is a plug for libraries and librarians, with Blume's conviction that books help solve problems, both nonfiction for facts and fiction for feelings. This excellent, ground-breaking new approach to family self-help belongs in all libraries and homes.

Linda R. Groen

SOURCE: A review of *Letters to Judy: What Your Kids Wish They Could Tell You*, in *Book Report*, Vol. 5, No. 2, September-October, 1986, p. 42.

Since her first letter in 1971, Blume now receives nearly 2,000 from young readers each month. She feels that it's easier for them to confide in someone they won't "have to face at the breakfast table the next morning." The letters are divided into chapters that deal with specific problems, including parents, school and friends, death, boys and girls, trouble in the family, and sexual development. Sensitive topics are handled in a matter-of-fact way. Although Blume seems to be writing to adults (particularly parents), she also addresses some comments specifically to the kids who will be reading the book. Blume does not offer specific advice as much as she shares her own experiences growing up and her experiences with her own children. A chapter of resources includes agencies and a few exceptional nonfiction books.

Carol Rumens

SOURCE: A review of *Letters to Judy*, in *The Times Literary Supplement*, No. 4365, November 28, 1986, p. 1342.

Every voluntary reader of fiction is no doubt self-searching to some degree, but the adolescent reader is particularly so. Provided it is open-minded, such reading entails deep imaginative contact. If a book isn't felt as some kind of personal, emotional discovery, it isn't read, but dead. Lucky the adolescent for whom the O or A level text turns out to be the set book of his or her soul.

Modern children for whom *Macbeth* doesn't quite fill the bill may turn to *Blubber* or *Are you there, God? It's me, Margaret* by Judy Blume, the American writer whose emotional "how-to" books for the under-sixteens are extremely popular on both sides of the Atlantic. Such books may require no great imaginative efforts from their readers, but they are far from stupid or dishonest. They faithfully re-create the realities of school and family life in good, brisk, colloquial prose. Anxieties are sensitively explored, and if the context is generally optimistic, it nevertheless retains a sense of uncertainty and flux as well as possibility; the false pink glow of happily-ever-after is usually nicely muted, if not avoided altogether.

All this began in the 1970s (and derives from 1960s barricade-storming as plainly as the surveys of Masters and Johnson do); by now it has become a minor industry. Two recent heirs are Paula Danziger and Norma Klein, a number of whose books have been brought out by Heinemann this year. The woe that is in marriage, and family life in general, comes through relentlessly in the work of both these authors, the mother's struggle for her own growth and autonomy often providing an interesting extra dimension, as in Klein's *Mom, the Wolf Man and Me* and Danziger's *Can you Sue your Parents for Malpractice?* I wonder, though, if they speak as intimately to their young readers as those of Blume.

Letters to Judy spells out the extent, and the pathos, of the response. "Some of your books almost tell my life", writes Emma, a black girl bullied by her white class-mates; "I feel you're writing about me" is indeed the refrain, and on both sides of the Atlantic. But of course this isn't simply a collection of fan-mail; invariably, the correspondents go on to describe problems of their own, adding that they "can't talk" to their parents. It appears that, while teenagers have always tended to suffer crises of one sort or another, the modern, two-generation family structure cruelly intensifies their sense of isolation. Parents are more likely to change partners, too, emerging from unassailable but comforting distance to become their children's sexual equals and rivals. None of the problems described could be termed trivial, least of all from the child's point of view, but some are more extreme than others, however casual the phrasing: "My mother was arrested for child abuse. She beat me and my heart stopped."

A number of the children suggest plots for further books, with touching apologies for "being pushy"; but of course the real need is to tell their own stories to a trusted listener. ("I will keep writing to you . . . will tell you one problem per letter.") Judy Blume, who trained as a teacher before she became a writer, makes a sensible and friendly guru. A trace of encounter-group jargon does not exceed the acceptable and the references to her own experiences as a child, a mother and a twice-divorced wife are easy and candid. Though she does not include her answering letters, the tone of her comments suggests their character, its genuine concern. Sometimes, when the correspondence has been sustained over a lengthy period, the letters have been put together to form "stories". At the same time, the writer is always alert to an emergency, urging counsellors and suicide hot-lines if necessary. A list of support groups and their telephone numbers is included in an appendix which, entitled "resources", might justifiably bear as its sub-title, "The limits of fiction".

This book is very much the product of a problem-solving society, imbued with its optimism and naivety. Most European writers, apart from the professional agony aunts, would probably feel like scurrying back to their ivory towers at even a trickle of such letters. While admiring the openness and human decency that sits down and replies in person to each *cri de coeur,* I feel a certain unease that a writer should be under such pressure, that huge social obligations should be raising their shark-like fins under the frail craft of fictional integrity. It is an expression of the utmost democracy; and yet, strangely enough, it suggests the kinds of demands made on writers in societies that are anything but democratic, where, though books are read, the literary imagination is all but dead.

JUST AS LONG AS WE'RE TOGETHER (1987)

Ilene Cooper

SOURCE: A review of *Just as Long as We're Together,* in *Booklist,* Vol. 83, No. 22, August, 1987, pp. 1741-42.

Gr. 6-8. Stephanie Hirsh, an eternal optimist, is looking forward to starting junior high. It bothers her that her father has to be on the West Coast until Thanksgiving, but at least she's home with her mom; her engaging younger brother, Bruce; and her best friend, Rachel Robinson. When Stephanie meets Alison Monceau, the Vietnamese daughter of an American actress, she happily incorporates the girl into her circle. But events are changing in Stephanie's life without her really being aware of them. Her father's absence turns out to be a marital separation from her mother, and Stephanie is inducted into the world of holidays split between parents, "flings," and adults caught up in their own lives. Moreover, Stephanie and Rachel have a falling out, and all of Stephanie's problems lead to a significant weight gain. It's been a while since Blume has written for this age group, and she shows the same easy touch that has endeared her to so many children. Unfortunately, it's hard to be an innovator when one has so many imitators— this predictable though likable story nestles right into the first-person genre. Conversations about first periods, career mothers, and boy girl relationships abound, but the serious problems, such as what it means to be overweight in a fanatically thin society, are never really addressed. While her plotting slides a bit, Blume's characters are engaging, and fans of the author will be happy to spend time with this winsome group.

Beryl Lieff Benderly

SOURCE: A review of *Just as Long as We're Together,* in *Book World—The Washington Post,* Vol. 17, No., November 8, 1987, p. 19.

Readers of my age—though probably not Blume's intended audience of grade-schoolers—will immediately recognize the title, a line from the old popular song *Side by Side.* Stephanie Hirsch, the young heroine, learns the ditty at summer camp. She particularly likes the part that goes "Through all kinds of weather, what if the sky should fall, just as long as we're together, it just doesn't matter at all." And the song comfortingly continues, "When they've all had their quarrels and parted, we'll be the same as we started." In this deceptively simple, multi-layered story, Blume puts these propositions to the test of experience.

This is, I hasten to admit, my first Blume. I'd long heard, of course, about her alleged penchant for off-color subject matter (of which I found no evidence) and her immense appeal to pre-teen readers (of which I found plenty). What I was not prepared for was her enormous skill as a novelist. While apparently presenting the bright, slangy, surface details of life in an upper-middle class suburban junior high school, she's really plumbing the meaning of honesty, friendship, loyalty, secrecy, individuality, and the painful, puzzling question of what we owe those we love.

We first meet 12-year-old Stephanie in the days just before she enters seventh grade. Her family has just moved to a new, somewhat smaller, house not far from their old house, and her father is away on an extended business trip to the west coast—thousands of miles from their Connecticut home. To someone with more worldly experience, these would be clear signs that something is up, that life will not be the same again. Other things are changing for Stephanie too. As her mother says, she's now "into hunks" in an innocent sort of way; she keeps a poster of the young Richard Gere right over her bed, and daydreams that he is her future boyfriend, but she calls him Benjamin Moore, after the paint used in her new room.

The move to her new neighborhood of Palfrey's Pond brings Steph closer to her lifelong best friend, the earnest, sensitive, studious Rachel Robinson. It also introduces her to a new classmate just arrived from Los Angeles, the savvy, breezy, resourceful Alison Monceau, a Vietnamese orphan adopted as an infant in Paris by a well-known American actress and her French first husband. Alison's family, now including her mother's second husband and a warm, funny step-grandmother, has come east to work on a TV series. So adept is Alison at friendship that the longstanding Rachel-Stephanie twosome quickly becomes an equally harmonious threesome. Even if you can't have two "best" friends, Alison points out, you can still have two "close" friends.

At first it seems that nothing much is going to happen. School starts. The girls speculate about a handsome ninth-grader on their school bus and about when their periods will come. But then, at Thanksgiving, Stephanie's life starts to unravel. Her father comes east for the holiday, but doesn't come home; his stay in California was no mere business trip, but the initial stage of a trial separation. In the first of a series of damaging secrets that destroy Stephanie's peace of mind, her parents neglect to tell the children outright about their problems and plans. To the anguish caused by the split itself, this adds the anguish of betrayal; her parents' inadvertent duplicity wounds Stephanie deeply. The wound festers during a disastrous Christmas visit to Los Angeles, where Steph and her brother encounter their father's rather obtuse new girlfriend.

But Stephanie huddled in around the hurt, fails to confide her troubles to her own friends. This leads to a sharp, painful rift with Rachel, who had kept a small but consequential secret of her own. As the months pass and her gloom deepens, Stephanie weighs the various claims that she makes on others and that others make on her. By surrounding her with many different ways of being together—intact families, broken families, adoptive families, old friendships, new friendships, puppy love, a first friendship with a boy—Blume astutely leads Stephanie through the maze of her own feelings to a kind of resolution.

In the end, as spring (and her period) come on, Stephanie is reconciled with her parents and with Rachel. (She also realizes she must don her "bee-sting necklace" containing allergy medicine that can save her life if she's stung; clearly her future will bring other problems her way, and she will learn to live with them, too.) And she sees that the song lyrics are at least partially true, but not in the simple way she had originally imagined. The relationships that matter can survive even if "the sky should fall," but the people won't necessarily emerge "the same as we started." The important thing, Blume seems to say, is working at staying together even as things change.

Ann A. Flowers

SOURCE: A review of *Just as Long as We're Together,* in *The Horn Book Magazine,* Vol. LXIV, No. 1, January-February, 1988, pp. 66-7.

A story of three very diverse girls emphasizes the differences in personality and rates of development among adolescents. Stephanie, the narrator, has been friends with Rachel since second grade. The two girls are looking forward to entering seventh grade when Alison, a Vietnamese adoptee, moves into the neighborhood. Alison becomes friends with both of them, and they all share interests in clothes and boys, school and games. Rachel is by far the most mature, a very well-organized, brilliant girl; Alison is funny, easygoing, and nonjudgmental; Stephanie is a pleasant child but deeply disturbed by her parents' separation. Her parents deal with it awkwardly, at first not telling her and then expecting her to accept the news gracefully. This problem and the normal stresses of adolescence eventually cause a rupture in the friendship, leaving Rachel out in the cold. The plot is almost entirely episodic; in fact, most issues remain unresolved, including the parents' separation and the rather shaky resumption of the three-way friendship. It would be hard to find a contemporary concern or trendy idea that the author does not mention—children's fear of nuclear war, transracial adoption, divorce, and weight control are among those included. A great deal of energy and discussion centers around the question of when Stephanie will get her first menstrual period. But there is no doubt that Judy Blume knows what thirteen-year-old girls think and talk about, and she does an excellent job of engaging our sympathies over Stephanie's grief and confusion.

Jan Dalley

SOURCE: A review of *Just as Long as We're Together,* in *The Times Literary Supplement,* No. 4426, January 29, 1988, p. 119.

Stephanie is at a difficult age, simultaneously entering her teens, a new home, junior high school and a new close friendship with another girl. When she discovers that her father's prolonged absence, supposedly on a business trip, is in fact a separation between her parents, she responds by indulging in a desperate spree of comfort eating.

Judy Blume's sickly tale of adolescent friendships and family relationships revolves around food, particularly junk food, in what adds up to a determined celebration of middle-class, middle-of-the-road American consumption: a whirling parade of pizza, popcorn and pretzels, macadamia peanut brittle, PeachBerry Smoothie, waffle cones with pecan praline yogurt, donuts by the boxful. Stephanie's family drama centres on the Great American Feast, Thanksgiving dinner, and many of the emotionally significant disclosures in the book are signalled in terms of food. On the night Steph's father is expected home, the first inkling that all is not well comes with Mom's announcement that "I've made reservations at Onion Alley for you and Bruce and Dad. . . . I'm going over to Denise's to help with the stuffing and the sweet potato pudding." And when Alison, Steph's popular and confident friend, tearfully announces her adoptive mother's late, unexpected pregnancy, we have had an early clue in the Frozen Yogurt Bar: "Gena's got a craving for pistachio."

The main alternative to the realm of the stomach appears to be the world of money, especially as something which occupies females in the new matriarchy which Blume outlines in a carefully throwaway manner (one classmate's mother is the family doctor; another's is a trial lawyer). Alison's grandmother, Sadie, who helps the girls make meltingly moist brownies that earn them the praise of their favourite teacher (and three return visits from the school hunk) at the seventh grade bake sale, is in strict contrast to Steph's Gran Lola, who "isn't the cooking kind of grandmother. She's a stockbroker in New York." Aunt Robin and "her live-in, Scott" are investment bankers whose compromise with gastronomy seems to consist of naming their poodle Enchilada. Stephanie's mother, Rowena, a "real go-getter" who runs a travel agency called Going Places, treads a careful tightrope between providing boxes of donuts for her family (but only plain or wholewheat, not glazed, chocolate or jelly-filled) and strenuous Jazzercise for her pear-shaped frame. Inevitably, when Steph begins to be known by the boys at school as El Chunko, Rowena also introduces her daughter to that other Great American Tradition: the Diet.

Matriarchy or no, the preoccupations of these teenage girls, in Blume's vision, are unchanged: shopping for clothes for the school dance, boys, the first kiss, and their own intense friendships. As well as venting her anger and confusion about her parents on her waistline, Steph takes it out on Dad's new friend Iris ("I've *told* Iris that we don't keep our peanut butter in the refrigerator but she doesn't listen") and, more importantly, on her own erstwhile best friend Rachel. It's all very professionally achieved, as one would expect from this highly successful author, but Blume's concoctions are unvaryingly smooth, bland

and glutinous. In revealing the web of hurts and jealousies and in supplying the final homilies on the nature of true friendship, she gives a lavish display of another trait the British like to identify as all-American: unabashed sentimentality.

Janet Hickman

SOURCE: A review of *Just as Long as We're Together,* in *Language Arts,* Vol. 65, No. 2, February, 1988, p. 192.

The fifth and sixth graders who are Judy Blume's most faithful audience will find many familiar motifs here, including the task of settling into a new home (even though it's just a few blocks from the old), anticipation of the changes of puberty, and being the child of parents who are parting. The strength of this new story about Stephanie is her friendship with Rachel and Allison, who are also beginning seventh grade. While all three girls live in the midst of privilege (Allison's mother is a TV star), each has her own problems. Stephanie's worst moments come when she discovers that her father isn't on the West Coast for business reasons, but that her parents are in the midst of a trial separation. She can't bear to talk about this with Rachel, her longtime confidante. Rachel is hurt by Stephanie's apparent closeness with Allison, and it's clear that two best friends are harder to manage than one. Amends are made in the end, and although Stephanie's parents are not reunited, she has learned to react to the situation in a different way. The dialogue is contemporary, and there moments of real humor. The three protagonists may seem a bit sheltered by their environment, but their fears and satisfactions are likely to ring true to preadolescent readers.

Pam Barnard

SOURCE: A review of *Just as Long as We're Together,* in *The Times Educational Supplement,* No. 3737, February 12, 1988, p. 27.

Stephanie Hirst is 12; a self-confessed, gullible optimist, curious about people and perceptive with her neat one-liners. She is the ideal first-person narrator: "In her closet everything faces the same way and hangs on white plastic hangers".

El Chunko, as Stephanie is rudely but aptly called by gauche male classmates, has a go-getter estate agent mother, a father trying out marital separation discreetly in Los Angeles and a 10-year-old brother whose frequent nuclear nightmares eventually find expression in an award-winning poster about "Kids for Peace".

Judy Blume's latest novel is about girl-friendship tested by the problems and the diversity of extrovert Stephanie, restrained Rachel, and Alison, Vietnamese and quirky. Their difficulties range from being gifted to learning about sexuality ("Jeremy Dragon has hairy legs—Rachel says that means he's experienced"), from being the adopted daughter of a TV star to starting menstruation half way through the first high school dance.

The narrative spans the girls' first two terms at the J E Fox junior high school. As seventh graders; entering their teen years and the culture of a new school, their blend of humour and seriousness about the trivial and the genuinely profound will be informative and fun for their British counterparts, among whom Judy Blume is a deservedly popular writer.

Books for Keeps

SOURCE: A review of *Just as Long as We're Together,* in *Books for Keeps,* No. 54, January, 1989, p. 21.

The Blume books keep on coming like chocolate bars, offering a comforting lack of variation and the apparent quenching of a kind of hunger. It's all to do with easing anxiety, naming the problems of schoolgirl adolescent life and weaving them into the comfort of everyday existence. Which is why we have so many facts of shopping trips and names of teachers, clothes, boys and rooms. The debate about different kinds of stuffing exists with the onset of menstruation and is handled in much the same way. The story? Well, parents separating, breaking and making friends, going out with boys. The title says it all and it will be popular but oh for the antidote—a strong dose of singleness.

FUDGE-A-MANIA (1990)

Kirkus Reviews

SOURCE: A review of *Fudge-A-Mania,* in *Kirkus Reviews,* Vol. LVIII, No. 18, September 15, 1990, p. 1321.

A well-loved author brings together, on a Maine vacation, characters from two of her books.

Peter's parents have assured him that though Sheila ("The Great") Tubman and her family will be nearby, they'll have their own house; but instead, they find a shared arrangement in which the two families become thoroughly intertwined—which suits everyone but the curmudgeonly Peter. Irrepressible little brother Fudge, now five, is planning to marry Sheila, who agrees to babysit with Peter's toddler sister; there's a romance between the grandparents in the two families; and the wholesome good fun, including a neighborhood baseball game featuring an aging celebrity player, seems more important than Sheila and Peter's halfhearted vendetta. The story's a bit tame (no controversies here), but often amusingly true to life and with enough comic episodes to satisfy fans. *(Fiction. 8-12)*

Ilene Cooper

SOURCE: A review of *Fudge-A-Mania,* in *Booklist,* Vol. 87, No. 4, October 15, 1990, p. 441.

Gr. 4-6. When Judy Blume first started writing, she had a unique voice. Her voice hasn't changed, but there have been so many Blume imitators—good and bad—that it is a little difficult to hear her above the others. *Fudge-a-Mania* is a perfectly respectable first-person novel, featuring those popular brothers Peter and Fudge, with a guest appearance by Sheila Tubman, otherwise known as Sheila the Great. Here, Peter and Sheila are forced to spend the summer together when their families share a vacation house, and readers will laugh at all the problems that pop up with the two enemies in such close quarters. As always with Blume, the dialogue is bright and snappy, the plotting episodic. It's not Blume's fault that she sounds like everyone else now, but it would be nice if she'd speak up a little so we could all remember what made her special.

Zena Sutherland

SOURCE: A review of *Fudge-A-Mania,* in *Bulletin of the Center for Children's Books,* Vol. 44, No. 3, November, 1990, pp. 54-5.

Gr. 4-6. Peter, the long-suffering brother of five-year-old Fudge, narrates the ebullient story of a very long three-week vacation. Long, that is, to Peter, because his parents are sharing a summer house with the Tubmans, and Sheila Tubman *(Otherwise Known as Sheila the Great)* is his arch-enemy. Blume manages to avoid slapstick, although she skirts it, probably to the delight of new and old Fudge and Sheila fans. Disasters (minor) accrue, Fudge and his new friend Mitzi are amusingly precocious, and there's wedding-bells romance between Peter's grandmother and Sheila's grandfather. Something for everyone.

David C. Mowery

SOURCE: A review of *Fudge-A-Mania,* in *Children's Book Review Service,* Vol. 19, No. 7, November, 1990, p. 32.

Three of Ms. Blume's popular characters—five-year-old Fudge, his older brother Peter, and Sheila Tubman—are back in this hilarious account of an August vacation in Maine. Much to Peter's horror and disbelief, he is not only stuck with Fudge for three long weeks, but Sheila and her family are right next door! True to her own inimitable style, the author fills this unforgettable adventure with memorable characters, laughter and surprises. *Fudge-A-Mania* is going to be contagiously popular and earn many new fans for Judy Blume.

▭ *HERE'S TO YOU, RACHEL ROBINSON* (1993)

Gary D. Schmidt

SOURCE: A review of *Here's to You, Rachel Robinson,* in *The Five Owls,* Vol. 8, No. 2, November, 1993, pp. 37-8.

Readers familiar with Judy Blume's novels—especially the recent *Just as Long as We're Together*—will be delighted with this new story of a family struggling to stay together. Narrated by the feisty Rachel, the story deals with subjects that one might expect from a Blume novel: relationships between siblings, emerging sexuality, changing relationships to parents, the intricacies of seventh-grade friendships, the effect of peers on how one understands oneself. As always Blume deals with these topics with wit and humor, but not condescension.

Rachel finds herself in the awkward—and very real—situation of succeeding brilliantly in school but struggling in her relationships. Seen as a very promising student, she is invited to a college-level academic program, encouraged to pursue her musical talents as well as her dramatic abilities, and recruited for a peer-counseling program. She is almost overwhelmed. At the same time, her close relationship with Alison and Stephanie is eroding; they are blocking her out

of their own friendship. She is angered by their attentions to her brother, as well as their willingness to dump her as a candidate for the class president.

But the tensions in her own family are particularly difficult. Her brother Charles, having been expelled from a private school, moves back home, bringing with him his cynicism and disdain for his parents and sisters. His cruel comments, delivered with a witty malice which is difficult to answer, hurts each of them, and he threatens to drive wedges between himself and the rest of his family. Despite herself, Rachel feels some concern for him, and even some admiration. But the wounds are deep. By the end of the novel Charles and his father have begun a kind of reconciliation based upon a commitment to their family's Polish roots, but nothing like this has developed between Charles and his sisters.

The novel ends ambivalently, with unresolved questions abounding. But this, Blume seems to be suggesting, is what life itself is like: nothing is neat and tidy. Family disruptions occur amid campaigns for class presidents, reconciliations amid class field trips, and new relationships amid Monopoly games. Struggling gamely to balance everything in her life, Rachel tells a tale of seventh-grade survival. Any young teen reader will immediately recognize her tensions, her hopes, her hurts, and her joys.

Wendy E. Betts

SOURCE: A review of *Here's to You Rachel Robinson,* in *Voice of Youth Advocates,* Vol. 16, No. 5, December, 1993, p. 287.

Blume's first young adult book in several years is a continuation of her last, *Just as Long as We're Together,* this time taking the point of view of gifted super-achiever Rachel Robinson. To her friends, Stephanie and Alison, Rachel has always seemed a model of perfection, always getting straight A's, talented in music and compulsively neat and organized. But there's a flaw in Rachel's perfect world: her older brother Charles, who seems to delight in tormenting her and the rest of her family with vicious remarks and self-destructive behavior. Between the pressures at home and the multiplying academic challenges offered to her at school, Rachel is becoming increasingly tense, with no release for her feelings except grinding her teeth in her sleep and daydreaming of romance.

Here's to You . . . is a typical Blume novel, with her usual trademarks: readable prose, casual but effective use of detail and an interesting mix of child and adult characters—all told from a first-person perspective designed to reflect the thoughts and experiences of "average" middle-class, adolescent girls. But Rachel is not meant to be a typical Blume heroine, and trying to fit her into the mold doesn't work: it's impossible to believe that a girl of her abilities and background would think, talk and behave so simplistically. Her narrative voice fails to ring true and the intellectual pressure she feels is not described well enough to be emotionally compelling, although her family troubles are strongly depicted. Overall, her intelligence and competitive drive seem as superficially bestowed as her hair color and virtually as unimportant in her life. As a "problem novel" *Here's to You* . . . isn't bad, but as a portrait of a gifted young adult it is a failure.

Daniel Menaker

SOURCE: A review of *Here's to You, Rachel Robinson,* in *The New Yorker,* Vol. 69, No. 42, December 13, 1993, p. 116.

Blume has blazed one of the widest trails in candid "problem" fiction for young people, of course, and this book is a sequel to her wildly popular *Just as Long as We're Together.* It features the same trio of teen-age friends—Alison, Stephanie, and the titular Rachel—and its central agon concerns thirteen-year-old Rachel's battles with her older brother Charles, who is living at home after being kicked out of boarding school. Along the way toward the inevitable dawn of reconciliation, the reader locks horns with bruxism, adoption, *foreign* adoption, possibly psychosomatic motion sickness, gender-role confusion, sibling rivalry, cystic acne, ethnic identity, single parenthood, and adultery. It all begins to look a little like wallpaper as it unrolls before us. But Judy Blume writes with humor and she knows how to work by implication, and her narrator, for all her intensity, recounts her trials in an appealing voice. So this is quite a good book on its own psychologistic terms, but it seems a bit too aware of what it's up to, and in that way . . . it exemplifies the salient and not always wonderful trend in children's-book publishing today.

James Gross

SOURCE: A review of *Here's to You, Rachel Robinson,* in *Book Report,* Vol. 12, No. 4, January-February, 1994, pp. 42-3.

Rachel Robinson is the protagonist and narrator of this very touching and realistic young adult novel of modern times with modern problems. Rachel tells of her life in the seventh grade, of her family, and of her friendship with Stephanie and Alison (which was reported from Stephanie's point of view in Blume's book, *Just as Long as We're Together*). Rachel is an overachiever in everything she does. She is well-mannered, "gifted" and advanced in her school work, and compulsive in her neatness and in her organization of all aspects of her personal life. She strives for perfection and has a seemingly perfect family, except for one big problem: her older brother Charles, who is definitely an underachiever in a high-achieving family. Rachel dreads the return of Charles to the household after it appears that he is finally going to be expelled from his out-of-state boarding school for "acting out." True to Rachel's worst expectations, Charles does return and proceeds to grate on everyone's nerves (causing Rachel to grind her teeth in her sleep) by picking on the other family members. He is expert at finding an especially sensitive area to criticize in a cruel manner and generally causes as much pain and disruption as he possibly can. The family attempts to deal with the problem by seeing a family counselor, which Rachel and her sister resent since they feel that Charles is the only one in the family who needs counseling. Rachel does learn to be less sensitive of Charles' behavior and to accept some of his critical pickings with a sense of humor. Unfortunately, this very well written realistic "problem novel" for young adults, could be a problem for the young adult librarian. The same "F-word" that keeps J.D. Salinger's *The Catcher in the Rye* off many library shelves is only used one time, as Charles toasts his sister, "Here's to you Rachel Robinson!" followed by "Here's to my whole f—ing family!" Unfortunately, while this quotation is probably a realistic portrayal of the sort of language that a young man like Charles would probably use, and probably a mild portrayal at that, the use of that particular word will keep this, an otherwise most outstanding novel, high on lists of future censorship problems. Therefore, I hesitate to give this book the "Highly Recommended" rating that I would otherwise gladly award it.

SUMMER SISTERS (1998)

Publishers Weekly

SOURCE: A review of *Summer Sisters,* in *Publishers Weekly,* Vol. 245, No. 13, March 30, 1998, p. 66.

Kid-lit giant Blume revisits familiar themes in her third adult novel (after *Smart Women*), an engaging coming-of-age story set during a series of summers on Martha's Vineyard in the late 1970s and early

'80s. At 12, Vix Weaver, the eldest daughter of a blue-collar Santa Fe couple, can't believe her luck when Caitlin Somers, the most popular girl in the sixth grade, invites her to vacation with the eclectically aristocratic Somers clan on the Vineyard. The girls declare themselves "summer sisters" and vow to "never be ordinary" as they forge a friendship marked by sexual awakening, angst and adventure. Vix continues to spend subsequent summers on the Vineyard with Caitlin and becomes an adopted member of Caitlin's oddball family. Caitlin's parents are divorced: Lamb (Lambert Mayhew Somers, III), Caitlin's father, is a laid-back and permissive ex-hippie; Phoebe, her flighty mother, flies off each year to the south of France. The girls are virtually unsupervised, and Vix grows up fast. Blume reproduces raunchy adolescent sex talk and describes the kinds of experimentation teens fantasize about. Lamb and his new wife provide Vix with a scholarship to a private school and encourage her to apply to Harvard. Over the course of their friendship, Caitlin and Vix experience first love, death and betrayal as they struggle to come to terms with their respective places in the world—and with their feelings about the same man. Blume keeps her story moving in straightforward prose, which occupies a step above serviceable Y A language and just skirts melodrama. Her facile portrait of an unlikely yet enduring friendship as it changes over time (the story concludes at a memorial service in 1990) will remind readers why they read Blume's books when they were young: she finds a provocative theme and spins an involving story.

Books

SOURCE: A review of *Summer Sisters,* in *Books* Magazine, Vol. 12, No. 2, Summer, 1998, p. 24.

Best-selling author, Judy Blume is on top form in this story of two women, who meet on the brink of adolescence, and then spend the pivotal summers of their coming-of-age years as inseparable companions on Martha's Vineyard. Caitlin Somers is the golden girl everyone would choose for a friend or lover but no-one ever really touches—until she impulsively invites Vix Weaver—a shy young woman from a struggling working class family—as her guest for an island summer. We watch as these two essential loners begin to forge the bonds of life-long friendship, and we wait for the confrontations that are inevitable between them and the people who shape their lives.

Carolyn Mackler

SOURCE: "Judy Blume on Sex, the Suburbs, and *Summer Sisters,*" in *Ms.* Vol. 9, No. 1, July-August, 1998, pp. 89-90.

When I was eight, my parents took me to New York City. As we were traipsing through Kennedy Airport in search of our gate, I trailed behind, absorbed in **Then Again, Maybe I Won't,** by Judy Blume. I came to a phrase I didn't understand.

"Mom," I shouted ten yards up to her.

She turned back to me, boarding pass in hand.

"What's a *wet dream?*"

She screeched to a halt. Glaring passersby craned their necks to steal a look at the smut she was exposing to her pigtailed, halter-topped daughter. Cheeks crimson, she took me by the shoulder and steered me from the gathering crowd. Clutching the book, I hurried along, realizing that I had happened upon something *very interesting.*

Similar stories can be told by millions who came of age in the last three decades, captivated by Judy Blume's realistic characters who have families, friends, problems, and—God forbid—a sense of sexuality. Sending tremors through an early 1970s children's fiction market that was still coping with Louise Fitzhugh's forth-right yet sterile mention of menstruation in *The Long Secret* (1965), Blume introduced preteens who prayed for their periods and recited mantras such as *we must, we must, we must increase our bust.* Blume's adolescents have masturbated, stuffed cotton balls in their bras, lubed their tampons with Vaseline, given fumbly hand jobs, and provided us with vivid, back-of-the-school-bus accounts.

And if there were a fiction category especially for those of us reared on Blume, her third and most recent "adult" book would be a charter member. **Summer Sisters** (Delacorte) surveys two girls' friendship between the ages of 12 and 30 (1977 to 1996). Victoria "Vix" Leonard, an observant sixth grader from the other side of the Santa Fe tracks, is lured to a summer on Martha's Vineyard by her tough-talking, aristocratic classmate, Caitlin Somers. From this first year when the girls vow to NBO (Never Be Ordinary) to subsequent summers and seasons, their families, futures, and first partners intersect in a coming-of-age saga. Vix is the everyfriend, girl-next-door type; Caitlin, clouded in mystery, represents, as Blume says, "the bad girl side of me, of all of us." In her most ambitious work to date, Blume time-travels from Abba to "Eye of the Tiger" to Joan Armatrading to *thirty-something.* **Summer Sisters,** with its fast-paced dialogue and uncannily accurate detail, is vintage Judy Blume, yet with a very nineties flair; characters now negotiate "first, last, and security" and exhibit a prudent awareness of STDs.

Blume, 60, divides her time between Key West, Martha's Vineyard, and New York City with her husband, nonfiction writer George Cooper. Frequently leaping out of her wicker lawn chair on the porch of her Key West home to grab munchies or a doodling notepad, Blume reminisces about her early days as an isolated housewife and young mother of two in 1960s suburban New Jersey. Starved for friendship and hungrily watching the feminist movement and sexual revolution erupt across the Hudson River, Blume felt trapped. "All I wanted to do was get out there and taste it and do it and be free," she says. "And I felt like this was it, this was the rest of my life." Realizing that she needed to satiate her creative drive in order to continue functioning, Blume began writing, first rhyming stories, then realistic children's fiction. Amidst biting criticism from fellow suburbanites (to the tune of "You're a nice girl, Judy, but I was an English major, and I can tell you don't have any talent"), her books began to take off.

It wasn't until much later that she started to think of herself as a feminist. "I went into all this with a naïveté. I was writing about what intrigued me, what I would have liked to read." Blume laughs. "I couldn't have called myself a feminist. That was too exciting. I mean, how could you possibly be a feminist and live in *New Jersey?*" Through a series of "evolving little bells," Blume began to come into her voice. "*Fear of Flying* by Erica Jong happened for me, *Ms.* happened for me, "I Want a Wife" by Judy Syfers happened for me, and even though I wasn't stomping in the streets, I was waving my own tiny flag, like the kind you get in a deli sandwich." Eventually Blume mustered the courage to ditch her decaying marriage *and* the suburbs.

Breaking acres of fresh ground with *Are You There God? It's Me Margaret* (1970) and *Then Again, Maybe I Won't* (1971), Blume created dialogue-driven, first-person, no-holds-barred accounts of the inner workings of junior high schoolers. She captured an authentic preteen voice and created complex characters who could feel several things simultaneously. *Margaret* is a candid peek into a sixth grader's daily life as she anticipates puberty, adjusts to moving to the suburbs, deals with family feuds, and embarks on a quest for spirituality. *Then Again's* 13-year-old protagonist, Tony, struggles with class issues, a friend's delinquency, and, yes, wet dreams. In Blume's books, the author's voice fades away while

the kids tell their own tales. She has tackled children's literature taboos such as racism, classism, religion, anti-Semitism, divorce, alcoholism, cliques, physical disabilities, and parental death. Her characters chat with God about breasts. They egg mailboxes on Halloween. They agonize over doing the right thing versus the overwhelming desire to fit in.

Blume rapidly developed a cult following among children. Young readers wrote to her to say that they read her books to find themselves, and that Blume's honesty about childhood being less than perfect validated their moments of unhappiness. They heard in Blume an adult voice that they could trust to be candid about puberty (one nine-year-old sent her a letter requesting "the facts of life, in number order"). As a reviewer once remarked, "News that a book describing the ordeal of puberty without mincing words could be had for seventy-five cents spread through every sixth grade in the land."

A quarter century later, Blume's 21 books (*Summer Sisters* makes 22) have sold upward of 65 million copies and have been translated into more than 20 languages. Journeying between books for children and adults, she has attained best-seller status in both categories.

She has also rung in at number one on more foreboding lists, like the People for the American Way's Most Frequently Challenged Authors between 1982 and 1996. "It all began in 1980," Blume recalls. "Literally the day after Reagan was elected, the censors crawled out of the woodwork and nothing was the same." Censors have yanked Blume's books off library shelves in countless school districts for reasons ranging from "lack of moral tone" (ill-behaved fifth graders don't get reprimanded for classroom taunting in *Blubber*), to the claim that "[*Margaret*] is built around just two themes: sex and anti-Christian behavior" (12-year-old wonders if she's Jewish or Christian and can't wait to grow breasts), to simply being authored by Blume, as in the harmless kitten of a story, *The One in the Middle Is the Green Kangaroo,* about a second grader coming to terms with his birth order.

Armed with pamphlets such as "How to Rid Your Schools and Libraries of Judy Blume Books," the Right has targeted *Deenie* (girl on the brink of adolescence develops scoliosis and has obscure nighttime communions with a "special place") and *Forever . . .* (high school seniors Katherine and Michael fall in love, "plan it," and then "do it" without punishment). Retorting the critics who have argued that *Forever* . . . is suggestive, Blume quotes her late friend and writing colleague, Norma Klein. "Norma used to say, 'I was curious about sex; I had books to read to satisfy my curiosity, so I didn't have to do it.'" Even so, Blume urges her readers to wait until they are older for her "adult" books and has added a bit to *Forever* . . . singing the praises of latex condoms (the 1970s protagonist goes on the Pill).

With *Summer Sisters,* Blume has dangled more bait over the ravenous censors. The seductive vibe between the young girls is strong: Caitlin counts Vix's (16) pubic hairs; they nickname their vaginas "The Power"; and they discover that by playing "boy/girl" games together, they feel "an electrical current buzzing through them." Twenty-something Caitlin is, Blume says, "bisexual, trisexual, whatever." Grown-up Vix has a "lush body," digs orgasms, and masturbates.

Blume, who has the gall to portray kid culture as it really is, not as some grownups wish it was, attributes her status as perennial target to adults' discomfort with their own sexuality and fear of "exposing their children to new ideas, ideas that are different from their own." An active spokesperson for the National Coalition Against Censorship, she includes kid-tailored messages about censorship on her Web site, and she is currently editing a book of short stories by young adult authors whose work has been challenged.

The 1996 recipient of the American Library Association's Margaret A. Edwards Award for Lifetime Achievement, Blume seems rather surprised by her enormous popularity. "When I wrote *Margaret,* it never dawned on me that 28 years later kids would still be reading it. But it's about feelings and anticipating growing up, and those things never change."

Additional coverage of Blume's life and career is contained in the following sources published by the Gale Group: *Authors and Artists for Young Adults,* **Vols. 3, 26;** *Contemporary Authors,* **Vols. 29-32R;** *Contemporary Authors New Revision Series,* **Vols. 13, 37, 66;** *Contemporary Literary Criticism,* **Vols. 12, 30;** *Dictionary of Literary Biography,* **Vol. 52;** *DISCovering Authors 3.0; DISCovering Authors Modules: Novelists Module, Popular Fiction and Genre Authors Module; Junior DISCovering Authors; Major Authors and Illustrators for Children and Young Adults; Major 20th-Century Writers; Something About the Author,* **Vols. 2, 31, 79.**

Shirley Climo
1928-

American folklorist, reteller, and travel writer.

Major works include *Piskies, Spriggans, and Other Magical Beings: Tales from the Droll-Teller* (1981), *The Cobweb Christmas* (1982), *A Month of Seven Days* (1987), *The Egyptian Cinderella* (1989), *City! New York* (1990).

INTRODUCTION

Shirley Climo is best known for her collections of folklore and for her multicultural retellings of fairy tales. A writer for children and young teens, Climo has gathered material from a wide spectrum of sources into collections devoted to such mythical beings as mermaids and fairies, has produced travel guides for children visiting American cities, and has written original mystery stories. Christine Doyle, a contributor to *Children's Writers,* has praised Climo as an author who is "extraordinarily skilled at using an already-existing frame as the basis for a story and embellishing it with details that make it come to life for the reader."

BIOGRAPHICAL INFORMATION

"Long before I could read," Climo told *Something about the Author (SATA),* "I'd begun telling my own tales to myself and to anyone else willing to listen." The daughter of a children's writer, Aldarilla Beistle, Climo was born in Cleveland, Ohio. She attended DePauw University from 1946 to 1949 and married in 1950. From 1949 to 1953 Climo worked as a scriptwriter for the weekly juvenile series Fairytale Theatre on WGAR-Radio in Cleveland. She put her career aside for the next two decades as personal priorities came first: "Between 1953 and 1976, I raised children," she noted in *SATA.* After that, "I fulfilled a typical writer-reentry apprenticeship doing a series of newspaper articles and selling a number of travel and humor pieces to adult magazines. I learned a great deal, but all along my target was not bigger but smaller." Climo found the inspiration to produce a work for the children's book market during a trip to Cornwall, England. A stay in a 400-year-old cottage set the stage for a retelling of ancient folktales that was published as *Piskies, Spriggans, and Other Magical Beings.* She continued in the folktale vein with her second book, *The Cobweb Christmas,* based on a German fable about spiders and the tradition of using garlands to decorate Christmas trees. Producing this book had an unexpected effect on the author: What had been a lifelong fear of spiders turned into fascination, leading Climo to another volume, *Someone Saw a Spider.* Climo expanded her output into a variety of genres over the years, always keeping her young readers in mind. She enjoys staying in touch with her audiences, and in conversations with children and adults, Climo has uncovered an interesting fact: "When I talk to fifth- and sixth-grade students about writing, most of them want to write for adults. When I speak to adult groups, most of them want to write for children. I encourage them all."

MAJOR WORKS

With her first two volumes, *Piskies, Spriggans, and Other Magical Beings* and *The Cobweb Christmas*, Climo reached back into history to retell folktales from England and Germany, respectively. In *Piskies,* the emphasis is on fantasy creatures who provide an entertaining introduction to the region's lore, history, and superstitions. She included humorous assistance with local dialect, resulting in what a *Publishers Weekly* review called "a folklore aficionado's paradise." With *Cobweb,* the author addressed an age-old question: why do people hang tinsel from Christmas trees? The answer, according to a 300-year-old German legend, centers on the kindly Cristkindel, who takes pity on the cold spiders that have been ejected from a newly cleaned house on Christmas Eve by bringing them inside with him. The spiders spin webs through the Christmas tree branches, which Cristkindel turns to silver and gold.

With a view toward multicultural storytelling, Climo produced three storybooks that recount the Cinderella tale, a legend that persists in many cultures. *The Egyptian Cinderella,* her first volume, presents a Greek slave girl who wins the heart of an Egyptian pharaoh with the help of a pair of magic slippers. In a favorable review of the book, *School Library Journal* critic Martha Rosen described *The Egyptian Cinderella* as "a stunning combination of fluent prose and exquisitely wrought illustrations." *The Korean Cinderella* was released in 1993, followed by *The Persian Cinderella* in 1999. In the latter book, young Settareh and her stepsisters go to buy cloth to make gowns to wear to a New Year celebration at the Royal Palace, but Settareh instead spends her money on an old blue jug. Luckily she finds a fairy inside, and the fairy grants her wish for a new gown. In this version, a diamond bangle that falls from her ankle replaces the glass slipper as the clue to her identity. A *Publishers Weekly* reviewer praised the work citing "historical details" that "readily transport readers to fifteenth-century Persia." Likewise, a *Booklist* article noted that while the pacing of *The Persian Cinderella* "isn't as successful as other versions," the book's lush illustrations and detailing "more than make up for it." In a similar vein, Climo produced the compilation *A Treasury of Princesses: Princess Tales from around the World* and a companion volume focused on mermaids.

For young tourists, Climo has written three books in the *City!* series, detailing the history and present-day attractions of San Francisco, New York, and Washington, D.C. In illustrating how, for example, the term "lobbyist" originated, the author "skillfully blends in nuggets of fascinating information," according to Christine Doyle of *Children's Writers,* "as she does when working with folk tales."

While many of Climo's books are aimed at younger children, she has also written works for middle-school readers, including such mystery titles as *Gopher, Tanker, and the Admiral* and *T. J.'s Ghost.* In *A Month of Seven Days* the author views the American Civil War through the eyes of a twelve-year-old girl in South Carolina. Zoe and her mother, left alone while her father fights for the Confederate Army, must fend off invading Yankee troops who attempt to commandeer their home. Zoe tries to protect her father by scaring away the superstitious Yankee captain, and in the process learns that even the enemy is human. While a *Publishers Weekly* review faulted the book for insufficient issue resolution, a *Kirkus Reviews* writer had fewer reservations, declaring that Zoe is a believable character, and that "her anger and bewilderment are well portrayed, as is the experience of being part of an occupied country."

AWARDS

Climo's literary honors include the Parents' Choice Award and a Pick of the Lists citation from the American Booksellers in 1982 for *The Cobweb Christmas* and the Storytelling World Award in 1997 for *A Treasury of Mermaids.* Several of Climo's books have been cited as "notable books in the field of social studies" by the American Library Association (ALA), including *King of the Birds, The Egyptian Cinderella,* and *The Korean Cinderella.* She has also received an ALA citation for "notable book in the field of science," and a Teacher's Choice selection from the National Association of English Teachers, both for *Someone Saw a Spider.* She has been nominated for state awards in Minnesota, Indiana, Oklahoma, and North Carolina for *A Month of Seven Days,* and in Georgia and Nevada for *The Korean Cinderella.*

TITLE COMMENTARY

PISKIES, SPRIGGANS, AND OTHER MAGICAL BEINGS: TALES FROM THE DROLL-TELLER (1980)

Virginia Haviland

SOURCE: A review of *Piskies, Spriggans, and Other Magical Beings: Tales from the Droll-Teller,* in *The Horn Book Magazine,* Vol. LVI, No. 6, December, 1980, p. 650.

Nine Cornish tales, fresh and rich in individuality of expression as well as of setting, all of them droll stories from the Land's End peninsula of Cornwall. A "droll-teller" was a kind of peddler, who told stories in exchange for a meal. The traveling, storytellers knew about the "little people": There were differences between the Piskies, who were mischievous but helpful, and the Spriggans, who were mean and ugly with "frightful . . . women" and "horrible . . . brats." Then there were the Knackers, who worked the mines and could be friendly if left to themselves but spiteful if spied upon. The stories also tell of changelings, giants, sea people, witches, and devils—the gamut of supernatural creatures, large and small. A welcome collection with illustrations which appropriately show fantastic faces and distorted features. Each story is preceded by an explanatory note and followed by lists of charms and superstitions.

Publishers Weekly

SOURCE: A review of *Piskies, Spriggans, and Other Magical Beings: Tales from the Droll-Teller,* in *Publishers Weekly,* Vol. 219, No. 12, March 20, 1981, pp. 62-3.

A folklore aficionado's paradise, Climo's versions of nine Cornish tales create intense reactions in the reader, effects increased by [Joynce Audy] dos Santos's artistry. The piskies, spriggans, knackers, fairies, etc., were magical beings starred in tales by the roving Droll-Teller, who paid for his keep with entertainment. One lusty, haunting story dwells on the travails of a doting mother, Janey Trayer. A spriggan steals her bonny child and leaves an evil changeling in its place. Janey's husband can't abide the brat and her neighbors, the wise sisters, urge her to work spells that will destroy the changeling and return her beloved son. But Janey is too soft-hearted, so the sisters take matters into their own hands. Climo also includes notes on the weird creatures, charms, spells, etc. (9-12)

THE COBWEB CHRISTMAS (1982)

Publishers Weekly

SOURCE: A review of *The Cobweb Christmas,* in *Publishers Weekly,* Vol. 222, No. 6, August 6, 1982, p. 70.

Prize-winning [Joe] Lasker illustrates Climo's sweet fairy tale with lovely scenes of a Yulctide long ago, in a snowy German woods. Known as Auntie (Tante),

an old woman lives in her small forest cottage where she prepares a special tree each year, for the children of a nearby village and all the animals. Tante decorates the tree with gifts for all but one Christmas Eve, she's so tired that she falls asleep before she puts anything on the little pine. Passing by the house, Cristkindel stops to chat with the spiders that Tante has swept out in her cleaning zeal. He pities the cold insects and takes them inside where they cover the tree with webs. Cristkindel quickly touches the webs, turning them silver and gold. When Tante awakens, she's elated by the glittering sight and all her guests declare this is the best Christmas tree ever. (4-8)

SOMEONE SAW A SPIDER: SPIDER FACTS AND FOLKTALES (1985)

Ilene Cooper

SOURCE: A review of *Someone Saw a Spider: Spider Facts and Folktales,* in *Booklist,* Vol. 82, No. 11, February 1, 1986, p. 808.

Gr. 4-6. Climo offers a mixed bag of information, stories, poems, and pictures about spiders. With obvious affection for her topic, Climo retells tales from Japan, Africa, America, Scotland, and Russia, showing the spider's wise, crafty, and magical sides. There are facts about spiders—body parts, web spinning, and mating practices—as well as spider folklore. For instance, a few hundred years ago, people thought you could cure whooping cough by dangling a spider over the sick person's head. Zimmer's black-and-white line drawings are humorous and, in places, as delicate as a spider's web.

Bulletin of the Center for Children's Books

SOURCE: A review of *Someone Saw a Spider: Spider Facts and Folktales,* in *Bulletin of the Center for Children's Books,* Vol. 39, No. 7, March, 1986, p. 124.

Retellings of folktales about spiders are linked by brief discussions of superstitions and legends about them; few facts are included, despite the implication of the subtitle. Although an appended section, "Extras and Explanations," contains notes on many other things, such as additional folk material or definitions of terms, some facts about spiders are included. This is useful as a source for storytelling, but what information it contains is scattered through the book and not made accessible by an index. A bibliography of source materials is provided.

📖 *A MONTH OF SEVEN DAYS* (1987)

Zena Sutherland

SOURCE: A review of *A Month of Seven Days,* in *Bulletin of the Center for Children's Books,* Vol. 41, No. 2, October, 1987, p. 24.

Gr. 5-7. Part third-person narrative, part journal, this Civil War story is set in Georgia in 1864. Father is serving in the Confederate Army, and Zoe (12-year-old protagonist, journal writer) is alone with her younger brother and pregnant mother when a Yankee captain and some of his men take over the house and demand cooking and other services. Zoe is both angry and fearful, but—like her sensible mother—she puts up with what she must. Unlike her mother, Zoe tries several schemes to frighten the superstitious captain. At the end of a week, the soldiers leave, but not before Zoe has learned that some Yankees are honest and kind and that some of her neighbors are secretly helping with the war effort, as she herself courageously does. This is written adequately, and the characters are well-defined if not always depicted with nuance, but the structure seems too dense, with too much happening in only seven days and too much depending on the gullibility of the Yankee captain.

Elizabeth M. Reardon

SOURCE: A review of *A Month of Seven Days,* in *School Library Journal,* Vol. 34, No. 4, December, 1987, p. 84.

Gr 5-8—Zoe Snyder, 12, spends the longest week of her life in June 1864, when invading Yankee troops take over her family's Georgia home and use it as their headquarters. With her father off fighting, Zoe and her mother must face the enemy alone, reduced to waiting on the Captain, Benjamin Hetcher. Hetcher is a superstitious sort, and Zoe sets out to scare him away with talk of the "haunt" who shares their home. In terms of historical fact, this is a trifle of a story—more an entertaining slice-of-life novel than anything else. Climo's stereotyped characterization of Hetcher, a silly creature more interested in a cup of coffee than the war, is somewhat offensive, but her other Yankees are more sympathetic and more human. Most of Climo's use of regional dialect is good, but some sounds like a Northerner's version of the dialect (as, when Zoe shouts at the troops, "You all stop that right now, hear!"). A story whose theme—summed up by Zoe when she tells one soldier, "Maybe underneath that ugly blue uniform you're not all that different from me"—makes a good balance to other Civil War stories.

Booklist

SOURCE: A review of *A Month of Seven Days,* in *Booklist,* Vol. 84, No. 7, December 1, 1987, p. 629.

Gr. 5-7. Papa is off fighting with the Confederate army, and the pompous Yankee captain Hetcher, on the march in Georgia, commandeers the family house for his headquarters. Twelve-year-old Zoe Snyder, her young brother, and her pregnant mother are forced to live in the cabin of their old Indian helper, Mr. Hodges, who, before leaving to fight for the Rebel cause, gives Zoe a tortoise shell talisman for luck. Zoe feels she needs more than luck, however, to protect her father, expected home any day, and connives a way to drive the superstitious captain out of their home. A problem of a different sort is the young bluecoat Joshua Boone, who shows her that soldiers are human regardless of their sympathies. Despite some artificiality in the writing and too many characters that don't always ring true, the story has tension and good pace. The Civil War from the Confederate viewpoint is not often covered, and this may help to balance collections. An author's background note is appended.

Publishers Weekly

SOURCE: A review of *A Month of Seven Days,* in *Publishers Weekly,* Vol. 232, No. 24, December 11, 1987, p. 66.

Zoe, 13, her little brother Jim Henry and their mother are all horrified when Captain Hetcher—a hated Yankee—sets up temporary military headquarters in their home. Putting up with the bullying captain's constant orders is bad enough, but Zoe and her mother share a worrisome secret: Zoe's father, on leave from the Confederate Army, may arrive home any day, and that means he'll fall into the hands of the Yankees. Determined to prevent this, Zoe comes up with a plan to get rid of the captain and his troops. Fans of historical fiction will enjoy this well-researched depiction of life in rural Georgia during the Civil War. But some readers may be disappointed that likable Zoe is never given the chance to become a truly compelling character. Her growing self-reliance, a confusing flirtation with one of the captain's young aides and her realization that Yankees aren't always inhuman monsters are just a few of the tantalizing issues that are brought to light but never satisfactorlly resolved. Ages 10-up.

📖 *KING OF THE BIRDS* (1988)

Publishers Weekly

SOURCE: A review of *King of the Birds,* in *Publishers Weekly,* Vol. 233, No. 2, January 15, 1988, p. 94.

Climo has created a lively, elegant version of an ancient legend: how the birds, long ago, determined their king. Mother Owl decrees that whoever flies highest and longest should reign; clever Wren wins the contest by hitching a ride, piggyback, with Eagle, and spreading his own wings only when the great bird tires. Wren's resourcefulness serves him well as ruler, for he puts an end to the birds' quarreling by assigning each its own place on the Earth—on land, in the water, on clifftops or in bushes—until peace is at last restored. [Ruth] Heller's brilliantly colored fowl lend majesty to this classic tale; her paintings are notable for both their detailed realism and striking composition. But, because most of the illustrations portray birds against plain backgrounds rather than fully rendered scenes, they do not capture the motion of the birds' flight nor reflect the escalating drama of the race—the only flaw in an otherwise satisfying work. Ages 4-8.

Zena Sutherland

SOURCE: A review of *King of the Birds,* in *Bulletin of the Center for Children's Books,* Vol. 41, No. 6, February, 1988, p. 114.

Gr. K-3. Although the paintings of birds are not always color-true (purple predominates over black in the raven's feathers) they are correct more often than not, and they are certainly handsome. Climo does a nice job of retelling the traditional story of how the small wren was chosen king of the birds "Long ago, when the oceans were only half filled with water and just a few stars lit the sky. . . . " This is also a *pourquoi* story, explaining how the wren got its color. The small bird used his brain when all the birds were in a race (literally) for title; he piggy-backed on the eagle and flew upward when the eagle tired, so that he was the last to return to the earth, scorched brown and gray by the sun. The story is retold with good pace and flow and with good balance of dialogue and exposition.

Booklist

SOURCE: A review of *King of the Birds,* in *Booklist,* Vol. 84, No. 12, February 15, 1988, p. 999.

Ages 4-8. In an afterword Climo comments that Aesop may have been the first to tell the legend of how the birds chose a king, which interestingly has a counterpart in a Chippewa Indian tale. This version begins: "Long ago, when the oceans were only half filled with water and just a few stars lit the sky, the birds quarreled loudly among themselves." Jostling for recognition and territory, each asserts its superior attributes. Amid the chaos and strife comes the sage directive of Old Mother Owl: whoever flies highest and longest will be King of the Birds. The nondescript wren, small but exceedingly clever, capitalizes on the strength of the mighty eagle, hiding among its long quills for a piggyback ride. When Eagle folds his wings to descend, Wren flutters his own and flies up, scorching his feathers by brushing against the sun. After he becomes their ruler, King Wren disperses all the birds to chosen habitats around the world. Rich and expressive illustrations depict the birds in their many vivid colors against white or subtly hued, atmospheric backgrounds.

Ellen Fader

SOURCE: A review of *King of the Birds,* in *School Library Journal,* Vol. 34, No. 11, August, 1988, p. 79.

K-Gr 4—When the birds cannot stop arguing, they realize that they need a ruler. Owl decides that "Whoever flies highest and longest shall be king." Wren bets Eagle and wins the honor by using his brain: he hides in Eagle's feathers and flies even higher when Eagle returns to earth. Many variants of this old tale can be found in collections long out of print, but few reward Wren for his deception by making him king or expand the story into a pourquoi tale by explaining how Wren brought peace to the kingdom of the birds by creating order. This folktale is not available in an illustrated version, and the appearance of this attractive volume will bring this engaging, smoothly told story to a new and younger audience. The bright, realistic, and often stunning paintings are merely decorations for the text and do little to enhance the natural drama of the narrative. The drawings of the birds are placed on a white background which provides no anchor, setting, or perspective for the creatures; they appear to sit or stand in air and fly in a vacuum. In spite of this, children will be captivated with this story of why Wren has such a drab coat, why he nests so near to the ground, and why his tail points straight to the sky.

📖 *T. J.'S GHOST* (1989)

Ilene Cooper

SOURCE: A review of *T. J.'s Ghost,* in *Booklist,* Vol. 85, No. 19, June 1, 1989, p. 1721.

Gr. 4-6. While her parents are away on a trip, T. J. goes to stay with old Auntie Onion and Uncle Will on the California coast. T. J. isn't expecting much out of her visit, but when a mysterious foghorn begins calling her name, she finds herself in the middle of an adventure. On the beach, she meets an Australian boy who is in search of a lost gold ring. Only there on foggy days, he seems to know little of modern life. When he tells T. J. he sailed on the *Coya,* which sank in 1866, she doesn't know what to believe but eventually realizes she must help the boy find peace. Based on the details of a real shipwreck, the story spins its web slowly at first, but readers will soon find themselves enmeshed. Climo nicely balances modern-day events, such as a trip to the Santa Cruz Boardwalk, with hints of the past. An eerie cover and frontispiece foreshadow the ghostly events.

Lisa Smith

SOURCE: A review of *T. J.'s Ghost,* in *School Library Journal,* Vol. 35, No. 15, November, 1989, p. 105.

Gr 4-6—While visiting her aunt and uncle on the California coast, T.J. meets a ghost boy on the beach who enlists her aid in recovering a lost ring. Well-drawn characters, a realistic setting, and smooth writing characterize this midly suspenseful, not-too-mysterious mystery. While the mystery is too easily resolved, and there's not much detection involved, it's an adequate choice for upper elementary or reluctant YA readers.

📖 *THE EGYPTIAN CINDERELLA* (1989)

Ilene Cooper

SOURCE: A review of *The Egyptian Cinderella,* in *Booklist,* Vol. 86, No. 1, September 1, 1989, p. 68.

Ages 6-9. As Climo explains in an author's note, this tale, based on fact (a Greek girl named Rhodopis was kidnapped and brought to Egypt), is one of the world's first Cinderella stories. In this version, Rhodopis is a slave ridiculed by the house servants and made to do much of the work. When she is spot-ted dancing by her master, he gives her a pair of dainty, rose-red slippers. Though Rhodopis loves them, the gift makes the other servant girls despise her even more. On the day the Pharaoh is to have a feast, Rhodopis is left at home to do the chores; insult is added to injury when a falcon steals one of her slippers. The bird drops the shoe at the Pharaoh's gala, the monarch mystically knows he is to find the girl who can wear it. Following a difficult search, he finally locates Rhodopis and makes her his queen. Oddly, this part of the story is also true: the real Rhodopis did marry the Pharaoh Amasis in fifth century B.C. [Ruth] Heller uses Egyptian motifs and stylings in her two-page spreads, but the artwork is neither as refined nor as delicate as one might wish. Colors are somewhat strident, and faces, in particular, appear stilted. Still, there are several striking spreads, and the book, besides its intrinsically interesting telling, offers a number of possibilities for use. Classes that explore variants of folktales and those that study Egypt will find this especially worthwhile.

Publishers Weekly

SOURCE: A review of *The Egyptian Cinderella,* in *Publishers Weekly,* Vol. 236, No. 13, September 29, 1989, p. 67.

The setting may be exotic and the glass slippers may have been replaced by leather ones with toes of rose-red gold, but this is a story no child could fail to recognize. Climo's intriguing variation on the Cinderella tale is based on a combination of fact (there was indeed a Greek slave girl named Rhodopis who married the Pharaoh Amasis), and fable—in this case, Egyptian. A trio of uppity servant girls assume the roles of the wicked stepsisters, a kindly master serves as the fairy godmother (to provide the slippers) and a handsome pharoah steps in as Prince Charming. The foreign locale comes complete with lotus flowers, a hippo, a great falcon (symbol of the Egyptian sky god Horus) and, of course, the River Nile. Climo hits just the right note in her imaginative retelling of the fairy tale. The text is incorporated in the design of Heller's stylized illustrations with their appropriately lush colors. Ages 4-8.

Martha Rosen

SOURCE: A review of *The Egyptian Cinderella,* in *School Library Journal,* Vol. 35, No. 14, October, 1989, p. 102.

K-Gr 3—A stunning combination of fluent prose and exquisitely wrought illustrations. Climo has woven this ancient tale, a mixture of fact and myth, with clarity and eloquence. The beauty of the language is set off to perfection by Heller's arresting full-color illustrations. The story of Rhodopis, a Greek slave girl in ancient Egypt, is an interesting variant of the traditional Cinderella legend. Because of her rosy complexion and fair hair, Rhodopis is scorned and teased by the Egyptian servant girls who work for her kind but disinterested master. Rhodopis' happy fate, becoming the wife of Pharaoh Amasis (570-526 B.C.), is accomplished through the intercession of the great falcon, symbol of the god Horus. When the majestic bird deposits one of Rhodopis' rosy-gold slippers, a gift from her master, in the lap of the Pharaoh, he determines this to be a signal from the gods to marry the maiden whose foot it fits. Powerful visual presentations reminiscent of the figures on Egyptian frieze paintings and carvings, colorful birds and animals that pulse with life, and information about Egyptian mythology and civilization are subtly interwoven into the traditional folktale. This will certainly be a winner for story hours, as well as a useful resource for the study of *Cinderella* through the ages and throughout the world.

CITY! SAN FRANCISCO (1990)

Phillis Wilson

SOURCE: A review of *City! San Francisco,* in *Booklist,* Vol. 86, No. 13, March 1, 1990, p. 1338.

Gr. 4-7. For a general use guidebook, Patricia Haddock's *San Francisco* is still a fine choice, but librarians will find that the Climo/[George] Ancona collaboration is a distinct and appealing entity. Coverage includes the city's unique history (six different flags have flown from Bay Area flagpoles), an account of the gold rush and its aftermath leading up to the earthquake of 1906 (a short author's note in the front briefly mentions the 1989 quake), and the city's present status as a mecca of ethnic variety. The writing is literate with imaginative use of analogy, and the chapter on exploring is child oriented. Unlike the large-scale glitz of many guidebooks, Ancona's eye seeks out the telling detail, a tight shot of the winding gears in the Cable Car Museum, for example, or a gold-rush days gravestone in Mission Dolores Cemetery, the kind of inquisitive views that children can ponder. Whether children travel in person, or thumb through the pages, they'll enjoy their visit to the Golden Gate city.

Elizabeth S. Watson

SOURCE: A review of *City! San Francisco,* in *The Horn Book Magazine,* Vol. LXVI, No. 3, May-June, 1990, p. 346.

"Ride a cable car . . . take a breezy ride on a boat to Alcatraz Island . . . walk across the Golden Gate Bridge . . . watch the waves on the Pacific coast. . . . ride the old carousel"—the author's suggestions for tourist activities in and around San Francisco are as diversified as they are interesting, and the book offers much more besides. The author has chosen and arranged her material to produce a superbly clear picture of the city—its geographical location, history, ethnic composition, and relationship to other cities that together with San Francisco make up the San Francisco Bay Area. The design is attractive and enticing, beginning with a terrific map of the Bay Area and a facing page of three photographs that show different aspects of San Francisco, and ending with an equally good map of the city. Ancona's photographs catch San Francisco's lively flavor, its diversity, and its breathtaking views. The photo quality and composition are excellent, extending the text and adding to the reader's understanding and appreciation of the subject. An extremely well thought-out and well presented look at one of our most interesting cities. Index.

Rosie Peasley

SOURCE: A review of *City! San Francisco,* in *School Library Journal,* Vol. 36, No. 6, June, 1990, p. 128.

Gr 4-7—Simply written and directed to young tourists rather than young researchers, this book is big on images and slim on facts. The first and last chapters are specifically directed to visitors, with the intervening chapters giving a brief historical overview of San Francisco yesterday and today. Climo does an adequate job of defining terms such as "coolie" that might be unfamiliar to young readers, but her repeated use of "what ifs," italicized words, and exclamations (*"fire!," "gold!," "silver!"*) seems like overkill. The book is attractive, with glossy paper, wide margins, and numerous color photographs. Many of Ancona's photos are lovely, but quality varies and some are too small to do their subjects justice, while the double-page layouts detract from the impact of any one photograph. Pleasant to look at, this volume seems like a coffee-table gift book for the young.

📖 CITY! NEW YORK (1990)

Denise Krell

SOURCE: A review of *City! New York,* in *School Library Journal,* Vol. 37, No. 3, March, 1991, p. 200.

Gr 4-5—It's a shame that the clear, lively writing is overshadowed by the focus on Manhattan, and an unbalanced format with an historical text coupled with modern photographs that resemble family travel snapshots. These crisp shots that sometimes crop off feet or bottoms of buildings are placed in page-filling groupings. In truth the book is two-thirds history about Manhattan and a little about New York State. Even the cover photo of skaters at Rockefeller Center misrepresents this as a travel guide. A chapter at the end has a scant list of attractions in each of the boroughs. In this final list, some of the most popular tourist attractions are omitted, including Chinatown and Yankee Stadium. Another incomplete chapter offers a list of facts about New York, city and state, that are readily available in any encyclopedia. Better guide books include *The Candy Apple: New York for Kids* by Bubbles Fisherand and *A Kid's Guide to New York City* (Gulliver, 1988).

📖 CITY! WASHINGTON, D.C. (1991)

Ilene Cooper

SOURCE: A review of *City! Washington, D.C.,* in *Booklist,* Vol. 87, No. 22, August, 1991, p. 2142.

Gr. 4-6. Climo continues her series on American cities that began with New York and San Francisco, providing an upbeat portrait of the nation's capital. This is primarily a historical travelogue, with the accent on how the city evolved and the many significant sights that attract tourists. Only a few sentences are devoted to Washington's myriad problems: "Some of the nation's wealthiest blacks live here, and so do some of the nation's poorest. What to do for those who live in poverty is one of the capital's challenging questions." Extending the sight-seeing feel are [George] Ancona's color photographs, usually appearing in a cluster, and Climo's suggestions for exploring Washington, including the most popular attractions as well as more hidden venues—with the permission of a congressperson, a visitor can eat lunch in one of the Capitol's restaurants. A friendly, informative introduction.

Margaret C. Howell

SOURCE: A review of *City! Washington. D.C.,* in *School Library Journal,* Vol. 37, No. 9, September, 1991, p. 262.

Gr 3-6—A series entry that adds to the wealth of material available on the nation's capital. As she did in **City! San Francisco** and **City! New York** (both Macmillan, 1990), Climo presents a brief history of Washington and its buildings and monuments. Her text is not very detailed but is enhanced with a number of vignettes that add interest and humor. There is a bit of information on the present city and its government and a thumbnail sketch of the sights visitors might wish to see. The book includes a serviceable index, quick facts, and several maps. There are a few minor errors: not all the books sent to the Library of Congress for copyright are kept in the collections, and the National Cathedral is basically an Episcopal church. Quibbles aside, this is a better basic introduction for younger readers than Kent's *Washington, D. C.* (Childrens, 1990). There are numerous full-color photographs; although they are small and reminiscent of those found in postcard packets, they extend the text both visually and with their captions.

📖 THE MATCH BETWEEN THE WINDS (1991)

Leone McDermott

SOURCE: A review of *The Match between the Winds,* in *Booklist,* Vol. 88, No. 1, September 1, 1991, p. 60.

Ages 4-8. Gentleness is often stronger than bluster, as many fables attest. This retelling of a folktale from Borneo makes the point using a match between the east and west winds. The west wind loves nothing more than whipping up nasty waterspouts and squalls, while the east wind brings only soft breezes and gentle rain. When the west wind challenges his wimpy (or so he thinks) cousin to a contest, the east wind poses a simple task: blow Kodok the tree frog off a palm leaf. Though the west wind huffs and puffs his way to a typhoon, Kodok remains unmoved. Only the east wind's soft lullaby succeeds, as Kodok slides off his leaf after falling asleep. Climo gives a bright, buoyant rendering of this simple fable. Though looking a little crowded at times, [Roni] Shepherd's gouache and watercolor paintings win favor with breezy lines and tropical colors. Young readers might wonder, however, how Kodok managed to cling to the tree during the typhoon—Climo doesn't mention that tree frogs have sticky feet.

Susan Scheps

SOURCE: A review of *The Match between the Winds*, in *School Library Journal*, Vol. 37, No. 12, December, 1991, p. 80.

Gr 1 Up—This tale is slight, but appealing to the eye. When the harsh West Wind awakens his milder cousin in the east, hoping to make some mischief, the East Wind challenges him to blow Kodok, the tiny tree frog, from his palm tree. Although the West Wind blows up a mighty typhoon, greatly disturbing the island's flora and fauna, it is the East Wind's gentle, calming breeze that causes the little frog to loosen his hold on the leaf and settle into the soft mud below for a nap. The bright, jewel-toned watercolor and gouache paintings that nearly fill each page have dominant hues of blue and green, creating a tropical mood. While most scenes of the island and the winds are painted in a dreamlike, impressionist style, those that illustrate the storm show distorted animals, birds, and people. One such painting of several people floating with animals in a torrent of water is a bit disturbing. Although a contest between the winds is a common folktale theme, the source of this retelling is not given.

THE KOREAN CINDERELLA (1993)

Janice Del Negro

SOURCE: A review of *The Korean Cinderella*, in *Booklist*, Vol. 89, No. 17, May 1, 1993, p. 1598.

Ages 5-8. Pear Blossom was named for the pear tree planted in honor of her birth by her aging father and mother. After her mother dies, her father marries again, and Pear Blossom is ill-treated by her stepmother and stepsister. Her stepmother sets her impossible tasks and threatens her with dire punishment unless she successfully completes them. With the help of a frog, some sparrows, and a black ox, Pear Blossom completes the tasks and finds good fortune in marriage to a wealthy magistrate, "and in the courtyard of her splendid new house, a dozen pear trees blossomed." Though characters' faces sometimes lack articulation, [Ruth] Heller's paintings are exotically lush and colorful as well as engaging. Climo includes an explanatory note about Cinderella variants (the Korean version in particular), and Heller explains the decorations, costumes, and settings she used in the illustrations. An agreeable retelling of the Cinderella story.

Publishers Weekly

SOURCE: A review of *The Korean Cinderella*, in *Publishers Weekly*, Vol. 240, No. 20, May 17, 1993, p. 79.

Following *The Egyptian Cinderella*, Climo and Heller conflate several Korean variants of Cinderella to offer up the story of Pear Blossom, a lovely girl who is sorely mistreated by her nasty stepmother and stepsister. Climo's engaging reworking lends familiar thematic elements an Asian twist: the evil stepmother saddles Pear Blossom with such impossible tasks as picking up scattered grains of rice and weeding an enormous rice paddy; the girl's magical helpers include a tokgabi, or goblin; she loses one straw sandal on the way to the village festival. At once comfortingly familiar and intriguingly exotic, the text is especially noteworthy for its instructive but unobtrusive incorporation of Korean words. Heller's illustrations, based on extensive research of Korean art, are filled with images of enchanted animals, traditional costumes and, of course, pear blossoms. Lavish geometric borders combine intense greens, oranges and purples; the spreads, while making use of Western perspectives, retain a busy, Asian sense of pattern. Endnotes by both author and illustrator amplify the cultural context. Ages 4-8.

John Philbrook

SOURCE: A review of *The Korean Cinderella*, in *School Library Journal*, Vol. 39, No. 8, August 1993, p. 156.

K-Gr 5—Climo combines three Korean variants on this folktale to create a retelling close to the French version. Here the Prince is a local magistrate, and the much-disputed glass or green slipper is a straw sandal. Previous English versions, e.g. Frances Carpenter's *Tales of a Korean Grandmother* (1972) and Edward Adams's *Korean Cinderella* (1982, both Tuttle) offer less detail. Climo gives more dialogue, more skillful character delineation, and better read-aloud possibilities. Heller's lush, full-color illustrations capture the vibrancy of traditional Korean culture with great accuracy. Very few faces, however, look Korean: the stepmother appears to be Latina, while Pear Blossom (Cinderella) and her stepsister often have a strongly simian cast to their features. While all of the supporting domestic details are truly Korean and beautifully drawn, the overuse of *tanchong* (colorful designs painted on the eaves and bracketing of temples, palaces, and some private homes) is unfortunate. Although Heller has depicted them perfectly, they have been wrenched from their settings, greatly enlarged, and sent cascading down or across pages, overwhelming the characters and engulfing the text. On occasion, they prove decoratively effective, but most often look like fancy gift wrap. Without this unfortunate excess and with better facial detail, this would have been a truly splendid creation.

STOLEN THUNDER: A NORSE MYTH (1994)

Publishers Weekly

SOURCE: A review of *Stolen Thunder: A Norse Myth,* in *Publishers Weekly,* Vol. 241, No. 10, March 7, 1994, p. 71.

Despite her wordy presentation, Climo brings an unmistakable verve to this retelling of a Norse myth. Opening passages set the story in context, introducing the various gods and goddesses before describing the theft of thunder god Thor's magic hammer. Overcome with foot-stamping fury, Thor accuses prankster Loki of the crime, but Loki guesses that a giant is the culprit and flies to the giants' icy land. His instincts proven correct, he negotiates a bargain with Thrym the Frost King: the return of the hammer in exchange for Freya, goddess of beauty. An unlikely scene of crossdressing follows, and all ends happily with Thor reunited with his precious tool. The artwork is alternately ethereal and solid, expressing mythic undertones as well as Climo's modern voice. Dark humor resonates, most noticeably in the frequent sneers that suggest that being a god is not all fun and games. Ages 6-10.

Deborah Abbott

SOURCE: A review of *Stolen Thunder: A Norse Myth,* in *Booklist,* Vol. 90, No. 17, May 1, 1994, p. 1596.

Gr. 3-5, younger for reading aloud. In this spirited Norse myth, a conflict rages between two larger-than-life characters. Thor, the most powerful god, who makes thunder with his magic hammer, Mjolnir, lives with the other gods high in the sky in Asgard. Thrym, the Frost King, lives in Jotunheim at the edge of the earth with the other giants. When Thrym slyly steals Mjolnir, a furious Thor sends the artful Loki to find the hammer. Wearing the special falcon cloak of Freya, the goddess of love, Loki flies down to Thrym

and dupes Thrym into a bargain: Freya for Mjolnir. Thor and Freya are horrified, but clever Loki proposes that Thor dress up as the bride. Thor, after feasting heavily enough to raise eyebrows, grabs back the magic hammer just before Thrym tries to kiss the bride, and felling the stunned Thrym, the Thunder-maker quickly exits, forcing Loki into silence about the dress-up escapade that led to their success. Climo carefully sets the stage, establishing setting and characters. Her dramatic text, jammed with snappy dialogue and colorful emotions, is framed in gold. The lovely full- and half-page paintings, also neatly framed, heighten both the distinctive characters and the fast-moving plot. An excerpt from Longfellow's "The Challenge of Thor" is included at the story's end. Although shorter in plot than many retellings, this book is a gem, guaranteed to spark interest in mythology. Use as a read-aloud and as a resource for mythology units and recommend it for pleasure reading.

Denise Anton Wright

SOURCE: A review of *Stolen Thunder: A Norse Myth,* in *School Library Journal,* Vol. 40, No. 7, July, 1994, pp. 92-3.

Gr 2-5—Evocative writing and dynamic full-color illustrations bring this Norse myth to life. When Thor's magical hammer is stolen, the trickster Loki goes in search of it and discovers the thief is none other than Thrym, king of the frost giants. He is unwilling to trade the hammer for anything other than the hand of the beautiful goddess Freya in marriage. After Freya refuses to consider such a proposal, Loki convinces Thor to shave his beard and disguise himself as the bride-to-be. The moment his hammer is safely back in his hand, Thor reveals his true identity and strikes the giant down with a thunderbolt. Climo's top-notch retelling relishes the humor inherent in Thor—that epitome of masculinity—pretending to be a woman. [Alexander] Koshkin draws unevenly upon a variety of influences from the art world: frescoes found in the early Christian cloisters, illuminated manuscripts, symbolist paintings, and even Japanese wood engravings. But ultimately, his exotic acrylic-wash illustrations, with their rich palette of reds and golds, possess a luxuriousness that is somehow appropriate for this story. Overall, an accessible introduction to Norse mythology for children who might otherwise think they are too old for picture books.

📖 *ATALANTA'S RACE: A GREEK MYTH* (1995)

Patricia (Dooley) Lothrop Green

SOURCE: A review of *Atalanta's Race: A Greek Myth,* in *School Library Journal,* Vol. 41, No. 4, April, 1995, p. 140.

Gr 3-7—By starting Atalanta's story with her rejection by her father (who wanted a boy), and carrying it past her race and marriage to her transformation into a lioness (because she failed to honor the gods), Climo hints at the rich psychological interest in her tale. A she-bear suckles Atalanta; a hunter raises her as a boy. Her athletic prowess first wins her notice, then acceptance, from her father; but what he really wants from her is a grandson. Melanion (Hippomenes in other versions) seems, at least, to love her for her own strong self. Atalanta, too, admires Melanion, and perhaps wishes him victory; although, as a true competitor, she tries her best to win. The apparent triumph of love is called into question by Aphrodite's revenge on the couple, both of whom are ungrateful to her for her gift. [Alexander] Koshkin's delicate but vibrant paintings, done in a style evoking the antique, set the raven-haired heroine and blond hero into an archaic Greek world of dress and decor. A slender architrave, pediment, and columns frame each picture. Aphrodite appears with her trademark swan and dolphins, while gorgeous double-spread endpapers depict the whole world of an ancient city-state. There are many retellings of Atalanta's story, but none surpasses this one.

Publishers Weekly

SOURCE: A review of *Atalanta's Race: A Greek Myth,* in *Publishers Weekly,* Vol. 242, No. 15, April 10, 1995, p. 62.

Climo and Koshkin, previously paired for **Stolen Thunder: A Norse Myth** reconfirm their compatibility with this stately picture book. Delving beyond the surface of the Greek myth of the fleet-footed princess, Climo's well-told tale raises issues of female worth and inclusion in male-dominated activities. She tempers the harshness of the ending (in which Atalanta and her true love are punished for failing to acknowledge divine help) in a thoughtful author's note that links the heroine to the modern Olympics, open to women athletes since 1900. Koshkin's striking, deep-toned, classically inspired paintings amplify the drama; framing each painting with architectural motifs, he matches Climo in her sensitivity to detail and ambience. Ages 6-10.

Carolyn Phelan

SOURCE: A review of *Atalanta's Race: A Greek Myth,* in *Booklist,* Vol. 91, No. 16, April 15, 1995, p. 1494.

Gr. 3-5, younger for reading aloud. Furious that the gods have sent him a daughter rather than a son, King Iasus of Arcadia orders the infant Atalanta abandoned in the forest. The baby, protected by a bear and raised by a hunter, grows into a beautiful young woman who can outrace any man in Greece. The time comes for her to choose a husband, but Atalanta refuses to marry any man who cannot outrun her. Through the intervention of Aphrodite, she finally meets her match. This dramatic picture book for older readers will find a ready audience in middle-graders studying Greek mythology, but younger children would also enjoy hearing it read aloud. Rich colors lend warmth to the stylized paintings that illustrate the myth.

Elizabeth Bush

SOURCE: A review of *Atalanta's Race: A Greek Myth,* in *Bulletin of the Center for Children's Books,* Vol. 48, No. 10, June, 1995, p. 339.

Atalanta's abandonment by her father, her childhood with the hunter Ciron, and the famous race against Melanion in which she loses her reputation as undefeated runner but wins a chance at love, are smoothly recounted in this retelling of the classical myth. The heroine is portrayed as headstrong and dangerously defiant: "I can take care of myself!" she claims, but Ciron warns, "Only with the help of the gods." While listeners new to this tale will be drawn into the excitement of the race, Climo never allows her audience to lose sight of Atalanta's pride, which ultimately brings Aphrodite's curse down upon the two lovers. Koshkin's figures are theatrically posed and set within architectural borders, narrow red columns with ornate capitals between a marble base and cornice. His Atalanta is a broad-shouldered, self-assured athlete—in strong contrast to the pert, leggy sprinter of Claire Martin's *The Race of the Golden Apples,* illustrated by the Dillons. A note on variations of the Atalanta myth is appended.

📖 *THE IRISH CINDERLAD* (1996)

Linda Perkins

SOURCE: A review of *The Irish Cinderlad,* in *Booklist,* Vol. 92, No. 14, March 15, 1996, p. 1265.

Ages 5-8. Becan, an Irish lad ridiculed for his huge feet, befriends a bull with magic powers who feeds him and bequeaths him his tail as a belt. With the belt, Becan vanquishes a giant, taking his sword and boots. With the giant's sword, Becan slays the dreaded Serpent, saving Princess Finola and losing a boot in his departure. According to the appended note, this "Cinderella" variant is based primarily on Douglas Hyde's "The Bracket Bull" and Sara Cone Bryant's "Billy Beg and His Bull." The retelling is satisfactory but lacks enough cultural detail to give it a distinctive Irish flavor. The illustrations are overly pretty and romanticized. When the text specifies a "blue-green sea," the picture shows a pinkish purple ocean. In a robust story of courage and danger, the dainty illustrations seem incongruous. This will be useful primarily in libraries where Climo's earlier titles, **The Egyptian Cinderella** (1989) and **The Korean Cinderella** (1993), are popular.

Marilyn Iarusso

SOURCE: A review of *The Irish Cinderlad,* in *School Library Journal,* Vol. 42, No. 6, June, 1996, p. 114.

K-Gr 2—A pleasant but rather bland condensation of a traditional tale. One of the sources cited, Sara Cone Bryant's "Billy Beg and His Bull" from *Best Stories to Tell to Children* (Houghton, 1912; o.p.), is much like Seumas MacManus's wonderful retelling in *In Chimnery Corners* (Doubleday & McClure, 1899; o.p.), in which Billy and the Bull are lifelong companions. The old versions have wonderful runs of poetic language and lots of action, a fair amount of which is violent. As well as gentling the story, Climo seems to want to democratize it. The hero is not a king's son but the son of a traveling peddler. He is described as being small in stature with inordinately large feet and the reteller makes much of the fact that he is ridiculed for his appearance. She even names him Becan, or "Little One." There is no magic stick that turns into a sword and gives the lad wondrous strength, and no belt from the bull's hide to make him invincible. Instead, the bull tells Becan to take his tail after he is dead because it will protect him. In fact, the tail kills a giant and the dragon almost on its own accord when the boy unleashes it. The tidy, full- and double-page illustrations are done in pastel colors and look like opaque watercolors. The people's faces are round and simple. It's fine for young picture-book readers and squeamish parents. However, Ellin Greene's retelling, *Billy Beg and His Bull* (Holiday, 1994), is much closer to the early versions, with its spirited text and earthy and humorous illustrations by Kimberly Bulcken Root.

A TREASURY OF PRINCESSES: PRINCESS TALES FROM AROUND THE WORLD (1996)

Susan Hepler

SOURCE: A review of *A Treasury of Princesses: Princess Tales from around the World,* in *School Library Journal,* Vol. 42, No. 10, October, 1996, p. 111.

Gr 2-5—These seven tales, each with a source note, have been retold from The Brothers Grimm; Afanasyev; the Arabian Nights; Greek mythology; and Mayan (Guatemalan), Xhosa, and Chinese classical literature. Each selection's prefatory note introduces the story and lists worldwide tales with similar motifs, a boon to scholars or teachers who wish to help children compare traditional literature across cultures. Each princess finds true happiness, whether it is in reunion with her family, the discovery of a faithful spouse, or the satisfaction of getting work accomplished. Climo's retellings move along briskly and Sanderson's seven richly realized paintings convey cultural aspects of each story's country of origin.

Publishers Weekly

SOURCE: A review of *A Treasury of Princesses: Princess Tales from Around the World,* in *Publishers Weekly,* Vol. 243, No. 43, October 21, 1996, p. 85.

In **A Treasury of Princesses: Princess Tales from Around the World,** Shirley Climo introduces new princesses to those maxed-out on Cinderella, Jasmine and their ilk: enter Mpunzanyana, White Jade, Gulnara, Vasilisa and others. The tone is traditional, in both the stories and the intensely hued, realistic paintings by Ruth Sanderson.

A TREASURY OF MERMAIDS: MERMAID TALES FROM AROUND THE WORLD (1997)

Publishers Weekly

SOURCE: A review of *A Treasury of Mermaids: Mermaid Tales from around the World,* in *Publishers Weekly,* Vol. 244, No. 39, September 22, 1997, p. 83.

A school of the mythic creatures gathers from diverse cultures in **A Treasury of Mermaids: Mermaid Tales from Around the World** by Shirley Climo, illus. by Jean and Mou-Sien Tseng. Folktale portraits range from the sirens who transfix Odysseus to New Zealand's Pania, who loves a mortal warrior, Karitoki. Full-page evocative watercolors and b&w spot illustrations reflect each mermaid's native culture.

Nancy Menaldi-Scanlan

SOURCE: A review of *A Treasury of Mermaids: Mermaid Tales from around the World,* in *School Library Journal,* Vol. 43, No. 10, October, 1997, pp. 144-45.

Gr 4-7—Climo has selected eight highly readable folktales from countries as far apart as Iceland and New Zealand and from cultures as diverse as Scotland and Japan. She includes both the familiar, such as **"Odysseus and the Sirens,"** and the unusual, such as **"Hansi and the Nix,"** with moods ranging from the humorous **"Mrs. Fitzgerald the Merrow"** to the heartrending **"Pania of the Reef."** Each tale begins with a one-page description of the story's motif and its place in the world of mermaid lore. The selections are approximately six pages each in length and are told in flowing language that is both easy to read and pleasant to hear. The plot lines are logical and the characters are clearly delineated within their cultural parameters. Words such as "ukpik" (Alaskan for "owl") and "kopu" (Maori for "morning star") are italicized and explained in context, while an appendix gives pertinent source notes. [Jean and Mou-sien] Tsengs' full-page watercolors capture the subtle colors of the creatures' watery environs while including details of both the settings and the tales' cultural backgrounds. Smaller and simpler pen-and-ink drawings focus on critical moments within each story. As with the author's *A Treasury of Princesses* (HarperCollins, 1996), this collection does a fine job of gathering a variety of tales into one place, and it is sure to satisfy young mermaid fans and add greatly to their knowledge of the lore (and lure) of these mythical creatures.

Karen Morgan

SOURCE: A review of *A Treasury of Mermaids: Mermaid Tales from Around the World,* in *Booklist,* Vol. 94, No. 6, November 15, 1997, p. 554.

Gr. 4-8. If you thought having Mary Pope Osborne's *Mermaid Tales* from around the world (1993) meant that you would not need to buy any more mermaid tales for a while, think again. This new set of eight stories expands our collective knowledge of mermaid and merpeople folktales. The two books overlap in the retelling of an Irish tale, but the versions are in-

terestingly different and may be fun for older students to compare. Climo's lyrical use of language and the dramatic, full-page color illustrations by Jean and Mou-sien Tseng make the book a strong choice for older readers, and because the stories come from around the world, the book will also be of use in multicultural units. Notes are appended.

THE PERSIAN CINDERELLA (1999)

Publishers Weekly

SOURCE: A review of *The Persian Cinderella,* in *Publishers Weekly,* Vol. 246, No. 23, June 7, 1999, p. 82.

Climo's *(The Egyptian Cinderella; The Irish Cinderlad)* adaptation of this Arabian Nights myth offers a capricious twist on the Cinderella story. In preparation for a No Ruz (New Year) celebration at the Royal Palace, Settareh and her stepsisters go to the bazaar to choose cloth for gowns. Settarah, however, gives alms to a beggar and buys a curious blue jug instead. But inside the jug is a pan, or fairy, who grants her wish for a gown. She captures the attentions of the prince, and a lost diamond bangle fallen from her ankle provides the clue to her whereabouts. On the day of Settareh's anticipated wedding to the Prince, the jealous stepsisters seek vengeance and usurp the magical powers of the pari. They fasten Settareh's hair with enchanted hairpins to transform her into a turtledove. But Prince Mehrdad's affections remain steadfast, and it is he who breaks the spell. Historical details in both the verse and illustrations readily transport readers to 15th-century Persia. "Carpets woven in jewel like colors brightened the walls, and the scent of ginger and cinnamon from the Indies and perfumed oils from Egypt hung in the air." Pomegranate trees, jasmine flowers and other Persian botanicals adorn [Robert] Florczak's *(The Rainbow Bridge; Birdsong)* effervescent landscapes framed with intricate borders. The characters, however, often appear to be pasted on, lending them a hyperrealistic quality. Still, the exotic setting and cultural details make this one of interest to any collector of Cinderella tales. Ages 5-9.

Susan Dove Lempke

SOURCE: A review of *The Persian Cinderella,* in *Booklist,* Vol. 95, No. 21, July, 1999, p. 1948.

Ages 4-9. Climo adds to her series of multicultural Cinderella books (*The Korean Cinderella* [1993]), once again choosing a version of the traditional story authentic to the culture. Here, the main character is named Settareh, and she has a star on her cheek. Instead of a fairy godmother, she has a pari (a kind of fairy) who lives in a blue jar; but when her jealous stepsisters use the pari against her, Settareh is turned into a turtledove. Persian stories are not as plentiful as those from other cultures, and though the pacing isn't as successful as other versions, the memorable details (such as the thousand matched pearls that shower upon the new couple once the spell is broken) more than make up for it. Florczak's illustrations are stunningly exotic and beautiful, with each fold of clothing, each reflection on a surface, and each leaf on a tree lovingly portrayed. The people look as life-like as photographs, each face unique. A fine addition for any folktale collection.

Donna L. Scanlon

SOURCE: A review of *The Persian Cinderella,* in *School Library Journal,* Vol. 45, No. 7, July, 1999, p. 84.

K-Gr 4—After giving most of her money to a beggar, young Settareh spends her last coins on a cracked jug instead of purchasing fabric for a new dress to wear to the prince's celebrations. Resigned to remaining home, she discovers that the pot is inhabited by a *pari* that is able to grant her every wish. She attends the festival, catches the eye of the prince, leaves behind a diamond ankle bracelet, and is found by the queen. Settareh unwisely reveals the secret of the jug to her stepsisters, who steal it and instruct it to get rid of the young woman. The jug self-destructs, leaving behind six jeweled hairpins that, once placed in Settareh's hair, turn her into a turtledove. When the grieving prince befriends the bird, he finds the pins and pulls them out, thus restoring his beloved. The story is well told, although the drama, and hence the pace, is somewhat subdued. The narrative reads smoothly and majestically and Climo explains her choices in a source note. Florczak's sumptuous illustrations have jewel-like tones that glow against the brownline-paper background, and traditional designs decorate the text. The illustrations are realistic and appealing, although in one scene, Settareh is wearing a blue veil with her face exposed when the text specifies that she and the other women draped themselves in black to conceal their faces. Despite this minor flaw, this is a suitable complement to Climo's other "Cinderella" stories.

Additional coverage of Climo's life and career is contained in the following sources published by the Gale Group:*Contemporary Authors,* **Vol. 107;** *Contemporary Authors New Revision Series,* **Vols. 24, 49, 91;** *Something About the Author,* **Vols. 35, 39, 77, 110.**

Russell Hoban
1925-

(Full name Russell Conwell Hoban) American novelist, short story writer, author of children's books, and illustrator.

Major works include the "Frances" series of picture books (1960-1970), *The Mouse and His Child* (1967), *Emmet Otter's Jug-Band Christmas* (1971), *How Tom Beat Captain Najork and His Hired Sportsmen* (1974), *Riddley Walker* (1981), *The Medusa Frequency* (1987).

For further information on Hoban's life and career, see *CLR,* Volume 3.

INTRODUCTION

Equally respected as a writer and illustrator of children's stories and adult novels, Hoban is known for the wit and elegance of his imaginative portrayals of modern life. Although Hoban has originated several well-known characters in children's literature, including Charlie the Tramp, Emmet Otter, the Mouse, his Child, and Manny Rat, he is especially recognized for a series of bedtime books about an anthropomorphic badger named Frances. Reviewers generally agree that these stories depict ordinary family life with much humor, intelligence, and style. While the Frances books have delighted readers since their first appearance in the early 1960s, critics have hailed his fantasy work *The Mouse and His Child* as a modern children's classic. Described by Penelope Farmer in *Children's Literature in Education* "like Beckett for children," *The Mouse and His Child* fascinates both child and adult readers for its multidimensional portrayal of its protagonists' search for a home amidst an often bleak landscape. Despite Hoban's use of black comedy that lends a surrealistic feel to the novel, his work has been noted for an optimistic viewpoint that highlights such traits as courage, hope, and humor. Hoban admits that when he wrote *The Mouse and His Child*, he was not specifically writing for children, although he subsequently has considered it his favorite work for children, noting, "Its heroes and heroines found out what they were and it wasn't enough, so they found out how to be more. . . . That's not a bad thought to be going with." Following the publication of *The Mouse and His Child*,

Hoban shifted his writing toward an adult audience with several well-received novels, most notably *Riddley Walker*, a highly acclaimed work set in the distant future after a twentieth-century atomic holocaust. Whether writing for children or adults, critics concur that Hoban's engaging works are infused with a powerfully mythic quality.

BIOGRAPHICAL INFORMATION

Born in Lansdale, Pennsylvania, Hoban exhibited an early talent for drawing and language and was rewarded with nickels from his father for his efforts. His parents expected Hoban to pursue a career as an artist, and, upon graduation from high school at sixteen, he attended the Philadelphia Museum School of Industrial Art. He worked as a successful freelance illustrator, television art director, and copywriter before he began writing children's stories. In 1944, he married his first wife, Lillian Hoban, an illustrator and children's book author with whom he collaborated on many works, including *The Mouse and His Child* and several volumes in the Frances series. While working as an illustrator, he drove throughout Connecticut, occasionally stopping at construction sites to sketch the machinery being used. A friend saw his work and suggested that it might make a good children's book. Published in 1959, Hoban's first work, *What Does It Do and How Does It Work?: Power Shovel, Dump Truck, and Other Heavy Machines*, was about construction equipment. After 1960, Hoban—having never fully enjoyed the illustration process—declined to illustrate his own works anymore, preferring instead to concentrate on the writing. Following a divorce and remarriage in 1975, Hoban relocated to London, where he began writing adult novels while continuing to write children's books.

MAJOR WORKS

Hoban's early career is noted for his successful picture books, which have been praised for their engaging depictions of ordinary childhood dilemmas and endearing, childlike animal characters. Drawing inspiration from his own four children, Hoban developed the character Frances the Badger, who endures such childhood experiences as bedtime fears, jealousy, and self-determination. The Frances series appeals to both children and their parents; one critic noted in a review of *Bedtime for Frances*, that "the exasperated humor of this book could only derive from actual parental experience." The familiarity of the characters along with the honesty with which Hoban portrays the situations the characters find themselves in has captivated readers for generations. Despite the positive reception of his picture books, and the Frances books in particular, critics were unprepared for the powerful impact of Hoban's fantasy novel *The Mouse and His Child*. Initially ignored by American critics, *The Mouse and His Child* gained great popularity in England, and it has since become a cult classic among preteens and adolescents. The picaresque story recounts the adventures of two wind-up toy mice who are discarded from a toyshop. Ill equipped for the baffling, threatening world into which they are tossed, the mouse and his child innocently confront its inherent treachery, violence, the unknown, and their own fears. The book explores not only the transience and inconstancy of life but the struggle to persevere as well.

With *The Lion of Boaz-Jachin and Jachin-Boaz* (1973) and *Kleinzeit* (1974), Hoban began to write allegorical novels specifically for a more mature au-

dience, although he retained the magical and bizarre worlds of his children's stories. Consistent throughout his adult novels is Hoban's search for the patterns that make life significant—and this often in the face of a threatening, desolate, or near mad world. Hoban's prose style, markedly individual, fresh, and often funny, is a linguistic match for his metaphysical themes. Nominated as the most distinguished book of fiction by the National Book Critics Circle, and for the Nebula Award for Science Fiction Writers of America, *Riddley Walker* received the John W. Campbell Memorial Award from the Science Fiction Research Association as the year's best science fiction novel. *Riddley Walker* imagines a world and civilization decades after a nuclear holocaust; the story of what remains is narrated in a fragmented, phonetical English by a twelve-year-old boy struggling to comprehend the past so that its magnificence might be recaptured. A popular work among young adult readers, *Riddley Walker* is often compared with other contemporary works such as Anthony Burgess's *A Clockwork Orange*, John Gardner's *Grendel*, and the works of William Golding, as well as with Mark Twain's *Adventures of Huckleberry Finn*. While the novel's philosophical themes, which explore such issues as humankind's continued existence on earth and the potential destructiveness of technology, are of interest to readers, the inventiveness of the language used throughout the narrative is most often discussed by commentators.

AWARDS

Hoban has received numerous adult- and child-selected honors, including the Library of Congress Children's Book Award in 1964 for *Bread and Jam for Frances*; the Boys' Club Junior Book Award in 1968 for *Charlie the Tramp*; the Lewis Carroll Shelf Award and the Christopher Award, both in 1972, for *Emmet Otter's Jug-Band Christmas*; the Whitbread Literary Award in 1974 for *How Tom Beat Captain Najork and His Hired Sportsmen*; the John W. Campbell Memorial Award for the best science fiction novel of the year from the Science Fiction Research Association in 1981 and the Australian Science Fiction Achievement Award in 1983 for *Riddley Walker*. Many of Hoban's books have received American Library Association (ALA) Notable Book citations. *Emmet Otter's Jug-Band Christmas* was named among the best books of the year by *School Library Journal*. *Riddley Walker* was nominated as the most distinguished book of fiction by the National Book Critics Circle and for the Nebula Award by the Science Fiction Writers of America in 1982. Hoban received Recognition of Merit from the George G. Stone Center for Children's Books in 1982 for his contribution to books for younger children.

AUTHOR COMMENTARY

Russell Hoban

SOURCE: "Russell Hoban Reads Russell Hoban: Children's Books," edited by Alida Allison, *The Lion and the Unicorn,* Vol. 15, No. 2, December, 1991, pp. 96-107.

What I want to do is come at you from several places at once. The emphasis is on my writing for children. It is not separate from my other writing, and, really, children don't live in a world that is separate from the grown-up world. It's just one world and my writing is just one way of writing. And some of it is within a child's frame of reference and some of it isn't. But all of it, and especially the children's writing, has to come from as deep a place in me as there is to write from.

Before I start, I want to show you the Mouse and His Child in what has become a little ritual, so you can see what got me started in novel writing.

[Hoban unwraps and winds up the clockwork toy after which he named his first novel, placing it on a table for the audience of around 400 to watch. There are Ooohs and Aaahs as the tiny toy father circles, applause as he lifts his little son, and laughter as the two wind down and stop. Hoban smiles and carefully rewraps the toy.]

I want to tell you something about how I work and how I get the story for a book together. I will be talking to you about *The Mouse and His Child,* but I want to begin with a lion because my first novel, so-called for grown ups, was *The Lion of Boaz Jachin and Jachin Boaz,* and the lead-up to that is perhaps a better example of the kind of thing that gets me started than the mouse and his child, so I'm going to read to you from it. But first I'll tell you something about it.

In Westport, Connecticut in 1968, I bought a book on Mesopotamian art, a big thick square book—I could hardly lift it up. And in this book there were wonderful clear photographs of sandstone carvings of a relief of a lion hunt in King Ashurbanipal's north pal-

ace at Ninevah. The photographs were remarkable because the sculptor was quite gifted, and his observation was accurate and strong and full of vitality. The human beings in this animal hunt—the huntsman, the men on the horses and leading horses, the men on top of the lion cages, and the men in the chariots—all of the people looked like nothing. The people were conventionalized and stereotyped and they all looked pretty much the same. The upper-class people had very fancy curled beards and hair and they were totally boring, but each of the lions was an individual tragic portrait very carefully observed. The sculptor had obviously looked at lions being hunted and being wounded and dying, and he had cared about the lions. He carved them with great force and with great artistry and I thought about it and thought about it, and mind you, this was only the book—I hadn't yet seen the real thing. The real thing was in the British Museum, far away. So I began to think about these lions. I read up on some Mesopotamian myth and got a little bit of material about what happens after death in that society about the netherworld of Cor and Ereshnigal and Nergal and the boatman who takes people across the river. Then I began to develop some mythology of my own to account for the feeling for the lions that was developing in me.

[Hoban then reads from some of his "made-up mythology" about the lion hunt of the king and the dying lions and the observant sculptor. Since the material has not yet been published, it will not be reproduced here.]

I wanted to start with that because I guess I want to stress that writing anything is a serious business that requires close attention and requires fidelity. As to fidelity, I'll read you a couple of lines from *The Medusa Frequency* [his 1987 novel] in which a not very successful writer, whose name is Herman Orff, finds the head of Orpheus, demigod and great singer and musician, buried in the low tide mud of the river Thames. They get into a conversation and Orpheus tells Herman Orff some of his troubles. At one point, Herman Orff says to this rotting, eyeless head covered with barnacles and slime that he's picked up, he says to it—because the head has been saying how it's been going from ocean to ocean, travelling all over the world—he says:

"Maybe you ought to stop trying. You're old, you're blind and rotten, you can't sing anymore. Why don't you just pack it in?"

"I haven't that choice. There's no way for me to cease to be. I'm manifesting myself to you as a rotting head but there's no picture for what I am. I am that which sings the world, I am the response that never dies. Fidelity is what's wanted."

"Fidelity? I got my head zapped looking for a novel and here I am listening to homilies from a rotting head."

"You don't know what you're looking for," said the rotting head. "Alone and endlessly voyaging I think constantly of fidelity. Fidelity is a matter of perception. Nobody is unfaithful to the sea or to mountains or to death. Once recognized they fill the heart. In love or in terror or in loathing one responds to them with the true self. Fidelity is not an act of the will. The soul is compelled by recognitions. Anyone who loves, anyone who perceives the other person fully can only be faithful, can never be unfaithful to the sea and the mountains and the death in that other person, so pitiful and heroic is it to be a human being."

I read that to make the point that, when I write, fidelity is what's wanted. The writing is an act of faithfulness to whatever it is that the writer has perceived.

Now I'll tell you a little bit about *The Mouse and His Child,* in which the approach was the same, really, as for the lion but perhaps a little simpler and more direct. And that simply was that, having seen these toys over three Christmases in a collection of other clockwork toys under my friend's Christmas tree, I began to feel there was a story in them. Toys are always interesting. For one thing, why do we make them? Why is it that people want to make little effigies in tin or in cloth, then put clockwork inside? They push wheelbarrows or climb up and down ladders or they shimmy up ropes and slide down boards or do gymnastics. Why is it we want to make little figures to do that? I don't know. These little figures, the ones we make from tin, they're almost a kind of metaphor. They're made from two halves that never match up quite exactly. And the two halves are fastened together with very fragile clasps of tin. If you try to repair a clockwork toy, the clasps break. You have the two halves of the shell falling apart and there's the clockwork and it seems to be saying something about the human condition. They wear out. . . . I have tin frogs that don't hop as well as they used to; neither do I.

So I looked at this toy and I thought I might get a story out of it. There's something about the way the father circles and lifts up the child. The arms come down, then he lifts it up again and turns the other way and gradually goes more and more slowly. I thought I might get a story of 36 pages or so, because up to then my limit had been 10 to 12 pages.

The Frances books, for example, they're always 10 or 12 pages of typescript. I began to work on the thing; I didn't think I'd be getting into a novel, but it began to grow and there began to be more of it. At that time, I was living in a house overlooking a pond in Wilton, Connecticut. The pond was full of things. Every spring the female snapping turtles would come up the hill out of the pond and lay eggs. In due course I'd see parades of little tiny snapping turtles coming down the hill to the pond. One night I picked each one up as it came down and I had a whole aquarium full of baby snapping turtles. I looked at them and they looked at me and I put them back in the pond. There were also some slimy jellyish things in the pond. One time I scooped up everything I could with the net and put it all in the aquarium in the window of the study where I worked. I ended up with all kinds of things coming to life there. That was where Miss Mudd came from, the dragonfly nymph in *The Mouse and His Child.* I actually did have a dragonfly nymph that looked very shabby and decrepit for a long time, then one day it climbed up a little stalk I had in the aquarium. It unfolded its iridescent wings and it waved them until they got dry and stiff and it flew away like a little Wright Brothers invention out of the window. I'd never seen anything like it before.

For the sequence in the book where the mouse and the child were at the bottom of the pond, I sacrificed another clockwork toy. This one was a juggler who had a red, blue, and yellow ball. I had that toy stand in the bottom of the pond and get rusty and eaten away and so forth. So there was a lot to do to get that book done. I had to keep being as faithful as I could to the essence of each thing that I saw or that occurred to me, to find out what the story was.

I thought of it then and still think of it now as an adult novel. It was the most book I could write at the time and I didn't make any concessions to a child's vocabulary. It's linear; the events follow one another like knots on a string. I was so unused to putting together anything of that length that I used to lay out pages and chapters on the floor of the living room. It was a very wide living room—28 feet wide. I'd lay them out the whole length of the room and I'd run back and forth trying to get my head around the whole story.

After three years I managed to get the story done, and it got a very brusque brush-off in *The New York Times Sunday Book Review.* It didn't attract a lot of attention anywhere in this country. It did rather better in England.

So, to get the reading of children's books started tonight, I'll read you a bit of the opening of *The Mouse and His Child,* then I'll move on to other picture books.

[Hoban reads from that Harper and Row paperback edition, starting with the epigram from W. H. Auden and ending with the dialogue between the mouse father and his child when the child asks who they are: "'We must wait and see,' said the father."]

[Hoban takes a moment to pick his next reading, selects *Ponders,* a more recent collection of stories, and introduces them.]

These were written long after I left the house overlooking the pond at Wilton, but the stories are about the animals that lived in the pond.

[There is much laughter as he reads all the *Ponders* stories, and Hoban responds to the applause when he finishes.]

All right, if you're going to keep nagging me, I'll read *The Dancing Tigers.*

[He does, to more applause and he continues.]

To finish on a somewhat bouncier note, I'll read *Monsters.*

[He does, and after the laughter and applause, he opens the evening to questions from the audience, most of whom are children's literature students who had read at least one of Hoban's books before he visited campus.]

Q: I read that you started out as an artist and that you gave it up for writing. Am I correct that you don't illustrate your own books?

A: I can't walk and chew gum at the same time. I'm sort of obsessive-compulsive and everything I do goes into one channel. For a time when I was drawing and painting that was about the only thing, but what happened was that all the eight years I was making a living as an illustrator, I only illustrated two of my own children's books. One was about heavy machinery and one was about an atomic submarine because I was never much good at cuddly animals. But I was already writing bits of things and I was beginning to sell a few things. I did a profile on Sandy Dennis for *Holiday* and a piece about a middleweight boxer on a trip to Boston. I found gradually that writing was what I really wanted, and once I got into writing, I just didn't want to do any-

thing else. Now writing takes up all of my time, thought, and energy and is the form in which all of my ideas get realized as much as possible. So I just don't do any drawing.

Q: Where did the idea of the tramp in **The Mouse and His Child** *come from?*

A: I think it's safe to say in general that when a writer starts a fantasy story involving a quest it's quite usual for some kind of a special stranger to come into it, as a catalyst of some kind, to get things going or provide an entrance into some sort of mystery. I think it's just inherent in that kind of story and that's what the tramp is for me.

Q: Did you like Jim Henson's version of **Emmet Otter's Jug Band Christmas**?

A: Yes. He did it very well and followed the style of the drawings. I didn't like what was done with *The Mouse and His Child,* but *Emmet Otter* was very nicely done.

Q: Why did you choose the name **The Marzipan Pig**? *The pig was killed off on the first page. Why not name it after something else, like "sweetness and love"?*

A: Well, it was a pig made of marzipan. Don't be angry with me for saying this, but I think you're being a little bit lazy with that question. Would you really want me to call the book "Sweetness and love"? The marzipan is where the sweentness originated in that story, and the traces of the marzipan sweetness went through, literally, many of the characters in the story and stayed as a continuing thread right to the end.

You know, to spell everything out for the reader is to take away the pleasure of discovering something for oneself. So it's called *The Marzipan Pig.*

Q: Where do you get ideas like having the owl (in **The Marzipan Pig***) fall in love with the taxi meter?*

A: I haven't seen any taxi meters here in the States, but in London the taxi meters have a kind of violet light that illuminates the meters. It's a fascinating light, it's a kind of a light that makes you want to follow it and get to know it and so the owl responded to that and he fell in love with it. It's a very lovable kind of violet light. [Laughter.]

Q: Did you fall in love with the meter?

A: Well, yes, to the extent that I'm in all my characters, yes, I guess you could say I fell in love with the meter to the extent that I wrote about an owl who fell in love with the meter. Nothing strange about that. [Laughter.]

Q: *How do you come to terms with what pictures other artists make to go along with what you've said?*

A: Mainly my selectivity goes into selecting the illustrator and I only work with illustrators who are going to be good for that particular story. I get Quentin Blake whenever I can and I have a pretty good idea of how he will handle it, and the same with the other illustrators. As for how I handle letting someone else do the pictures, pause and reflect for a moment how long it takes to paint a picture as opposed to writing a page of words.

Q: *Can you expand on what parts of the film* **The Mouse and His Child** *you didn't like?*

A: Not really, because there were so many things I didn't like. [Laughter.] It's a strange cultural phenomenon, really, and it's been happening for lifetimes. Film people find something that a writer's done and they say, "Oh terrific. This is really great stuff"—grovel, grovel—and "Can we make a film of your book?" and "We'll give you money—here's money for it." They take your book and you say "thanks" and take the money, then they say, "Well, what we need to do now is make it a little more accessible and the trouble is you've got good dialogue that's not cinematic, so let's put in some bad dialogue and make it cinematic," and they put in bad dialogue that's cinematic and they take out good characters that aren't cinematic and they take out episodes and finally they wind up with a whole other thing. Then you say, "Well, how's it doing, is there any profit?" because in your contract you take a percentage of the profit and they say, "Well, no profits," and well, there it went.

Q: *Do any of your family write?*

A: Most of them. I have four children by my first marriage. Phoebe Hoban does quite well as a journalist, does a lot of work for *New York Magazine,* and Julia Hoban has done a number of children's books for Harper and Row. My daughter Esme hasn't had anything published yet, but she's done a dissertation in linguistics and my son Brom is now doing some freelance writing for a magazine in Texas, so that eventually all of them will be published in one way or another. The three sons of my second marriage don't have any writing inclinations so far, but it's early days; one is 18, one is 16, and one is 12.

Lillian Hoban is my first wife. She illustrates and writes books on her own; she used to illustrate my books. And Tana Hoban is my sister; she does children's books with photographs.

Q: *Did you always enjoy writing? Did you get A's in English?* [Laughter.]

A: Yes, I did. I was always interested in writing and I always got good grades in English and I won short story and poetry contests. When I got out of high school I remember wondering whether I ought to go to art school or college. My mother wanted me to go to college and become well-rounded, so I became a proto-drop-out; I went to Temple University for five weeks, then I dropped out and went to art school for a year and a half, then I went into the army.

Q: *Can you tell me more about the Bonzo Dog Food cans from* **The Mouse and His Child?**

Q: When I was a small boy living in Pennsylvania, there was a brand of dog food we got. It was called Marco dog food and it had the same label that the dog food can in *The Mouse and His Child* had—a little black and white dog standing on his hind legs wearing a white cap and an apron. And he was carrying a tray on which there was a little black and white dog standing on his hind legs carrying a tray on which there was a dog food can and so on to infinity. And I still marvel at that device because I would put my face as close as I could to that label and try to see where the cans ended. [Laughter.] And of course after about the third can you couldn't make out a can anymore because the picture broke up into colored dots, but I understood that metaphysically, the cans continued to recede to infinity in the colored dots. A heavy concept for me to deal with and it's stayed with me a long time. [Laughter.]

Q: *Why did you choose to let Manny Rat live at the end of* **The Mouse and His Child?** *[Laughter.]*

A: It just seemed it was inevitable that he would go on living. When I put together a story, I don't think it's for me to say, well, this one should live and this one should die. If the story comes out in such a way that one of them should die, well, then they die. But if I create a character who seems as if he will go on living, well, he goes on living. Manny Rat seemed to want to go on living, and he was not without charm, I thought. [Laughter.]

Q: *Have you ever worked with children in writing?*

A: I have, but not a lot. Years ago I made some school visits and I didn't work with small children but high school age. The little workshop session I had with them went quite well. They all came up with good things. I don't know, I'm really not too keen on working with children; I think it may be overworked. I think there's too much of a trend for Show-and-Tell-ism.

I'm an American but I've been out of the country for a long time and many of the things I used to take for granted I don't anymore. I get big brown envelopes from teachers with sheets of large ruled paper inside and letters from their classes. The envelope will say on the outside, Mrs. Such and Such's class, second grade. And Such and Such School. And there are these sweet letters from the kids—where do you get your ideas and please write back. And the teacher has an explanatory letter and she says, "We've done two units on you." [Laughter.]

I don't like the industrialization of everything. I don't want units done on me. [Laughter.] I'm glad people buy the books, don't get me wrong—that's what I live on. But I don't want "We've done two units on you." I get the feeling that this working with kids has been overdone in America. Let's say someone turns a kid loose and the kid is walking along the beach picking up stones. You just know that some grown-up is going to come along and say, "Isn't that nice, picking up stones. Now let's sort the stones into colors and let's put them in a box and let's write about sorting stones. Let's work with that." Then I just know someone in the Media Department is going to come along with a video camera and say, "Let's make a film about the teachers and the kids working with the stones." And then I just know that someone else is going to come along and make a movie about the video of the teachers and the kids working with the stones. I just wish that that kid who picked up the stone could be left alone.

I'm sure you've heard this joke that a teacher told me: two kids are sitting by the window in the classroom and a traveling carnival goes by with vans and the equipment for the rollercoasters and everything is bright and colorful and musical and one kids says, "Hey, look at the carnival going by!" And the other kids says, "Sh! We'll have to write about it!" [Laughter, applause.]

And kids that have been industrialized like that, what happens when they grow up and retire and go abroad? They set about industrializing Europe. They have cameras and video cameras and they produce "product." They visit cathedrals and they say, "We did ten cathedrals last week," and they produce video tapes and slides and it's a cycle from infancy to the coffin, industrializing everything.

Q: Where do your stories come from? Is it like day-dreaming? Or is it more methodical?

A: It happens in all kinds of ways. One way it doesn't happen—and people will sometimes go so far as to ask this question—"Do you wait for inspiration or do you work every day?" Well, I work every day. If I waited for inspiration, I'd be in a lot worse shape than I am now. I have a fixed routine, and even the days when nothing's coming, I put words down on paper; I do what I can, however I can. I use an Apple II and I type out notes, I ask questions, "What about this? What if such and such happened?" There have been times when I've talked to myself on a tape recorder, trying to encourage thoughts to come up and, from time to time, because I'm that sort of an animal, ideas come to me.

I don't always finish the ones I start. Sometimes it takes me a certain distance and then it fades away and I'm left stranded. Other times it'll go a certain distance and stop for a while and years later I can do something with it. It works all kinds of ways. If you're not in the business of writing every day, you wonder how it happens. If you are in the business of writing every day, it's just an inevitable process that you maintain, an alertness to anything that could possibly lead to a story. And also, I encourage mental drift, sort of.

By now everybody knows about the two hemispheres of the brain. The left hemisphere is more for the rational and the right hemisphere is more for the visual and the irrational and the intuitive. I don't know about other people, but I find that when I fall asleep, if I'm lying on my left side I get more verbal ideas, and if I'm lying on my right side I get more visual things. [Laughter.]

I always try to make use of whatever mental state is happening and sift through images. I have a large accumulation of books of all kinds. I have scientific books in which I can understand only one paragraph or two. But that paragraph might make it worthwhile because it might start a train of thought. I buy loads of art books and natural history books. Our shelves are bending under videos of nature films. I'm always thinking of every kind of thing interesting to a nonspecialist thinker; that's how ideas come to me.

Q: Is a story like **Monsters** *something that you could get done in an afternoon?*

A: Oh yes. I've done numerous picturebook texts in one day and I've had texts that might be only six to ten pages that I couldn't get together for months. I tell everybody that over my computer monitor I've taped a quote from Barry Lopez, from his book *Arctic Dreams*. He says that the polar bear is not unfailingly successful in its hunting and that, depending upon the condition of the ice, and the age and sex of the seal, and the age sex of bear, the success rate might be anywhere from 2 to 25 percent. And I look at that and I say "Yeah!"

Q: Obviously you do research, but once you start a work, do you find you have to really deeply research?

A: Oh yes. For example, the book **Pilgermann** got started on a trip to Israel when I went to visit my daughter, who was living there then. We went to visit the ruins of a stronghold of Teutonic knights of the twelfth and thirteenth centuries and that got me going, that gave me the protagonist, the narrator. Then I found I got into a thing on the First Crusade. That involved three religions, Christian, Islamic, and Judaic. Although I'm a Jew, I didn't know anything about Judaism and I had to swot up all three religions. I had to read the Old Testament and the New all over again. I accumulated notes and made notes on the Koran. I then also had to read up on a lot of history and I had to get into all sorts of technology too. For example, the stirrup was instrumental in social and historical changes. Before the invention of the stirrup, you couldn't have the attacks of armored knights, which were the tanks of their time. You couldn't wield a lance and a sword in that way without the leverage of the stirrup. So it was the invention of the stirrup that engendered a whole age of chivalry at a certain time.

I spent thousands of pounds on books for that novel. I always buy books like a drunken sailor because I feel I have to show the gods and forces who help writers that I'm not holding back. I spend money right, left, and center. I buy books till I come home with my knees buckling. Anyhow, that one took only two years but it involved very concentrated research. I took naturally to it in that I'm good at connecting things, finding how one thing leads to another. I hate to just sit there and just read, but if I have to do it I have to do it.

Q: Do you have any children's books in the making that we can look forward to?

A: Yes, at the moment my most recent published book is **Jim Hedgehog and the Lonesome Tower.** That's number two in the Jim Hedgehog series. The first was **Jim Hedgehog's Supernatural Christmas,** which has been published in England but not yet here. It will be here soon. I have a picturebook text that my London publisher wants to do in two-color, but I'm shopping around for someone to do full-color. I have yet another one that's in production

where I've done a semifinal text and the illustrator has begun. So I always have children's books in the works. I try to keep a novel going, too. Right now, I'm about 100 pages into one. I'm hoping to get another 100 pages done, then I'll have 200 pages. [Laughter.] [Applause.]

GENERAL COMMENTARY

Gillian McMahon-Hill

SOURCE: "A Narrow Pavement Says 'Walk Alone': The Books of Russell Hoban," in *Children's Literature in Education,* Vol. 20, 1976, pp. 41-55.

> Most adult books are about clockwork dolls who copulate. **The Mouse and His Child** happens to be about clockwork mice that walk, and therefore it is a children's book.

Especially in these days of rational woodpulp, this admirably terse statement does not encourage yet another investigation of the confusing kernel of that elderly chestnut, 'when is a children's book not a children's book?' At the Exeter Children's Literature Conference in 1973 Russell Hoban was asked if he thought that **The Mouse and His Child** was 'a children's book'. Again the response was flippantly expressed, but essentially unanswerable: he replied that he had wanted the manuscript to be published, that Faber was interested, and if Faber had marketed tables and chairs, he would have sold it as a table or, if they preferred, as a chair.

Nobody, one would have thought, who has read **The Mouse and His Child** could deny that it deals with areas of concern to adult readers (even though, when I read extracts from it in Assembly at school a year or two ago, I was asked by one member of staff What It All Had To Do With God). In speaking of its subject-matter Hoban himself said:

> I wrote a book called **The Mouse and His Child** in which I made a world-picture that was an attempt to see the thingness of things in a very narrow compass, a microcosm. It was published as a children's book, and, for the most part, reviewed as such.

The phrase 'narrow compass' must be read very carefully: there is no suggestion in this work of narrowness in the sense of restriction or limitation. All the significant detail of one particular and small, but carefully defined, area is examined with precise imagination. The ramifications of what is observed are no less far reaching because the protagonists are clockwork mice that walk. Without reaching for the nutcrackers, the initial point which needs to be made is that Russell Hoban writes books, some of which children enjoy reading or having read to them, and that the best of these books offer material of interest and importance to the adult reader. Again, the author's own words are useful:

> Books in nameless categories are needed—books for children and adults together, books that can stand in the middle of an existential nowhere and find reference points.

Since writing that article, Russell Hoban has produced three books specifically for adults, as well as more stories intended for children. This study will include a consideration of the three adult novels because they are facets of one creative whole, and to consider some parts in isolation is not very satisfactory. All the books help to elucidate each, and the four long works—*The Mouse and His Child, The Lion of Jachin-Boaz and Boaz-Jachin, Kleinzeit* and *Turtle Diary*—are equally important.

The Mouse and His Child, for several reasons, seems the best starting point. It is both a chronological and creative beginning. Hoban himself looks upon it as the start of his mature writing, his first 'real' book, and what is found there can be seen to be developed and expanded in the later work. This article hopes to explore some of the directions in which this first 'real' book leads, to see the line that runs from it through all the subsequent writing. Earlier writing— the Frances Books, the Brute family stories and other picture-books—already manifests the same rhythmic, controlled and witty use of language, the same brevity, precision and careful observation which are so representative of the more recent writing; but the early work does not arrive at the heart of the matter very often. Frances' world is very well ordered, very cosy, and evasive in its cosiness. Even the Brute Family (before they change their name to Nice), who eat sand and gravel porridge and stews of sticks and stones, reveal what is only the reverse side of the same coin. Sister Brute wants a doll, so her mother gives her a heavy stone which she christens 'Alice Brute Stone'; there is a dog too:

> 'Love me,' said the dog,
> 'or I will kick you very hard.'

> .   .   .   .   .

> One day Sister Brute
> said to her mama,

> 'All I have is tiredness
> and kicks and bruises.'

> 'Maybe that is because you have
> been loving only a hard stone
> and a kicking dog,' said Mother Brute.

> 'What else is there to love?'
> said Sister Brute.

> 'I don't know,' said Mother Brute.

Another much more sophisticated reaction to the world of Frances is seen in the splendid antiestablishment tale of *How Tom Beat Captain Najork and his Hired Sportsmen.*

Russell Hoban's specific way of looking at things invests everything he writes with a very particular life of its own. The peculiar qualities of his style, although easy to locate, are, it would seem, sometimes difficult to define successfully (one hapless individual found his way into *Private Eye's* 'Pseuds' Corner' with his review of *Lion*). Hoban's work has been compared in originality—quite unhelpfully, I feel—to the writing of C S Lewis and Tolkien; it has been called 'gently fierce', of 'exceptional originality', allegorical, mythological, strange, magical, irreverant, illuminating. However, none of this helps very much in moving towards a definition, much less an analysis, of Hoban's particular skill in self-expression.

The Mouse and His Child possesses all the representative stylistic qualities of the earlier children's books, in a new and powerfully imaginative synthesis. This extraordinary book needs little introduction: the toy father mouse, forever looking in the opposite direction from the son whose paws he holds, is a familiar figure and the quest of the clockwork mice to achieve self-winding is by now well known. In looking at this book, and indeed at any of Hoban's writing, the first aspect of his style to make itself apparent is the spareness of expression, the very precise, brief wit, the effective understatement. The opening paragraph of the book well illustrates this quality:

> The tramp was big and squarely built, and he walked with the rolling stride of the long road, his steps too big for the little streets of the little town. Shivering in his thin coat, he passed aimlessly through the crowd while rosy-faced Christmas shoppers quickened their steps and moved aside to give him room.

Already the reader has been given, in these few words, a detailed picture of the tramp, the town, the shoppers. It is the same with the initial description of the dolls' house in the toyshop where the mice find themselves, a dolls' house which is ultimately to play an important role in the lives of the mouse and his son:

'Why haven't they bought you?' asked the little tin seal. 'How come you've stayed here so long?'

'It isn't quite the same for me, my dear,' replied the elephant. 'I'm part of the establishment, you see, and this is my house.'

The house was certainly grand enough for her, or indeed for anyone. The very cornices and carven brackets bespoke a residence of dignity and style, and the dolls never set foot outside it. They had no need to; everything they could possibly want was there, from the covered platters and silver chafing dishes on the sideboard to the ebony grand piano among the potted ferns in the conservatory. No expense had been spared and no detail was wanting. . . . Interminable-weekend-guest dolls lay in all the guest room beds, sporting dolls played billiards in the billiard room, and a scholar doll in the library never ceased persual of the book he held, although he kept in touch with the world by the hand he lightly rested on the globe that stood beside him. . . . In the dining room, beneath a glittering chandelier, a party of lady and gentleman dolls sat perpetually round a table. . . .

It was the elephant's constant delight to watch that tea party through the window, and as the hostess she took great pride in the quality of her hospitality. 'Have another cup of tea,' she said to one of the ladies. 'Try a little pastry.'

'HIGH SOCIETY SCANDAL, changing to cloudy, with a possibility of BARGAINS GALORE!' replied the lady. Her papier mache head being made of paste and newsprint, she always spoke in scraps of news and advertising, in whatever order they came to mind.

This cameo is perfectly constructed and wittily expressed; it presents the cosy and well-ordered world which instigates the mouse son's search for a mother and sister and the domestic joy they will bring, and his father's desire to possess a territory of his own. It forms a savage contrast with what they actually encounter in the outside world. This passage makes wry comment on the ultimate futility of social pretensions of genteel life, and incidentally, of academic achievement.

In their strange, pathetic, amusing and sometimes very depressing odyssey, the two mice encounter many living creatures, speaking toys, and inanimate objects, all of which are ciphers, more or less animated, vivid images representing philosophical concepts, human characteristics and emotions, particular ways of living. One image which is central to the story and is developed in various ways is that printed on the label of BONZO Dog Food tins:

BONZO Dog Food said the white letters on the orange label, and below the name was a picture of a little black-and-white spotted dog, walking on his hind legs and wearing a chef's cap and an apron. The dog carried a tray on which there was another can of BONZO Dog Food, on the label of which another little black-and-white spotted dog, exactly the same but much smaller, was walking on his hind legs carrying a tray on which there was another can of BONZO Dog Food, on the label of which another little black-and-white spotted dog, exactly the same but much smaller, was walking on his hind legs carrying a tray on which there was another can of BONZO Dog Food, and so on until the dogs became too small for the eye to follow.

This is a particularly strong and successful example of one aspect of Hoban's technique. It is no small accomplishment to encapsulate infinity in an image so tangible, so contained and so precise.

At the 1974 Exeter Children's Literature Conference, Russell Hoban led a writer's workshop. One of his most frequent pieces of advice, as the participants read their work was that the writer should concentrate on careful, realized detail, because where the particular was probably observed, the general would follow of its own accord. The writer must describe the 'thingness of things', understand their concrete, particular presence. If he examines the general before realizing specific details, then the result will be a woolly mess. This concern with specifics is, of course, a familiar one: it is at the root of Blake's belief in minute particulars, Keats' negative capability, Hopkins's theory of inscape and instress. The BONZO Dog Food label is a perfect example of this precept: a discussion based on the nature of infinity might well have proved difficult to follow, for those of less than C Serpentina's intellect. Expressed in terms of a tin of dogfood, it is more readily accessible to most of us.

So, of course, is that embodiment of pure philosophical and academic thought, the turtle C Serpentina himself, the author of the 'riotously entertaining' play *Beyond the Last Visible Dog,* in which Furza and Wurza, living in dustbins, represent the ISness of TO BE, cloaked in fun and farce. C Serpentina's particular, subtly apposite physical characteristics make him vivid in a way in which his ideas, expressed in the abstract, could never be. The strengths and weaknesses of his point of view are embodied in the nature of his existence:

'Earliness,' said a voice that boomed and quivered in the deeps. It was a slow and heavy voice and the sound of it was like the sound of gravel sliding from an iron bucket. 'Earliness in the sense of untimely awakening,' it said. '*See above.*

One arises to consider the corporeal continuity of AM.' The voice came closer. 'One becomes aware of appetizing aspects of IS. *Which see.*' KLOP! A pair of sharp and horny jaws closed on one of the mouse father's legs. '*Note well,*' said the voice. '*In the work cited. Inedible.*'

'Get us out of the mud, please,' gurgled the father, 'and stop bending my leg.'

'If you're capable of speech, you're capable of being eaten,' said the voice. KLOP! The jaws opened and closed again on the mouse father's leg.

'Compare,' said the voice. '*In the same place. Still inedible. Very well then, let us talk.*'

'What is there to say when one's head is in the mud?' said the father.

'What is there *not* to say!' came the answer from the gravelly voice. 'The relation of self to mud is basic to any discussion of TO BE. Basic. At the bottom.'

'Our heads are at the bottom,' said the mouse child. 'We're upside-down.'

'The upside-downness of self,' said the voice. 'a good beginning. Continue.'

The discussion continues, as C Serpentina snaps up tasty morsels and watches the father and son with an eye that 'seemed the very eye of time itself, set like a smoky gray jewel in some old and scaling rock'. The passage requires no comment: Its wit and precision are manifest.

It is tempting to quote further large sections of the book to illustrate each of its special qualities, but space is limited and the book itself is available. Any passage quoted is bound to contain one aspect of all the elements which contribute to the very special flavour of the whole. Everything in the world of the mouse father and his son is regarded with the same discerning eye and noted with the same wry brevity and clearly defined, witty perception. This wit is very much the wit of the performer. It is significant that Russell Hoban often reads his work aloud to an audience, and welcomes the chance to do so. His language is essentially language to be read aloud: his timing is perfect; his rhythms are meticulous; no word is wasted, no idea over-expressed. It is these attributes which have made the texts for his children's picture books so distinctive and memorable. The same techniques when adapted to a longer work produce powerful and equally distinctive results. Before he became a professional writer, Hoban was an illustrator and then a copywriter for an advertising agency in the United States. Both these trainings are mani-

fested in the qualities of observation, careful recording and pointed brevity which mark his writing. This brevity of expression is associated with another piece of advice which Hoban gave to the writers' workshop. He stressed the need to let the reader draw his own conclusions: some work must be left for him; everything should not be explicitly expressed. This idea is developed in later work, so that a kind of shorthand becomes apparent, at times almost as cryptic as the style used with such power by Alan Garner in *Red Shift,* as the consideration of **Turtle Diary** hopes to indicate.

The mouse father and son, walking through their world (when someone is kind enough to wind them up), are searching for answers: What lies beyond the last visible dog? How can they achieve self-winding? Where can the mouse child find a mother and his father discover a territory? The world in which their odyssey takes place is one of patterns, of linked occurrences and interlocking shapes. As more and more parts of what they encounter are entwined and form one whole cosmos, so the answers they are seeking become less finite and conclusive. When Manny Rat, the erstwhile villain, helps them to achieve self-winding, even that is not the final answer: the mechanism at last becomes unwound again, but, as their friend the frog remarks, 'I don't suppose anyone is ever completely self-winding. That's what friends are for.' The mouse child has discovered that, out beyond the dots that form the last visible dog, is nothing, and beyond that (on the reflective surface of the tin underneath) 'there's nothing on the other side of nothing but us'. But he has found it out on his own; his father was only too keen to help, to do it for him, to contemplate infinity in his place, but he had his back to it and so his son approached the task alone. The ultimate answers, then, are inconclusive, are, in fact, not ultimate answers, but the final scenes of the book are still as cosy as anything in the Frances stories, and disconcertingly so:

[Manny Rat] stopped for a lingering look at the mouse and his child, self-windingly and interminably walking their boundaries single file, prevented from going over the edge by a guard rail he had built.

The child wore his little drum as if in constant readiness to sound a call to arms. The father paced the platform with the air of a newly prosperous landowner surveying his broad acres. Behind them, wound by Frog, strolled the elephant and the seal. The elephant, now that she was Mrs Mouse, had begun to take some little pains with her appearance. Wearing a black eye-patch over the missing eye and a bright kerchief knotted over the missing ear, she achieved a look both charmingly rakish and surprisingly chic. The seal spun a gay parasol on the rod that projected upwards from her nose, and the whole little party, in their manifest contentment, mutual esteem, and pride of place burned their image unforgettably upon the brain of Manny Rat.

Surely the reader's sympathies are more than partially with Manny Rat in his desire to blow this scene of domestic bliss into little bits. His final position of reformed rathood, as the mouse child's 'Uncle Manny', is very depressing—or rather, it would be, were it really as credible as is his more scurrilous behaviour throughout the book, were it more vivid than his vision of the mouse and his child after his provision of electricity to the dolls' house:

> Manny Rat giggled as he imagined the mouse and his child, charred spectres, treading endlessly the ashes of their territory.

With Manny Rat's plan foiled, the new world of the mouse and his child is very cosy . . . but then, they have had to stand in the mud for many months, either with back to, or facing, infinity; they have helped in a search for the Hows and the Whys and the Whats; they have looked at the other side of nothing. So I suppose they deserve a gentle slice of middle class comfort under the flag of the Last Visible Dog. But their enjoyment of it, after so many harrowing revelations, is a letdown, and the story's ending does not stand up to what the bulk of the book has been saying so strongly. A return to a parody of Frances' world is less than one could hope for and less than the rest of the book deserves.

The theme of the odyssey of father and son is continued in *The Lion of Jachin-Boaz and Boaz-Jachin,* the first of the adult novels. The world of this book is even more difficult to evoke without the use of pretentious language. The book creates a universe of very special magic, in which everything forms part of a pattern in a more complex way than in *The Mouse and His Child.* There the father and son faced in opposite directions but were forever linked. Here it is their names which are linked and face in opposite directions, while they themselves are bound spiritually but lead separate lives. However, although their lives are ostensibly more naturalistic and set in a recognizable human world, their journey is as allegorical as that of the two mice—even more so in some ways. The novel's allegorical qualities should not be laboured too minutely; they are there, and they form definite patterns which speak more than adequately for themselves. Suffice it to say that

Jachin-Boaz is a mapmaker, and a very special mapmaker, whose maps chart experience as well as recording the physical attributes of places. Jachin-Boaz leaves his wife and goes to another country, taking with him the complex map which he had been making for his son, who is left behind with his mother:

> I sit in this shop like an old man, selling maps to help other people find things, thought Boaz-Jachin, because my father has taken my map for himself and has run off to find a new life with it. The boy has become an old man and the old man has become a boy.

The novel hinges on antitheses of this nature: Russell Hoban's understanding of the world involves a knife-edge juxtaposition of humour and horror, of reality and seeming nonsense—which is, of course, the ultimate reality. When Jachin-Boaz is committed to a mental hospital for seeing, and really being savaged by, a lion (an animal now extinct), he is rather jealous to discover that other inmates can see his own private lion too:

> 'Why can they see it, the other? . . .'
>
> 'Sorry about that, old man,' said the letter writer.
>
> 'But you've got to expect that sort of thing here. After all, why have they put us in the fun house? The straight people agree that some things are not allowed to be possible, and they govern their perceptions accordingly. Very strong, the straight people. We're not as strong as they. Things not allowed to be possible jump on us, beasts and demons, because we don't know how to keep them out.'

Lion examines the problems of the people who are not strong. The significances of a world where anything is allowed to be possible and everything is liable to break out in conversation are a cumbersome burden sometimes, as Boaz-Jachin discovers:

> 'Every fucking things talks to me,' he said. 'Leave me alone for a while. I'll talk to you some other time. I can't be rushed all the time.'

Another aspect of a world where everything can offer significant communication is found in language which works in unorthodox ways. When Jachin-Boaz sets off to find his father and claim his map, he meets a lorry driver who cannot speak his language: they converse together, each in his own tongue, to great mutual satisfaction. Cynically, the explanation is that no one listens to the person to whom he is talking anyway and that conversation exists to formulate private thoughts, not to communicate them to others. More hopefully the explanation is that communication is a more complex matter than mere verbal-connection, and things can be 'said' in a variety of ways. The decision as to which explanation is applicable here is, characteristically, left to us. One of the significant things about the conversation is that each is saying the same thing to the other. Language is used in a more depressing way by the doctor treating Jachin-Boaz in the hope of eradicating his feelings of being-with-the-lion. He has a friendly chat with Jachin-Boaz, confidently expecting him to be a sensible chap from now on:

> 'That's when a good tock and some tick and tocket will tick tockets, and then a fellow can tick himtock toticker.'

Everything has its own language, as meaningful as the listener and the speaker choose to make it, as we find in greater detail in *Klenizeit.*

Some things have to be made amusing in order to be rendered tolerable, especially if one has little control over beasts and demons. Boaz-Jachin initially releases the lion by offering to a lion-relief from the palace of an ancient king a sequence of life-giving drawings, and subsequently both father and son experience the feeling of being-with-the-lion, an occurrence which, in its forcefulness, brings with it complex memories and fierce emotional experience. The lion is at the centre of things, and at one point the centre, for Jachin-Boaz, moves back to childhood, in a vivid and sad memory. At dawn in a city street (in a place which could be London) he tries to tell the lion about this past experience, but the lion runs off:

> Jachin-Boaz followed. When he got to the embankment there was no lion. Only the rain, the pavement and the street wet and glistening, the hiss of tyres on the road.
>
> 'YOU weren't listening!' shouted Jachin-Boaz to the empty air, the rain.
>
> 'There was a time when I wanted something and I knew what it was. I wanted a black-and-silver cowboy suit with two pistols.'
>
> 'Cheer up, mate,' said the police constable with whom Jachin-Boaz collided while going down the steps. 'Perhaps Father Christmas'll bring you one.
>
> 'You've plenty of time till December.'

The combination in that passage of the policeman's total failure to comprehend the situation, while remaining wryly friendly, even compassionate, the unspeakably pathetic nature of certain childhood memories, the awful humour of some very sad things, is presented here in a most moving manner. This is, indeed, the thingness of things.

It is easy to see how the writer of *The Mouse and His Child* moved into creating the world of Boaz-Jachin and his father, where 'everything that is found is always lost again, and nothing that is found is ever lost again.' It is a longer, but still traceable, step from that cosmos full of maps, where 'there are no maps', to the bizarre world of Kleinzeit. His world is more brash, more urbane, funnier, than the universe of Jachin-Boaz (sometimes, indeed, in *Kleinzeit* the brilliant verbal technique is self-indulgent in its witty extravagance). In some ways it is a less remote universe, more recognizable and accessible, but it nevertheless carries that same unmistakable aura of magical terror and absurdity. It is still easy to identify as a world where things not-allowed-to-be-possible jump out. Kleinzeit is surrounded by the ridiculous and the terrible aspects of living all the time. Everything talks; everything is significant; everything is part of the pattern. The structures which might seem to hold our lives together are not ultimately as meaningful as other, less easily identifiable inner structures, which, once apparent, are always present.

Thus, when Kleinzeit feels a 'clear brilliant flash of pain from A to B', it turns out to be his hypotenuse which is playing him up (' "We don't know an awful lot about the hypotenuse" Dr Pink said'). All the terrifying mumbo-jumbo of modern medicine—its jargon, its drugs, its technical complexity, its appalling paraphernalia—is put sharply into a new and sardonic perspective. Inhabiting our bodies is a depressing, disgusting, alarming, and, of course, very funny business, especially when Hospital, and the bed in Hospital, are so very loquacious:

> Kleinzeit awake, watching the blips on Flashpoint's monitor: blip, blip, blip, blip. Flashpoint asleep. The distant horn sounding in Kleinzeit's body. Not yet, O God. The stench of bedpans. A sky like brown velvet, the red wink of an aeroplane. So high, so going-way! Gone!

Suddenly the hospital. Suddenly crouching. I am between its paws, thought Kleinzeit. It is gigantic. I had no idea how long its waiting, how heavy its patience. O God.

I can't be bothered with details, said God.

Blip, blip. Blip . . .

'Bowls and gold!' cried Flashpoint, twisting in the dark. 'Velvet and hangings, youth and folly.'

It's happened, thought Kleinzeit. Hendiadys. . . .

There was a terrible rushing tumbling gurgling sound. 'Burst spectrum,' said Dr Krishna.

'Arrow in a box,' said Flashpoint quietly.

It is difficult to quote briefly, because this novel, more than any that precede it, is closely and tightly written. Everything is significant; everything relates to everything else. The echoes in the passage quoted are heard throughout the book. In Kleinzeit's world all things are part of a pattern; all his experience carries echoes of other times and places. The thingness of things is all-important. This is the real structure of his life, not the ostensible order of Doctors Pink, Krishna and Company. As Boaz-Jachin did, so Kleinzeit resists this pattern; it is too difficult, too frightening. Significance is wearying. But once the connections have revealed themselves, they have to be acknowledged, as Kleinzeit comes to accept. Whoever is the only connector of this significantly patterned universe, it is certainly not God, as Sister and Kleinzeit find out in their conversations with him. He is just another part of the whole thing, one of the many voices, one of the fragments which must be connected.

One insistent echo in this world of connections is a verbal one. At the beginning of the book, the last piece of copy which Kleinzeit writes at the advertising agency before he is sacked, involves the phrase 'a barrow full of rocks'. He writes this on a piece of yellow paper which he finds in the Underground. Rhythms and assonances echoing this phrase, and the yellow paper it was written on, subsequently pursue Kleinzeit: 'HARROW FULL OF CROCKS'; 'Arrow in a box'; 'YARROW; *Fullest Stock'*; 'SORROW; FULL SHOCK'; and so on. The phrase seems to be linked with the red-bearded tramp who threw down the paper in the Underground (as was the tramp in *The Mouse and His Child,* this tramp, too, is in some ways a prime mover, the instigator of proceedings); he is one of the connections which Kleinzeit must make. As in *The Mouse and His Child,* where the protagonists experienced fragments of the pattern and gradually saw more of the whole, so for Kleinzeit fragments begin to connect. He resents this order. He wants answers and wants to know what is going on, but he does not want the complications of a pattern.

Kleinzeit confronts the red-bearded man and makes explicit the business of the string of echoing phrases that the yellow paper instigated. I wonder, in fact, if he needed to be quite so explicit; in this passage Hoban comes as near as he ever does to forgetting his own advice. I do not feel that the reader is left with enough to do. By this time he has made the connection for himself; so it need not be stated again in such direct terms: in reading, he, like Kleinzeit, has already experienced the echoes. However, the scene is an important one. Kleinzeit clamours for answers but has to discover, as the mouse and his son

did and as Jachin-Boaz and his son did, that there are no ultimate answers and that acceptance of what is is necessary. At the end of the book he still has his pain shooting from A to B and he still has all his organs grumbling but intact, but now no one seems worried about it. He himself is not really any different from how he was at the beginning of the book. He has not been presented with answers, but his perception has changed. Now he has beautiful Sister from the hospital to live with him, he is on social chatting terms with Death, and he has his yellow paper to write upon.

This yellow paper is central to, and recurrent throughout, the story, like the ever-receding dogs on the BONZO tin. Kleinzeit has a very special relationship with his yellow paper; but so, it seems has Word, who visits the paper while Kleinzeit is away in hospital:

> Like thunder and lightning the seed of Word jetted into the yellow paper. Now, said Word, there you are. I've quickened you. Let them die in their hundreds and their thousands, from time to time one of them must wiggle through. I see to that.
>
> The yellow paper was weeping quietly. He wanted . . . He wanted . . . it sobbed.
>
> Yes, said Word. He wanted?
>
> He wanted to be the only one, he wanted to do it all himself.
>
> Nobody does it all himself, said Word.

This is an account of the familiar experience, expressed by many writers, of being the instrument of their words, rather than their originator: 'Not I, not I, but the wind that blows through me.' Thus the third piece of advice which Russell Hoban offered the Workshop was that the writer must let it happen, must 'wait in the silence', not create intellectual barriers, not think for hours before letting the words out onto the paper, not construct it all before he picks up the pen. 'I write what wants to get written', he himself once said. (Word, incidentally, is a crass, brash, flashy, insensitive fellow, who cannot be bothered to get people's names right. He is far from perceptive and is unintelligent and unselective in his use of language.)

Language plays the games on Kleinzeit that it did on Jachin-Boaz. Phrases recur and echo through his life; phrases also change their meaning horribly. When Jachin-Boaz ran away, headlines in other people's newspapers began to say 'JACHIN-BOAZ GUILTY'. When Kleinzeit looks at the side of a delivery truck it says 'MORTAL TERROR' although the driver says he's from Morton Taylor. Later, in hospital, Kleinzeit is chatting to a fellow patient:

> 'I'm a traveller for a clock company,' said Drogue. 'Speedclox Ltd. I was out with the new line, coming down the M4 when a tremendous lorry hurtled by . . . '
>
> 'Morton Taylor?'
>
> 'Not at all. Why should I be afraid of a passing lorry?'

Even if he is, and not through choice, a part of the game, Kleinzeit learns to play these jokes himself, as well as experiencing them. At the beginning of the book, the mirror tyrannizes Kleinzeit:

> He put his face in front of the bathroom mirror.
>
> I exist, said the mirror.
>
> What about me? said Kleinzeit.
>
> Not my problem, said the mirror.

Later, things are different. He knows how to punish the mirror, play it at its own game:

> Right, said Kleinzeit. He went into the bathroom without turning on the light, washed his face and brushed his teeth in the dark, peed by ear.
>
> What's happening? said the mirror. Who am I?
>
> Morton Taylor, said Kleinzeit with a sinister chuckle, and went to bed.

Turtle Diary, in some ways Hoban's finest writing yet, provides the best marriage of his concise, poetic and rhythmic expression with his dry, witty observation. This particular synthesis was foreshadowed in **The Sea-Thing Child,** a beautiful, brief fable, both sad and funny, which he wrote after **The Mouse and His Child.** This latest novel, **Turtle Diary,** incorporates all the themes examined so far, in a very subtle and delicate manner, different from the style of the earlier stories. There is no 'happy ending': the previous books all offered this in some way, even if it was not really an intrinsic part of the story. Thus, what Kleinzeit learns about patterns, about acceptance and resignation, what Jachin-Boaz and his son learn about maps and lions, what the mice learn about self-winding and territories, is centrally important; but in each case they are given some sort of present as well, a cosy ending. Here, for one of the protagonists at least, things are rather more bleak. The resignation and acceptance are all. The observation is as sensitive and as humorous as always and more carefully and closely expressed than

ever. Stylistically the novel is both more ambitious and more accomplished than anything previously written. It is the only book which Hoban has chosen so far to write in the first person; however, he has written the story from the point of view of two different people, so that alternate chapters are told by William G and Neaera H. He has used this technique successfully, for the most part maintaining the individual characteristics of each speaker with skillful care. The added complexity which this brings to his familiar preoccupations is an exciting development.

Some aspects of the book initially seem far more conventional and less eccentric than earlier works. The story line is more central and ostensibly important; the world is, or at least seems, a more naturalistic one. It is a world which contains London, with the Zoo, Madame Tussaud's, the British Museum and Hungerford Bridge; the protagonists are presumably telling the story to 'ordinary people', explaining how they feel; the language is less extravagant, less concerned with its own wit. All this makes the representative originality of vision all the more forceful and impressive when it appears in its new and subtler forms. What finally matters to the novel is not the outcome of the story, for itself, but what the story says about the central characters. It is their inner world which is important, as always.

As always, too, this is a world of significant connections, and this time we see two separate people, not one person with his son, or one man alone, finding the patterns, discovering the integral parts of the whole, noting the awful ironies and sardonic jokes of being alive. William G and Neara H have a similar approach to living—they are 'from the same picture', so they see the same patterns, but, of course, in different ways. Nothing the delicate disparities in their understanding of their mutual experiences is one of the chief delights of the book. 'As a man is, so he sees': the way in which a human being's mind colours the world he sees is one of Hoban's central themes. Both central characters are always aware of the shaping patterns, the messages the world has to offer; they frequently note the same idea, at widely spaced intervals in the book.

Although (on self-admission) Russell Hoban seems closer to William G in attitude, it is Neaera H who says several things which are central to most of Hoban's writing:

> But more and more I think that madness is the world's natural condition and to expect anything else is madness compounded.
>
> More and more I'm aware that the permutations are not unlimited. Only a certain number of things

can happen and whatever can happen *will* happen. The differences in scale and costume do not alter the event. Oedipus went to Thebes. Peter Rabbit into Mr McGregor's garden but the story is essentially the same: life points only towards the terror.

Ultimately such a division is simplistic and dangerous, but in some ways it can be said that, while it is more often Neaera H who provides these thematic statements, it is William G who observes the grim humour, hears the implicit language and messages around him. He is the one who sees that a manhole cover bears the number K257:

> All right, I thought as I stepped on it, go ahead, play Mozart. It didn't. When I got home I looked up K257 in the Kochel listing in my *Mozart Companion.* It was the Credo Mass in C. *Credo,* I believe. What does the manhole cover believe, or what's being believed down in the hole? I don't like getting too many messages from the things around me, it confuses me.

The apposite observation, the wry and resigned comment, is all delightfully familiar. What is new in this novel is the detailed organization and structuring of the protagonists' thoughts. They are skillfully ordered so that the novel progresses in certain ways, considers specific themes, while the two people seem just to be thinking aloud, responding to a situation as it develops. The way in which their similar opinions on certain topics are introduced is superbly managed. Because so much of their narrative is just a statement of aspects of their inner selves, the task is much more complex than the mere telling of a story from two points of view. Two thought-patterns have to be developed concurrently, and the external 'story' that is happening to both characters is only one of several stimuli working on them. Thus, always, although they reach similar or coordinated conclusions, it is from different directions, and in different ways. There is ample opportunity within this structure for things to become boring, repetitive or muddled, and this never happens. It is always an accomplished and controlled look at the familiar world of Russell Hoban where a wide pavement says 'walk together' and a narrow pavement says 'walk alone'.

A. Joan Bowers

SOURCE: "The Fantasy World of Russell Hoban," in *Children's Literature*, Vol. 8, 1979, pp. 80-97.

Russell Hoban, who is best known for his numerous children's books, including *Bedtime for Frances, Henry and the Monstrous Din, Harvey's Hideout,*

and the novel *The Mouse and His Child,* has in recent years been writing adult novels as well: *The Lion of Boaz-Jachin and Jachin-Boaz, Kleinzeit,* and *Turtle Diary.* Although the "child is father to the mouse," as the mouse child says, the children's and adult books of Hoban, like those of most other authors who write for both audiences, have usually been discussed independently of each other. It is my contention that Hoban's works represent a unified aesthetic whole and that in both adult and children's books Hoban typically expresses his psychological and metaphysical concerns in fantasies involving animals. His children's books become increasingly fantasy-like as his philosophical concerns become more evident. Similarly, his adult fantasies, together with his essay **"Thoughts on Being and Writing,"** become a kind of "gloss" reflecting upon and illuminating his children's books.

If one looks at Hoban's most famous children's books, one realizes that they are essentially didactic. Frances the Badger, like any imaginative little girl, may be able to put off bedtime by going beyond requests for milk, kisses, cake, and toothbrushing to vivid thoughts about tigers, giants, and cracks in the ceiling, but in the end it is her association of the moth's bumping against the window with her father's spanking which keeps her in bed. Harvey Muskrat and his sister Mildred are made to write 500 sentences saying that they will not call each other names. In this case direct punishment does not work. Since "the Rabbit children are all too fast . . . to run around with" and their father has warned them "not to get mixed up with Weasels" and their best friends are away on vacation, they must learn to appreciate and respect each other if they are to have playmates for the summer. For Arthur Crocodile to learn his table manners it takes both family nagging and the incentive of trying to impress a member of the opposite sex. After Arthur learns his table manners, he makes a remark typical of many of Hoban's characters in its insight into human, rather than reptilian, nature: "and I think the nicest part of manners is teaching them to other people, the way I did to Sidney" (by an offstage pummeling to repay Sidney for making fun of his newly acquired social graces).

Such insight into the sometimes quasi-sadistic aspects of punishment and discipline perhaps explains some of Hoban's increasing aversion to didacticism. In his book *How Tom Beat Captain Najork and His Hired Sportsmen,* Tom's "fooling around" is ultimately vindicated. His aunt, a draconian villainess named Aunt Fidget Wonkham-Strong, who wears an iron hat and causes flowers to droop, tries to curb Tom's playful instincts by making him "learn off pages 65 to 75 of the Nautical Almanac." When this fails she brings in Captain Najork and his Hired Sportsmen to teach Tom a lesson. Tom's long experience at various kinds of "fooling around" helps him defeat Captain Najork, win the Captain's boat from him, and take off for a new locale where he advertises for, and obtains, a different aunt—Aunt Bundlejoy Cosysweet. In this instance didacticism seems directed towards adults and their treatment of children.

Didacticism is a legitimate concern in both children's and adult books. Yet if one seeks more in a book, in Tolkien's words, "beauty that is an enchantment, and an ever-present peril . . . joy and sorrow as sharp as swords," as well as "the satisfaction of certain primordial human desires," then didacticism is not enough no matter how cleverly handled. Hoban himself is well aware of this, and even his most didactic writing is more than Emily Post disguised as Beast Fable. Throughout his simplest books Hoban makes use of motifs and themes which become increasingly fantastic and symbolic as his work acquires more complexity.

An example of such a motif is Hoban's use of stones. In **Nothing to Do** Father and Mother Possum enjoy a walk by the edge of the water, "watching their shadows move over the stones that were silvery in the moonlight." They express their enjoyment of "round stones that have been polished smooth by the river," and Father Possum later pretends that one of these is a magic stone which can give his son Walter "something to do." In **Egg Thoughts and Other Frances Songs** Frances sings:

> I just found a lucky stone-
> Maybe I'll be smart tomorrow.
> With today one day behind me
> Maybe my good luck will find me.

Stones and good luck pieces are significant for numerous Hoban charcters, including the fortune-telling frog in **The Mouse and His Child.** But they achieve their greatest symbolic resonance when they become the priestly oracle stones Urim and Thummim of Judaic tradition in **The Lion of Boaz-Jachin and Jachin-Boaz.**

A similar metamorphosis takes place in Hoban's treatment of things mechanical. His first book, **What Does It Do and How Does It Work?,** is a pedestrian account for very young children of how machines such as tractor shovels, bulldozers, and dump trucks look and operate. There are no animals or humans, certainly nothing fantastical. **Henry and the Monstrous Din,** however, ostensibly a didactic tale about

the need for Henry to stop making noise, contains a wonderful mechanical monster as well. Henry's "monstrous din" literally becomes a "Monstrous Din" (or Djinn?), a huge, flying monster, which takes him on an adventurous tour of the city, including a double-feature Monster Movie.

Mechanical toys are particularly evocative for Hoban. His book of poems **The Pedaling Man** contains a poem about the rigors endured by a pedaling-man wind vane and a poem about a mechanical frog that says, after a fall, "Since then the two halves of my tin have been awry; my strength / Is not quite what it used to be; I do not hop so well." Finally, there is **The Mouse and His Child,** light years removed in both concept and execution from **What Does It Do and How Does It Work?** Here Hoban has created an entire world of animal characters and wind-up toys which pursue their quests within the limitations of a mechanical toy. As a reviewer for the *Times Literary Supplement* states: "Mr. Hoban rides his fantasy with a tight rein. Granting himself one single improbable assumption—that among the rubbish dumps and the wildernesses beyond the urban world there is a world of animals and toys made in its distorted image—he pursues the implications of his invention with remorseless logic."

Hoban's language itself changes and becomes more humorous and fanciful in the course of his works. In **A Birthday for Frances,** Frances, who has obviously heard her parents spell out words when they don't want her to know what they are talking about, tells her mother that she is going to have "h-r-n-d and g-k-l-s," which she later says means "cake and candy," for her birthday. Similar nonsensical wordplay occurs in some of the poems in **The Pedaling Man,** though it does not always succeed. The imaginary creature "Skilly Oogan," for example, is described in trite and plodding couplets:

> Sometimes he hides in letters that I write—
> Snug in the envelope and out of sight,
> On six-cent stamps he travels in all weathers
> And with the midnight owl returns on silent feathers.

A more effective use of the nonsensical occurs in the poem **"Typo."** The narrator thinks he has typed "nothing," but "nitgub" is actually on the paper. Then the typewriter speaks:

> "I like it," said the typewriter.
> "It strikes a happy note.
> It has more style than *nothing*,
> Has a different sort of sound.
> The color is superior;
> The flavor's nice and round.

Have you plumbed its deepest depths,
Its mystery explained?"
"All right," I said, "I'll take it.
Nitgub ventured, nitgub gained."

This verbal whimsy reaches its peak in *Kleinzeit,* the most "absurdist" of Hoban's books. In this book, even Word himself, a character more or less situated in Kleinzeit's mind, calls Dante's Inferno, "Auntie's Inferno," and says:

It's that other chap who wrote the Bible. Firkin? Pipkin? Pipkin? Wilkins.

Milton, you mean? said Kleinzeit.

That's it, said Word. Milton. They don't write like that any more. As it were the crack of leather on willow. A well-bowled thought, you know, meeting a well-swung sentence. No, the pitches aren't green the way they were, the whites don't take the light the same way. It mostly isn't writing now, it's just spelling.

It wasn't Milton wrote the Bible, said Kleinzeit.

As a final example of a motif which Russell Hoban expands and invests with deeper meaning in the course of his writing there is, of course, his use of animals. Richard Adams has written tellingly of the difficulties involved in using animals in fantasy literature: "How exactly do you go about an anthropomorphic fantasy? Beyond one end of the scale altogether—a sort of ultra-violet—stands Henry Williamson. *Tarka the Otter* is superb natural history, but for that very reason it is neither a novel nor an anthropomorphic fantasy; nor is it meant to be either. It is simply an account of the life and death of a real otter. . . . At the extreme other end of the scale is Kenneth Grahame, whose animals are simply humans disguised in animals' bodies. All anthropomorphic fantasies have to pick a point along that line."

I would suggest that Russell Hoban's books begin at the infrared or Kenneth Grahame end of the scale but proceed to move beyond the spectrum as defined by Adams. Certainly Frances the Badger, Walter Possum, Harvey Muskrat, et al. are disguised girls and boys. Only an occasional reference to something like a "paw," in addition to the illustrations, maintains the animal pretense. Frances is interested in china tea sets and skipping rope while Arthur Crocodile actually speaks of teaching good manners to "other people." But, whereas Hoban sometimes uses symbolic stones or good luck coins in his early animal stories, animals themselves become symbolic in his later fantasies. Lions and animals or birds associated with the sea, such as the turtle, albatross, and sea gull, become especially significant. Far from retreat-

ing down the spectrum to natural history, Hoban expands the treatment of his animals into the realm of myth and metaphysics.

Having discussed some of the common motifs in Hoban's earlier books, I would like to turn to three books that I consider transitional in Hoban's development: *Ugly Bird* (1969), *The Sea-Thing Child* (1972), and *The Mouse and His Child* (1967). These are transitional not because they represent a midpoint between "low art"—writing for children—and "high art"—writing for adults—but because they reveal Hoban struggling with themes he had previously hinted at but not explored. Hoban himself does not denigrate writing for children: "It seems to me . . . that more and more adult novels are not essentially literary. Many of them simply communicate experience, and that of itself is not art. . . . There are empty spaces now in literature, vacated by the so-called adult novel, and some of those spaces now become new territory for children's writers." He then discusses three writers: one has turned from adult novels to children's books, one has remained a children's book writer, and one "is an example of what talent can do to a children's book writer: it can drive him out of children's books as he follows the development of his material wherever it takes him. . . . Comedy is a serious business in that it relies on dead accuracy of insight—the laughs don't happen unless we recognize ourselves and others in each situation. And the depth of recognition . . . requires adult experience."

This is the metamorphosis which Hoban has undergone and which is illustrated in his "transitional" books. Of these three, *Ugly Bird* is most like Hoban's earlier books about Frances the Badger and Harvey Muskrat. It is a short picture book which at first deceptively suggests an echo of Hans Christian Andersen's *The Ugly Duckling*. In its dedication, however, "For every child who has heard the world say Yah yah," Hoban seems to be acknowledging a cruelty in the world which is only hinted at in the childish squabbles of Frances and her friends. Ugly Bird has to learn who he is and how to appreciate himself, but he does not achieve this self-knowledge by literally becoming more beautiful, like a swan. Instead he "ate his worm and grew . . . flapped his wings and saw that he was falling up" and embarked upon a fantasy adventure in which he became a number of things, from stone and pebble to fish and bee. The discoveries he makes, however, are internal, not external. As he tells his mother at the end, "I know who I am and what I am, . . . Some of who is handsome and some is shiny and some is little and some is buzzing." As this quotation and the following examples reveal, Hoban's style and syntax have become more imaginatively suited to the fantastic. Ugly Bird played "leapstone and skipfrog" with a frog; as a pebble he was swallowed by a turtle who said "Good aftersnap," and as a bee he "took a honeycomb and combed the honey. He took a honeybrush and brushed the honey." This whimsical use of language is appreciated as much by the adult who reads the book as by the child who is read to.

A further point of interest in *Ugly Bird,* the symbolic importance of which can remain unnoticed if one reads only a few of Hoban's books, is Ugly Bird's descent to the bottom of the pond. Twice he sinks to the bottom of the pond, once as a stone and once as a pebble. The first time, he becomes a fish and swims away; the second time, he is swallowed by a "sleeping snapping turtle" who deposits him on the nearest log after the pebble begins dancing the "chachacha" in his stomach. Such humorous treatment should not blind one to the importance Hoban attaches to this image, one which he has touched upon in prior books, which will be continued in *The Sea-Thing Child,* and which will reach its culmination in *Turtle Diary.* Hoban, like Tolkien, seeks "the satisfaction of certain primordial human desires," not in fairy tales but in the mythic symbol of a sinking back into and an acceptance of the past—symbolized by mankind's evolutionary origins in the ocean—in order to live fully here and now. As he states in his essay **"Thoughts on Being and Writing"**:

> The inanimate was disturbed into the animate, non-life was disturbed into life, and in us is a longing for the peace that was before that original disturbance. In all of us, I think, there remains some awareness, rudimentary and inchoate, far down, dim in green light through the ancient reeds and tasting of the primal salt, in which there is no "I," no person, no identity, but only the passage, moment by moment, of time through being undisturbed by birth or death. We push away from it but it is there, containing self and struggle both. Far down and dim it is, not ordinarily accessible to us. I think we have to learn to feel for it, to go beyond our swimmer's fright, to dive for it and touch it before returning to the sunlight and the present, to touch it as a child in a dark room gets out of bed to touch the clothes tree that bulks monstrous in the dimness, magnetic with terror.

A book in which Hoban attempts, with mixed success, to develop this image exclusively is *The Sea-Thing Child.* A critic calls it a "frail, elusive fantasy" which "is not quite a poem; it is insufficiently developed to make a novel, too long to be a short story. Classification does not matter if a work is strong

enough to transcend form, but the indeterminate form of this curious piece is symptomatic of a fundamental uncertainty." Such criticism is justifiable, even though Hoban's central image is provocative, since Hoban is artistically weakest when he attempts poetry or something as self-consciously lyrical as *The Sea-Thing Child;* and he is strongest when he writes the rich humorous prose which seems to come most easily to him and which often achieves lyricism without any apparent effort. *The Sea-Thing Child* (illustrated with a few black and white pictures by his son Abrom Hoban) is a small, 35-page book, though textually much longer than Hoban's usual picture books. The sea-thing child itself is a frightened, indeterminate kind of creature who, unlike Ugly Bird, knows who he is and what he is but is too much afraid of life to act upon his knowledge. Instead of going to the sea, his natural element, he surrounds himself with a stone igloo.

It takes an encounter with an albatross who has been everywhere and has spoken with walruses and green turtles to shame the sea-thing child into destroying his igloo. The albatross even expresses envy of the sea-thing child: "'But you can go under, too. You can do the deep swimming. Envy you that, I do.'" When asked if he is never afraid, the albatross responds, "'How can you get lost when you're where you live? . . . Mind what I say, . . . and get off the beach before you go barmy and start building stone igloos.'" Finally, of course, the sea-thing child leaves even the circles he has drawn around himself in the sand, in place of the stone igloo, and flies back to the sea in which he was born. To be able to live fully he must become willing to accept what he is and follow the instincts which lead him back to the sea and down to the depths. The encounters between the sea-thing child and the fiddler crab, who eventually learns to be honest with himself about his fiddling—or lack of fiddling—embody some of the uneasy tension in the book between comedy and high seriousness. It is as if Hoban were not yet fully convinced of the remark which he later makes that comedy itself "is a serious business." The comedy in *The Sea-Thing Child* is not self-confident enough and the seriousness is too strained.

My final example of a transitional book, *The Mouse and His Child* (1967) actually precedes both *Ugly Bird* (1969) and *The Sea-Thing Child* (1972) but will be discussed here because of its greater length and complexity. Even as the sea-thing child must make a kind of existential leap of faith to fly back into the ocean, so Hoban as well as the mouse and his child strike out in both fear and hope for new directions. Acknowledging the need for such a leap,

Hoban quotes the following verse from W. H. Auden's poem "Leap Before You Look" at the start of his book:

> The sense of danger must not disappear:
> The way is certainly both short and steep,
> However gradual it looks from here;
> Look if you like, but you will have to leap.

Critics, particularly in England, were delighted as well as surprised by what they perceived as a new kind of writing. Ann Thwaite, writing for the *New Statesman* (May 16, 1969), says of *The Mouse and His Child:* "Demanding, disturbing, memorable, like all the best children's books it is a book for anybody. I am sure it is a classic; *The Wind in the Willows* of this post-Buchenwald generation. Buy it and read it aloud by firelight to children warmed with mugs of Sainsbury's malted bedtime drink. Alone, in a cold bedroom, it could be too hard for them to take." A reviewer for the *Times Literary Supplement* calls Hoban's style "exquisitely apt" and ends by saying that "Like the best books it is a book from which one can peel layer after layer of meaning. It may not be a Children's Book but, my goodness, it is a *Book.*"

Although, as we have already seen, motifs in *The Mouse and His Child* such as mechanical toys, good luck coins, and going to the depths of the pond are common enough in Hoban's picture books, what seems to have caught critics off guard and made them question the appropriateness of the book for children are the book's unrelenting portrayal of nature's cruelty and the numerous philosophical or mock-philosophical discussions which run throughout. This is no idyllic pastoral of rural life but a remorseless portrayal of "Nature, red in tooth and claw." Neaera H., the children's-book writer/illustrator "heroine" of *Turtle Diary,* at one point complains about the publisher's pressures to grind out more children's books with sweet, cuddly animal heroes. Instead, she says, "my next book will be about a predator." *The Mouse and His Child* contains the predator Hoban had ignored before. One episode, in particular, shows Hoban's portrayal of the bloodthirstiness inherent in nature. Two armies of shrews are battling for control of a piece of ground when a pair of weasels arrive:

> The weasels flowed like hungry shadows down into the hollow, and once among the shrews, struck right and left with lightning swiftness, smiling pleasantly with the blood of both armies dripping from their jaws. Not a single shrew escaped. . . . [The weasel couple] nuzzled each other affectionately as they ran, and their heads were so close together that when the horned owl swooped down out of the moonlight his talons pierced both brains at once.

Such grim realism about the facts of animal life may seem quite removed from Frances the Badger and her eating habits; yet, as Hoban states, "today's children do not live in an expurgated world. With their elders they must endure sudden deaths and slow ones, bombs and fire falling from the sky, the poisoning of peaceful air and the threatened extinction of this green jewel of Earth. They must endure the reality of mortal man."

The mechanical toy mouse and his child have much to endure. Like Ugly Bird, at first they do not know where they are or what they are; and to find out they must first break the clockwork rules that restrict them and embark upon a painful epic quest for family and home. That they achieve at least a modified version of their dream is the result both of their pluck and determination and of their encounters along the way with friendly, philosophical, not to mention prophetic animals. Not all the animals are described in terms of their predatory natural instincts. Indeed, the Dickensian villain Manny Rat (who becomes "Uncle Manny" at the end by making the mouse and his child self-winding, thereby making one assume that Hoban is well aware of "Manny's" derivation from "Emanuel"), the charlatan fortune-telling Frog who becomes truly prophetical, and the hapless Muskrat of Muskrat's Much-in-Little course in "pure thought," are fully realized and delightful characters. Needless to say, the most important animal character for Hoban—and the epitome of "deep" thinking—is the huge snapping turtle which the mouse and his child encounter at the bottom of the pond. C. Serpentina "was very old and ponderously fat, and the eye that watched them seemed the very eye of time itself, set like a smoky gray jewel in some old and scaling rock. . . . 'One has no need to get out of here,' said Serpentina. 'One is at home on the bottom. One sees below the surface of things. One thinks in depth and acquires profundity, the *without which nothing* of . . . ' SCRUNCH! A fish had swum near him, and he struck with terrible, snaky swiftness. CHOMP, CHOMP, CHOMP, ULP. 'Contemplation,' he said, finishing the sentence and the fish together." This is a particularly fine example of how Hoban blends both symbolism and realism in an inimitably humorous style.

Though the episode is couched in humorous language, C. Serpentina and a tiny ugly water bug named Miss Mudd (who becomes a beautiful green dragonfly in the process) help the mouse and his child contemplate the infinity which lies "beyond the last visible dog" on a Bonzo Dog Food can. The label on the can, which reappears frequently, portrays a black and white dog carrying a tray on which is a can of dog food with a label showing a black and white dog carrying a tray on which is a can of dog food, *ad infinitum*. It is the *ad infinitum* which interests the mouse child and he eventually comes to the philosophical realization, seconded by C. Serpentina, that there is nothing whatever "beyond the last visible dog." The mouse child, however, is not satisfied with this answer and feels that if he is big enough to contemplate infinity, he is big enough to "look at the other side of nothing." With the help of Miss Mudd he peels off the label from the shiny tin can and makes a further discovery: "'there's nothing beyond the last visible dog but us,' he said. 'Nobody can get us out of here but us. That gives us Why. Now we have to figure out the Hows and the Whats.'" Surprisingly it is this philosophical acceptance of their own ultimate "aloneness" which provides the impetus for the mouse and his child to find a way up and out of the pond and to continue their quest.

This feeling of utter "aloneness," in contrast to the cozy secure world of many children's books, leads to Hoban's adult books. In these he can deal with sexual matters that are taboo in young children's books as well as with his increasingly complex philosophical concerns. *The Lion of Boaz-Jachin and Jachin-Boaz* (1973), *Kleinzeit* (1974), and *Turtle Diary* (1975) portray poignantly the "aloneness" of a divorced man who, in leaving wife and children, becomes divorced from his past as well. But beyond this they portray the "aloneness" of human beings in the universe. They abound with references to the sterility and emptiness of Sundays when presumably the reason for considering them "holy days" no longer exists.

The Lion of Boaz-Jachin and Jachin-Boaz, for example, takes place at a time and location where lions no longer exist; yet Hoban's quotation of Job's cry to God does not leave much doubt as to the symbolic association of the lion: "Thou huntest me as a fierce lion: and again thou shewest thyself marvellous upon me" (Job X: 16). Even when the lion re-appears, after its ritualistic Jungian re-creation from the carving of a lion hunt, it is scarcely the orthodox Christ-lion of C. S. Lewis's Aslan. For Hoban the lion seems to represent a primal life force, or Being itself, which is rather like fate in its association with a turning wheel:

> The lion was. Ignorant of non-existence he existed. Ignorant of self he was a sunlit violence with calm joy at the center of it, he was the violence of being-as-hunter constantly renewed in the devouring of non-being. . . . He ate meat or he did not eat meat, was seen or unseen, known when there was knowledge of him, unknown when there was not. But always he was.

For him there were no maps, no places, no time. Beneath his tread the round earth rolled, the wheel turned, bearing him to death and life again.

After their encounters with the lion, whose only time is now, both the mapmaker father (Jachin-Boaz) and his son (Boaz-Jachin) reject maps and the past which they symbolize and immortalize. Instead, father and son arrive at an inner peace by learning to live in the "now." In his mystical experience of closing his eyes in the presence of the lion, Jachin-Boaz perceives the familiar primal image of ocean depths: "He dropped through blackness, sank through time to green-lit ooze and primal salt, to green light through the reeds. Being, he sensed, is. Goes on. Trust in being. He rested there, prostrate in his mind, awaiting his ascent." For the son also at the end of his quest "the aloneness became comfortable, the darkness was simply where he was. . . . he was thinking less words than he used to. His mind simply was, and in it were people he had been with, the times he had lived." The past has become a living part of the present, not sterilely fixed on a map.

For the characters in Hoban's adult books to arrive at this acceptance of their "aloneness" they must not only descend figuratively to the ocean depths and accept their past but also renounce the magic stones and what they symbolize in the form of external or supernatural help that are so familiar in Hoban's children's books. Both Boaz-Jachin and Jachin-Boaz come to reject amulets and magic stones in their realization that "Being" is all that there is. Neaera H. and William G. in *Turtle Diary* eventually throw away their "magic stones" as well. Even though they are both desperately looking for "signs and wonders"—to such extent that William G. sees in the "K257" inscribed on a manhole cover the opus number for Mozart's Credo Mass in C—Neaera H. admits that her "Caister two-stone confers no magic, it's only a touchstone for the terrors that I try to cover up with books and papers and plants in the window."

Neaera H. and William G. discover that they both feel awe at the self-possession and instinctive navigational ability of sea turtles, of turtles' inerrant seeking and finding across thousands of miles of ocean, a seeking and finding which humans seem not to possess. Their adventure of returning the sea turtles from the London Zoo to the sea, which Hoban describes in terms of Mircea Eliade's work on shamanism and man's primitive urge to commune with other forms of life, is not the ecstatic experience which they had expected, however. As William G. wryly admits,

"'You can't do it with turtles.'" Yet the two are more alive and can relate better to other people after their experience. They reach a qualified or muted "happy ending," similar to that of Boaz-Jachin and Jachin-Boaz, in which they no longer "mind being alive." Perhaps the fact that Hoban has yet to write a book with a tragic ending, in spite of his unflinching portrayal of mankind's "lostness" in the universe, is a hold-over from his children's books as well as a measure of his unquenchable sense of humor.

Kleinzeit is something of an anomaly in relation to Hoban's other books, though it, too, has a humorously qualified "happy ending" in which the best wedding gift "God" can give to Sister is to delay an electrical strike for a week. This is Hoban's most "absurdist" book and his most ribald; it contains much broad and black humor as well as fanciful wordplay. In *Kleinzeit* the central symbol is shifted away from familiar sea and animal imagery. For Kleinzeit (whose name means "small time," not "hero" as he tells Sister) to come to terms with his past, he and Sister must re-enact, in Hospital and (London) Underground, a modern re-creation of the Orpheus and Eurydice myth. Even as the head of Orpheus (in the version of the myth recounted by Hospital) swam back to the place of his dismemberment and "remembered" himself, so Kleinzeit must force himself to "remember" his past. Obviously, though the metaphor is altered, Hoban is still concerned with descent to the depths of the ocean or the Underworld (Underground) which each person must experience. Yet within the mythic structure of *Kleinzeit*, Kleinzeit as Orpheus the Singer/Poet writes poems about sea turtles, including a *Dies Irae* variation on the green turtle theme." Ultimately Hoban's world view is remarkably consistent.

One might ask what this has to do with Hoban as children's book writer. Hoban's philosophical concerns have become increasingly complex in the course of his writing; his later books are as much metaphysical as fantastical. As his characters are forced to endure a mythical descent into and acceptance of their past, they are compelled to face the pain of their own childhood and to reassess what it means to be a child, to have a child, and to write for a child. Jachin-Boaz, for example, identifies himself with the young heroes of the fairy tales from his youth: "Always the father was dead at the beginning of the story, and the young man went out with his few coins, his crust of bread, his fiddle or his sword. Sometimes he found or won some magic thing along the way. A map, perhaps. . . . Now he, Jachin-Boaz, was the old man out in the wide world seeking his fortune, the old man who wanted a new story and

would not agree to be dead." What Jachin-Boaz finds is not magic but the knowledge that he has been expecting his son to be something that he is not in the same way that his father had made painfully unrealistic demands of him when he was a child. Even as he learns "to be" fully in the here and now, he learns that one must allow others, including one's children, "to be" as well, without imposing one's aspirations upon them.

In **"Thoughts on Being and Writing"** Hoban discusses the birth of his son, Jachin Boaz, named for the two pillars on the porch of Solomon's Temple (and accounting for some of the autobiographical sense of fathers and sons, sons and fathers, which permeates *The Lion of Boaz-Jachin and Jachin-Boaz*). In describing Jachin Boaz's birth, Hoban reveals his philosophy of how new life fits into the past. Life, he says, "has used Gundula and me to bring Jachin into the morning mist and the noonday sun with Venus's people and the non-colossal Egyptians. He's life's child before and after everything else; he does not personally belong to Gundula and me. He's ours to love and have fun with and take care of until he can take care of himself, but he's not really ours, and both of us know it." Once more, in having a child as well as in his recent fictional descriptions of being a child, Hoban opts for freedom rather than authoritarianism.

Predictably, then, Hoban's children's books have become less didactic and more fanciful. While he has certainly not abandoned children's books, his most recent works seem directed more towards whimsical funtasy than the good manners of the early Frances the Badger books; and, if one accepts some of Neaera H.'s comments on children's literature as his own, any sense of authoritarian "mission" which he may have had with respect to writing for children has undergone a profound sea-change. Neaera H. feels that what she does "is not as good as what an oyster-catcher does. Writing and illustrating books for children is not as good as walking orange-eyed, orange-billed in the distance on the river, on the beaches of the ocean, finding shellfish." Neaera's most bitter and disturbing remarks on the subject of writing for children come after she receives an offer to publish a critical book (*From Oedipus to Peter Rabbit: The Tragic Heritage in Children's Literature*) which she had drunkenly suggested to her publisher at a cocktail party. Expressing her genuine feelings on the subject, she states that

> possibly the biggest tragedy in children's literature is that people won't stop writing it. . . . People write books for children and other people write

about the books written for children but I don't think it's for the children at all. I think that all the people who worry so much about the children are really worrying about themselves, about keeping their world together and getting the children to help them do it, getting the children to agree that it is indeed a world. Each new generation of children has to be told: "This is a world, this is what one does, one lives like this." Maybe our constant fear is that a generation of children will come along and say: "This is not a world, this is nothing, there's no way to live at all."

Hoban, in his bleaker moments, may or may not feel like Neaera H., but he can only make such thinking explicit in his adult novels while allowing the changing form of his children's books to mirror his growing philosophical unease. One can only wonder what further changes Hoban may make in both his adult and his children's books. It will be enjoyable to watch the future literary development of this immensely talented and wryly sympathetic author.

David Rees

SOURCE: "Beyond the Last Visible Dog," in *Painted Desert, Green Shade: Essays on Contemporary Writers of Fiction for Children and Young Adults,* The Horn Book Inc., 1984, pp. 138-52.

Russell Hoban is the author of several novels for adults, one full-length story published on a children's list (*The Mouse and His Child*), and for more than twenty years he has been the writer of texts of picturebooks for young readers. It is the last-named area that he would probably regard as the measure of his contribution to children's literature, for *The Mouse and His Child* was written for adult publication and only became a juvenile by accident.

A number of changes have taken place over the past two decades in the world of picturebooks, the most interesting being the advances made in the reproduction of artwork in color, and the fact that many artists who, a quarter of a century ago, would have been regarded as decorators of other people's work, now write and illustrate their own stories. A picturebook these days can be a beautiful object, a work of art in its own right: the subservience of the illustrator to the author is no longer considered a necessity; he doesn't exist merely to render in visual terms another person's words. It is possible now—and it happens occasionally—for the words to be subservient to the pictures, indeed to be almost irrelevant. Some of the productions of Brian Wildsmith, for instance, seem like glossy coffee-table books for the young—striking and original pictures occupying most of the available space, with an odd word or two at the foot of the page. *The Haunted House* by Jan Pienkowski was not intended to have a text at all; it was added at the last moment to avoid a curious state of affairs in the United Kingdom's taxation—books there are not subjected to Value Added Tax; but *The Haunted House,* a pop-up, would be regarded by the Inland Revenue as a toy if it had no words, and toys *are* subject to V.A.T.

Good artists are not automatically good writers, however. John Burningham's work is a constant pleasure to the eye, but the stories that accompany his pictures can be thin; the well-known *Mr. Gumpy's Outing,* for example, is not particularly memorable in its choice of words, and its narrative is somewhat predictable. Charles Keeping, perhaps more interested in words than John Burningham, also does not always succeed in writing a story that is as convincing as the dazzling colored pictures that he paints. *Charlie, Charlotte and the Golden Canary,* for instance, is marred by a rather sentimental story line. There are some artists, however, who do solve the problem brilliantly. Ezra Jack Keats is one, and Maurice Sendak is probably the supreme example: the narrative structure and the way the pictures convey the emotions within the words in *Where the Wild Things Are* and *In the Night Kitchen* and hardly be bettered, whatever strange judgments may be made about them by adults who fear that toddlers will be frightened or disturbed. (In my experience, no child I've come across has been alarmed by monsters in *Where the Wild Things Are,* nor upset by nudity in *In the Night Kitchen;* adult hang-ups are the voice behind such reservations.)

Russell Hoban began his career as an artist. He attended the Philadelphia Museum School of Industrial Art, and later, after working as the television art director in a big advertising agency, he became a freelance artist. But it is not as a painter and illustrator that he is known. Soon after he established himself as a writer of picturebooks, he gave up the idea of wishing to illustrate them; the early *What Does It Do and How Does It Work?*—not a story but an explanatory text about power shovels and dump trucks—shows that a considerable talent in picturebook illustration has disappeared from children's literature. For many years the illustrator of his stories was his first wife, Lillian, but recently a number of different artists, both British and American, including Quentin Blake and Emily Arnold McCully, have illustrated his work.

The writing in Russell Hoban's picturebooks has changed and developed greatly over the years. The earlier books for the most part contain realistic narratives—some of them rather didactic in intention—whereas the more recent ones can be wildly fantastic, showing vivid and bizarre flights of imagination and a delicious sense of humor. Even the seven very popular Frances books are more concerned with teaching something to the child reader than in telling a story for its own sake. Frances—indeed all the characters —are badgers, but their behavior is entirely middle class. To all intents and purposes Frances is a little girl who has to learn a series of lessons—how to cope with jealousy on her younger sister's birthday (*A Birthday for Frances*), how to outwit false friends (*A Bargain for Frances*), or how to make real friends (*Best Friends for Frances*). Parents and teachers no doubt like these tales because they are useful. That is a perfectly proper function of some books, some people think, but it is only a secondary function. Story is more important, and story in the Frances tales, though suited to the pre-school intentions of the books, is not always particularly interesting:

> It was a pleasant summer morning, so Frances took her bat and her ball and some chocolate sandwich cookies and went outside. "Will you play ball with me?" Frances's little sister called to her as she was leaving. "No," said Frances. "You are too little." Gloria sat down on the back steps and cried. (*Best Friends for Frances*)

Frances has to discover how to find room in her games for her little sister, not just on those occasions when there is no one else to play with, but also when she wants to play with badgers of her own age. In the end she is happy to do so:

> "It was only yesterday that you got to be big enough to play baseball. But I will give you half the daisies Albert gave me." So Frances gave Gloria half the daisies, and Gloria stopped crying. Then Harold came over, and everybody played baseball—Gloria too.

The lessons Frances learns are those the vast majority of children need to learn; yet one can have picturebooks that are not only didactic, but put forward the wrong kind of lesson. Russell Hoban's *Tom and the Two Handles* seems to me to be a little dubious in its morality. Tom's friend Kenny gives him a bloody nose, but when he tells his father he's going to get his own back by doing the same thing in return, Dad says they ought to talk it over and become friends again. Kenny punches Tom a second, a third, a fourth time; so Dad decides to teach Tom how to fight. Eventually—

"Well," said Tom, "after I gave Kenny a bloody nose, I knocked him down. Then I sat on top of him. And I told him there was more than one way of looking at it. I told him that he could say I gave him a bloody nose. Or he could say that he had a bad time with his best friend and we could make up. So we made up."

Dad approves of all this, but I'm not sure that I think it's a good—or, indeed, a likely—way of helping a shaky friendship to become whole.

As soon as the need to teach disappears from Russell Hoban's texts, the writing improves. One notices it even in books he had published at the same time as the Frances stories: it is as if he is released from some kind of unwelcome pressure; the prose becomes more flowing, more sure of itself. The cadences are more musical, and there is room for humor and for making the reader enjoy turning the page to find out what happens. *Ugly Bird* appeared in the same year as *Best Friends for Frances* and it's a much better book. Again, it is worthwhile quoting the opening sentences to see the difference:

> Once there was a very ugly bird baby, and his mama loved him. But all the other birds said, "My goodness, what a very ugly bird baby that is!"
>
> "Never mind," said Mama to her baby as she petted him. "They just don't know."
>
> "Don't know what?" said the ugly bird baby.
>
> "Don't know who you are and what you are," said Mama.
>
> "Who am I and what am I?" said Baby.
>
> "When it's flying time we'll both find out," said Mama. "Eat your worm and grow."

Baby does find out, in a pleasingly unpredictable way, who he is and what he is, but the really imaginative surprises and delights come in the later books, particularly *Arthur's New Power, The Twenty-Elephant Restaurant,* and *How Tom Beat Captain Najork and His Hired Sportsmen. Arthur's New Power* is a joky, satirical piece about domestic electrical gadgets that become substitutes for conversation and the finer things of life; Father Crocodile comes home one evening to find his house in darkness because his wife, son, and daughter have used too much power:

> "While she was ironing, she was watching the Early Horror on TV," said Arthur, "plus wearing her Slimmo Electronic Wonder-Massage belt and listening to her stereo with headphones. If you unplugged Emma, she wouldn't know what to do."

"What about Mom?" said Emma. "She was plugged into her bio-feedback machine, listening to her alpha waves and watching the yoga lady on the kitchen TV and mixing kelp-and-carrot cocktails in the blender."

"You see what I mean?" said Arthur. "And everybody yells at me for plugging in one little amplifier."

This is all the funnier when one remembers that these are crocodiles talking! Quite gratuitously they are crocodiles—they could just as easily be hippopotamuses or boa constrictors—but the fact that they are crocodiles seems to add an extra touch of craziness to the story.

The plot of *The Twenty-Elephant Restaurant* is even more bizarre. A man and a woman are fed up with their dining room table being wobbly, so the man makes a new one steady as a rock; "elephants could dance on that table," he says. In his wife's reply lies the nature of the book's ludicrous humor: she takes his image as literal, and asks, "How many?" They discuss how many and advertise in the paper—"Elephants wanted for table work. Must be agile." Eventually they open a restaurant with twenty tables; on each one is a full-size dancing elephant. The business is a huge success, but after a while the dancing tilts the foundation of the building, so they move on with their elephants to a new site and stay there until *that* building is also disturbed. And so on: it has the possibility of as many repetitions as the Last Visible Dog in *The Mouse and His Child*—the label on a tin of dog food has a picture of a dog and a tin of dog food; on the latter is a label with a dog and a tin of dog food: et cetera. The humor reminds one of the work of the Absurdist drama of the 1950s and 1960s—Ionesco's *Rhinoceros*, N. F. Simpson's *One-Way Pendulum,* or some of the situations in the plays of Samuel Beckett. It doesn't, of course, have the same profundity or the same pretensions; it's just a crazy flight of fancy for kids. And adults.

The finest of all these picturebooks is the most well known of all—*How Tom Beat Captain Najork and His Hired Sportsmen.* This story had some rather curious origins. The organizers of the Exeter, England conference on children's books in 1972, asked Russell Hoban to write something that could be used as the basis for an exercise in mime, movement, and dance. He sent them *How Tom Beat Captain Najork and His Hired Sportsmen,* then existing only in typescript; so its first admirers were not readers but an audience watching a performance. Several eminent children's writers, publishers, and librarians played

the parts, a somewhat bewildered but most convincing Brian Alderson taking the role of Captain Najork. Later the book was published with the superbly effective Quentin Blake pictures. Every sentence in this story is a gem:

"Very well," said Aunt Fidget Wonkham-Strong at table in her iron hat. "Eat your greasy bloaters."

Tom took his boat and pedalled to the next town down the river. There he advertised in the newspaper for a new aunt.

or

The hired sportsmen brought out the ramp, the slide, the barrel, the bobble, the sneeding tongs, the bar and the grapples. Tom saw at once that sneedball was like several kinds of fooling around that he was particularly good at.

The plot tells us how Tom's aunt, annoyed that her nephew does nothing but fool around, sends for Captain Najork to teach him a lesson by beating him at fooling-around games. But the Captain loses every time, and Tom leaves to find a new aunt, Bundlejoy Cosysweet. "She had a floppy hat with flowers on it. She had long, long hair." He tells her his conditions—no greasy bloaters, no cabbage-and-potato sog. And he does lots of fooling around. "That sounds fine to me," she says. "We'll have a go." The captain marries Aunt Fidget Wonkham-Strong, so they all live happily ever after.

Underneath this dotty and enchanting story lie some serious themes—childhood innocence pitted against adult incomprehension; repressed adults disliking nonconformity; a genuine aunt not necessarily being a blood relative. The child reader will not, of course, be aware of any of this, but, as Ted Hughes said in "Myth and Education," literature for the young is often a blueprint or do-it-yourself kit for experiences that children cannot yet have the equipment for dealing with in real life. Since they may absorb ideas subconsciously, it is very important to consider what kind of experiences we want them to encounter when they read a book. The underlying themes of *How Tom Beat Captain Najork and His Hired Sportsmen* are far more worthwhile than those of, say, *Tom and the Two Handles,* just as the idea behind *Where the Wild Things Are* is valuable in its suggestion that fear is more to do with what is going on inside us rather than what is outside us: much more therapeutic than a conventional story of beasts and monsters. Picturebooks at their best should put us in touch with as universally interesting matters as any of the major novels we may read in the years of our maturity.

Russell Hoban did not write *The Mouse and His Child* with a young audience in mind; it was intended to be a novel for adults. His publisher, however, decided to issue it as a children's book as it is a story about talking animals and toys. It's impossible, of course, to know precisely what alterations, if any, were asked for when the publisher decided to place this novel on a children's list, but the adult reader may well wonder how a seven-year-old can deal with some of the difficulties it presents:

> "The upside-downness of self," said the voice. "A good beginning. Continue."
>
> "We cannot continue," said the father, "unless we are put back on dry land and wound up."
>
> "'Wound up?'" said the voice. "Define your terms."
>
> "I don't want to," said the father. "I don't like this sort of talk."
>
> "What other sort of talk is there?" said the voice.
>
> "Here below the surface one studies the depths of TO BE, as manifest in AM, IS and ARE. And if you don't hold up your end of the conversation I may very well snap you in two even though I don't choose to eat you."

The influence of Lewis Carroll is obvious here, as it is in other parts of the story; other influences elsewhere in the writing are Hans Andersen and Samuel Beckett, the latter a particularly unusual person to see lurking behind the pages of a so-called children's book.

Maybe the difficulties shouldn't worry us: there is much here that a child can enjoy, the ideas and the pace of the narrative, for instance. It's a "chase" plot, the villain pursuing the good characters through a series of dangerous situations, until the concluding chapters when the individuals with whom we identify—the mouse and his child—win out, and the baddie, Manny the rat, is rendered powerless. This is a common enough story line in scores of children's books. The mouse and his child are wind-up toys, thrown out with the garbage when they are broken. Manny, the boss of the town's dump, repairs them and forces them to work for him, but with the aid of an old fortune-telling frog, they escape. Manny vows revenge and sets off in pursuit, declaring that he will smash them to bits with a large rock. The mouse and his child, helped by the frog, a kingfisher, a friendly bittern and a clockwork elephant, defeat the rat and his allies in a full-scale battle: Manny's teeth are knocked out so he is now useless as a leader. He starts working for the mouse and his child, but his wicked nature is untamed—he has a complex plan to electrocute his enemies, which, happily, fails.

Manny is an interesting villain:

> A large rat crept out of the shadows of the girders into the light of the overhead lamps, and stood up suddenly on his hind legs before the mouse and his child. He wore a greasy scrap of silk paisley tied with a dirty string in the manner of a dressing gown, and he smelled of darkness, of stale and moldy things, and garbage. He was there all at once and with a look of tenure, as if he had been waiting always just beyond their field of vision, and once let in would never go away.

But he is not wholly evil; in some ways he is pleasant and amusing, and capable of having his better nature appealed to, not unlike the ambiguous figure cut by Long John Silver in Stevenson's *Treasure Island:*

> The house, he saw, had not burned down, and he found that he was glad. "Say vat again," he murmured faintly.
>
> "Say what?" asked the mouse child.
>
> "What you called me," said Manny Rat.
>
> "Uncle Manny?"

Manny Rat nodded, and smiled a toothless smile, and felt the darkness that dwelt in him open to the light.

The reader, towards the end, feels that the author is becoming more interested in Manny than in the mouse and his child, rather as Milton in *Paradise Lost* found Satan more interesting to write about than God; this impression is confirmed by the fact that Russell Hoban at one time planned a sequel, called *The Return of Manny Rat*. This exists only as a fragment: it describes how Manny gets a new set of teeth made of papier mache, gnaws his way into a church, finds himself completely baffled by the organ—he thinks the stops are door-knockers, and wonders what sort of creature Diapason is—and experiences the greatest moments of his whole life when he hears the organist play Bach's Passacaglia and Fugue in C minor. Maybe there wasn't a possible narrative to develop, but it is a pity that this extremely amusing piece, though published, remains unfinished.

The influence of Hans Andersen makes itself felt particularly in the opening chapter of *The Mouse and His Child*—the toyshop with the toys that speak after midnight, Christmas, snow—and the effect is almost like a Christmas card in words:

> The sound of music made him stop at a toyshop where the door, continually swinging open and shut in a moving stream of people, jangled its bell and sent warm air and Christmas carols out

into the street. "Deck the halls with boughs of holly," sang the loudspeakers in the shop, and the tramp smelled Christmas in the pine wreaths, in the bright paint and varnish, in the shining metal and fresh pasteboard of the new toys.

Russell Hoban often uses Christmas as a background—*The Mole Family's Christmas* and *Emmet Otter's Jug-Band* Christmas are picturebook stories set at this time of the year. The author, like Katherine Paterson in *Angels and Other Strangers,* employs the season of good will to emphasize the loneliness of certain individuals. It is a recurring theme in his work; father-son relationships are also a recurring theme—they are at the center of *The Mouse and His Child* and also his novel for adults, *The Lion of Boaz-Jachin and Jachin-Boaz.* Much of the time the mouse and his child are friendless, vulnerable, indeed pitiable in their inability to help themselves. Russell Hoban seems to have a particular interest in a child's loneliness and naivete—the big outside world is awesome and frightening in its complexity. *Ugly Bird,* for instance, also touches on these ideas.

The major problem confronting the mouse and his child is movement. They can only dance in a circle, and when Manny repairs them, they are able to travel only in one direction, the father walking forward, holding up his child at arm's length, and the child cannot look at what is ahead of the father. Their greatest wish is to be self-winding, so that they can deal with life more easily, and it is Manny, eventually, who gives them this ability. The limitations on movement are reminiscent of ideas in the plays of Samuel Beckett—in *End Game,* Clov can only hop, and Hamm can only move when Clov pushes his wheelchair; in *Happy Days,* Winnie is buried in the first act up to her waist in a mound of sand, in the second up to her neck; in *Play* the three characters are incarcerated in urns and can only move their heads. The mouse and his child spend several months upside down in mud at the bottom of a river, and when Serpentina the turtle turns them the right way up, they still cannot move. The play—The Last Visible Dog—presented by the amateur theater group, the Caws of Art, seems particularly close to Beckett; in it Furza and Wurza live in tin cans half buried in mud, just as the legless Nagg and Nell in *End Game* live in trash-cans at the front of the stage. The Caws of Art is one of the areas of the novel that is above the head of the young reader—it is a wickedly funny parody of a second-rate experimental drama group that has lost any real rapport with its audience:

> "Out among the out among the out among the dots."

After which Crow stepped out of his role and said, "You feel it building?"

"No," said Mrs. Crow. "I'll be honest with you. I don't feel it building."

"Never mind," said Crow. "Just let it happen. Your line."

"Where among the dots?" said Mrs. Crow.

"Out among the dots beyond . . . "

"Yes, yes. Go on. Beyond?"

"Beyond the . . . "

"Don't stop now. . . . Beyond the . . . ?"

"BEYOND THE LAST VISIBLE DOG!" shouted Crow.

"There!" he said to his wife. "See how it pays off? Up and up and up, and then Zonk! BEYOND THE LAST VISIBLE DOG!"

"It's getting to me now," said Mrs. Crow. "But what does it mean?"

Crow flung wide his broad wings like a black cloak. "What *doesn't* it mean!" he said. "There's no end to it—it just goes on and on until it means anything and everything, depending on who you are and what your last visible dog is."

"'Beyond the last visible dog,'" said the mouse child to his father. "Where is that, I wonder?"

"I don't know," said the father, "but those words touch something in me—something half remembered, half forgotten—that escapes me just as it seems almost clear."

Difficult also for the young reader is the distressing scene in which the shrews attack and kill another colony of shrews; they in turn are eaten by the weasels who are promptly slaughtered by an owl. This may be unpleasant, but only temporarily; we are not asked to be directly involved with the shrews, the weasels, or the owl, who are essentially minor characters, and in any case animals eating each other is a fact of life that a child has to learn to accept:

> Behind them on the snow lay fallen shrews and wood mice, their open mouths still shaping final cries of rage and fear, their open eyes fast glazing in the moonlight. The mouse child stared beyond his father's shoulder at the astonishing stillness of the dead. The father looked at the spears he carried; he had felt the weight of enemies upon them, and for the first time in his life knew what it was to strike a blow for freedom.

It was a good decision to publish *The Mouse and His Child* as a book for the young reader; it is a fine work, entertaining and thought-provoking. The qualities of its writing are outstanding, particularly the sensitive descriptions of nature:

Winter had left the pond. The trees had lost their bare sharpness, and their branches were blurring into leaf. Skunk cabbages pushed their coarse green points up out of the black, boggy earth, and the nights grew clamorous with spring peepers. Robins were hard at work among the earthworms; the rattling cry of the kingfisher sounded along the banks; mallards cruised among the reeds; and from the surrounding swamps came the whistle of the marsh hawk and the pumping of the bittern. The fish that swam past the mouse and his child moved more swiftly now, and the sunlight filtering through the depths seemed warmer than before. Grown frogs and young tadpoles, newts, snakes, and turtles, awakening from hibernation, swam up to the surface as spring came to the pond.

This compares very favorably with the famous description of spring in the concluding pages of E. B. White's *Charlotte's Web*. *The Mouse and His Child* thoroughly deserves the status it has achieved as something of a modern classic in children's fiction. No doubt there will be many more picturebooks to come from Russell Hoban, but one hopes that he will also give us another full-length novel: it's long overdue.

Jack Branscomb

SOURCE: "The Quest for Wholeness in the Fiction of Russell Hoban," in *Critique*, Vol. 28, No. 1, Fall, 1986, pp. 29-38.

One of the contemporary masters of fantasy writing, Ursula LeGuin, has remarked that the theme of most great works of fantasy is the journey to self-knowledge; and, she claims, "fantasy is the medium best suited to a description of that journey, its perils and rewards" ("The Child and the Shadow"). Russell Hoban seems to find both the theme and the approach congenial. In four of the five adult novels he has written since 1973, he has experimented with various modes of fantasy. *The Lion of Boaz-Jachin and Jachin-Boaz* (1973) presents a family psychodrama in which the timeless rage of sons against fathers is embodied in a stone lion that comes to life. *Kleinzeit* (1974), a comic reworking of the Orpheus myth, and *Pilgermann* (1983), a Jewish *Pilgrim's Progress,* veer strongly toward allegory. Hoban's finest novel, *Riddley Walker* (1980), is a blend of mysticism and apocalyptic science fiction.

The central subject of all the novels is the individual's quest for knowledge of self and psychic wholeness. The protagonists, usually middle-aged men, find themselves cut off from parents and wives—the past—and from children—the future. They develop, not toward conventional happiness, but toward reintegration of the self, recovery of the past, openness toward the future, and freedom to act in the present. The complexity of Hoban's treatment of theme and symbol has increased greatly over the past twelve years, but his concerns and methods have remained essentially the same.

Hoban's reputation first began to move beyond the relatively narrow field of children's books, his earlier specialty, when he published *The Mouse and His Child,* a novel for children, in 1969, the year in which the Pennsylvania-born writer moved to Britain. With the publication of his adult novels since then, his circle of admirers has steadily grown, especially in Britain, where he has been something of a cult figure (Prescott). *Riddley Walker* in particular was enthusiastically received on both sides of the Atlantic. Joel Conarroe, for example, writing for *The New York Times Book Review* called it "miraculous" and praised it as the best novel of 1981. Despite the reviewer's praise, however, Hoban has received little critical attention. The first scholarly article to deal with Hoban's adult fiction presented the novels before *Riddley Walker* as a gloss upon his children's books (Bowers). More recently, Hoban's remarkable linguistic innovations in *Riddley Walker* have received much deserved treatment (Maynor and Patteson). Little has been done to suggest Hoban's development of his major themes or to detail the intricate patterning of the novels of their complex allusiveness.

As is often the case in fiction with a strong element of fantasy, Hoban's novels rely heavily on spatial, often visual, patterning. Hoban's background as an illustrator may contribute to the unusually strong sense of controlling images at the heart of the novels. In *The Lion of Boaz-Jachin and Jachin-Boaz,* an ancient carving of a lion hunt expresses the theme and structure of the entire novel, and a medieval painting of the Legend of Saint Eustace at Canterbury Cathedral plays a similar role in *Riddley Walker.* The tendency is clearest of all in *Pilgermann,* in which Tarot figures and an ornamental design worked out in a tiled courtyard are central symbols of the book, and Hoban allows his narrator, Pilgermann, a number of intrusive lectures on paintings and sculptures.

Whether based on a visual image or not, Hoban's novels are dominated by patterns whose effect is both spatial and temporal. As Pilgermann says, "I can't tell this as a story because it isn't a story; a story is what remains when you leave out most of the action; a story is a coherent sequence of picture cards." As a matter of fact, Hoban relies heavily on "picture cards," relatively discrete, two-dimensional episodes in his novels (nowhere more than in *Pilgermann*), but his main concern is always with the action, the rhythmic energy underlying the picture cards, which is universal and timeless. Hoban's protagonists find themselves, surprised and often against their will, in the midst of a pattern, whose working out is the novel. The patterns Hoban draws upon come from actual images, from well known myths and Jungian psychology, sometimes from more esoteric systems like the Tarot. Whatever the source, Hoban's main interest in them is psychological. His protagonists come to recognize that they are fragmented or incomplete. They launch themselves or are thrust into searches for wholeness which turn out to be circular, leading them into the past before allowing them to escape into the present. Ultimately, their quests lead them to acceptance of their place in time, reintegration, and painful self-knowledge.

The circular pattern of psychological flight and recovery is clearly defined in Hoban's *Lion of Boaz-Jachin and Jachin-Boaz.* The novel explores fundamental conflicts between parents and children, particularly fathers and sons: the rage of the son against the father who seems always beyond him, escaping and denying the son his individuality; and the angry resentment of his father for the son who represents time and death for his parents. The cumbersomely symbolic names of the father and son, Jachin-Boaz and Boaz-Jachin, refer to the two colossal pillars in front of Solomon's temple, and their meaning, "beginning" and "negation" (Butler), indicates clearly the circular pattern that Hoban sees in the relationship between the generations. Father and son are the antagonists in an endless round of beginning and negation which can be overcome only through an openness to the pattern which allows them to live in the present.

The pattern of endless conflict in *Lion* is revealed in an image, a seventh-century B.C. Assyrian bas relief of a lion hunt. The crucial part of the image is that of a dying lion attacking the wheel of the king's chariot:

> Always and always the leaping dying lion never reaching the splendid blank-faced king for ever receding before him, for ever borne away in safety by the tall wheel for ever turning.
>
> "The wheel," said Boaz-Jachin.

Both father and son realize that the center of the image is the wheel of time, generation, and death.

Mere recognition of the destructive cycle is not enough, however; Jachin-Boaz must enter into the quest for reconciliation which is the only escape from the cycle. A middle-aged Jew from the Near East, he flees to London to escape from his wife, his son, and the death-in-life he has made for himself. He has spent his life as a map-maker, abstractly charting the world for others and especially for his son, and in his flight he continues to cling to his master map. He fears both the past, his disappointed parents, and the future, death; but not until his son liberates the lion of the sculpture and sets out in quest of his father does Jachin-Boaz begin to confront the heart of the problem: the lion itself, the rage of the son against the father. Reconciliation comes only when Jachin-Boaz burns his map and confronts both his son and the lion. He sees:

> Frowning brows. Amber eyes luminous and infinite. Open jaws, hot breath, pink rasping tongue and white teeth of the end of the world. Jachin-Boaz smelled the lion, saw the muscles taut beneath the tawny skin. Immense, the lion, dominating space and time. Distinct, forward of the air around him. Immediate. Now. Nothing else.

The circular pattern of destruction ends as father and son meet and for the first time accept one another and the possibility of living in the present.

The need for the individual to enter into a cyclical pattern larger than himself is even clearer in Hoban's next novel, *Kleinzeit,* in which the hero finds himself caught up in the cyclical return of the archetypal poet, Orpheus. Hoban's treatment of the theme in this case, however, is comic. Most of the characters are allegorical: Word, the god of poetry; Hospital, the place where would-be Orpheuses attempt to put themselves together; Death, who takes the form of a chimpanzee. Kleinzeit, as his name suggests, is a small-time person living in a nonheroic age. Like Jachin-Boaz, he is a displaced person, divorced, alienated from his children, cut off from his own past, working at a meaningless job writing advertisements. Psychologically fragmented as he is, Kleinzeit feels the need for wholeness, represented by a compulsion to write poetry, and so he finds himself in Hospital, in a ward filled with secret scribblers like himself, all of them terminal cases.

The allegorical characters make it clear that Kleinzeit is a small part of the larger pattern, the most recent of innumerable vessels of poetry. At one point, while Kleinzeit is away and his poetic mistress, a ream of yellow paper, is crooning, "Lover come back to me," Word appears:

He's not here today, said Word. I am.

Not you, whimpered the yellow paper. Not the enormity of you.

No, no, please, you're *hurting me. . . .*

Like thunder and lighting [sic] the seed of Word jetted into the yellow paper. Now, said Word, there you are. I've quickened you. Let them die in their hundreds and their thousands, from time to time one of them must wiggle through. I see to that.

Both the yellow paper and Kleinzeit's Eurydice belong to him only temporarily and only if he is able to fulfill the role of Orpheus, the critical stage of which is the regeneration of himself as a poet and a man.

The time of regeneration, Hospital explains, comes after Orpheus is torn apart by the Thracian women and his head has floated across the sea to Lemnos. Eventually it swims back to the place of dismemberment, where Orpheus must be restored:

There is a sighing perhaps, you can't be sure. Someone unseen walks away slowly.

He's found his members, said Kleinzeit. He's remembered himself.

What is harmony, said Hospital, but a fitting together?

The image of dismemberment, particularly in the forms of decapitation or castration, is frequent, almost obsessive, in Hoban's novels; it suggests, as in *Kleinzeit,* a radical loss of wholeness due to excessive rationality or sensuality. The goal of all Hoban's questers is the reachievement of wholeness, a remembering. As Kleinzeit is a poet, his remembering is triggered through poetry, by his discovery of some lines from Milton's "L'Allegro": "Untwisting all the chains that ty/The hidden soul of harmony." They serve as the catalyst for his recovery of his own forgotten past and the achievement of a moment of harmony within himself. Death presents Kleinzeit with a gift: Kleinzeit takes ink and a Japanese brush and draws on a piece of yellow paper "in one smooth sweep a fat black circle, sweet and round." This image, Kleinzeit's mandala, sums up both the cyclical pattern of Orpheus and Kleinzeit's personal achievement: the effortless, Zen-like expression of interior harmony which makes it possible for him to be a whole person and a poet.

In the culminating scene of *The Lion,* Jachin-Boaz "ceased to be himself, and only was." This process of "remembering" oneself by losing oneself in larger

mythic patterns receives its most ambitious treatment in Hoban's more recent novels, *Riddley Walker* and *Pilgermann.* The context of the quests becomes enormously greater as Hoban explores the themes of time and timelessness, freedom and predestination, wisdom and sin and plunges far more deeply into arcane allusions than in his earlier novels. It is both legitimate and useful to treat the two books as complementary. In the Acknowledgements to *Pilgermann* Hoban tells the reader, "*Riddley Walker* left me in a place where there was further action pending and this further action was waiting for the element that would precipitate it into the time and place of its own story" (vii). The precipitating element was Hoban's visit to a ruined twelfth-century castle built by the Teutonic Knights of Saint Mary in Galilee—a sight which parallels a climactic visit to the ruined Cathedral of Canterbury in *Riddley Walker.* The quests of the two heroes, Riddley Walker and Pilgermann, taken together form a single exploration, generally Jungian in approach, of the individual's attempt to discover himself and place himself in space and time.

Riddley Walker is a post-apocalyptic fantasy set in Kent some 2,400 years in the future. Riddley is one of a group of foragers who dig for usable scrap from the time preceding "Bad Time," the nuclear holocaust. By chance he gets caught up in the "Mincery's" (Ministry's) attempts to rediscover the secrets of computers and nuclear power ("the 1 Big 1") through the ritual questioning and sacrifice of the "Ardship of Cambry" (Archbishop of Canterbury), the symbolic heir of the technocrats who controlled and ultimately unleashed the destruction. He is deeply moved by the remnants of force which he feels in a ruined nuclear power plant, but ultimately rejects the pursuit of this power in favor of the spiritual power that he discovers in the ruins of Canterbury Cathedral. At the end of the novel, he is still on the road, walking and looking for answers to the unsolvable riddles of sin and guilt.

Riddley's "roading" is circular, following the circuit of nine villages in which the Mincery holds its questionings of the Ardship every twelve years. As in *The Lion of Boaz-Jachin and Jachin-Boaz,* the circular pattern here suggests the futile, destructive, repetitive nature of the human search for knowledge and power. The circuit has its roots in the legendary wanderings of Eusa (U.S.A.), the mythic discoverer of the "1 Big 1" and the unleasher of Bad Time. As archetypal eater of forbidden fruit, he wandered from city to city, mutilated, blinded, and finally killed, and so has been passed down as the central sacramental figure of the culture. Because the Ardship of Cambry is Eusa's spiritual heir, he must follow the same circle every twelve years, reinacting Eusa's search for knowledge, his suffering, and his death at the hands of the representatives of the people. The pattern even exists in a children's circle game, whose name sums up its futility: "Fools Circel 9wys."

The circle is without meaning, but Riddley must first come to terms with it before he can escape from it. The story begins with his coming of age (at the age of twelve in his society), the accidental death of his father, his growing alienation from the other members of his tribe, and his final escape from them. This separation of the young man from his society marks the first stage of the Jungian process of individuation, by which he develops a personality of his own. He is taken up by the representatives of Nature—one of the packs of wild dogs that live in the burnt-out cities of "Inland" (England). The dogs, formerly the friends and servants of man, but now vicious and uncannily intelligent, represent Nature alienated and ravaged by man's exploitation of knowledge for power.

Having separated himself from the society of men and at least partially established a connection with the greater natural world. Riddley encounters his Jungian shadow, the repressed part of his own personality which he must recognize as part of himself. Riddley's shadow is the Ardship of Cambry, Lissener, whom Riddley rescues from the Mincery's inquiries. The two are the same age, twelve at the full of the last moon, but their natures are opposite. Riddley is a talker, an explainer of riddles, and potentially an artist. Lissener is abstract, a seeker of power, a descendent of Eusa and the "puter leat" (computer elite) before Bad Time. He is also deformed, like the rest of the Eusa folk preserved at Canterbury, and like them he is psychically fragmented. Whereas before the holocaust "the Puter Leat . . . had the woal worl in our mynd," now the remnants of the Eusa folk have only bits of knowledge and periodically "do some poasyum" (symposium) "rubbing up to 1 a nother skin to skin and talking vantsit theary." Riddley ultimately rejects Lissener's aims, but through him he comes to be something of a listener and experiences the awesomeness of intellectual achievement and domination of Nature represented by control of atomic energy.

Riddley's discovery of the appeal of this kind of power comes as he and Lissener enter the ruins of a power plant. Looking at the shining, broken machines, Riddley whispers, "'O what we ben! And what we come to!' . . . How cud any 1 not want to get that shyning Power back from time back way

back?" The scene is reminiscent of an experience which took place some 2,500 years before Riddley's: Henry Adams' visit to the hall of dynamos at the Paris Exposition of 1900. "The planet itself," writes Adams

> seemed less impressive, in its old-fashioned, deliberate, annual or daily revolution, than this huge wheel, revolving within arm's-length at some vertiginous speed, and barely murmuring. . . . Before the end, one began to pray to it; inherited instinct taught the natural expression of man before silent and infinite force. (*Education.*)

Unlike Riddley, Adams had experienced the frightening sense of multiplicity of the nineteenth century as well as its energy; the perception made him a prophet of the turmoil which Riddley's culture remembers as Bad Time.

As a balancing, human force, Adams in "The Dynamo and the Virgin" looks back to the cathedrals built to honor the Virgin Mary in the twelfth and thirteenth centuries. He finds that "the Virgin had acted as the greatest force the western world had ever felt, and had drawn man's activities to herself more strongly than any other power, natural or supernatural, had ever done" (*Education.*) For the Ardship, Canterbury, the final stop in the Fools Circel 9wys, signifies death and mutilation at the end of another cycle of the fruitless search for power. But for Riddley, the discovery of the ruins of Canterbury Cathedral provides a mystic experience of the energy felt by Adams in the cathedrals of France; it is both the starting point of the holocaust and the seat of a power even greater than that of the atom. Entering the city Riddley is more aware than ever of the ghost of the nuclear power that was centered there. This energy Riddley identifies with the Spirit of God, a "Big Old Father" which he imagines taking him sexually. But even more intense is the feminine power that he feels when he comes to the ruins of the cathedral: "the woom of her what has her woom in Cambry." Hoban's use of the architecture is precise. Riddley sees first in the foundations of Trinity Chapel the rudimentary outline of a female fertility figure. Though dedicated to the Trinity at Canterbury, the chapel in this position was usually in England dedicated to the Virgin (Woodman). Like Adams, who sees in the Virgin the most powerful incarnation of the female sexual principle (*Education*), Riddley responds sexually to force which he sees as fundamental to all of nature: "Shes that same 1 shows her moon self or she jus shows her old old nite and no moon. Shes that 1 same thing and all of us come out of. Shes what she is." The womb of the goddess Riddley finds in the still intact cathedral crypt, which contained the Virgin's altar (Woodman). Standing among the forest of stone columns in the crypt Riddley, like Adams, glimpses a lost wholeness:

> Them as made Canterbury musve put ther selfs right. Only it dint stay right did it. Somers in be twean them stoan trees and the [nuclear] Power Ring they musve put ther selfs wrong. Now we dint have the 1 nor the other.

Like Jachin-Boaz, Riddley breaks free of the destructive cycle he has been following and discovers himself by allowing himself to merge into a new pattern. Near the end of the novel he says, "Its not sturgling for Power thats where the Power is. Its in jus letting your self be where it is. Its tuning in to the worl its leaving your self behynt." In the rejection of power, Riddley, like Henry Adams, finds the freedom to pose the riddles about human nature which he knows he will never be able to answer.

In *Pilgermann,* Hoban returns to Riddley Walker's quest and explores the second phase of the process of individuation, in which the individual, having established his ego in relation to the external world, begins to turn inward to explore hitherto unrealized areas of the Self. The events of the novel take place during the First Crusade, in the years 1096-98, in central Europe and in Antioch. The narrator and central character is a Jew who calls himself Pilgermann; he has left ego so far behind that he no longer remembers his historical name and exists now as "waves and particles" in the "space called time." The story he tells of his pilgrimage to Jerusalem is also an account of his exploration of himself, a process of self-sacrifice by which the pilgrim must lose the things he values most in the physical world to discover new areas of the spiritual world.

Although *Pilgermann* is clearly not a "historical" novel, the setting in time and place are highly significant in showing the relationship between this novel and *Riddley Walker.* The parallels with Henry Adams' *Mont-Saint-Michel and Chartres* and *The Education of Henry Adams* are again close and instructive.

Mont-Saint-Michel, "a study of thirteenth-century unity," and *The Education,* "a study of twentieth-century multiplicity," are "two points of relation" (*Education*) by which Adams might view the movement of forces in history and, more important, understand his own sense of personal failure as a man born in the wrong era (Hochfield). *Mont-Saint-Michel* begins with a study of the vigorously masculine Nor-

man architecture of the eleventh century and goes on to the twelfth and thirteenth-century cathedrals dedicated to the Virgin. *The Education* deals with the failure of Adams' experience to equip him to live in the nineteenth century's world of force and leads him back in time to contemplate the lost unity of the thirteenth century.

The relationships of unity/multiplicity and of masculine/feminine and the artistic attempt to place these principles in time by means of two related books are also central to Hoban's two novels. Set far in the future, *Riddley Walker* moves back in time to find its spiritual core in the "woom" of Canterbury, the crypt whose construction was begun in 1096 (Woodman). *Pilgermann,* narrated by the "waves and particles" of *Pilgermann* in the twentieth century, is set in the year 1096 and reaches its climax when the virile Frankish soldiers of Christ conquer Antioch. The movement from the eleventh century to the twentieth and from the forty-fifth century back through the twentieth to the eleventh links the novels and reinforces the sense of cyclical recurrence which is both a form of bondage and a path of release in Hoban's works.

To emphasize the aspect of spiritual questing of Pilgermann's journey, Hoban relies heavily on images from the twenty-one cards of the major arcana of the Tarot pack to embody stages of the quest. The Tarot pack has, in addition, been seen as related to the symbolism of medieval alchemy and Jungian psychology, (Douglas), both of which are important in *Pilgermann.* Cards which are particularly important are the Fool, the High Priestess, the Hanged Man, and Death, though several other cards also appear in the novel. The most important of the Tarot figures is the Fool, who appears both at the beginning and the end of the deck. Like Pilgermann, he is a spiritual quester. Also crucial is the High Priestess, sometimes identified with divine Wisdom, or Sophia, who links the physical and the spiritual worlds and, like the Virgin in *Riddley Walker,* represents "the great feminine force controlling the very source of life" (Thorndike, quoted by Douglas). In the course of his wandering, Pilgermann also encounters a second Sophia, lustful and murderous, who embodies the negative aspect of the High Priestess, "the weaver of illusions who destroys her lovers" (Douglas). The Hanged Man, who saves Pilgermann's life and thereby starts him on his pilgrimage, is a figure of redemptive self-sacrifice. Death, who becomes Pilgermann's companion, is both the destroyer of old life and the initiator of the new.

The cards in themselves are static. As Pilgermann says, "A story is a coherent sequence of picture cards," minus the crucial motive force—the action. In this novel, the action is the questing spirit of the pilgrim himself. Pilgermann is launched into his journey by the pogroms which accompanied the beginnings of the Crusade in Germany. He has lusted after and seduced a gentile woman, Sophia, and immediately thereafter has been caught and castrated by a Christian mob. This loss of physical potency, contrasting with the recovery of sexual power by Jachin-Boaz and Kleinzeit, emphasizes the exclusively spiritual nature of Pilgermann's quest. After various adventures, he ends up in Antioch befriended by a philosophically inclined father-figure named Bembel Rudzuk shortly before the city is besieged by the Crusaders. Together they design a large tile courtyard whose pattern is an endlessly repeating mandala that expresses both motionlessness and motion. The impulse to try to represent such a mystery, like Jachin-Boaz's map, turns out to be ill-advised; Pilgermann learns that his quest for enlightenment must be experiential, not symbolic.

Pilgermann's willing death in the capture of Antioch is the culminating experience of the pilgrim, corresponding to Riddley Walker's discoveries of the female power in Canterbury. Pilgermann finds himself fascinated by the leader of the Crusaders, Bohemond, the gigantic embodiment of violent maleness in the novel:

> the enemy as messenger of God, the enemy as teacher. Sophia was the beginning of my holy Wisdom and Bohemond would be the end of it.

Like Hoban's earlier heroes, but transcending them, Pilgermann finds himself by losing himself in the cyclical patterns of existence, represented here finally by the rhythmical circling of migrating birds which he sees just as he throws himself to certain death at Bohemond's hands:

> the last thing I see with my mortal eyes, very, very high in the sky and circling in the overlapping patterns of the Law, is that drifting meditation of storks that I have known from my childhood, each year returning in their season to their wonted place.

The sense of paradoxical affirmation found in this death scene is one of the most fundamental effects of Hoban's novels and the source of much of their power. The individual's quest for wholeness must lead him through "fools circels" until he perceives that the circle is also a part of liberation. Only then can he discover his Self and accept his life and death.

Alida Allison

SOURCE: "Living the Non-Mechanical Life: Russell Hoban's Metaphorical Wind-Up Toys," in *Children's Literature in Education,* Vol. 22, No. 3, 1991, pp. 189-94.

Toys have been one of the tools of Russell Hoban's trade as a children's writer for more than three decades now. More precisely, Hoban has used toys *as* tools, metaphorically: tools for self-discovery, tools for finding the road to independent existence, to what he calls "self-winding." For the kinds of toys he has consistently used as characters have been wind-up toys, mechanical toys—metaphors for wind-up, mechanical lives. Since Hoban's first novel, the 1967 ***The Mouse and His Child,*** is about two wind-up mice joined at the hands and geared to dance forever round and round in circles, their difficult journey into self-winding is a convenient example of Hoban's characteristic preoccupation. But it is not his only book specifically to feature mechanical toys; another is the 1979 ***La Corona and the Tin Frog.***

In fact, Hoban had long been concerned with the workings of things; a gifted artist, one of his early careers was as an illustrator of sporting events, and for pleasure, he sketched athletes, such as boxers and hockey players, and machines, such as bulldozers and power shovels, because he enjoyed observing how they moved. Not surprisingly, then, his first children's book was ***What Does It Do and How Does It Work?,*** published in 1958, quickly followed by ***The Atomic Submarine.*** But his interest wasn't really in machines per se, but in the *idea* of the mechanical, and its complement, the idea of breaking out of perfunctory existence. Though the investigative bent in his first two books was strictly Hoban, after them, he abandoned both nonfiction and illustration and began the career most of us are familiar with, as the author of nearly seventy children's picture books and seven novels.

Certainly Hoban's writing since the late sixties, since ***The Mouse and His Child*** and its critical and commercial success, has taken on a more overtly philosophical tone, whether in children's books or in the novels for adults he began at about the same time. The tension between mechanical as opposed to conscious behavior, the movement of breaking out of traditional grooves, is a major topic in his work. As Hoban put it during a 1985 interview in Australia, pulling the actual mouse-and-his-child toy out of his rucksack to illustrate the point:

> Well, wind-up toys, I find, are a really good metaphor. . . . This toy is covered with felt, but underneath, it is the classical tin toy that's made in two

halves, fastened together with clasps. The two heads never meet quite precisely and if you undo the clasps to repair the thing, somehow you never get it back together properly. . . . [Though the tramp] mended them, they no longer danced in circles, they walked straight ahead. In other words, they stopped playing around and moved out into the world.

Though Hoban's writing falls with such apparent ease into these two major categories (pre-*The Mouse and His Child* and post-*The Mouse and His Child*), this division is deceptive because, before he moved out of his own familiar groove, out of what had become mechanical and repetitive writing, many of the books he wrote shared the same theme with the later books. In many of the early books, too, the ones represented by the Frances the Badger stories, the young character is testing the limits, striking out for new territory, and asserting a sense of independence. The major difference is not in theme, but in resolution.

It is the difference in denouement that truly represents the two basic kinds of Hoban's books. And few critics have been as perceptive about the difference as he has himself, perceptive about its philosophical import and its impact on his royalty checks. His Frances books sell much better even twenty years after their publication than most of his new books. Asked about a comment he'd made that he was working his way from "popularity to obscurity," he told me last summer, "I can only write what comes to me in the way it comes to me. I'm stuck with it, stuck with the progression of ideas and the development of those ideas that go on in my head."

Hoban's best selling books, the titles he is most readily associated with, continue to be the ones he wrote in his first decades as a children's writer. He calls these "pleasant little cautionary tales." Didactic, reassuring, they are very much loved by children, critics, and teachers—and rightly so. Told with great charm, Hoban's imaginative Frances series captures the dilemmas, language, and relationships of the four-to eight-year-olds who are his subjects.

But to be realistic about children is to acknowledge that they don't always like the familiarity within which they live. Frances, sweet as she is, is a bit of an iconoclast in rebelling against bedtime, in insisting on her bread and jam sandwiches day after day, or in refusing eggs in her memorably inventive sotto voce song:

> Poached eggs on toast, why do you shiver
> With such a funny little quiver?

Other Hoban characters of about the same period, the Little Brute family, are as funny and nasty a group of uncivilized eccentrics as one could encounter. Charlie the Beaver packs his sack and leaves his loving home to tramp through the forest like any pint-sized philosopher questioning the values he has inherited from his parents. Arthur, the hilariously slobby and inconsiderate alligator from *Dinner at Alberta's,* will not take to table manners merely because his sister complains he drops bits of ravioli on her head. No, he, like Frances, like Charlie, like the littlest Brute child, must have his own reasons. These characters share, no less than any of Hoban's later ones, the drive to check the world out for themselves. Hoban has expressed bemusement that children should prefer his didactic books one reason might be that the parents in them have the patience to let their children find their own reasons. Hoban's description of these books as *"pleasant* cautionary tales" is accurate. Patience and wisdom and respect for the child permeate the stories and thus serve to teach adult readers, too.

But all of these early characters have one thing in common: They all return home. Their stories share a resolution in which they are reintegrated into the comfortable little norms of their habitual world. Despite the rebellions, their stories are cozy and safe. Though at her own pace and through no more compulsion than subtle parental guidance, Frances does abandon her individualistic if restricted diet of bread and jam. Charlie, though he does spend the night in the woods, returns home and enters the world of industrious and eager beavers. Smitten with the lovely eyelash-batting Alberta, Arthur, the seemingly irredeemable slob, does learn table manners. The littlest Brute captures a "wandering good feeling" and goes so far as to bring it home and civilize the rest of her griping, growling family, which is forever transformed into the Nice family.

The lesson here is not at all a bad lesson, that children will be loved even when they test moving away from the main arena of family and society life. But the situations are as safe for the adults as they are for the children; the adults are certain their insubordinate children will shape up. The adults in the books, and the adult readers, if not the child readers, *know* the little heroes will come home. Home waits and, with it, security for parent and child. Parents know a six-year-old's running away from home can be halted with the promise of a good dinner and a face-saving device or two. From the standpoint of the relative risk, these stories are like traveling to the Third World with an American Express card and claiming to have lived with the people: They're not too convincing.

Nor are they metaphorical. They are straightforward stories about children, depicted in illustration as animals, but nice normal little animals nonetheless. They will probably grow up to be nice little parents who read books like these to their children, as I do, as probably most of us do. But if these were the only kinds of books Hoban wrote after three decades at it, he might well be undergoing the crisis of personal significance he scripts for his children's book writer Neaera H. in *Turtle Diary.* Hoban does continue to write stories more or less like these, which he calls commercial, alongside his more extraordinary ones. From a literary standpoint, though if not a commercial one, the books Hoban calls "antididactic" are the best, and fortunately, there are many of these.

The first hint of Hoban's more profound literary talent came even before *The Mouse and His Child.* As Joan Bowers pointed out, the 1966 story *The Sea Thing Child* is his first mythopoetic and metaphorical work. But it's *The Mouse* with which he startled critics and readers alike, and in which he presented in metaphorical form a well-developed philosophy from which he has not deviated. He has developed certainly, leaped and bounded breathtakingly with such books as *Riddley Walker,* but the basic idea of self-winding is common to all of his adult novels and to his more creative, philosophical, and metaphorical efforts for children.

In *La Corona and the Tin Frog,* Hoban presents the idea of bondage to the unexamined life in many images and structural devices. The book itself is a frame story, symbolic of enclosure. La Corona, the lady painted on the cigar box, is trapped in her own frame. The tin frog is trapped within his habitual fears, and his fears are real; as with the clockwork mouse and his child, the possibility of defeat is no fantasy. Even the clock in the story admits that sometimes he wonders whether he keeps time or time keeps him.

Mightn't we ask ourselves the same question? Hoban does: "The nature of clockwork toys is very provocative of thought. Why," he asks, "do we make clockwork toys that replicate some simple human action?"

Why indeed? The winder has such power, the wind-ed such bondage to the clock of its inner works. When it winds down, it simply stops; it dies. The clockwork characters in Hoban's books are so compelling, their breaking free is so important, because they *do* replicate human actions; they *do* represent the human situation. The characters in the beginning of *La Corona and the Tin Frog* represent human life at its worst, its most mindless, its least free. Their

longings are ineffectual because they haven't acted. They undergo a tremendous lot to free themselves of their clockwork, their frames, and their fears, but free themselves they do, breaking right out of the story and into an open future.

Similarly, in *The Mouse and His Child,* what the father and son undergo in becoming self-winding is the main story, but other characters' odysseys are equally illuminating, for example, that of the elephant. True, she is a "silly female" character, not especially likable. Fortunately, the female wind-up seal is spunkier or one might be very uncomfortable thinking about gender stereotypes in Hoban's book. But the elephant, too, undergoes profound change in her being, physical and emotional change of metaphorical significance. She suffers, she learns, she grows out of her limitations. At the start, she is a plush pomposity, self-deluded and haughtily sniffing as she delivers such typically Hobanesque puns as, "One does what one is wound to do." As the book progresses, she is literally weathered. Her pretensions fall away as her fancy outer trappings fade and vanish. Once bound to the appearances of things, she loses an eye and perceives true value; she sees clearly, finally, the love that's been staring right at her for chapters and chapters. She uses her refined taste for the common good, welcoming into her territory those whom she would earlier have excluded. Adaptable, inventive, and plucky, all the clockwork toys in Hoban's story move, metaphorically, beyond their limits.

"Metaphorically" is important; clockwork toys they are, and clockwork toys they remain—just like us. There are no miraculous metamorphoses; there is just working with what one has. Hoban commented that children could enjoy the story of *The Mouse and His Child,* but only adults could extract all its "juice." For adults, Hoban's metaphorical books are provocative because, as adults, we can, if we choose, be instructed by the tin frog and the mouse child about shedding pretensions, about seeing clearly, about moving and self winding—about, in short, living a nonmechanical life. Clockwork toys, remember, "replicate human actions"—and we are wound and bound by time as they. If that weren't true, there would be a lot more Methuselahs running around than there are. There is a sadness to childhood, Hoban wrote, and the sadness is from not knowing how little time there is, or, rather, how much. We are all being toyed with in the sense that we are all wound up for an unknowable amount of time. This is the ultimate limit beyond which we cannot move, but within that limit, Hoban said, "the action itself is enough reward. . . . We can't reasonably ask for more."

We can, however, by living like machines, "wind up" with a lot less. We can stop, dead in our tracks, even before our time runs out—or like La Corona, like the elephant, like the mouse child, we can leave the familiar behind, realizing that the quest to be self-winding is an ongoing tool for the sharpening of the self, a quest that we never outgrow.

TITLE COMMENTARY

THE MOUSE AND HIS CHILD (1967)

Kirkus Reviews

SOURCE: A review of *The Mouse and His Child,* in *Kirkus Reviews,* Vol. XXXV, September 15, 1967, p. 1134.

"Be naked" our departing predecessor pinned to the bulletin board, and we have never felt so vulnerable as in anticipating the response to Russell Hoban's arresting departure from juvenile precedent. "I want to find the elephant . . . to be my mama," says the mouse child, remembering the toy shop, to the other wind-ups, "and I want the seal to be my sister, and I want us all to live in the beautiful house." Mouse & Child's frustrating, harrowing, sometimes funny quest is also a flight—from Manny Rat, the ultimate under-worldling who is both Lucifer and Luciano. Through trashcan and dump, past murder and robbery and war, into the obscurities of the Caws of Art (two crows on a bare stage), Muskrat's Much-in-Little ("Why times How equals What"), and the contemplation of infinity (by the turtle author of "The Last Visible Dog") they pace their little circles, searching for a way to become self-winding, the child clinging to his faith in a future. At last, beyond the last visible dog (on the disintegrating label of a can) the child finds the answer—"nothing but us." Irony, satire, parody—and an implicit, unrestricted compassion (except for fools). The two windups survive shattering and reassembling, finally reform Manny Rat and establish family and fellowship in their own territory. "Be happy," the tramp blesses them in what could be a blessing for the book—and we will "be naked" and say that man *and* child will recognize themselves in [*The Mouse and His Child*]. A rich, disturbing, very touching book.

Booklist

SOURCE: A review of *The Mouse and His Child,* in *Booklist,* Vol. 64, No. 10, January 15, 1968, p. 593.

An intricate but skillfully executed fantasy chronicles the hazardous and heroic adventures of a broken windup mouse child and his father in search of happiness and security. Love and valor ultimately triumph over violence and evil in a realistically created world of humanly characterized windup toys and real animals including a malevolent rat, a fortune-telling frog, a scholarly snapping turtle, and a play-producing crow. Limited in appeal but for the special reader a rare treat and for the perceptive adult a delight to share. Small black-and-white drawings fittingly complement the spirit of the story. Grades 4-6.

Bulletin of the Center for Children's Books

SOURCE: A review of *The Mouse and His Child,* in *Bulletin of the Center for Children's Books,* Vol. 21, No. 9, May, 1968, p. 143.

Hands clasped together, the mouse and his child are never parted in all their search for love and security; they are a single unit, a wind-up tin toy. Broken and discarded, the toy is repaired by a tramp, and then the father and child have a series of adventures—many of them in an effort to escape the vengeance of Manny the Rat, vicious head of a gang of foraging rats. In the end, the mouse and his child achieve the serenity of being part of a household, a queerly assorted but compatible world of toys and animals. The book has some marvelously tender scenes, some that are humorous, some that are pointed and sophisticated. The unusual reader who sees the subtle comment on society will enjoy the book, but it will probably be limited in appeal to the general reader because of the long drawn chase, and because of the odd blend of a cast of characters best suited to the rather young child and a plot in which the nuances and the complications—as well as the vocabulary—demand on older reader.

Times Literary Supplement

SOURCE: A review of *The Mouse and His Child,* in *The Times Literary Supplement,* No. 3501, April 3, 1969, p. 357.

Russell Hoban is known best in this country for his gentle bedtime stories about little Frances, who is so like little girls all over the world but who turns out in the illustrations to be a badger-cub. They are charming picture-books, distinguished from others of their kind by the shrewdness which lies below the surface sentimentality. Excellent as they are, they give no hint that the author had in him such a blockbuster of a book as *The Mouse and his Child.*

The book looks harmless enough. Mrs. Hoban's illustrations are a little like Shepard's without Shepard's precision; here, one thinks, is something "after" and probably a long way after *The Wind in the Willows.* The story starts quietly, too, in the shop where a clockwork mouse and his child stand outside a dolls' house "owned" by a clockwork elephant who is, being unsold, "part of the establishment". It is a vision of security which the mouse-child remembers through all the hazards and disasters that follow. For the mice are sold, played with and broken, and thrown out for scrap. Repaired, inefficiently, by a passing tramp, they take the road.

The long episodic story that follows is beyond summarizing. This is not to say that it is loosely constructed. Each stage of the toys' odyssey is purposeful, and the author brings the threads together with the greatest skill. There are some memorable inventions. Manny Rat, who runs a racket in scrap, is most subtly conceived; a villain, certainly, but one in whom self-interest is matched with more complex motives. He is a ruthless hater and a mechanical genius, one who has, as he says after he loses his teeth in the Great Battle for the Dolls' House, "a feel for fings". He ends up as lecturer in practical physics at the Muskrat Foundation and as the mouse-child's Uncle Manny, but one would never entirely trust him.

Manny, malignant and dedicated, spans the whole story, but there are other rich creations. Frog, who wears an old glove as a body-belt and tells fortunes, survives the hazards of the wilderness to become Chairman of the Committee for the Surveillance of Territories and the Resolution of Inter-Field Enmities (STRIFE for short). Frog is a bit of a charlatan but a practical realist.

> He had attained his present age . . . by paying closer attention to not being eaten than his enemies could bring to bear on eating him.

He is kindly withal: when the mice's clockwork runs down he says "That's what friends are for" and he winds them up again.

Frog is lovable, and so in a terrible way is Manny Rat. One feels only awe for C. Serpentina, "thinker, scholar, playwright" (the description is his own), the ancient turtle who lives in masterly inactivity—apart from eating—at the bottom of the pond, and whose expressionist drama—*The Last Visible Dog*—is presented, with disastrous consequences, by the Caws of Art Experimental Theatre Group—artistic director Crow. Under the tutelage of this formidable philosopher the mouse and his child sit at the bottom of the pond and ponder—and reject—his dictum that "Nothing is the ultimate truth and this mud is like all other mud".

The appeal of C. Serpentina is entirely cerebral and static. There are still moments like this in the long story and also scenes of swift action. There is a terrifying episode when the wanderers get caught up in a battle between rival armies of shrews. The mice—tin and consequently inedible—are mustered, together with Frog and other unfortunates, as rations. The shrews fight for territory, a place "where everything smells right". "Rations don't have territories", and neither do toy mice, until after long suffering and great courage they win their own.

The story is rich in memorable invention, but this would count for nothing if the style were not so exquisitely apt. There is no fine writing, but Mr. Hoban matches every nuance of his narrative with words so completely right as to be quite unobtrusive. This is a perfection so flawless as to pass unobserved until, the turmoil and passion of the story over, one thinks back to the masterly means by which these ends were reached.

Nothing could be farther than the untidy muddle of this anguished world from the miniature perfection of the Borrowers, but it is to Mrs. Norton, together with even more distinguished and "adult" writers, that the mind returns again and again in the course of *The Mouse and His Child.* It is partly a matter of scale. Everything in the story is precisely to size. There is a marvellous consistency in each one of a multitude of details. There is something too in the nature of the fantasy. Like Mrs. Norton, Mr. Hoban rides his fantasy with a tight rein. Granting himself one single improbable assumption—that among the rubbish dumps and the wildernesses beyond the urban world there is a world of animals and toys made in its distorted image—he pursues the implications of his invention with remorseless logic.

This is to take quite seriously a story which deserves and demands such a reception. The story is also, for full measure, hugely funny, provocative, pathetic and heroic. Some of the fun is satiric with adult overtones. The metaphysics—however mock—may be beyond the range of those who revel in the knockabout. Like the best books it is a book from which one can peel layer after layer of meaning. It may not be a Children's Book but, my goodness, it is a *Book*.

Joanne Lynn

SOURCE: "Threadbare Utopia: Hoban's Modern Pastoral," in *Children's Literature Association*, Vol. 11, No. 1, 1986, pp. 19-24.

Though Russell Hoban's **The Mouse and His Child** has attained status as a modern classic on both sides of the Atlantic, it is usually labeled as "disturbing," possibly unsuitable for children, even when it is admired. Dennis Butts calls it "powerful, comic disturbing"; Margery Fisher's list of adjectives is "brilliant, puzzling, disturbing"; Ann Thwaite's is "Demanding disturbing, memorable." But all agree on its importance. Marcus Crouch is perhaps only the most extravagant in calling it "one of the most revolutionary books in the whole history of children's literature"; John Rowe Townsend puts it forward unequivocally as a "modern classic."

Curiously, however, most commentators have stopped short of genuine interpretation. After the notation cited above, Margery Fisher begs off the task of interpretation, saying that there "seems little profit in speculating on the exact meaning or intention of particular scenes or characters." Barbara Wersba complains about the "metaphysical" epigraph (a quotation from Auden), allowing that, though "the writing is beautiful, the satire often profound . . . the puzzle remains unworked." One of the best of the novel's recent critics, Fred Inglis, deplores what he calls a "rather studied sequence of emblems and allegory" in Hoban's "awkward and effortful reaching for significance," concluding that the book bears "a heavy-handed as well as an obscure little message if you try to unpack its meaning." He fails, however, to read, or at least to communicate, the "message" he has discerned, disproportionately emphasizing what he labels "Symbols and structures: Advanced" over Hoban's skill in handling important contemporary themes within the confines of a children's tale. Indeed, **The Mouse and His Child** occupies a pivotal position in Hoban's career. Now that he has established himself as an accomplished, witty and serious novelist (at least in England), it is time to recognize the place of **The Mouse and His Child** in the context of Hoban's career and in the larger context of children's literature, giving it a literary home, and taking a hand at the unpacking job thus far avoided.

In form, **The Mouse and His Child** was a distinct departure from Hoban's early picture book collaborations with Lillian Hoban. (The anthropomorphic tales of Frances the badger are gritty little evocations of American family life that have a secure place of their own.) Yet the angle of departure is not entirely abrupt, nor have Hoban's adult novels abandoned the central concerns of **The Mouse and His Child.** Like the Frances books, it evokes a keenly observed domestic scene. Like **Turtle Diary,** it explores the fragility of human relationships. As in **Kleinzeit,** Hoban is concerned with a painful sense of fragmentation, and the apocalyptic fears and tentative hope of **Riddley Walker** are here prefigured also. To freight Hoban's funny and poignant book with a load of interpretation is to risk burying its beauty and wit in C. Serpentina's turtle pond pedantry. Yet it seems fair to take on Hoban's own terms Muskrat's "much in little": "Writing about anything," Hoban once wrote, "one writes about everything. The most limited history, the very smallest and most neatly painted door, opens on immensities" (**"Death"**). In a burst of irritation at people who ask, "but is it a children's book?" the disenchanted Protagonist of **Turtle Diary** observes:

> People write books for children and other people write about the books written for children but I don't think it's for the children at all. I think that all the people who worry so much about the children are really worrying about themselves, about keeping their world together and getting the children to help them do it, getting the children to agree that it is indeed a world. Each new generation of children has to be told: "This is a world, this is what one does, one lives like this." Maybe our constant fear is that a generation of children will come along and say: "This is not a world, this is nothing, there's no way to live at all."

The Mouse and His Child is very much an exploration of how one tries to live in a world that has come to seem "not a world" much of the time. Hoban chose to cast his existential leap of faith in the form of an anthropomorphic fantasy: mechanical toys, animals, birds, amphibians, even an insect, play out the drama against a backdrop that pits the natural world against that which man has made. As Hoban employs it, anthropomorphic fantasy, a common vehicle for children's books, is a form of modern pastoral. William Empson was the first to broaden the traditional definition of pastoral, seeing it as a means of putting the "complex into the simple," creating "momentary havens" to withstand an oppressive awareness of darkness and confusion (Tolliver). In modern critical usage, the term pastoral is not strictly generic: to the traditional generic elements of form, structure and subject matter it adds purpose and point of view as valid shaping forces in literature, and thus bypasses the confusions of mixed critical "kinds." Like traditional pastoral, modern pastoral is a figure for the contemplative life, "a withdrawal from action that affords a perspective on battlefield and marketplace" (Lincoln). The vulnerable protagonist is separated by physical and/or chronological barriers from active participation in the adult world until he has achieved an insight about or acceptance of his human condition. As the shepherd of traditional pastoral is removed by occupation from participation in urban life, so the child is barred by age, thus making him a natural agent for the modern writer who casts his evaluation of contemporary life in the form of a fantasy for children.

Russell Hoban's "rustics," a wind-up mouse attached at the hands to the child he mechanically tosses in the air," are thrust willy nilly into the *vita contempla-tiva.* A toyshop and city dump, metonyms for modern urban existence, contrast with rural scenes in meadow, woodland, stream and pond. Rural scenes, however, are not views of Arcadia, as we shall see below. A satanic rat pursues the innocents through rural landscape in episodic catastrophe: a war between shrews and woodmice, a provincial theatrical performance, a winter of labor for a muskrat at a beaver pond, a sojourn in primal ooze contemplating a dog food can. Each episode offers criticism of modern life as well as developing insight for the mouse's child.

The original doll house is occupied by papier-mache inhabitants who are content to communicate in conversation derived from the newsprint of which they are made: "'Bargains galore,' replied the lady . . . 'PRICES SLASHED,' said the gentleman . . . 'EVERYTHING MUST GO.'" A proprietary plush elephant voices their general acceptance of the world-as-it-is: "One does what one is wound up to do" (*Mouse*). One dances or one balances a ball on the end of one's nose; one speaks without thinking, in the idiom of consumerism. Toyshop and house are Plato's Cave. The mouse child's initial vision of Eden is the Victorian doll house presided over by Mama Elephant. This vision must be revised. Doll house and nurturing "mama" are, in their bright perfection, not sufficient but stultifying. The elephant must undergo her own humiliations; the house must undergo almost complete disintegration and an equally thorough refurbishing by the "rustics" (windup toys and animals). Only then are they sufficient to the mouse child's dream. When the toys are sold and perform under Christmas trees as they were wound up to do, their lives are patterned, predictable, repetitive. The

mouse child's cry of protest against the clockwork "rules" is responsible for this destruction and relegation to the trash heap. O *felix culpa!* This first "smashing" liberates the mouse and child from convention, separates them from the town, and thrusts them into the scenes which will force reflection on the world in which we live.

"Mended" by the mysterious tramp who leaves out the crucial parts that keep them dancing in circles, the mouse and his child, now "lurching straight ahead," have broken the closed circle of safe domesticity but are vulnerable to the ravages of the second, and more negative, urban image. The smoldering landscape of the junkyard is the landscape of hell. Composed of the detritus of technological, commercial society, it is powered by "wind-ups," slaves to technology, commanded by vermin, led by the mafioso villain, Manny Rat. The order he rules in the junkyard is characterized by exploitation and tawdry commercial exchange for objects of sensory desire: "a headless pink celluloid hula doll" entertains paying customers at the dance halls; Manny Rat plots robberies out of a passion for treacle brittle.

Subsequent escape into the countryside does not provide idyllic refuge, but a series of brutal lessons in reality. Each succeeding escape is toward a traditional pastoral haven. But Hoban quickly peels away the illusion of safety, revealing hazards in Arcadia. Though Joan Bowers observed that the rural scenes are "no idyllic pastoral of rural life but a remorseless portrayal of 'Nature, red in tooth and claw'." we must remember that even traditional pastoral is not a literature of escape. The pastoral withdrawal is not to Eden; pastoral protagonists are vulnerable to attack by enemies and the elements (Lincoln). The wintry thickets, woods and meadows are scenes of a fierce territorial battle between woodmice and shrews—a war which no one wins. At the moment of apparent victory, two shrews are caught by a pair of weasels, "smiling pleasantly with the blood of both armies dripping from their jaws" (*Mouse*). Satiated and blissfully oblivious, the weasels "nuzzled each other affectionately as they ran, and their heads were so close together that when the horned owl swooped down out of the moonlight his talons pierced both brains at once". The mouse and his child are not observers of this drama of merciless territorial imperative. It takes place above them, as counterpoint to the mouse child's longing for home and his father's recognition of their placelessness in a hostile universe. Only author and reader share the double perspective of impersonal nature and intimate need, a technique discussed further below. Grimly, father mouse reflects: *"What chance has anybody got without a ter-*

ritory!" (**Mouse**), as he waits, immobile, to be woundup once again.

The reappearance of Manny Rat now drives father and child to the territory of the Caws of Art Repertory Company, a pine woods by a stream. The promise of pastoral comedy, rural games, companionship and safety is soon dispelled. Production of *The Last Visible Dog,* Hoban's parody of Beckett's *Endgame,* satirizes intellectual pretension as much as boorish philistinism. Two thespian crows, eager to bring culture to the rustic masses, appear onstage in "two large rusty grapefruit cans," half buried in "mud, ooze, rubbish" at "the bottom of a pond. . . ." The provincial audience of outspoken animals—martens, porcupines, weasels—soon makes clear that it "don't want none of your modern filth here." The weasel aserts his critical opinion by killing a rabbit actor whose part in the production has bored him. By an inadvertent comic turn, the mouse and child stumble across the stage, and the avant garde gives way to schlock melodrama. Brilliant improvisation by father mouse and child, their first self-determining act, frees them once more. Manny Rat appears and is caught in the net of living theater. Father mouse intones: "'Does he hound us still? . . . he who drove us forth to wander denless through the world?. . . . He hounds us still!' the child replied. . . . 'Banker Ratsneak . . . come out and face your victims!'" The lines between art and life are blurred. Typecast by his victims, Manny plays his role so well he is mobbed and beaten by the dangerously ignorant audience. Another rustic retreat fails, but the mouse child's imaginative improvisational flight thrusts the protagonists into yet another haven, another possibility for growth: Muskrat's home beside the beaver dam.

Lame Muskrat now takes them into his tunnel under the stream bank on the promise not only of safety, but of the hope of achieving self-winding, a more urgent goal now than the need for place. Muskrat's scientific services are offered in trade for a winter's labor at his project in applied physics. In the end, both Muskrat and Manny Rat contribute to the solution of the problem of self-winding. Neither can solve it alone. In contrast to Manny Rat's exploitation of power, however, Muskrat at least offers something in return for the wind-ups' labor. Muskrat's formula, "Why Times How Equals What," will eventually help the mouse child to the solutions of a series of problems. Meanwhile Muskrat's scientific detachment has become tainted with competitiveness, and is as destructive as Manny Rat's megalomania. Muskrat has divorced "pure thought" and mechanical ingenuity from a sense of values. In his eagerness to show up the active beavers who "do things," Muskrat wipes

out his own world along with the beaver dam. His tree-felling project is successful, but at the cost of a flood which carries mouse and child away from the clutches of their resurgent enemy. "Saved" by the flood, they come to rest in the mud of C. Serpentina's turtle pond, and are forced to spend the rest of the winter upended, in uninterrupted contemplation of a Bonzo dog food can.

The oozy retreat of C. Serpentina demonstrates another paradox of creation and destruction. The turtle-playwright is simultaneously creative, pedantic, and predatory. His play title, *The Last Visible Dog,* is a clue to the mouse child's solution of life's mystery, but the ponderous mud turtle is utterly self-absorbed, indifferent to the wind-ups' plight:

> "One arises to consider the corporeal continuity of AM. . . . One becomes aware of appetizing aspects of IS. *Which see."* KLOP! A pair of sharp and hory jaws closed on one of the mouse father's legs. *"Note well,"* said the voice. *"In the work cited.* Inedible."

Ironically, here in the mud and dimness of the pond, the protagonists achieve the *vita contemplativa:* the mouse child steadily regards the receding images of the dog on the Bonzo dog food can, discovering the dual meaning at the heart of the book. At the end of his involuntary mediation on infinite images he announces his illumination. "Nothing is what is beyond the last visible dog." But there is *etre* as well as *neant* in his budding existentialism. The label falls off the can, offering the more important revelation: "There's nothing on the other side of nothing but us!". The mouse child's naive assertion of faith in himself, and in fate, overrides C. Serpentina's sterile pedantry and the mouse's father disconsolate realism.

Armed with the tentative tool of insight, the mouse child now combines abstract thought (C. Serpentina's play), rational pragmatism (Muskrat's formula), and chthonic forces (a lowly midge, a "resurrected" frog), to produce an intricate sequence of invention (aided by happy coincidence) that raises them from the mud. The mouse child's stubborn passion to find a "place" brings birds and wind-ups (Nature and Culture) into bizarre coalition for an onslaught against the vermin who hold their "place," the once glorious doll house, now mounted on a pole by the railroad over the junkyard, appropriated by Manny Rat. Re-emergence from their winter in the pond has prepared the mouse and his child for a return to urban scenes, in the direction of the *vita activa.*

As essential to significant pastoral as withdrawal from society is the return. Protagonist and reader at the end emerge with a sense of man's place in the world afforded by reconnection with real (not idealized) nature. The necessary withdrawal leads to return and reintegration with the real world, where finding a "place" is tempered by rigorous experience (Lincoln). The epic battle for the doll house (*Mouse*), initiates the pastoral return. Hoban focuses on mechanical ingenuity, collaborative action, reunification of lost friends and allies, and above all on the inspiriting possibility of reclaiming the doll house. The house in the hands of Manny Rat has fallen on evil days: "Stark against the red sky, its mansard roof crudely mended with tin and all its chimneys and dormers jammed roughly back in place," painted black, its windows, balusters, scrollworks, and cornices that once constituted the glory of its Victorian complacency are gone: "The whole house bristled with bent nails clumsily driven and smashed into the splintered wood. Nothing was straight, and everything awry." The work of putting it straight is accomplished by the combined talents of the cast (reassembled now, both socially and individually, in the case of the wind-ups who must literally be put back together). Even the spare parts stashed by Manny Rat in another Bonzo dog food contribute.

After much scrounging and labor by the victorious commune of protagonists and allies, the house stands firmly at last over "rubbish mountains" and "tin can slopes." Painted in motely from tag ends in discarded paint cans, glazed with shards of curved, colored bottle glass, crooked, wonky, askew, but glowing, "the place" nevertheless "seemed reborn of itself." In his discussion of Elizabethan pastoral poetry, Frank Kermode notes that the notion of a lost Golden Age motivates the pastoral dream: "We have abused Nature, by breaking its laws . . . and we are therefore steadily deteriorating so that our only hope is for a fresh start after some kind of redemption." In *The Mouse and His Child* civilization has not only deteriorated, it is choked with the by-products of man's abuse of nature. The Inn of the Last Visible Dog is a limited and conditional "fresh start" following the redemption brought about by the mouse child's faith, and the collaboration of forces both rational and intuitive.

Definitions of pastoral, traditional and modern, remind us that pastoral is an urban product, and that the contrast of the simple with the complicated involves the reader in an ironic perception of the world we have made. As characters, the rustics (shepherds or children), rarely offer full explicit insight. Hoban guides the reader's critical perception of the world not only by the mouse child's developing sensibility, but by a technique of descriptive and narrative summary. As in the shrew/weasel/owl passage noted above, the reader is removed from the main action to a bird's-eye view from the from the top of Olympus. In the middle distance, the bluejay reporter squawks out dispassionate capsules in staccato bursts: "MUSKRAT KILLED BY FALLING TREE . . . DIVING BEETLES ROUT BACKSWIMMERS IN WATER POLO. TADPOLES HIT BOTTOM IN LITTLE LEAGUE STANDINGS . . . WIND-UPS IDLE" (*Mouse*). In longer descriptive/narrative passages at crucial junctures, detail and action rather than explicit authorial comment offer a view of the world beyond the protagonists' immediate arena. Halfway through the novel, such a passage becomes an extended metaphor, cosmic counterpoint to the main action.

After Muskrat's inadvertent deluge, we observe from our vantage point that the destruction is local: "The world went its way." Back at the dump, however, we discover that the doll house has almost been destroyed "by a nursery fire that started with its youthful owners playing with matches." It has become "a trysting place for young rat lovers, then a social and athletic club." All that remains of its former splendor is "the globe the scholar doll had had beneath its hand, and that was now a football for the rats" (*Mouse*). The doll house, which has figured as a smug imperfect Eden, and will later become a revised version of the mouse child's dream of "place," collects the burden of Hoban's meaning. Before we can accept a place in the revised Eden, we are confronted with a vision of the irresponsibility of a civilized world which can unleash technological and political power but cannot control it, a world run by human beings too morally immature, too driven by appetite to reckon with the limits of what man has made. Surely the image of its "youthful owners" suggests man playing with the matches of ecological imbalance or nuclear destruction, the risks of ignoring Nature's larger patterns and man's place in them. The poor tired planet ("globe") is reduced to a political football for rats. Hoban does not delay overmuch in these passages: we are soon returned to the intimate perspective, the thick of the action, but the image persists, emanates.

Were the novel patterned solely after heroic quest, modeled on the *marchen,* it would end with the retaking of the doll house. But reintegration is yet to come. Self-winding must be accomplished and a reconciliation with the forces of evil achieved. Now toothless after battle, Manny Rat "who had reveled in darkness" reappears, ironically offering light. His shrewd intuition and inventing cunning must supplement formulae and naive faith in the matter of self-winding: "vere are fings vat simply cannot be figures out." "Reasoning won't do at all. . . . You have to have a feel for fings." Hoban holds sentiment at bay: the stern vision that acknowledges "nature red in tooth and claw" accepts the paradox of good out of evil, recognizes the danger of blind trust. Though all seems homey, hospitable, in the new-christened Inn of the Last Visible Dog, Manny Rat's "conversion to goodness, auspiciously as it had begun, had suffered a jolting setback with his gift of self-winding . . . the strain on his moral fiber was too great." His attempt to destroy the doll house in a last blaze of illumination is foiled, but the suggestion of inevitable imperfection, the tragic possibility of life, remains. Idyllic resolution is conditioned, too, by the discovery that neither mouse nor child is, after all, eternally self-winding. Self-actualization is not enough; they will forever depend on others as well as a kind fate. In the last scene, the melancholy tramp suddenly emerges as an equivocal Jehovah, gazes through the windows of the house that now "blaze like a beacon," and murmurs tentatively, half in benediction, half in exhortation: "Be happy."

One may, in the end, acknowledge a chorus of critical carping at self-conscious symbols in a children's book, as one acknowledges the chorus of Oceanids in *Prometheus.* One notes also that no critics have complained that the book fails. Hoban's use of the informing spirit of pastoral, whether consciously worked out or seized on through happy intuition, offers simple characters to express the complex world we share with our children. The Inn of the Last Visible Dog is Hoban's qualified version of Utopia: a society which, accepting the limitations of human nature, can yet build a workable "place," a place in which human society rises above the junkheap of technological civilization and creates from however disparate materials and human capacities a world that glows with possibilities of the worth of human existence. If I have called Hoban's Utopia threadbare, it is because threadbareness and patching are perhaps, at present, the best vision one can manage, even in writing for children, of a worn and weary world very dangerously close, in its drunken slouch toward Bethlehem, to falling on the red button marked Apocalypse.

Geraldine DeLuca

SOURCE: "A Condition of Complete Simplicity': The Toy as a Child in *The Mouse and His Child,*" in *Children's Literature in Education,* Vol. 19, No. 4, 1988, pp. 211-21.

The toy is one of the humblest of creations in children's books, emerging from its factory or wrapped box as blank a slate as ever there was, a mere imita-

tion of the living—not in the eyes of the child, perhaps, but certainly in the hierarchy of characters that children's book writers have at their disposal. It is also one of the most vulnerable, subject to breakage, mishandling, abandonment; inevitably to be left on a shelf as the child grows older, a perfect subject for abuse, and thus also a ready subject to express the extreme dependency and vulnerability, and the need to be accepted and loved, that are central facts of childhood. There are certain obvious directions in which stories about toys can go, most, it seems, involving some sort of transformation. In the much-celebrated *Velveteen Rabbit,* the maudlin nature of which has always disturbed me, the child reader is assured that destroyed toys are reborn as living things—precisely because some child has loved them; *Pinocchio* must prove himself worthy to become a real boy—and again, there is much for the puppet and the reader to endure: the world is infinitely threatening and there are terrible consequences for mistakes.

A writer has a number of interesting problems to solve in creating characters out of toys. They have a peculiar status: they are just objects, but as Piaget tells us and as we can all remember from our own childhood, children regard them as alive and having feelings. But to what extent are they alive? How are they like us and how are they like whatever creatures they are fashioned to look like? How like something entirely different? What might it mean to be a toy, an object, manufactured? What aspect of life do they seem particularly suited to represent. Winnie-the-Pooh eats honey all day or thinks about it, but is utterly unaggressive. He is a poet, a singer, a friend of Piglet, he is Christopher Robin's favorite, an image of Milne's own fondest childhood remembrance. But toys are not universally or equally special or favored. They aren't even, in the same work, necessarily "alive" to the same degree.

In a picture book called *Peabody,* published in 1983, the author, Rosemary Wells, plays off the "aliveness" and humanness of one toy against the mechanical nature of another. In this book, a little girl temporarily rejects a stuffed bear named Peabody for a walking, talking doll named Rita. We are to identify with Peabody, the "natural" toy, soft, cuddly, and simple; and are to rejoice when the stiffed-legged, marching intruder, Rita, who says over and over, "Good morning, I love you, good morning, I love you"—is finally drowned in the bathtub by the girl's little brother, whereupon the girl turns back, without a moment's regret, to the bear. The doll is obviously to be regarded as some sort of monstrous mechanical excess, its manufacturer's attempts to humanize it a kind of hubris that intrudes on the child's provenance as animator and thus limits its appeal—as in fact is usually the case with toys that have batteries in their stomachs. Still the girl in the story doesn't seem to mind, either that the doll is mechanical or that it gets broken.

And what a confusing message: are some toys "real" and some okay to drown? And what accounts for the difference? Are some toys inherently more lovable, more essentially true to their toy nature? Like *The Velveteen Rabbit,* this book suggests that it is the status conveyed by the child that gives the toy its value—which is certainly true—but also that it is okay to destroy those that don't quite make it in the child's or author's mind. Also true, maybe—certainly common—except when you bring them to life. What happens, I can't help wondering, to the toys in the nursery in *The Velveteen Rabbit* that don't get to sleep next to the little boy, that don't get loved? Do they go to heaven or do they stay in some nursery limbo, like unbaptized souls?

Russell Hoban's **The Mouse and His Child** is the kind of book that raises such questions, not about toys alone, but about the world, about a human society that is based on a caste system of wealth and intellect, where the main characters are outcasts, the weak and insignificant, the toys of the humblest status—decorations, that even get played with. The story is about how they survive in a world given to sentimentality and to the avoidance of real feeling and responsibility, that has such wonderful little symbols of filial love to put under its Christmas tree, but that is perfectly comfortable with carelessness, corruption, brutality. The mouse and his child are windup toys, joined at the hands and fashioned to dance in a circle. This is what they have been "wound to do," says Hoban with the allegorical tone that pervades the book. They have no names; they are simply the thing itself. How does this world treat its child, the book asks. And the child here, in a Darwinian universe, represents the "other," innocence as other, something transcendent, to be relearned, understood, cherished.

For as long as they are toys functioning as toys, Christmas decorations brought down from the attic once a year, the mouse and his child have no existence to speak of. There is no human child in the story who loves them, though the book's dedication mentions one of three fathers, "Harvey Cushman, under whose Christmas tree I first saw the mouse and his child dance." So the child for whom they are alive is Hoban himself. But it is only when they inadvertently violate the "clockwork laws" by crying,

thus attracting the attention of a cat who knocks them over and breaks them so that they are thrown into the garbage, that they really begin to "live." Soon afterward, they are retrieved from the garbage by another outcast, a tramp, and set on their way as picaresque heroes in a universe where the predators are small animals, all stuck in various low slots on the food chain, and many of them ultimately ennobled by the hapless but determined little toys, who don't turn into real mice, but who do change form in other significant ways.

The father and child begin, after the first bit of damage is done to them, to move in a straight line—an obvious advance. Toward the end of the book they become physically separate, and finally, with the aid of their original enemy, Manny Rat, they become self-winding. Ever more battered and rusted as time goes on, the toys' very existence is constantly threatened, but in their tenacity, they achieve a kind of unique, almost mysterious status in the world as "in their long exposure to the weather, moss had rooted in the crevices of their tin, and . . . covered them like soft green fur." This observation, to underline the windups' achievement in transforming their enemy, is from the rat himself. At the end of the book they are decrepit—the father ceases to be self-winding— but they are almost ecstatically alive:

> "We aren't toys anymore," says the father. "Toys are to be played with, and we aren't. We have endured . . . the painful spring, the shattering fall, and more. Now we have come to that place where the scattering is regathered."

Hoban's story begins at Christmastime, outside a toy store. A tramp "whose steps [were] too big for the little streets of the little town" shivered and "passed aimlessly through the crowd while rosy-faced . . . shoppers quickened their steps and moved aside to give him room." How quickly and deftly Hoban gets us to look at ourselves from the "larger" perspective of the tramp, the outcast, the only human involved in the story. Through his eyes, we look in at the toys and "at a splendid dollhouse . . . very large and expensive, a full three stories high and a marvel of its kind." It is there that the mouse and his child are lifted out of their box and born into consciousness. Both the father and the child are new to the world, it is clear, but it is the child's innocence that is focused on here. Since the "works" for the two are inside the father and since he is larger, he is somehow established as wiser, knowing that he must be responsible, worrying about the child, experiencing the world as an adult, though he clearly has no experience.

To the child, the toy store is a world of a seemingly timeless and protected opulence, though Hoban is quick to make us feel the pride that goeth before a fall of the snobbish elephant, and the vapidness of the dollhouse dolls whose papier-mache newspaper heads announce whatever gossip or cliche happens to be printed on them. But to the mouse's child they are wonderful: they imprint on his imagination the American dream: a mother, a family, a big house, community—or, as the animals later teach him to call it, territory. Yet if Hoban satirizes many aspects of the dream, he never mocks the child's hopes, and finally what the child achieves is larger, more generous than what he had been given to see in the toy store.

Immediately after being set down on the road by the tramp and told to "Be tramps," the mouse and his child are captured and enslaved by Manny Rat, the villain from whom they keep escaping throughout the story and with whom their fate is inevitably linked. The toy mice and the real rat represent two kinds of energy; as Blake would say, "without contraries is no progression," and just as the windups can't escape from their problems but rather have to face them, the rat, for all his furious intensity, can't smash them. Ultimately they have to reckon with each other. Michael and Margaret Rustin suggest that the rat's fury is an expression of violence against his own feared weakness. When the mice do finally disarm him—they knock out his teeth—they give him something to replace his rage: he becomes "Uncle Manny" in the child's family.

The toys have adventures with a fortune-telling frog, a troupe of animal actors performing an absurdist play; a lame philosopher-muskrat devoted to "pure thought"; a "deep thinking" sea turtle named "C. serpentina." Always the mouse searches for his original family: the toy elephant who once sang him a lullaby, the toy seal he imagines as a sister, and the splendid doll house. But nothing escapes the ravages of time and fortune in this book, and that, in Hoban's view, is perhaps okay. For misfortune deepens these characters; despite their increasingly tattered condition they attain a kind of luminosity. And when the mouse and his child finally recover their family and the dollhouse, it is at the dump again, where, as T.S. Eliot puts it, "the end of all our exploring/Will be to arrive where we started/And know the place for the first time."

Their conquest of the rat suggests that they have achieved the autonomy and the knowledge that self-winding represents. And it is appropriate that the rat is the one who finally discovers how to do it—in a way that the friendlier but more effete characters could not even begin to contemplate. In fighting him they have found the power in themselves that he in some sense represented. Thus, when the toothless rat comes back to plead for inclusion in the family, he argues: "Fink of it! Fink how I have helped you! Where would you be now if you had not had me to fight against! Could you have won vat victory if vere had been no Manny Rat to be defeated?'" And the rat, in turn, recognizes his kinship with the wind-ups: "They were not unlike him, he realized for the first time; almost they were tin caricatures of himself."

The rat, it must be said, does have a final go at burning down the house, as if Hoban couldn't quite get comfortable with the reformation he had allowed to happen. Or perhaps he is making the point that what is once established in us as a way of being is not easily put aside. But this time the elephant saves the house and the rat from his folly. The rat is almost electrocuted, in the farcical manner of a cartoon and, as in a cartoon, he recovers. We have taken a step out of the dog-eat-dog world, have moved from tragedy to comedy, and Hoban is now protecting his creatures' welfare. Beneficence has the upper hand. The book closes with the same picture of the face of the tramp, looking in at the window of the repaired dollhouse, now a hotel welcoming "migrants yes," transcending the idea of territoriality and property that define the animal world and to a great degree our own. It is once again Christmas, and now we understand it more fully.

Hoban's book is undeniably harsh at times, initially unrelenting in its insistence on a Darwinian universe, where the animals matter of factly prey on each other and where the toys seem to be lower still. Some of the early incidents in the book are quite startling in their demonstration of cruelty. For example, as the mouse and his child are introduced to the world of the dump, they soon get a sample of Manny Rat in action. It is reported to him by one of his lackeys, Ralphie, that a one-eyed, three-legged donkey—one of the many disabled that populate this book—is complaining that he can't work because his spring is broken:

> "It's nothing," said the frightened donkey as he heard Manny Rat approach his blind side. "I've got plenty of work left in me. I was just feeling a little low—you know how it is."
>
> "You're not well," said Manny Rat. "I can see that easily. What you need is a long rest." He picked up a heavy rock, lifted it high, and brought it down on the donkey's back, splitting him open

like a walnut. "Put his works in the spare-parts can," said Manny Rat to Ralphie.

As the Rustins note, the scene evokes not only the gangster story, but also, on the darkest level, the world of slavery or the holocaust, moments of monstrous evil hardly relieved by the reminder that the donkey is finally only a toy. And there are other moments of breath-taking harshness as when two weasels, predators themselves, enjoy a meal of newly dead shrews and decide to settle down and make a home in the shrews' territory. Hoban writes, "They nuzzled each other affectionately as they ran, and their heads were so close together that when the horned owl swooped down out of the moonlight his talons pierced both brains at once."

But just as the book insists on the reality of what appears to be an unconquerable evil, it insists also on the existence of goodness and the potential for transformation, and is in total sympathy with the child's need for hope. The toys in this context represent a spirit that lies outside the cycle of predator and prey. They are easily exploited but, as the gaint snapping turtle discovers, they have the advantage of being inedible. Thus they demonstrate something else, a larger way of being that paradoxically derives from their obvious helplessness: they need each other, they need family—and they need someone to wind them up. They represent the interdependence of creatures in a nobler way than the Darwinian. They suggest how we may rise above the animal, get beyond the physical needs, understand something about our higher nature. Fred Inglis writes that "the best children's books reawaken our innocence," and that is the function of the toys here. They are outside the animal world, symbolizing human aspiration and caring.

The child's strength here is in his ability to arouse something noble in adults. Thus the story asserts that the perspective of innocence is as real and as powerful as the perspective of experience, that experience needs innocence, that the two can move toward each other in a way that strengthens both against evil. In Hoban's adult novel, **Turtle Diary,** he uses two large sea turtles to suggest the same idea as the two middle-aged protagonists, one a children's book writer, renew their own lives by stealing the turtles from the zoo and returning them to the sea. Like the child, the turtles have their right to freedom: "they can find something and they are not being allowed to do it," thinks Naeara H. "What more can you do to a creature, short of killing it, than prevent it from finding what it can find?"

For most of the book, the mouse and his child, joined at the hands, face and support each other; their fates are linked, their visions complementary; as the father looks back at the evil that pursues them, the child looks ahead to his dream of a family; when the father, defeated by the odds or by rusty springs or by the sense of his own ridiculous position in the universe, is ready to settle forever into the primal mud at the bottom of a pond, the child keeps him going. And the child's strength, in turn, derives in part from the closeness of his father. He is not alone in this story until he is ready to be.

One aspect of the book that has been criticized for going over the child reader's head (the Rustins) is Hoban's parody of modern intellectuals comfortable in their nihilism, exempting themselves from the effort to change anything yet still seeking recognition, respect, and self-advancement for their statements of the futility of it all. For children, there is a complex message: that adults can be self-absorbed and lazy, that they forget about the particular kind of powerlessness and bewilderment that children experience. The hopeful part of this particular fable is that some adults are awakened by the presence of the child from whatever cynical sleep they've slipped into and that the child can then get the support he needs for both to work together. As to the reader's missing the jokes, one could say the same of the Alice books, to take just one obvious example. There's enough broad humor in these episodes, it seems to me, so that at the very least something entertaining will come across to the child.

The first creatures to whom the windups turn for help in their dual quest to become self-winding and to find their family are an acting troupe called the "Caws of Art" led by two crows and a parrot. While the windups explain their plight, the crows see only their potential as actors. "Let's see what you can do," says the crow:

> The mouse and his child walked across the snow until they bumped into a twig and fell down. They lay there, the father's legs moving slowly back and forth while the company watched in silence. . . . "Can you help us?" asked the father. "We must keep moving on; we cannot stop here."
>
> "Pathos," said Crow. "Real pathos."
>
> "They've definitely got something," said Mrs. Crow, as she helped the mouse and his child to their feet. "The patter about the seal and the elephant needs working up, but the walk is good and the fall is terrific. . . ."

When they tell the crows that Manny Rat is pursuing them, the crow says complacently, in the manner of an adult denying a child's real fear, or a racist reasoning that slave owners wouldn't abuse their own property: "Oh, it can't be so bad as all that. . . . Why in the world would he destory windups? He fixes them up and sells them. And he's not the rat to destroy his own profits . . . ".

The troupe are getting ready to perform a play entitled "The Last Visible Dog," a parody of Beckett with three characters: a rabbit named Gretch who stands silently, "investing his silence with heavy meaning," and the two crows, playing Furza and Wurza, who sit in two cans and contemplate "A manyness of dogs. A moreness of dogs. A too-muchness of dogs . . . ". When they finally perform the play for the local animals, the animals are outraged. "That's what this play is," shouted an angry marten. "Too much of a dog!" And in the riot that ensues, they kill the rabbit. As he lies dead, "his life-blood staining the moonlit snow around him" the field mouse critic observes, "One so seldom gets anything really *complete* from these road companies."

The muskrat, to whom the windups next turn for help, is a logician engaged in "pure thought," spurning applications as beneath him, yet at the same time hungry to compete with the industrious beavers who are furiously felling trees and building dams outside his window. Thus, completely ignoring the windups' real need, he involves them in a ridiculous, tedious scheme to chop down a tree, having arrived at the formula—"Tooth k times Gnaw times Time times Tree equals Treefall" for chopping it down, and rigging up the windups to spend months walking around the tree, attached to an ax. They are once again going in circles, which can be seen as a setback but can also be a recognition of the seeming repetitiveness involved in our striving.

Later, through the vicious yet fortunate intervention of the everpresent rat, they are propelled forward again, this time into the lake where at its bottom they meet C. Serpentina, another "deep" thinker who tells them, "Here below the surface one studies the depths of TO BE, as manifest in AM, IS, and ARE." When they tell him they want to become self-winding so they can go someplace, he says,

> Go where? This mud being like other mud, we may assume that other mud is like this mud, which is to say that one place is all places and all places are one. Thus by staying here we are at the same time everywhere, and there is obviously no place to go. Winding, therefore, is futile."

And later: "there is no way out: Each way out of one situation necessarily being the way into another situation." Given this fact, the turtle has chosen to con-

template infinity as it is manifested on a can of Bonzo Dogfood, the label of which has an infinitely regressing picture of a dog carrying a can of dogfood—thus the title of the play, written by the turtle: "The Last Visible Dog." When they ask the turtle to help them get out of the pond, the turtle replies,

> "For shame! . . . Each of us, sunk in the mud however deep, must rise on the propulsion of his own thought. Each of us must journey through the dogs, beyond the dots, and to the truth, alone." Having said which, he dug himself into the mud, closed his gray eyes, and went to sleep.

The turtle is thus ostensibly no help, and the windups spend another long stretch of time stuck in the mud at the bottom of the pond. But the child, in fact, does what the turtle's speeches suggest he might: he discovers what is at the end of the last visible dog. Watching the label peel off the can of submerged dogfood he comes to the dots of the disintegrating picture and then finally arrives at the can itself wherein he sees his own reflection. "'There's nothing beyond the last visible dog but us,' he said. 'Nobody can get us out of here but us.'" The father is ready to concede to the turtle that "Nothing is the ultimate truth, and this mud is like all other mud," but the child is adamant: "I don't care if it is. . . . I want to get out of here." He has answered for himself one of those monumental questions children so easily ask, and with the help of another seemingly insignificant creature, a dragon fly in its larval stage—named Mudd, appropriately enough, he pulls his father and himself out.

At the point at which the windups leave the pond, the dragon fly metamorphoses into its adult form. As it does so, it splits open, believing it is dying. This kind of splitting apart occurs several times in the story, expressing Hoban's sense of growth as a kind of continual death of one self and emergence of another, assuring the reader that growth experiences may often seem devastating at the time. And in between there are long patches of dead time where nothing seems to be happening; but it is then that the child discovers that he has himself.

In an essay on Robin Hood as the figure of the outlaw self, a kind of chaotic and necessary life force—something not yet fixed and rigidified, something still idealistic—Hoban writes: "Books in nameless categories are needed—books for children and adults together, books that can stand in an existential nowhere and find a centre that will hold." Hoban is really not so far from Beckett or Sartre in his existentialism, but like other modern children's book writers whose books raise the same issues—St. Exupery, E. B. White, William Steig—he needs to emphasize that commitment, engagement, the choice to love another are what empower and enrich our lives. That is what the mouse child inspires and what he learns. He contemplates the nothingness of existence and finds himself. He also finds adults who are moved enough by his predicament to put aside their skepticism or their isolation and throw in their lot with his. The muskrat, the crows, the turtle, for all their culture, miss he main point. It is only when the spectacle is on the stage they've constructed, that they recognize that something worth watching is happening.

At various points during the book, Hoban directs our attention to the stars. It is predicted by the fortune-telling frog early in the book that the mouse and his child have broken the circle of their early condition and that a straight line of great force will emerge. He also predicts to the rat that "a dog shall rise; a rat shall fall." The dog is the dog star, Sirius, that rises over the dump. And the mouse's child is conscious of it very early in the story:

> Low above the horizon wheeled Orion the Hunter, and near the luminous scattering of the Milky Way, in the Great Dog constellation, blazed Sirius, the brightest star of all. Manny Rat liked dark nights best; he grimaced at the stars and turned away.
>
> Standing as he was on uneven ground, the child was tilted at such an angle that he too saw the Dog Star, beyond his father's shoulder. He had never looked up at the sky before. . . . At first the icy glitter of the far-off star was terrifying to him; he sensed a distance so vast as to reduce him to nothing. But as he looked and looked upon that steady burning he was comforted a little; if he was nothing he thought, so also was this rat and all the dump. His father's hands were firm upon his, and he resolved to see what next the great world offered.

One can do any number of things with the concept of nothingness, and what the child chooses to do is to assert his own equality with everyone else, to regard the infiniteness of space as an opportunity, a metaphor for possibility. Moreover, the dog star with its obvious link to the can of dog food that keeps appearing throughout the novel and with the animal world in general—it is *their* star, as it were—suggests transcendence. When, for example, the mouse child first asks the frog to be his uncle, the frog replies, "Ah! . . . I had better make no promises; I am at best an infirm vessel. Do not expect too much,"

and at the first sign of danger, he seems ready to save his own skin. But ultimately he chooses to risk his life for the windups; he achieves a larger sense of self.

At the point in the novel where the mouse and his child are close to their home, they are dropped from the sky by a bird whose help they had enlisted, and when they fall they split apart. Now they are separate, as children finally need to be separate, and it is only a matter of time until the child's tenacity infects the others and they are strong enough to defeat the rat. As the child transforms the adults around him, they become the motley family that he needs them to be, they find whatever heroism is latent in them, they take chances, they transcend their former existence. Hoban's point is that the child's vision, his youthful belief, is a vital part of any civilization. It is not the child's burden to transform the adult characters. But his presence moves them, as it should.

This story, then, for all its violence and satire, does seem to me to be expressing an archetypal viewpoint about children, telling them an important story. And its child has all the fragility, openness, neediness, imagination, resilience that we associate with innocence. There is certainly a leap of faith involved in accepting the ending of the story, given its grisly beginning. But perhaps that is just what Hoban is suggesting we need: otherwise we're stuck in the mud with the wise/foolish turtle, convinced that what we know is all there is to know, that the realm of possibility ends at the boundaries of our own isolated existence, worse, that conditions are what they are and it is hopeless to strive to change them. The benefit of this kind of story is that it tells up bluntly what is out there, but also affirms in the strongest of terms what is possible—even for the most seemingly insignificant of creatures. It allows us, in 200 pages or so, to live through the process of moving from adversity to prosperity, and gives us, children and adults, the courage to believe in the risks we need to take to shape our own lives and of the necessary interconnectedness of all of us in moving where we need to go. It also demonstrates how one goes about understanding what is set before us. The journey may bring us back to the same place, but only by leaving and returning do we come to know it.

Valerie Krips

SOURCE: "Mistaken Identity: Russell Hoban's *Mouse and His Child*," in *Children's Literature,* Vol. 21, 1993, pp. 92-100.

The longing for a past of innocence and wholeness haunts many a narrative, not least those that find themselves, either by design or accident, ranked among books for children. Such a longing often finds expression in an idealization of the child and of childhood itself. This idealization, which reaches back at least as far as Rousseau, still animates certain contemporary ideas of the child and provides a subtext both for fiction written for children and for criticism of that fiction. When criticism finds child protagonists to be the site of "hope" or "deep feelings," or when an interpretation credits a child with the ability to reshape or revitalize his or her world simply because he or she is a child, then we are almost certainly in the presence of idealized innocence.

Russell Hoban's *Mouse and His Child* appears apt for such a reading. Its theme, a child's longing for a home and family, is familiar enough, while its happy outcome echoes any number of stories in which an inventive and persistent youngster succeeds where adults have given up or have already failed. However, Hoban's text, rather than affirming familiar ideas, in fact reevaluates the status of children and childhood, rejecting ideas of wholeness and innocence in favor of struggle and empowerment. Interpreted in this way some of the apparent difficulties in the book, such as Hoban's allusions to existential philosophy and modernist writing, as well as his use of narrative repetition, are demystified. It is in these details that the book's careful reworking of the theme of childhood develops much of its argumentative power and generates the conditions in which a radical rethinking of the idea of an innocent child can be undertaken.

Hoban's book is not an easy read; nor is childhood an easy time as Hoban remembers and reimagines it. It is a time when the child is beginning to create a self, a me, and to find a place in the world into which (willy-nilly) she or he was so abruptly born. The challenges of self-creation are met by Hoban's protagonist with verve, dignity, and determination: the mouse-child's progress is something like a pilgrimage. Its ending is not easily thought of, however, within the conventional frameworks of reconciliation and affirmation that bring other childish success stories to a close: the self-hood the mouse-child achieves is the site of loss as well as gain, and the "happy ending" is shown to be provisional. Nor is Hoban's rethinking or reimagining of childhood limited to the characters and events in the book; as the reader imagines this text and creates its meanings, she or he must also struggle to become its reader, its partner in narrative. The reader's struggle interweaves with that of the mouse-child: both reader and character are trying to find a place—the reader in the book, the mouse-child in his world. What, then, is offered?

What sort of world, what sort of place, can the child reader find in Hoban's work?

No human child is represented directly in *The Mouse and His Child*. Instead, the narrative of the coming-into-being of a human subject takes as its protagonist a clockwork mouse-child, attached by his hands, apparently for ever, to his father. Born into the world in a toy shop, the mouse-child wants to know what and where he is. His father cannot help; they must "wait and see." The child hears the word "mama," and although he does not know what the word means, "he knew at once that he needed one badly." In an interesting reversal of a well-established psychoanalytic view of childhood development, Hoban's mouse-child encounters language, the system that will enable him to represent, and thus to some extent overcome, his primary loss of the mother before he is aware of his lack of her. So, in a moment of remarkable power and economy, the text indicates both that the mouse-child's existence begins with lack (expressed here as the absence of a mother) and that his attempts to remedy this will be made within language, a system that precedes him (he has language as soon as he is aware) and, to some extent, defines him (he knows what he wants within its frameworks: "He had no idea what a mama might be, but he knew at once that he needed one badly"). The narrative of human subjectivity brought into focus here suggests that human beings find and locate themselves in a world in which there is an imperfect match between what their unsocialized selves demand and what the social structures of their world will allow them to have or to be.

The mouse-child, who doesn't know who or what he is, who doesn't know what being someone means, sets out from the toy store in which he comes into being. Made of matched halves of tin held together with tags, he and his father have no place, society, or name to call their own. Their only family is each other. What the mice lack is summed up in their desire to be self-winding and to have their own territory. With a nice irony Hoban's metaphors point to the contradiction in their situation: mechanical, they seek to carve out a place for themselves within the plenitude of an organic world. As the text contemplates their mechanical state it questions oppositions which appear natural, asking what in the organic is mechanical, where in clockwork can we find a human face?

The mouse-child's entry into history as an independent subject is made in a meditative mode. Submerged at the bottom of a pond, he has been staring for months at a nearby tin can that once contained Bonzo dog food. The label on the Bonzo can shows a dog carrying a tray upon which rests another can showing a dog bearing a tray, and so on, until the dogs "become too small for the eye to follow." The toy mice encounter Bonzo cans soon after being sent out into the world. But then it was the father who faced a can filled with clockwork dumped after being torn from the bodies of toys worn out in the service of a tyrant rat called Manny. The mouse father knew only that he and his son must try to escape: "He could not look beyond that, and did not attempt to." When their positions are reversed and it is his son who faces a Bonzo can, the mouse-child also wants to escape, but to do so he contemplates infinity.

By the time the mouse-child confronts his own Bonzo can in the water an exploration of the relation of container to contained, one of the book's central themes, has found expression through the agency of the cans. In a literal reading, the cans are a double of the mice, who are also made of tin. Like the mice, the cans undergo a subtle transformation. Originally receptacles for dog food, then containers for clockwork, the cans next appear unlabeled, props in a Becket-like play entitled "The Last Visible Dog." They later provide armor for Manny Rat and a mirror for the mouse-child. Initially both can and label depend for their meaning upon something inside. The can that the mouse father contemplates when he stands immobile and helpless in Manny Rat's camp has meaning as a container of mechanical spare parts, similar to those he bears inside himself. By the time it is his son's turn to stand staring at a can, meaning has been transferred from an inner essence to an outer representation. What is important for the mouse-child is not what the can contains but what is on the outside: its label. This label, which shows the dog and its tray, contains all the meaning that the mouse-child will allocate to the can. For him it becomes both sign and symbol: the last visible dog.

One day the tattered label is gone, and the mouse child sees that beyond the last visible dog. "on the other side of nothing," as he puts it, is his own reflection. It is a moment doubly inscribed. On the other side of nothing lies the child himself, a knowing subject, recognized, in Kantian style, through the play of his own faculties. At the same time the child sees himself reflected in a mirror. He is also, then, in Lacan's psychoanalytic account, the narcissistic infant who, having until this moment experienced his body as fragmented, suddenly sees himself whole, apparently coordinated and in control. The infant then "jubilantly assumes" the plenitude seen, mistaking representation for reality. The development of the

Lacanian mirror-stage, we are told, "projects the formation of the individual into history"—that is, sets in motion the subject's activity of anticipation and retroaction, of placing her or himself within chronology (Lacan). For the human subject this is a moment, as one of Lacan's commentators puts it, of "high tragedy," since the unity the child sees is illusory. It is nevertheless one that will haunt his life forever as he attempts to recapture, to live up to, the idea of wholeness he once had. Gallop calls the mirror-stage a "lost paradise" and sees it in terms of a rewriting of the tragedy of Adam and Eve. It is an innocence short-lived indeed, both for the human child and for Hoban's young toy mouse.

The mouse and his child are surrounded by minor characters who provide a set of relations in which the toy mice can find a place. These relations are envisaged by the text in both an embodied form (the mice find a wife and mother, uncles, and a sister) and an abstract one. The necessary correlation of these concrete and abstract forms is achieved in a remarkable way through the bodies of the toy mice. The mice are broken and remade three times during the story. After their first awakening in a toy shop they are sold, broken, and thrown out in the rubbish. They are found by a tramp, the same person who witnessed their coming-into-being as they danced in circles in the toy shop window. He refashions them, ensuring that they will walk in a straight line instead of a circle. After their adventures in a wider world the toy mice return to the rubbish dump in the claws of a hawk who, discovering that they will make no sort of meal, drops them. The impact breaks them apart: never again will father and son be joined. But their individual bodies are remade, and "as his two halves came together the mouse child *returned to himself*" (emphasis added). In their final remaking, Manny Rat implants in the mice the clockwork mechanism that will make them self-winding. The mice then "return to consciousness": their evolution seems complete. It is this idea of a completeness that the text interrogates.

Hoban's analysis of identity takes account of misidentification, of the sort of mistake represented by the mouse-child's appropriation of the reflection he saw in the Bonzo can as his "self" rather than a representation of it, and of the assumption by father and son of a "self-winding" that is really nothing of the kind. Such mistakes are important enough to warrant an allegory of their own, one that warns against taking things literally.

The mouse and his child spend some time in the company of a muskrat, a scientist manque. The muskrat has a project: to fell a tree. His elaborate thinking on the subject finds eventual embodiment in a formula to do with teeth and gnawing—he has in mind the way beavers get wood for their lodges. The muskrat, who is lame, can only think when he walks. He sends the mice on circuits of his room; they walk so that he can think. The result is a formula: $XT = Tf$. The muskrat then harnesses the mice to an ax; they act as a motor, going round and round like clockwork. When the tree falls, the muskrat misidentifies the role his formula has played: he thinks the tree is felled because he produced the formula. The text makes it absolutely clear however, that the relation of formulated thought to result is not causal and that the muskrat's formula is neither an explanation of the tree's felling nor a recipe for repeating the effect.

The mice, in their turn, retrospectively "identify" what they achieve with what they set out to do. They reinterpret the past in the light of the present and identify events as grounded in an originary moment, as something they were "wound" to do. This interpretation depends, as the muskrat's formula shows, on an arbitrary allocation of significance or meaning to events that, rather than being linked in a causal chain, are contiguous and contingent. In other words, the relation of event to event is not one of "because" but rather of "then." It is an abstract point that has concrete results: the mouse and his child interpret a series of events as deterministic when in fact the relation they attribute to them is their own creation, part of the story they tell of their own subjectivities and their lives. In revealing this misidentification the text is at pains to illustrate the retrospective and retroactive nature of self-understanding, as well as the disjunctive nature of the self. It does so not only in the allegory of signification that is the muskrat's story but in its narrative of the bodies of the mice themselves.

Each time the mice are broken and remade their appearance changes, and importantly, while they are being reconstituted, the mice cease to exist. So what the mouse-child experiences as a return to himself is in fact a fresh beginning, a resurrection. Each time the mice come back to life they are changed beyond the possibility of a return to their former state, and each return marks a new stage in their life experiences and possibilities. A gap opens between the mice who existed before remaking and those who "return" to life. In a clear subversion of certain humanistic accounts of the subject that stress continuity and the presence of some essential and unchanging core, Hoban introduces the idea of a subject created by disjunction and discontinuity. Again, this idea of the subject can be usefully imagined within the interpretive frameworks of Lacanian theory.

The mirror-stage, which we imagine the mouse-child entering when he sees himself in the Bonzo can, marks the first step in a process that will impose a gap, or splitting, within the child's psyche, a splitting that results in the creation of the unconscious. This gap or disjuncture, according to Lacan, will never be closed. The child will henceforth experience itself as split between "me" and "I," where the child's "I" is a representation of self created in the mirror of language. The idea of wholeness, of a complete, unsplit entity that includes unproblematically both me and I is therefore, according to this account, a fantasy. Yet, it is a fantasy in which the subject continually indulges, imagining a past moment of primordial wholeness with the world—a wholeness that can, by association with ideas of anterior perfection, become a synonym for innocence. It is such a fantasy of subjectivity that this text interrogates: an interrogation made not only within the narrative itself, but in the position it makes available for its reader.

The story of the toy mouse and child is embedded within a narrative frame that describes the margins of the world of the toys and their friends. The frame finds expression in the tramp who utters the text's last words: "Be happy." The tramp, we recall, was first encountered in the book's opening paragraphs, and it was he who saw the mice come into the world. His return at the end of their story points to the possibility of return, of closure. But in narrative terms this is a promise unfulfilled. The omniscient and therefore authoritative narrator, who introduced the reader to the tramp as well as to the mice, leaves us looking over the tramp's shoulder into the toys' world without returning us to the toyshop window, where we looked at the tramp looking at the toys. The reader, in other words, is left in an immediate relationship with the tramp and given no final narratorial guidance about how to read him or what he says. Is "Be happy" a command or entreaty, a statement of fact or the invitation to another pilgrimage?

This ambiguous moment represents a revelation long deferred in the cause of narrative, of telling a story: just as the reader has been shown how the mice mistake the source of their "identity," so the source of the text's authority is reassessed. The frame that is the text, and the textual frames that were opened at the book's beginning, fail to close over the characters created, fail to shut them into a fictional world held in the eye of omniscience. Instead, as the text inhibits the expected closure, the narrator relinquishes his power, inviting the reader to engage even more closely with the book, whose ending now depends not on the past of the narrator but upon the reader's present. So as the mice are dependent upon their relations for self-winding and the tramp is dependent upon the narrator, the narrator, absent at the end, reveals that the novel's meanings are dependent upon the reader.

Hoban's book positions its reader as an active partner engaged in the creative work of the text. In recognition of the partnership required for reading, texts have been likened to musical scores. Just as a musician must bring creativity to bear upon a score, so, it is argued, must the reader invest creativity in the story. This model of reading is particularly useful when applied to a complex narrative with great possibilities for interpretation; in which, for example, the reader can apply intertextual knowledge (for example, recognize the reference to Becket) as well as respond to unusual turns in narrative technique, such as repetition within a realistic discourse, and such overt textual devices as framing. It is, of course, precisely the inclusion of such possibilities within Hoban's text that have led to discussions of its difficulty for younger readers. Yet although it remains unlikely that many younger readers will have enough intertextual knowledge to be able to take up the allusion to Becket, to read this reference as a shortcoming or as a sign of misunderstanding or miscoding at the site of the implied reader is to reconstruct the narrative in terms of an interpretive strategy that the text itself has investigated and found wanting.

The story of a subject who is perpetually becoming rather than being, who is in a process that ensures that he will continually reassess, rework, and reconstruct his own identity, will be told in conventional narrative form at its peril, particularly if its implied audience is of all readerships the least experienced. The way Hoban's book tackles the narrative difficulties and opportunities afforded by telling such a story has been outlined in part here. Many of the strategies discussed point to the text's desire to interrogate received ideas about what it means to be a person or subject, the role of history in that project, and the reader's role in textual interpretation. Intertextual references that may or may not be available to the child implied reader (or an adult reader, for that matter) form part of the text's web of cultural reference, which is at times overt and at times worked out in terms of metaphor and simile, as, say, the muskrat's story speaks indirectly about misidentification of cause and effect. Whereas the audience of the Becket-like play in which the toy mice become involved, however, was not "ready for this yet," according to the fieldmouse critic, it is clear that Hoban's implied reader is ready or, rather, is made ready by the struggle that is involved in creating a meaning and a place in this text.

Hoban's messages about the retrospective and retroactive nature of understanding demand that the reader continually reassess where she or he is in the text, both in terms of the narrative and of the subjectivities suggested within it. *The Mouse and His Child* is a modern allegory of subjectivity; the role of allegory is not to make each of its discrete utterances plain but rather to enable its audience to make meaning under its guidance. Hoban's writing and use of symbolism are certainly more self-conscious than is generally expected in contemporary children's novels. As we have seen, however, the text is at pains to avoid conventional reconstructions of its meanings; what may be thought of as heavy-handed can also be read as the text's determination to disrupt a too-simple reading of its representations, symbolic or narrative. The reader is forced to pick a way through the complications of Hoban's story, through difficult language, obscure symbolism, and the disruptions in the lifeline of the protagonist. How the reader strings this together to make a story is explained by the text in its own story of the mice, who are joined by their relations. This analogy, complex in the abstract, is lived by the reader in the concrete, who connects one element of the story to another by relating language, theme, and narrative to create meaning. That this work is not easy is in itself a warning against a natural or straightforward reading both of narrative and of symbol. Hoban's book makes the reader aware that knowing what or where one is and what it means to find a place in any story, including the one we tell about ourselves, is as difficult as it is necessary.

RIDDLEY WALKER (1981)

Marion Glastonbury

SOURCE: A review of *Riddley Walker,* in *The Times Educational Supplement,* No. 3358, October 31, 1980, p. 22.

Forlorn figures stumbling through mud; crows cawing; fires in the night. The scene recalls the pilgrimage of the Mouse and his Child, and can be located, thanks to the map provided, in post-nuclear Kent where the Isle of Thanet has been torn from Inland and the ruins of Canterbury Cathedral stand as a Power Ring at the Centre.

Twelve-year-old Riddley Walker inherits the role of "Tel-Man" or seer from his father, who dies demolishing machinery in the rubble of a byegone techonological age. Caught up in the rivalry of gang leaders, Riddley is led by a pack of wild dogs across ravaged terrain, where nomads compete for subsistence with foragers from fortified stockades. Literacy is almost extinct but the lore of the community is preserved and reenacted in travelling puppet shows. These are the property of the rural elite and tell the story of Eusa who was tricked by the diabolical Mr Clever into splitting the "'addom, the Little shining Man at the Hart of the wood".

Riddley's quest for the truth within this Foundation Myth, his efforts to discover both what the world is coming to and what it has lost, are prefigured in a children's song:

> Horny Boy rang Widder's Bel
> Stoal from his Father's Ham as wel
> Bernt his Arse and Forkt a Stoan
> Done it Over broak a boan.

You will notice that this conundrum incorporates the place names Herne Bay, Whitstable, Faversham, Folkestone and Dover. You will also, if you are paying proper attention, spot the symbolic significance of St Eustace, depicted in a fifteenth century wall painting, on his knees before a stag with the radiance of the crucifixion between its antlers. At a loss to interpret this Riddley asks: "Howd you say a guvner s a little t" and is told "St is short for Saint. Meaning this block Eustace he dintjus tern up he wer sent".

Riddley's sub-literate narration is initially painful for us fast readers and good spellers. But the heavy head-work required to decipher it is justified, in the long run by the unexpected meanings that seep through the cracks when conventional orthography is fractured. Hoban the master wordsmith has fun with the remnants of our administrative system: "loakel tharty; trufax from the Mincery; Pry Mincer and Wes Mincer; the fissonal seakerts; clinnicking and national healsing; and with the terminology of science: gallack seas; the sadellite bird; Saul and Peter (salt petre); party cools; vantsit theary trylnarrer; the woal chemistry and fizzics of it.

While engaged on this elaborate invention, Hoban wrote an introduction to Grimms Tales in which he expounded the ideas that the novel seeks to embody. Thus, domestic unity encompasses human existence. The myths that are in us prove our affinity with the cycle of the collective mind, illustrate the cosmic pattern, the infinite rhythm, of which our destinies are apart. "All of us have been, all of us are, everything".

Unfortunately, when a metaphysician casts his net over the whole of human consciousness, as it was in the beginning, is now and ever shall be, and returns

in triumph to share what he has caught, he appears to everyone but himself to be empty handed. The secret is incommunicable; the revelation void. So, in this creation, despite wonderful energy, an intricate structure, poignant characters, and a compelling landscape the message, of survival through renunciation "The onlyes power is no power", cannot escape bathos.

Among the archetypes that haunt this author's imagination is a ravening succubus, the rampant incarnation of female lust who turns up here as the legendary Aunty astride a red-eyed rat, destroying her helpless partners with "teef be twean her legs". The narrator insists that he didn't invent her: she came into his head, and, indeed, we have met her before as Aunt Fidget Wonkham Strong in the Captain Najork stories. Those of us whose dreams are happily free from castrating harpies often have to put up with them in literature, where, I'm bound to say, they look more like a grotesque figment of disordered male fantasy than an Eternal Truth. Russell Hoban's Aunty doubtless had her origins in infancy, but she is misplaced in picture books for children. She belongs, if anywhere, on a bomb site.

Publishers Weekly

SOURCE: A review of *Riddley Walker,* in *Publishers Weekly,* Vol. 219, No. 17, April 24, 1981, p. 70.

In a year distinguished by original and exciting new fiction, **Riddley Walker** is still something very special. We do not know quite where we are as it opens. A youth is having his "naming day" at the age of 12. He kills a wild boar. He is taken into the tribe of men. But this is not a caveman society. It is all that is left of Britain, near what is left of the ruins of Cantebury. As Riddley Walker sets out on his quest we follow with increasing fascination. He is a dreamer, a questioner; he wants to know what has happened, what was in the past, what may lie ahead. He makes up rhymes; he becomes an interpreter of the handed-down and garbled Punch and Judy shows by which the authorities manipulate and tantalize the survivors. For this *is* a world of survivors in which we find ourselves. In a largely male society (the women seem to exist only for breeding purposes) Riddley and some of his friends begin to piece together dim remembrances of the past as handed down legends. They move toward a future that involves the discovery of gunpowder. What is marvelous about Hoban's creation is the effect it has, how it draws us into an atavistic dreamworld to which we intensely and instinctively relate—and it does so in a language all its own that soon becomes ours.

Julia M. Ehresmann

SOURCE: A review of *Riddley Walker,* in *Booklist,* Vol. 77, No. 18, May 15, 1981, p. 1213.

"We aint as good as them befor us. Weve come way way down from what they ben time back way back. May be it wer the barms what done it poysening the lan or when they made a hoal in what they callit the O Zoan." In this deeply imagined work, the narrator, Riddley Walker, gallantly struggles to figure out the koans of soul and the purpose of life. His is a feral existence in a post-Armageddon world. A vague collective memory of civilization (as we know it) taunts him and his fellow hunters, with the legend of St. Eustace, martyr saint of hunters, plaguing his bafflements. Part of the spell—a sort of black enchantment—lies in Hoban's specially concocted, purely phonetic language; to be comprehended it almost needs to be read aloud, yet its childlike freshness constantly overturns assumptions of meaning. Although the story line (and therefore the interest) peaks too early, *Riddley Walker* is an eerily powerful, bewitching book.

A. Alvarez

SOURCE: A review of *Riddley Walker,* in *The New York Review of Books,* Vol. 28, November 19, 1981, pp. 16-17.

> I reckon I got to light out for the Territory ahead of the rest, because Aunt Sally she's going to adopt me and sivilize me, and I can't stand it. I been there before.

Since Russell Hoban is an American—now settled in London—who has also written books for children, it seems natural enough that *Riddley Walker* should pick up where *Huckleberry Finn* leaves off:

> On my naming day when I come 12 I gone front spear and kilt a wyld boar he parbly ben the las wyld pig on the Bundel Downs any how there hadnt ben none for a long time befor him nor I aint looking to see none agen. He dint make the groun shake nor nothing like that when he come on to my spear he wernt all that big plus he look-it poorly. He done the reqwyrt he ternt and stood and clattert his teef and made his rush and there we wer then. Him on 1 end of the spear kicking his life out and me on the other end watching him dy. I said, "Your tern now my tern later."

The voices are very similar, at once young and knowing, innocent and disillusioned, the voices of survivors fumbling with a language they have never been formally taught.

Hoban, however, has transformed Huck in a minatory contemporary way, much as William Golding, in *Lord of the Flies,* rewrote *The Swiss Family Robinson.* Riddley Walker is Huck Finn after an atomic disaster, mourning his jaunty self, stripped barer than he could ever have imagined, with no Judge Thatcher or Aunt Sally waiting in the wings to rescue him. He is also a creature of a distant and desolate future, though just how distant he himself does not know. The story he tells takes place at least two and a half millennia from now in the year 2347 OC, "which means Our Count." When OC began is not certain. The date 1997 has been found cut into stone and in some unspecified year after that came Bad Time, the nuclear holocaust which poisoned the land and "made a hoal in what they callit the O Zoan":

> Then every thing gone black. Nothing only nite for years on end. Playgs kilt peopl off and naminals nor there wernt nothing growit in the groun. Man and woman starveling in the blackness looking for the dog to eat it and the dog out looking to eat them the same. Finely there come day agen then nite and day regler but never like it ben befor. Day beart crookit out of crookit nite and sickness in them boath.

It was years before the survivors were organized enough to begin counting again. But dates no longer matter; they are known only to the men from "the Mincery"; Riddley and his like reckon by moons, which are adequate enough when full manhood begins at twelve and few people survive their thirties.

Since Bad Time they have evolved only as far as the Iron Age. They live in fenced settlements, farming in a primitive way, foraging, digging in the muck for fragments of pre-holocaust metal, under orders from men from "the Mincery." Off in the woods are the "chard coal berners" who pursue their mystery in isolation, and hidden away in forbidden areas are the "Eusa folk," a tribe of deformed monsters descended from the original nuclear victims and made to interbreed to preserve the last scattered imprints of a now vanished science:

> Faces like bad dreams. Faces with 3 eyes and no nose. Faces with 1 eye and a snout. Humps on backs and hans growing out of sholders wer the leas of it.

Their leader is ritually beheaded every twelve years, like a sacrificial ruler from *The Golden Bough.* His title is the "Ardship of Cambry."

"Ardship of Cambry": Archbishop of Canterbury. Hoban has created his own language for Riddley, as Twain did for Huck and Jim. But instead of dialect and misspelling, Riddley Walker writes down words as he apprehends them: "Fork Stoan" for Folkestone, "Do It Over" for Dover, "Sams Itch" for Sandwich, "Horny Boy" for Herne Bay, "Fathers Ham" for Faversham. What he writes reflects the brute physical world he inhabits. His rotted-down Mummerzet-Cockney resonates with older words, handed down and distorted because no longer understood: "gallack seas," "nebyul eye"; the medicine man goes "clinnicking and national healfing"; the titles of the two leaders are "Pry Mincer" and "Wes Mincer." There are also echoes of lost scientific jargon: "programmit" for planned, "what I pirntow from my innermost datter" (what I print out from my innermost data) for what I secretly believe.

Hoban has said **Riddley Walker** took him five and a half years and went through fourteen drafts. It is easy to see why. The book is an artistic *tour de force* in every possible way and the language he has invented for it reflects with extraordinary precision both the narrator's understanding and the desolate landscape he moves through: contaminated ruins, bleak encampments and marauding packs of killer dogs where there was once the fertile, cozy, affluent county of Kent, "the garden of England."

The basic plot of the novel concerns the rediscovery of gunpowder. A dead sailor is washed ashore carrying two bags of mysterious "yellerboy stoan." These turn out to be sulphur, the missing "gready mint" which, when combined with "Saul & Peter" and "chard coal," produce the "1 Littl 1," the first explosion from which nuclear fission, "the 1 Big 1," may eventually emerge. But at some point during the fourteen rewrites Hoban seems to have become bored with a simple story and gone, instead, after the harder artistic choices implicit in the language and world and sensibility he has created.

He has said the book was sparked off by a fifteenth-century wall painting in Canterbury cathedral, *The Legend of St. Eustace,* in one section of which the saint kneels before "a stag, between whose antlers appears, on a cross of radiant light, the figure of the crucified Saviour." By Riddley's time the painting has gone, like the wall it adorned, but the description remains, written down in what is, for him, barely decipherable twentieth-century English. It is one of the few written fragments surviving from before the Bad Time and over the centuries it has been combined with garbled memories of the atom bomb. In their myth, the radiant image of Christ becomes "the Littl Shyning Man the Addom," torn in two by Eusa, who

then must suffer for his crime down the ages. And will continue to suffer until he gets his "head back"—that is, until both he and the "Littl Shyning Man" are whole again.

Riddley's discovery is that redemption will not come through "clevverness"—reinventing gunpowder—but through getting back in touch with the secret resources of the mind, "the 1st knowing" which humans once shared with the animals:

> The man and the woman seen the fire shyning in the dogs eyes. The man throwit meat to the dog and the dog come in to them by the fire. Brung its eyes in out of the nite then they all lookit at the nite to gether. The man and the woman seen the nite in the dogs eyes and thats when they got the 1st knowing of it. They knowit the nite the same as the dog knowit.

The book ends with Riddley setting out with a little band of followers to preach this gospel of "1st knowing" through the riddles of a Punch and Judy show.

Russell Hoban has transformed what might have been just another fantasy of the future into a novel of exceptional depth and originality. He has created a hero who, deprived of all other references, reads the world through his instincts, his imagination, his unconscious, without losing touch with his own reality or becoming either more or less than he is: a twelve-year-old who has become a man and is fighting to maintain his clarity and independence in a devastated land. He is also an orphan haunted by an unspecified sense of grief; the Iron Age he lives in is made even more desolate by the vague memory of what has been lost and will never be recovered, a civilization that had "boats in the air and picters on the wind." He survives by looking at what is in front of him and seeing it as though for the first time:

> Looking at that black leaders eyes they myndit me of gulls eyes. Eyes so fearce they cudnt even be sorry for the naminal they wer in. Like a gull I seen 1 time with a broakin wing and Dad kilt it. Them yeller eyes staret scareless to the las. They jus happent to be in the gull but they dint care nothing for it.

Again and again, Hoban transforms Riddley's broken dialect into prose which reflects every tremor of his fierce and unanswerable world. It is an extraordinary achievement, comparable, in its way, to *Huckleberry Finn* itself.

Dennis Butts

SOURCE: *"Riddley Walker* and the Novels of Russell Hoban," in *Use of English,* Vol. 33, No. 3, Summer, 1982, pp. 20-7.

One cannot say that Russell Hoban's work is neglected. His adult novels are usually received sympathetically, and he is, of course, extremely well-known as a children's writer. Few families with young children will not have made some contact with his delightful series about Frances the Badger or about Tom and Captain Najork, to give two examples. But for all the apparent interest in Hoban's adult novels at the time of publication, they are, I believe, in danger of being underestimated by those who care about serious fiction at a time when the contemporary novel seems to be going through one of its periodic doldrums. The publication of Hoban's fourth and most recent novel, ***Riddley Walker*** provides an opportunity to offer some kind of interim judgement.

The first thing to say is that Hoban is an extraordinarily fresh and original kind of writer, whose books are racy, readable, and full of jokes, and who, in a period dominated by tired realism or overblown symbolism, isn't afraid to take risks and innovate, with stories about children's clockwork toys, or men in pursuit of imaginary lions, or a science-fiction account of England in the year 4344 A.D. He is a man who has read T. S. Eliot and Freud, and knows about architecture and animals, and Bach and Mozart, but always wears his learning lightly, and reads more like Woody Allen than the deeply serious novelist I think he is.

The humour is omnipresent but deceptive, for whether Hoban is writing in semi-realistic vein as in ***The Turtle Diary*** or quasi-allegorically as in ***Kleinzeit,*** his humour is nearly always based upon a response to the incongruities of life, which, for the most part, is seen as a bleak and destructive business. Hoban's world is one of human violence and natural disasters, in which men and women cause each other pain deliberately and accidentally, in which lovers betray each other, and parents and children give each other grief, in which the environment is being destroyed, and in which there is much cruelty, both human and animal. Even the apparently innocent landscape of the children's book, ***The Mouse and his Child,*** becomes a bloody battleground, as two weasels find when they come across armies of warring shrews:

> 'I know you'll like this place,' said the female to her mate. 'I came here the other night, and it's really a darling little hollow. There's always something good. Mmm! Smell those shrews!' . . .
>
> The weasels flowed like hungry shadows down into the hollow, and once among the shrews struck right and left with lightning swiftness, smiling pleasantly with the blood of both armies dripping

from their jaws. Not a single shrew escaped. When the weasels had satisfied their thirst for blood they bounded away, leaving behind them heaps of tiny corpses scattered on the snow.

> 'This is a *nice* territory,' said the female. 'It's the nicest we've had yet. I'd kind of like to settle down here for a while'.
>
> 'It's not bad', said her mate. 'Not a bad little territory at all. I could see us making a home here.' They nuzzled each other affectionately as they ran, and their heads were so close together that when the horned owl swooped down out of the moonlight his talons pierced both brains at once.
>
> 'My land', wheezed the owl as he rose heavily with the weasels' limp bodies dangling from his claws. 'Two at once! The missus won't believe me when I tell her. Yessiree!' he chuckled, 'as territories go, this is a mighty good one!'

Hoban's world then, for all its jokes and humour, with its headline-shrieking bluejay and its crows' theatre, the Caws of Art, is a dark one—too dark for children, say some readers of ***The Mouse and his Child.*** But Hoban's vision is not wholly pessimistic. His main characters usually survive and even achieve a kind of happy ending in the earlier books, though Hoban's vision has gradually darkened, and by the time Riddley Walker tries to wrest some kind of meaning from his journeys there is not much light at the end of his tunnel.

Yet all this has been present in Hoban's work from the beginning, and if ***Riddley Walker*** represents, as I believe it does, a major development in Hoban's career, there is no doubt that many of its metaphysical and literary concerns have been present from the earliest children's books. Thus ***The Mouse and his Child*** uses the picaresque form to portray the adventures of a clockwork toy-mouse and his son as they wander through modern civilisation and come close to disaster and failure many times. They meet a variety of toys and animals including a prophetic Frog, an aristocratic toy Elephant, and a philosophical Muskrat; they constantly need rewinding and founder for a time in a muddy lake. Above all they are pursued by Manny Rat, a ruthless and ingenious predator, who can be viciously cruel, for example, to a broken-down toy-donkey:

> 'You're not well', said Manny Rat. 'I can see that easily. What you need is a long rest.' He picked up a heavy rock, lifted it high, and brought it down on the donkey's back, splitting him open like a walnut. 'Put his works in the spare-parts can', said Manny Rat to Ralphie.

As this powerful and disturbing narrative develops, however, we become aware that the pilgrimage of the Mouse and his Child is centred upon three very human needs, the desire for territory or a home of their own, the desire to become self-winding and independent, and finally the desire to discover meaning in life, to know what is beyond 'The Last Visible Dog' they see mentioned everywhere. Despite the violence of Hoban's vision, the Mouse and his Child do find happiness at the end of the story—in the apparent security of a renovated Doll's House, where they are surrounded by many friends including the apparently reformed Manny Rat. But they have also learned that 'there's nothing on the other side of nothing but us'. The lucky coin with which the Mouse knocked Manny's teeth out is no more than that, a lucky coin.

The Lion of Boaz-Jachin and Jachin-Boaz develops these themes in ways which are curiously both more recognisable and yet more elusive. The setting is clearly contemporary, modern Israel perhaps, and despite the unfamiliarity of the two protagonists' names, the father and son are clearly recognisable contemporary figures, the father having come to a middle-aged crisis of marriage and identity, the son to an uncertainty of vocation and of confused family relationships. What gives the book its bite, however, is that both father and son leave home, they being perfectly normal human beings in every other respect, in search of lions which no longer exist, but which now begin mysteriously re-appearing to the father and then finally to the son. The book contains a variety of episode and invention characteristic of all Hoban's work, while the comedy, mostly achieved through minor characters' ability to perceive or not perceive the lion which haunts Boaz-Jachin, is still pretty effective, if not as copious as elsewhere.

What gives the book its extraordinary power and intensity, of course, is the richly evocative figure of the lion itself, and what he means for father and son. There is a curious, but, in its context, quite natural episode in *The Mouse and his Child* when the crashing down of a tree throws the toy-heroes into the middle of a muddy pond, where, being immobile, they are apparently doomed to stay forever. Yet it is here, in fact, that the mouse-child has his revelation about personal responsibility, and begins that movement towards self-development which is to lead to their ultimate salvation. Hoban is an admirer of Freud, as we know—he has written eloquently about this in '**Thoughts on Being and Writing**' (1975)—and it is a part of his belief that we all need moments when we are aware of time undisturbed by birth or death or death in order to sustain ourselves in the Present. We need an awareness of the Past, the primal Past Hoban might say, in order to live today, but

we must not be overwhelmed by that Past and ignore the Present. The Mouse's immersion in the mud is one way of suggesting that return to the primal Past, and Boaz-Jachin's encounters with the lion is another way of dramatising an experience with Time. Boaz-Jachin is haunted by memories of his broken relationship with his father and with his wife, as in his profession as a map-maker he earns a living recording the Past. But, as his son says, 'A map is the dead body of where you've been'. The lion, then, who might also be interpreted as something like God or Energy in Blake's sense of that word, can most clearly be identified as something like Being itself, as something which has to be accepted wholeheartedly if father and son are to forgive each other and be reconciled: 'The lion was. Ignorant of non-existence he existed . . . He ate meat or he did not eat meat, was seen or unseen, known when there was knowledge of him, unknown when there was not. But always he was'.

Kleinzeit deals with similar themes in a similar engaging mixture of realism and allegory. The hero—his name means 'hero' he says, but it really means 'small time'—falls ill and struggles against the oppressions of death and hospitalisation in our contemporary National Health world, where part of his difficulty arises from the gloom of fellow-patients with names like Schwarzgang, and encounters with witty and wisecracking allegorical figures like Word, Hospital and God Himself.

An unsuccessful husband and unemployed advertising man, Kleinzeit longs for success as human being and as writer, but, like Orpheus, in one version of the legend, has to be led into the Underworld and back again before he can regain his health. This episode is entirely typical of Hoban's rich mixture of symbolism, mythology and witty realism, Kleinzeit's descent into the Underground (or Hades) being accompanied by a Eurydice figure, who is also his hospital Sister and with whom he earns 1.27 by playing the glockenspiel to commuters, as at the same time, by learning to accept the painful memories of his past life he begins to cure the ailment which lies at the heart of his psychic illness. And yet there is no sense of strain about the whole of this extraordinary book, only the fluency and poise of a really gifted writer.

Turtle Diary also deals with problems of loneliness and alienation, though in a somewhat schematic way. I think, as if Hoban was only marking time before making another creative leap in his work. William G., a divorced bookseller, and Neaera H., a children's writer, finding themselves dissatisfied with their lives, come together in middle age not, as the realistic novelists would lead us to expect, in order to copulate, but in a mad conspiracy to kidnap the sea turtles from London Zoo, and liberate them into the ocean at Polperro. The grace and instinctive skill of the turtles, the way they swim 1,400 miles to lay their eggs and breed on Ascension Island, obviously has something of the symbolic meaning of Boaz-Jachin's lion. More particularly, their ability to immerse themselves in the green deeps of the ocean helps William and Neaera to come to terms with their own painful memories of the Past and to accept the Present more positively. At the end of the novel Neaera is beginning a relationship with George Fairbairn, and William is on friendlier terms with his eccentric neighbours, in fact.

Even so, while the book is the most accessible of all Hoban's novels so far, there is a certain sense of slightness and self-consciousness about it all. The comedy of William's neighbours works well enough, but the nature of the protagonists' dilemma is perhaps too familiar by now, and the symbolism of the turtles too predictable to be as effective as the lion earlier.

It is wonderfully witty in places, of course, like all Hoban's books, as when Neaera turns on the people who write books about people who write books for children. This is almost on a par with the jokes in **The Mouse and his Child** where the philosophical Muskrat discovers the Law that 'Why Times How Equals What', for example, or the many word-jokes in **Kleinzeit,** which are not unlike the black humour of *Crow* or *Mercian Hymns*. There is the continuing fascination with animals—badgers, mice, rats, lions, now sea turtles; and there is the perennial fascination with maps and journeys, from the toyshop to the Doll's House, from the Mediterranean to the Thames, from London Zoo to Polperro and back. And finally there is the same preoccupation with loneliness and alienation, with the problems of survival and fulfilment in an increasingly hostile world, and the need for human integration to be achieved by the symbiosis of the Past and the Present, often realised by scenes of immersion and regeneration.

All Hoban's books have engaged with these matters to a greater or lesser degree, and to some extent, therefore, **Turtle Diary** was predictable in its conception, and disappointingly self-conscious in its execution. Perhaps Hoban himself felt something of this. There was a gap of five years before **Riddley Walker** appeared, and its intensity and ferocity come as something of a revelation, even if the links with the earlier books are quite clear.

The increasing bleakness of Hoban's vision is the first thing that strikes the reader of his latest novel. The world is much more violent, and human happiness is much rarer to purchase. The England of 4,000 A.D., long since devastated by a nuclear explosion towards the end of the twentieth century, has fallen back into barbarism. It is a country divided into fenced regions which are patrolled by hevvys with bows and arrows, and roamed by wild dogs and occasional boars. The towns are 'dead', and farming is extremely primitive. Organised government has virtually disappeared—there is constant fighting and feuding between rival gangs—and even language itself has disintegrated so much that it is often quite difficult to follow the story told by Riddley which begins: 'On my naming day when I come 12 I to gone front spear and kilt a wyld boar he parbly ben the las wyld pig on the Bundel Downs . . .'

Interest in and jokes about language have always been one of Hoban's major interests—he even used Word as a character in **Kleinzeit**—and part of the energy of **Riddley Walker** comes from the extraordinary way Hoban sets himself to reveal the collapse of our civilisation, with all its complex culture and technology, through the limited linguistic resources of his teenage hero. It is not so much the vocabulary that is different, as in *The Clockwork Orange,* as that the spelling and syntax have become much more phonetic, and that there has also been a general impoverishment. There just don't seem enough words to describe exactly what has happened. Place-names, too, have been reduced or confused by folk-etymologising, and well-known resorts such as Herne Bay and Folkstone have been transformed to Horny Boy and Fork Stoan.

The most amazing example of the way in which Riddley and his contemporaries have misinterpreted their civilisation is their attribution of their nuclear disaster at the end of the twentieth century to the workings of Eusa at Cambry (or Canterbury); and it is part of the book's energy and humour to show how this misinterpretation happened, and how the explanation of the disaster by reference to a fourteenth-century wall-painting in Canterbury Cathedral is both hopelessly erroneous, and yet, paradoxically, at the heart of the tragedy which Hoban is describing.

The story is essentially about the journeys and discoveries of twelve-year-old Riddley as he makes his way through the revaged Kent countryside between Burnt Arse, Fork Stoan and Cambry, and back again. He witnesses the death of his father, the torture of sixteen-year-old Belnot Phist, and finally the bloody conflict between Abel Goodparley and Ernie Orfing, Pry Mincer and Wes Mincer respectively.

Riddley's father was a Connexion Man, that is he walked the roads and explained things to people, and when Riddley succeeds his father it is obvious that he too is possessed with instinctive gifts which afflict him with visions and with the ability to interpret them. (Hoban's interest in Shamanism appeared as early as the fortune-telling Frog in *The Mouse and his Child,* and he quotes Eliade's work directly in *Turtle Diary.*) So Riddley's travels, another of Hoban's recurring motifs, gradually help him to understand what was the nature of the nuclear disaster which devastated England in 1997, and which, in folk-memory, is explained in terms of the legend of St. Eustace as portrayed on the wall-painting in Canterbury Cathedral. And if this muddling confusion, this attempt to explain a historical event by using erroneous evidence, is one of Hoban's greatest jokes in the novel, through it Riddley's visit to the Cathedral helps him to see how evil men are still eager to rediscover the source of the explosive power that could wreak such havoc, in order to use it again, against each other. Thus, within the space of a few horrendous days the twelve year-old illiterate comes to perceive, first that 'The Onlyes Power is no Power', and ultimately that 'It's the not sturglin for Power that's where the Power is'.

Most important of all, and what is the radical development in Hoban's latest novel, is the way Riddley comes to feel not only the need for continuity between the Past (with its wonderful and not necessarily destructive technology) and the Present—a familiar Hoban theme—but concern at the loss of a power which he finds in Canterbury, and which is other than technological. The revelation comes to him as he wanders around the magnificently-described crypt of the Cathedral: 'It were a wud of stoan it were stoan trees growing unner the groun. . . . Stoan branches unner a stoan sky . . . ' And then the intuition comes:

> Becaws it come to me what it wer wed los. It come to me what it wer as made them peopl time back way back bettern us. It were knowing how to put ther selfs with the Power of the wood be come stoan. The wood in the stoan and the stoan in the wood. The idear in the hart of every thing.
>
> If you cud even jus only put your self right with 1 stoan. Thats what kep saying its self in my head. If you cud even jus only put your self right with 1 stoan youwd be moving with the girt dants of

the every thing the 1 Big 1 the Master Chaynjis. Then you mit have the res of it or not. The boats in the air or what ever. What ever you done wud-be right.

> Them as made Canterbury musve put ther selfs right. Only it dint stay right did it. Somers in be twean them stoan trees and the Power Ring they musve put ther selfs wrong. Now we dint have the 1 nor the other. Them stoan trees were stanning in the dead town only wed los the knowing of how to put our selfs with the Power of the wood and Power in the stoan. Plus wed los the knowing whatd woosht the Power roun the Power Ring.

It is a tremendous discovery, and, given the circumstances of Riddley's upbringing, a moving one. This assertion of the existence of a non-human, almost numinous, power in the Past, and the continuing human need for it in the Present also seems to me qualitatively different from the need for connections between Past and Present which Hoban has urged in his previous novels.

There is no really happy ending to Riddley's story, just this incoherent, eloquent, struggling attempt to express the inexpressible by an illiterate young boy. Then he goes off with a suspiciously reformed Ernie Orfing—by now Goodparley is killed in an explosion, too—to wander the countryside as Punch and Judy showmen, and to assert the existence of non-material values as best they can.

Punch and Judy shows are not great Art, but their crudely-comic puppet-plays offer some sort of spectacle, like but different from the world of daily experience. They may even remind us of what Mircea Eliade has written of the effect of shamanic spectacles, all tricks and magical feats, in the kinds of primitive society that Riddley's England has become. 'They stimulate and feed the imagination', Eliade says, 'demolish the barriers between dream and present reality, open windows upon worlds inhabited by the gods, the dead, and the spirits'.

Riddley Walker is an exciting, difficult, disturbing book, and, though it has clear connections with earlier novels, its ambitious scope marks it as an important stage in Russell Hoban's development. It is demanding in more senses than one, not easy to get at or assent to without some effort. But it is a real book, and Hoban is a real writer. I would like to end by quoting something he himself said about writing: 'There are aspects of life that require not simply to be communicated as experience, but to be made into art, and if some writers won't do it then others will'.

Janet Julian

SOURCE: A review of *Riddley Walker,* in *Kliatt Young Adult Paperback Book Guide,* Vol. 17, No. 1, January, 1983, p. 18.

Riddley Walker is a remarkable book, compared by critics to *Huckleberry Finn, A Clockwork Orange, Lord of the Flies,* and Tolkien's novels.

The story is set in England in the distant future after a nuclear holocaust. That civilization is back in the Dark Ages is immediately apparent from the language, a peculiar combination of computer lingo, phonetic spelling (smoak = smoke, agen = again, ther = their, noatis = notice), old words half-remembered (parbly = probably, persoon = pretty soon, Sams Itch = Sandwich, Horny Boy = Herne Bay), religious/political terms (Prime Mincer and the Ardship of Cambry), and new coinages such as doing the juicies (sex) and getting ready for Aunty (dying).

The plot concerns Riddley Walker, newly orphaned at 12, who goes on a quest. During his travels he becomes the pawn of several power groups who are trying to rediscover the scientific secrets of airplanes, computers, and nuclear energy. In the end they reinvent gunpowder, starting mankind on another cycle of progress and destruction. Riddley, however, eschews violence, having found that THE ONLYES POWER IS NO POWER. He becomes a member of a traveling Punch and Judy show, maintaining a failed and morally bankrupt culture, but at least doing no one harm.

The end is the weakest part of the novel. Like Twain at the end of *Huckleberry Finn,* Hoban doesn't quite know what to do with Riddley. This letdown at the end of an adventure story is common enough, but not inevitable. Even so, the novel is well worth reading. Twice.

Natalie Maynor and Richard F. Patteson

SOURCE: "Language as Protagonist in Russell Hoban's *Riddley Walker,*" in *Critique,* Vol. 26, No. 1, Fall, 1984, pp. 18-25.

Russell Hoban's *Riddley Walker* is perhaps the most sophisticated work of fiction ever to speculate about man's future on earth and the implications of a potentially destructive technology. Like Walter Miller in *A Canticle for Leibowitz,* Hoban hypothesizes that many centuries after a nuclear cataclysm, there will be major changes not only in habits of living, political structures, and religious beliefs, but also in language. Unlike Miller, however, Hoban constructs that future language; indeed, his entire novel is written in a much-altered version of English, by a first-person narrator, shortly after the rediscovery of writing. The novel's prose style evokes simultaneously medieval usage, the patois of pre-school children, fragments of cybernetic jargon handed down from our own era, and essays written for remedial English classes. But the style of *Riddley Walker* is also distinctive, consistent, and almost hypnotic in its poetry. It is, finally, what lingers longest in the reader's imagination.

Riddley Walker is more than a stylistic *tour de force,* however. Although Hoban is reluctant to label his novel science fiction, it does in fact stand squarely in the post-apocalyptic tradition of SF. As in many works of this sub-genre, the plot involves a society in which most of the past's technological wonders have been lost. Again as in *A Canticle for Leibowitz,* a period of hostility toward science has been followed, at long last, by a period of renaissance, in which certain elements of society attempt to dig out the secrets of the past. *Riddley Walker* is set primarily in what is now Kent, and the autocratic rulers of that little world are determined to retrieve the "clevverness" of "time back way back." To this end teams of men dig up machines long buried, while the authorities try to determine what those devices are and how they were used. Two of the digers are Riddley Walker, the novel's narrator, and his father. After the elder Walker is killed, Riddley embarks on a series of adventures culminating in the rediscovery of gunpowder and Riddley's determination to have no part of such destructive "clevverness."

Throughout the narrative there are scattered interpolated stories that combine folklore with bits of half-remembered history. The most important of these is "The Eusa Story," which contains an allegorical explanation of the holocaust, the "1 Big 1." To "fyn that 1 Big 1," Eusa was told by "Mr. Clevver" that he first "mus fyn the Littl Shynin Man the Addom." As the story goes on, it becomes apparent that the tale of the Bad Time has been confused with the legend of St. Eustace, a painting of which can be found in Canterbury Cathedral. In the painting, the crucified Christ appears to Eustace between the horns of a stag; in the Eusa story, "the Littl Shynin Man the Addom" appears. Eusa can obviously be identified with Eustace. He may be, as well, the U.S.A. (with its nuclear arsenal at this very moment poised to destroy the planet), or even St. Augustine of Canterbury. Eusa is said to have been the "1st Ardship of Cambry"; hence, EUSA may have been extracted from *augusT*-IN*e.* More interesting is the association of "the Littl

Shynin Man the Addom" with Christ (the second Adam). The deity becomes a kind of power or force within the entire universe. Metaphysical truth may well be concealed within the webs of historical error.

As even this brief outline makes evident, the political and religious implications of *Riddley Walker* are complicated and fascinating. But it is nevertheless the novel's language that remains its most arresting feature. From the first sentence ("On my naming day when I come 12 I gone front spear and kilt a wyld boar he parbly ben the last wyld pig on the Bundel Downs any how there hadnt ben none for a long time befor him nor I aint looking to see none agen") to the last ("Stil I wunt have no other track"), *Riddley Walker* is composed in a strange dialect that reflects Hoban's perception of English culture two thousand years after the holocaust. As Hoban has pointed out, "it really would have been bizarre for them to be speaking in BBC English in the world they lived in" (interview). Although Hoban claims that the language in *Riddley Walker* does not follow a consciously devised system, he does believe that the dialect contributes significantly—that it is, in fact, "one of the protagonists of the story" (interview).

Life for Riddley and his associates is primitive. Their society is still in the process of moving through the usual stages of cultural evolution, having progressed from foraging to farming, with hints of a new technological age to follow. Yet vestiges of past civilization remain—Punch and Pooty (Judy), pot smoking, guards at the edges of Widders Dump Form (farm) enjoying "a nice cup of tea," titles like "Pry Mincer" (prime minister).

The language contributes to this picture of primitive life, with its violations of today's standard English, its heavy reliance upon the concrete, and its child-like phonology and syntax. And the language also contains vestiges of the past, of the technological age that preceded the holocaust.

Most linguists agree that there is no such thing as a "primitive" language or dialect, that there is no correlation between the language used by a group of people and the cultural evolution of that group (except, of course, in lexicon). Nevertheless, Hoban has managed in *Riddley Walker* to suggest a primitive culture by distorting the English language, or, as Hoban puts it, by attempting to "corrupt the language in what seemed to be a natural and believable way" (interview). Although no language or dialect is inherently better or worse than another, most educated societies have standard codes adhered to in writing and

in educated speech. Standard English ("BBC English," "Edited American English") does exist as such a code. By creating a dialect that deviates sharply from standard English, Hoban has portrayed a society in *Riddley Walker* that most readers will view as lacking education and sophistication.

Deviations from standard English are evident in virtually every sentence of the book, although many are simply deviations in spelling and punctuation, obvious manifestations of the loss of writing. Many other deviations, however, are clearly patterned on so-called errors made by uneducated speakers in twentieth-century England and America: "He dint make the groun shake nor nothing like that when he come on to my spear he wernt all that big plus he lookit poorly."

Hoban's picture of a primitive society is strengthened by the literal nature of the characters' thoughts and descriptions. Such literalness suggests both the mental processes of children and the speech habits of lower classes in society. The place names, for example, have been changed in much the same way that a child might construe the name Chicago as The Car Go. Herne Bay becomes Horny Boy, Dover becomes Do It Over, Godmersham becomes Good Mercy, Faversham becomes Fathers Ham, to name only a few. Many of the characters' names also suggest a kind of literalness: Fister Crunchman, Rightway Flinter, Follery Digman. There is, moreover, a child-like simplicity in such designations as Bad Time (the holocaust) and Littl Shynin Man (the atom). The bits of knowledge remaining about life before Bad Time are also couched in literal terms, suggesting that more general terms are no longer available: "boats in the air" (airplanes, spacecraft) and "picters on the wind" (television). This absence of abstract concepts is suggestive of the "restrictive code" defined by Basil Bernstein. When using restrictive code, the speaker relies heavily on context, on tangible objects around him, a reliance that has been associated with lower socio-economic levels in English and American society.

A sense of frustration results from the inability of Riddley and his people to discuss the abstract. Early in the book Lorna says, "You know Riddley theres some thing in us it dont have no name." Later, in talking about the "1st knowing," she says, "its what there aint no words for." Naming seems to be a sort of obsession throughout the book, beginning with Riddley's "naming day" in the first sentence. After his father's death, Riddley starts climbing on "that girt big black thing . . . looking to see if it had a name stampt in or raisd up in the iron of it," and, unsuccessful in this search, he says, "My dad ben kilt by some thing I dont even know the name of aint that a larf." Much later, looking at the black dog that had led him to the Ardship of Cambry, Riddley thinks:

> That dog, I wunnert what the name of him myt be. Which I dont mean name like my name is Riddley or formers myt call a pair of oxen Jet & Fire. I knowit he dint have no name the other dogs callt him by nor I wunt try to put no name to him no moren Iwd take it on me to name the litening or the sea. I thot his name myt be a fraction of the nite or the numbers of the black wind or the hisper of the rain.

Riddley is also interested in place names. His questioning of Wayman Footling about Hagmans Il, formerly Hogmans Kil, is not unlike the inquisitiveness of a young child. Later, pronouncing the word Canterbury, the old name for Cambry, Riddley thinks, "the new name werent no good it wer a stanning in the mud name it dint have no zanting to it."

The phonology and syntax in *Riddley Walker* are at times suggestive of early stages in language acquisition of a child. Jill and Peter de Villiers list seven phonological processes common in young children. Six of these processes are recurrent in the language in *Riddley Walker:* (1) reduction of consonant clusters (*dint for didn't, hisper* for *whisper*), (2) deletion of final consonants (*leas* for *least, trubba* for *trouble*), (3) devoicing of final consonants (*behynt* for *behind, ternt* for *turned*), (4) substitution of stops for fricatives (*diffrents* for *difference*), (5) fronting of consonants (*teef* for *teeth*), (6) phonological assimilation (*minim* for *minute*).

In addition, the syntax in *Riddley Walker* suggests that of a child going through the necessary experimentation in mastering sentence construction: case errors ("Dad and me we jus come off forage rota and back on jobbing that day,"), double negatives ("That dont mean nothing tho"), tense errors ("When Dad ben a live I all ways ben there when he done the wotcher"), grammatical conversions ("Arnge flames upping in the dark and liting all the faces roun").

The unusual language of *Riddley Walker* is obviously the first thing a reader notices. But it is not merely a decorative twist. The language is, as Hoban has said, a protagonist in the book in its intrinsic relationship with theme and setting. Not only does the language suggest early stages in language acquisition, but it also contains echoes of earlier stages of

English: *childer* (children), *lorn* (forlorn), *afeart* (afraid). These echoes are strengthened by thematic parallels with medieval literature. In spite of Hoban's denial of any Chaucerian echoes (interview), there are obvious hints of Chaucer in *Riddley Walker,* not the least of which is the pilgrimage Riddley makes to Cambry. In addition, there are parallels with Old English literature. The words spoken at Durster Potter's funeral, for example, are reminiscent of Wiglaf's speech after Beowulf's death:

> That nite we done the berning and thinet hans and the res of it. Wording roun and it come to Jobber Easting he ben a frend of Dursters he said, "Bye bye Durster theres some of uswl keap it in memberment how you got dog kilt nor no l to lif a han for you." He ben in that same rota when Durster got kilt. He come roun that ben with the others when Durster ben all ready dead so he knowit there bint no l only me there to lif a han. Nex wordit Coxin Shoaring a nother frend of Dursters. He said, "Bye bye Durster theres others may be shudve give you crowd on that long road you gone."

The attempt to place guilt on Riddley for not helping Durster is similar to Wiglaf's derision of the thanes who hid while Beowulf and Wiglaf fought the dragon:

> The people's king had indeed no cause to boast of his comrades in fight. . . . The few protectors pressed round the prince, when the time came upon him. Now the receiving of jewels, giving of swords, all the splendid heritage, and life's necessities, shall pass away from your race. Every man of the people shall wander, stripped of his rights in the land, when chieftains from afar hear of your flight, the inglorious act. Death is better for all earls than a shameful life.

And Riddley's feelings of loss and his thoughts about life before Bad Time are not unlike the *ubi sunt* theme so prevalent in Old English literature:

> You try to think of how it musve soundit when the Power Ring ben there and working not just crummelt stannings and a ditch. . . . Old foller in the air the after blip and fading of what ben.
>
> • • • • •
>
> How cud any l not want to get that syning Power back from time back way back? How cud any l not want to be like them what had boats in the air and picters on the wind? How cud any l not want to see them shyning weals terning?

Riddley's grief may be compared with the well-known lamentation in "The Wanderer":

Whither has gone the horse? Whither has gone the man? Whither has gone the giver of treasure? Whither has gone the place of feasting? Where are the joys of hall: Alas, the bright cup! Alas, the warrior in his corslet! Alas, the glory of the prince! How that time has passed away, has grown dark under the shadow of night, as if it had never been!

Frustration is a strong theme throughout the book. As Hoban says, "these people are frustrated and embittered, and they feel inferior and full of despair at ever being able to get the boats in the air and the pictures on the wind and all that" (interview). Linguistic problems contribute to this frustration: failure to find names for the abstract, failure to translate accurately the Legend of St. Eustace, failure to understand fully the bits and pieces of scientific knowledge remaining from before Bad Time. It is this last failure, of course, that has saved them so far from repeating the catastrophe of Bad Time. But the prospect of future success in their self-destruction is strong. And language once again is clearly a protagonist.

Remnants of technical jargon keep the reader aware of the cause of the "fall." And the piecing together of these remnants will ultimately cause the next holocaust. Computer jargon appears throughout the book: *input, progam* (program), *randem* (random), *Puter Leat* (Computer Elite), *pul datter* (pool data), *pirntowt* (printout). Examples abound: "Hes inputting all kynds of knowing out of his head in to the box," "wunnering what that black leader had in mynd becaws he cernly had some progam he wernt just randeming," "It wer lik I jus ben progammit to go there and get him out," "He wer so much out of Luck his numbers all gone random and his progam come unstuck," "he cudnt put out no mor input," "We ben the Puter Leat we had the woal worl in our mynd we progammit pas the sarvering gallack seas we progammit the girt dants of the every thing," "We pult datter and we pirntowt".

A more frightening kind of jargon has also been passed down to Riddley's generation—that of gun powder, bombs, and nuclear power. Granser demonstrates the mixing of gunpowder for Riddley and Goodparley:

He wer pounding the yellerboy stoan to a fine powder (sulphur). Then he done the same with some chard coal (charcoal). Done it with a boal and pounder. He had the Saul & Peter (saltpeter) all ready that wer kirstels like salt. He took littl measuring and measuring out yellerboy and chard coal and Saul & Peter. Mixing them all to gether then and me watching.

Erny Orfing speaks of bombs:

Wel the hevvys took the yellerboy stoan and the other gready mints and they done that mixter like the dyer tol them which they packt it in a iron pot and they had what they callit a fews which the dyer give them it wer a bit of chemistery roap.

And Orfing speaks of nuclear power:

This other tho youve got to have the Nos. of the mixter then youve got to fynd your gready mints then youve got to do the mixing of the mixter and youve got to say the fissional seakerts of the act.

There are, of course, hints of the dangers in nuclear power. Early in the book, in telling "Why the Dog Wont Show Its Eyes," Lorna tells of Bad Time:

They had the Nos. of the sun and moon all fractiont out and fed to the machines. They said, "Wewl put all the Nos. in to 1 Big 1 and that wil be the No. of the Master Chaynjis." They bill the Power Ring thats where you see the Ring Ditch now. They put in the 1 Big 1 and woosht it roun there come a flash of lite then bigger nor the woal worl and it ternt the nite to day. Then every thing gone black. Nothing only nite for years on end. Playgs kilt peopl off and naminals nor there wernt nothing growit in the groun. Man and woman starveling in the blackness looking for the dog to eat it and the dog out looking to eat them the same. Finely there come day agen then nite and day regler but never like it ben befor. Day beartht crookit out of crookit nite and sickness in them boath.

Bad Time is also described in "The Eusa Story." And Riddley expresses misgivings on several occasions. For instance, when Goodparley urges Riddley to watch Ganser make the gunpowder, Riddley says, "I dont want to know." But the race to rediscover "fissional seakerts" continues, often with familiar arguments:

Ice that Powers luce itwl fetch itwl work itwl move itwl happen every 1 whats in its road. *Some* 1s got to happen it. If it aint me or you it cud wel be come 1 wersen us cudnt it. So I wer on for letting it happen.

The discussions that these people have about "yellerboy stoan," "chard coal," "Saul & Peter," "mixing of the mixter," and "fissional seakerts" evoke in the reader's mind images of children playing with chemistry sets. And the strange dialect contributes significantly to these images. The language spoken by the characters is obviously an important feature in every good work of fiction. It is not possible to imagine

Huckleberry Finn, for instance, or *The Catcher in the Rye* (to cite two books that **Riddley Walker** resembles in certain respects) in a "neutral" linguistic context. And when the cultural milieu is radically different from any that has actually existed, the linguistic representation of experience becomes paramount. In **Riddley Walker,** moreover, language both conceals the civilization of "time back way back" and contains keys to its rediscovery, for the language of the novel is, like all living tongues, as much a record of the past as it is of the present.

David Dowling

SOURCE: "Russell Hoban's *Riddley Walker*: Doing the Connections," in *Critique,* Vol. 29, No. 3, Spring, 1988, pp. 179-87.

In an interview in 1984, Russell Hoban said, "Rational thinking is not enough to get us through what we have to get through." All his novels, and a good many of his children's stories, have been about the nonrational or numinous forces hovering around human lives. Always he has been devoted to portraying what it is like to live from day to day, moment to moment, and his problem has been to reconcile this naturalistic gift with his urge to edify and illuminate. His voice therefore hovers between the playful and profound, between the patent wish fulfillment of fairy stories and the shamanistic preaching of parable. This tension has led him more and more to experiment with the reading process, but not until **Riddley Walker** (1980) did he find the perfect balance. In that novel, he broadened his previously domestic canvas to the sweep of a post-disaster wasteland. He simultaneously reinvented the English language, questioned the whole status of storytelling in a society, and evoked in the reader that anguished conflict between despair and belief that makes it the perfect companion text for our age—for getting through what we have to get through.

It may seem a long way from the children's story **Bedtime for Frances** (1963) to **Riddley Walker,** but Hoban has always endorsed the child's viewpoint for its anarchic challenge to adult ways of doing things. In his third novel **Turtle Diary** (1975), the narrator criticises the way we impose upon children our way of doing things by saying: "This is a world, this is what it does, one lives like this." Perhaps one day there will come a generation that will reject a hand-me-down world, saying, "This is not a world, this is nothing, there's no way to live at all." Hoban's characters are always working their way towards an un-

cluttered view of things, based on the essential vision of existential freedom—even in his children's books. In **The Mouse and his Child** (1967), the child, after confronting a *mise en abyme* in the form of a series of infinitely receding pictures on a can of dog food, concludes: "There's nothing beyond the last visible dog but us. Nobody can get us out of here but us."

In his early novels, Hoban portrays adults working through to this child's view of the world. The transition from "children's" to "adult" fiction was easy for Hoban, since he never believed in such distinct genres. He has called for "books in nameless categories . . . books for children and adults together." While it was in fact "adult" events like gall bladder surgery and the break-up of his marriage that inspired these first novels, the Hobanian hero characteristically fights free of grown-up fears and blinkers, to see the world with a child's innocence. The next step is typically either a wise resignation or a daring revolutionary gesture.

The Lion of Boaz-Jachin and Jachin-Boaz (1973) was based on the wall carvings of King Assurbanipal in his Sumerian palace at Nineveh. There the hunted lion seems to embrace the hunter's spear willingly; so in the novel, antagonism becomes symbiosis. A father deserts his son and upsets the normal fictional pattern by setting out himself on the road to enlightenment. The jealous son eventually confronts him, and father and son discover that in embracing the lion, which is between them, they are embracing each other: "The lion, father, son, sent his roar." The novel retells the Oedipal conflict in Biblical terms: the lion does not lie down with the lamb, but is seen as a kind of necessary violent relationship or "Holy Ghost" between Father and Son, uniting them by defining them. It is a vision of violence dear to Hoban's heart.

The necessity of accepting oneself and one's predicament is also the theme of **Kleinzeit** (1974). Here an advertising executive comes to terms with a serious illness by tuning in to the world about him as it speaks to him. In this wildly animated universe, Hospitals, Undergrounds, and glockenspiels all have advice to give, and the hero's task is to discriminate the static from useful information. But Word himself is hopelessly allusive and elusive, and much of the novel is an attack on coded meanings of any kind.

Set up as a detective novel, **Kleinzeit** eventually frustrates the hero's and reader's sleuthing and even the notion of "narrative" itself. The most useful advice seems to come from Hospital, who re-interprets the

Greek myth of Orpheus into a circular tale, based on man's eternal restlessness. Kleinzeit, who learns that his name means "small time" and not "Hero" (as he thought) reconciles himself with morality by accepting his limitations, faults, and physical decay.

As if conscious of the preacher in him, Hoban gave his next novel, *Turtle Diary* (1975), a downbeat ending. The central characters William and Neaera, who come together to free some turtles from an aquarium into the ocean, may find themselves, but they do not stay together. Although reader and writer (Hoban called the two heroes the "yin and yang of me") desire closure, we are left only with a revolutionary gesture. The turtles are free, but we do not know whether William and Neaera have freed themselves.

Throughout Hoban's novels runs a biological theme of our rightful place in nature. *The Lion* . . . alludes to Joseph Wood Krutch's *The Great Chain of Being* (1956), an eminently Hobanian meditation on biology. For Hoban, as for Krutch, all is related and all is wonderfully unique: whatever the robin is saying in his song, "it fills his universe with joy." That pantheism is extended in *Turtle Diary* by reference to Mercias Eliade's *Shamanism: Archaic Techniques of Ecstasy* (1970). According to Eliade, the "secret shamanic tongue" of the spiritual world is often animal. The shaman can assume animal form in order to keep evil powers at bay and reveal to the tribe the continuity of biological life.

Increasingly, Hoban was led to ponder his own role as novelist/shaman. He regards himself as a "mystic . . . someone who thinks that the things that really matter are not those that admit of rational explanation, and whose thinking does not go along rational lines, but is extra-rational or super-rational." As in William Blake, the child, the seer, and the animal come together in Hoban's writing; and as in Blake (or Walt Whitman), the problem of voice becomes acute. In what language can one "sing the universe"?

Hoban rejects the solution of Whitman and the later Blake, the orotund note of Old Testament bombast. He prefers small voices: in *The Lion* . . . , the son hitches a ride with a lorry driver and they converse for some time, each in their own language, and to their mutual satisfaction; in *Kleinzeit,* the tiny voices of the yellow paper or glockenspiel counterpoint the bullying rhetoric of Hospital and Word. Even in *Turtle Diary,* Hoban resisted concocting a turtle language, leaving us only with the often bland diary entries of the two protagonists. The novelist himself is silent.

At this point in his development, Hoban was looking for a way to speak to us in tongues, like the shaman, without forsaking everyday human dilemmas or the everyday English language that are the stuff of his, and most, fiction.

In *Riddley Walker,* he found a way. Five and a half years in the making (according to Hoban he went back to page one at least 14 times), the novel is set in South East England at least two thousand years after the "Bad Times" or nuclear holocaust of 1997. It is a recognisable world, but the lines of communication have been tangled by time and by radiation. The distinction between matter and spirit is blurred. As Krutch says in *The Great Chain of Being:*

> The matter that disintegrated privately over the American desert and publicly over Japan ceased in those instants to occupy space. At those instants, therefore, the meaning of the term "materialist" disappeared as completely as the disintegrated atoms themselves.

Living in the environs of the wrecked nuclear power station of Cambry (Canterbury), Hoban's motley characters are victims of generations of radiation sickness. They have mutated into a new level of human being. Their extended sensory awareness is abetted by drugs, and by the constant danger of attack by other tribes or by wild dogs. In their extremity, they are looking for spiritual answers and are ready to adopt new messiahs who might interpret their riddles.

At the same time, of course, they live in a harsh, materialistic world. This is reflected not so much in the familiar wasteland, but in the verbal landscape inhabited by readers and inhabitants alike. Their language is the only intricate structure linking Riddley's tribe, however tenuously, with the dim past, with us. (Hoban may have got the idea for this mutated language from Jack London's 1910 story "The Scarlet Plague," which also features a wise man called Granser in the ruins; but London's wise man is a professor of literature, while Hoban's mixes up gunpowder.) While several characters ransack language for its half-life of scientific knowledge, much of the language itself reflects the devolution of post-disaster society into brutishness. Even on the surface, words tell us where we have been. As Riddley puts it, places "become the name of what happent in them." For example, Horny Boy (Herne Bay), Monkeys Whoar Town (Monks Horton), Do It Over (Dover), and Nelly's Bum (Nailbourne) suggest brutish sexuality; Sel Out (Selindge), River Sour (River Stour), and How (instead of Wye!) suggest cynicism and bewilderment; Widders Bel (Whitstable), Crippel the Fark (Capel le Ferne), Sams Itch (Sandwich), Dog Et (Dargate), and Dunk Your Arse (Dungenesse) suggest a brutish struggle for survival. The characters' names also tenaciously name their world and its qualities, in forceful dactyls or trochees, e.g., "Fister Crunchman, Belgrave Moaters." Even Riddley's rudimentary spelling and grammar seem to reflect a rough language too crude for what the characters want it to perform.

However, Riddley's vocabulary also has a vitality and richness that make his prose dance on the page. Hoban uses at least ten literary devices to create a "nukespeak" invigorated by Cockney English:

-phonetic spellings (lykens/lichens, sepert/separate, pernear/pretty near)
-homonyms or puns ('it seams', minim/minute, fizzics/physics)
-metathesis (sturgling, parper, arnge)
-childish pronunciation (nindicater, amminals)
-onomatopoeia (the dogs 'grooling and smarling')
-archaic English (withering, glimmers)
-computer jargon (puter leat/computer elite, to input and printout)
-contemporary slang (just so much cow shit, pressurs little barset, pissing down, thats a larf innit)
-Clockwork Orange-ese (vackt, zanting).

So vivid is this language that when we encounter our present-day English in the brochure about St. Eustace, it seems lifeless by comparison.

As in *Kleinzeit,* the central characters of *Riddley Walker* are searching language for a key. They dig in it, as fiercely as they dig in the muddy ground to unearth relics of the nuclear age, bits of machinery that are frustrating traces of a former order and power. At the outset of the novel, the eponymous hero's father is killed while unearthing one of these machines, and Riddley clambers over it searching for some kind of name or "on-with," as he puts it. He is also given the father's mantle of formal interpreter or "telman" for the tribe. While he ponders the meaning of new and old stories, other more pragmatic characters are searching language for the embedded formula for gunpowder, which will give them a different kind of power.

Riddley faces a deconstructionist nightmare. He already lives in a deconstructed world where no position is privileged, no code to decoding apparent. Apparent key words like "aulder/older, hart/heart, wood/would" and "saviour/saver/savor" replicate and mutate dizzyingly even as he contemplates them. Everything and nothing seems to be connected; Riddley's task as "connection man" is both easy and impossible. The task of supplying useful stories or meanings to the tribe is constantly threatened, on the one hand by the scheming pragmatists who simply want a weapon of power, and on the other hand by the wise woman Lorna Elswint who tells Riddley at the beginning of his quest that "theres something in us it dont have no name," some unspeakable mystery at the heart of things. To put it in current terminology, Riddley has to choose between an endless regression of traces and the metaphysics of presence.

In *Riddley Walker,* Hoban has dramatised his own creative dilemma: whether to present transparent fables of discovery and harmony, or to scatter opaque clues that gesture but leave the mysterious heart of things intact. The *mise en scene* of the wasteland usefully gets rid of all the "dreck" of everyday life, in the same way that Beckett's lonely road imbues a boot with all kinds of symbolic possibility; it foregrounds the predicament of human consciousness, alone on a hostile planet. At the same time, radioactivity ties the human beings to the physical setting and the irresistible "call" of the power station at Cambry. Similarly, the language emerges out of the ashes of our own tongue, bare and brutal; and yet it beckons with its traces of connection and coherence.

For Riddley, single words hold no possibility; in combination, a pattern may emerge. The typical syntax of Riddley's narration, comprising two sentences run together with double negatives, also suggests the difficulty of making headway at the level of single words or definitions. No, the answer lies in stories; Riddley challenges the vertigo of unresolvable equations by listening to and telling stories—finally, by becoming the hero of the one he is telling us.

It is Riddley's conception of "story," rather than the machinations of the various gunpowder-seekers, which forms the true narrative line. He begins, "On my naming day . . . " but, like Tristham Shandy, is lured into telling a story first. It is not until chapter two that he sounds the Melvillean note—"Walker is my name and I am the same"—having gained confidence by beginning not with definitions (as *Moby Dick* does) but with narrative. Lorna laments, "That's what happens to people on the way down from what they ben. The storys go"; but there are plenty of stories to go on with, and Riddley tells us nine during the course of the novel:

"Hart of the Wud"
"Why the dog wont show its eyes"
"The Eusa Story"
"The Lissener and the other voyce out of the worl"
"The Bloak as got on top of Aunty"
"The legend of St Eustace"
"Punch and Judy"

"Stoan"
"Punch and Judy"

The sequence is significant. The first three stories are, or claim to be, parables of our fall from grace through the invention of nuclear power. In each story, a parent takes life from a child. The fourth story is Lissener's and is devoted to the importance, not of making connections or telling, but rather of listening, sustaining the world by careful attention to it instead of acting upon it and threatening it: we must "lissen everything back."

The centre story is offered as an explanation of the name "Hagmans II" (Hinxhill)—a man is seduced by the inescapable aunty, Death, in disguise. But this story is undercut by the revelation that the name Hagmans II may be a corruption of "Hogmans Kil," whose source is a completely different story about a woman who killed her brutish husband there.

In the first half of **Riddley Walker,** then, we see a progressive reduction in the power of stories to provide meaningful answers to the people's predicament, until the *aporia* of Hagmans II opens up a bewildering world of hearsay and etymological obscurity.

The second half of the novel reinstates story, but in a performative context. Goodparley decodes the Eustace story for his own ends, seeing secreted in the life of the saint the chemical formula for gunpowder. The Punch and Judy show is a dramatic performance, which is followed by Riddley's own lyrical outpouring in "Stoan." The only non-narrative piece, it is an expression of his feeling of oneness with the universe brought on by his proximity to both the cathedral and the power station at Cambry. Finally we are left with Riddley's own performance of the Punch and Judy show, which does not simply present Punch's violence but engages in dialogue with the audience.

Riddley, then, proceeds from being a listener to being a teller to being a performer, in a steady evolution from a faith in received meaning and encoded connection, to an acceptance of mystery and an extreme epistemological scepticism. From the pragmatic Goodparley who tells Riddley that words "move things you know theywl do things. Theywl fetch," he moves to Lissener's position. Lissener warned him early on that "storys jus what ever it is and thats what storys are"; interpretation is all.

Hoban the storyteller also practises what he preaches. In the last sections of the novel as the narrative speeds up and Riddley, like the reader, looks for alle-gorical twists in the storyline, Hoban deliberately frustrates the reader. Young Riddley, his father dead and the omens propitious, has set off on his walk towards the "riddle" of his Sphinx. His destination is Cambry, ancient centre of pilgrimage, and centre also of Hoban's carefully plotted, wheeling narrative, which takes the characters around the outer ring of Cambry's fields of force. Already won over to the beauties of technology by seeing the shining machines at Fork Stoan (Folkestone), Riddley feels the life force as he stands in the centre of the ruined nuclear power station at Cambry. He connects where before man had divided, and he sings his "Stoan" song.

From here he moves into his second experience in the crypt of Canterbury Cathedral. He stands among the "stone trees" of the fan-vaulted architecture, gazing at the sculpture of the Green Man with vines growing out of its mouth, and becomes converted to pantheism. As it is epitomised in the pun of "wood" with "would," Riddley acknowledges the "wanting to be" of all life.

An epiphanic conclusion? Not quite, for the Eusa story, central myth of the tribe, describes the wanting to *know* of the scientist who wrenches apart the atom (the little Shining Man). There are sinister sides, after all, to both the power station and the cathedral, something over-reaching and phallic in nuclear missiles and towering spires. Lissener, the "Ardship of Cambry" who advocated a mystical passivity, is blown up by the newly invented gunpowder, along with Goodparley. Riddley's final companion is not Lissener but Orfing, who moralises, "Its the in side has got to do the moving." The finger of Riddley inside Punch seems to be preaching a new doctrine of potentiality: "The onlyes Power is no Power."

How can we square this eventual vagueness, this retreat away from moral *dicta* into performance and caution, with Riddley's previous exultation at human beings' technological and spiritual power? We can do so as readers only by a radical revision of our normal response to fiction.

Riddley, despite appearing to be sublimely indifferent to the desperate quest of others all around him for the formula for gunpowder, actually plays a major role in the plot that leads to its discovery. It is his wanderings that eventually bring together the three deadly ingredients of charcoal, sulphur, and saltpetre in the scientist Granser's crucible. Yet his pilgrimage is not so much towards Cambry as away from the site of his father's death. He stumbles upon his moments of enlightenment and stumbles away from them again. Denied the expected narrative denoument, the reader begins to wonder whether *Riddley Walker* is not so much a detective thriller as an absurdist play in the tradition of *King Lear* and *Waiting for Godot.*

Echoes of Shakespeare's play can in fact be heard throughout, from the desolate English countryside to the cruelly blinded (Lissener), and blinding leading to insight (Goodparley). Riddley's conclusion shimmers before the mind, now profound, now banal, like Shakespeare's "Ripeness is all":

> May be there aint no such thing as a Big 1 or a Littl 1 its just only all 1 and you see what diffrent things you see in the chaynjing lites of the diffrent times of the girt dants of the every thing.

Hoban lives in a post-fission world, and in *Riddley Walker,* he uses the basic facts of nuclear physics brilliantly to suggest the fallacy of all answers. Riddley sees his world driven by dualities: Pry Mincer and Wes Mincer, Lissener and Granser, power plant and cathedral. Like most thinking people in his land, he is searching for a synthesis of these dualities (all the characters have a pattern of three stripes gashed across their chests suggesting this quest). For the materialists, the goal is the third ingredient of gunpowder; even Riddley wants to resolve the duality of power plant and cathedral into pure "power." Like the scientist Eusa in the central myth of the tribe, he wants to stop at the "aul or nuthing No." The reader, too, expects ambiguity to be resolved by the narrative drive to a conclusion.

We have seen that such a conclusion never comes. Hoban's epigraph from the Gospel of Thomas suggests why. It describes the "lion" side of human beings, and we recall the resolution of *The Lion* . . . But Hoban prefers Thomas to John who, in his Book of Revelation, has the "Lion of the tribe of Judah" loosen the seals of the Book (*Rev.* 5:5) and decides who will be saved (the lambs) and who will be damned (the lions). There is no apocalypse in Hoban, no division of the world into "aul" and "nothing," saved and damned—only the yearning for one. Knowledge brings both glory *and* damnation; during his epiphany Riddley describes the tree: "Pick the appel off it. Hang the man on it." Hoban, and finally Riddley, refuse to enter the fiction of resolution into an answer, a third term. Instead of synthesis, we have, to the last, oscillation. History repeats itself, Riddley's people rediscover gunpowder, and Hoban refuses to say whether this is for good or ill.

Jacques Derrida has called Einsteinian physics the essence of variability: "finally, the concept of the game." *Riddley Walker* is truly a nuclear novel, turning the act of reading itself into a game, a demonstration of the uncertainty principle. As Penelope Lively said in her 1981 review of the novel, "The matter of the book—for all its chilling supposition—is the human mind." The urge is strong in Hoban to create a hero/listener, a shaman figure who will show us how to "do it," how to get in touch with the "girt dants" of everything. In *Riddley Walker,* he resists that impulse when it is at its strongest, for in the end Riddley simply walks away, having presented his play, his "riddle." We the audience are left with a Punch and Judy show, a demonstration of man at his most brutal, acquisitive and warlike. Where we go from there is up to the individual. Neither resigned nor revolutionary, Riddley shows us his "fit-up," the skull of Punch beneath the skin, and asks us to decide for ourselves what kind of power we want to live our lives by.

The amazing, unique verbal texture of *Riddley Walker* reminds us that wherever we walk we will inhabit text, with its information, its ambiguities, its recipes for disaster, but above all its energy and invention. That text faithfully captures Hoban's feelings about living now: "Horror at the actuality of history and joy in being alive and conscious go together quite naturally." Having teased us with answers, it leaves us with the question that Thomas asked of Christ:

> But when you have become two, what will you do?

Leonard Mustazza

SOURCE: "Myth and History in Russell Hoban's *Riddley Walker,*" in *Critique,* Vol. 31, No. 1, Fall, 1989, pp. 17-26.

In his review of Russell Hoban's *Riddley Walker* (1980) for *Time* magazine, Paul Gray asserts that our interest in the novel derives from "the fascination of watching a strange world evolve out of unfamiliar words." Riddley's world—the world as it exists many centuries after a nuclear holocaust—and his odd language, composed of slang British English and a few technical terms, are indeed strange and wonderful. We must also admit, however, that the contours of the language and the vision of the world are familiar enough: the language, though nonstandard, is decipherable; and the primitive society of foragers and farmers is recognizable in terms of the anthropological progress of our species. The technologically advanced world of the nuclear age—our age—has been blasted back into the primitive past, and the novel shows us humanity trying to make its painful way back—crawling toward technical know-how, pursuing progress. In this regard, none of what we see in the novel is that unfamiliar.

The remarkable achievement of *Riddley Walker* lies, I think, not so much in the ways it departs from recognizable models but in the ways that it beautifully mirrors the movement forward of the species. In fact, what we are witnessing in the book is a society on the verge of, from an anthropological perspective, dramatic change—change from a nomadic hunting-and-gathering society into a culture of permanent agricultural units and towns, and, even more significant, change from a primitive into a modern culture. Hoban reflects this attitudinal change in a variety of ways, the most overt being in the attempt by the country's leader (the Pry Mincer) to recapture the lost "clevverness" (technological know-how) of those "time way back" (before the holocaust); to discover the secret to the "1 Big 1" (nuclear weaponry), which he believes will enable England (Inland) to become a dominant world force; and even to rediscover some of the technological wonders of the past, such as putting boats in the air (aircraft) and pictures on the wind (television). Apart from the character's conscious decision to pursue information and power, Hoban also reflects societal change in a more subtle way: in the society's attitudes toward myth and history—concepts that, among other things, have been used to lend meaning to human endeavors. I will focus on this more subtle shift toward modernity of outlook—the movement from traditional society's reliance upon myth as unifying intellectual force toward the prestige afforded to history by modern societies.

In *Myth and Reality,* Mircea Eliade identifies the ways in which primitive or traditional societies regard mythic stories:

> [Myth] relates events that took place in primordial Time, the fabled time of the "beginnings." In other words, myth tells how, through the deeds of Supernatural Beings, a reality came into existence, be it the whole of reality, the Cosmos, or only a fragment of reality—an island, a species of plant, a particular kind of human behavior, an institution. Myth, then, is always an account of a "creation"; it relates how something was produced, came to be.

As such, myth partakes of both the religious and the historical, bodies of knowledge that are of a piece in such societies, contrary to the attitudes of modern people, who tend to separate the mythic from the historical or the actual. Put another way, while a modern person might be inclined to compartmentalize as much as possible matters of fact and matters of belief, the traditional person would regard the myth as essentially historical, as the only reality. Moreover, Eliade writes that the "foremost function of myth is to reveal exemplary models of all human rites and all significant human activities—diet or marriage, work or education, art or wisdom." Myth, then, operates in various ways: as sacred history, as guide to behavior, and as prescription for holy rites. The last of these is more than merely ceremonial. Rather, the rite is always meant to be a reenactment of the mythic events, and, in this dramatic ritual, the participants are said to be "seized by the sacred, exalting power of events recollected or reenacted" (Eliade). Such powerful reenactments enable those whom Eliade identifies as *homo religious* to emerge from profane chronological time and enter the frame of sacred time.

If we place *Riddley Walker* within the intellectual framework of Eliade's description of myth, we can recognize how remarkably accurate Hoban's description of the primitive society is. We notice fairly early in the narrative that Riddley and the people of his society readily subscribe to myths of different kinds. One example is found in the story entitled "Hart of the Wood," which concerns the origin of charcoal. The story is about a man, a woman, and a child who survived "Bad Time," the nuclear blast occurred centuries before. Emerging from a devastated town, they go to a nearby forest and forage for whatever food they can find. Little is there besides dead leaves, and those are indigestible, as they soon discover. "Starveling wer what they wer doing," Riddley says, indicating the futility of their activity. In the course of their stay in that forest, they encounter a man Riddley describes as "the clevver looking bloak." The man claims to know how to build a fire, and he offers to share his knowledge with them if they will share something with him: their child as a meal. Without much soul-searching, the people agree, and they eat the child, the stranger's portion being the heart. After the meal, the man makes the cryptic prediction that charcoal burning, now extinct, will one day return, and the burners will make their charcoal piles in the shape of the child's heart. The parents do not comment but proceed to build a fire "to keap the black from moving in on them." Their quest for survival, however, is doomed nevertheless: "They fel a sleap by ther fire and the fire biggering on it et them up they bernt to death. They ben the old ls or you myt say the *auld* ls and be come chard coal. That's why theywl tel you the aulder tree is bes for charring coal."

What we see in this story and in other such mythic accounts interspersed throughout the novel are not really sacred myths of the sort that Eliade describes but, rather, small etiological narratives similar to the Ovidian tales of transformations. As in Ovid's *Metamorphoses,* these stories account for various mundane phenomena, and they are couched in narratives that are usually tragic. Riddley merely passes these stories along to the reader—stories that he has picked up from his cultural surroundings—and he neither challenges nor vouches for their veracity.

Indeed, the most interesting aspect of these myths is that Hoban artfully permits them to stand as they are, having his characters accept them as would a person in an archaic society. Such a person would never subject the myth to literary or historical analysis. Only once does Riddley try to analyze the origin of a myth, when a man he meets tells him a story concerning a place name that disagrees with his own myth regarding the town's naming. Riddley questions the source of the man's information, and the response he receives might well serve as a definition of origins for all the myths in archaic society:

> . . . you cant make up nothing in your head no moren you can make up what you see. You know what I mean may be what you see aint all ways there so you cud reach out and touch it but its there some kynd of way and it comes from some where. . . . That story cudnt come out of no where cud it so it musve come out of some where. Parbly it ben in that place from time way back or may be in a nother place only the idear of it come to me there. That dont make no odds. That storys jus what ever it is and thats what storys are.

The innocent acceptance of the source and "truth" of myths, which we might see as evolving from something like the Jungian collective unconscious, reflects fairly accurately the approach that an archaic society would take to its stories of origin, sacred or otherwise.

These smaller inset myths, however, are clearly secondary to the unifying cultural myth, the Eusa story. Riddley is emphatic about the sacredness of that myth: "Every body knows bits and peaces of it but the connexion men and the Eusa show men they have the woal thing wrote down the same and they have to know it all by hart." Following the death of his father near the beginning of the novel, Riddley takes his place as his group's "connexion man," a kind of priest and mystic, whose main task is to interpret the meanings hidden in the sacred reenactments of the Eusa myth. The reenactments themselves take the

form of a puppet show dramatizing the life of Eusa. These shows are put on only by itinerant representatives of the government, the Mincery; on the occasion of Riddley's elevation to connexion man, a show is put on by no one less than the heads of the government—the Pry Mincer and Wes Mincer, Abel Goodparley and Ernie Orfing. We can see in this ceremony, replete with its fixed hierarchical functions and its arcane aspects, the features of highly ritualistic religious observances, and, in this case, the central myth and the celebration of its mysteries derive added prestige by being the official state religion. Now that Riddley joins the ranks of the privileged "clergy," he must set himself apart from the community while serving it, and this separateness is effected by his taking of the scar—an *E* carved onto his stomach. Thus, Riddley becomes "anointed" and assumes his place as priest and liaison ("connexion man") between his community and the political-religious hierarchy.

More important than the ceremonial aspects of worship, however, is the sacred myth itself, which Riddley relates to the reader. Hoban goes to great lengths to show the importance of this myth to the traditional society by linking it, through the use of allusion, to the Bible. The text of the Eusa myth is written down (unlike the lesser myths Riddley relates) and is organized into thirty-three numbered paragraphs. Riddley claims that "its all ways wrote down in the *old spel*" (emphasis added), "old spel" being clearly reminiscent of the term *gospel.* Like the four gospels of the New Testament—the sacred texts that tell of the life of Christ as God and man—the Eusa story speaks of a man whose life changed the world as Riddley's society knows it.

As with all myths, the Eusa story is concerned with both the mundane and the supernatural. In primordial times, the "Big Man" of England, Mr. Clevver, finds his country besieged by enemies, so he turns to Eusa, "a noing man [who was] vere qwik he cud tern his han tu enne thing," and asks him to build "masheans uv Warr" for the country's defense. Eusa agrees, and he goes in search of the secrets of potency. Shrinking himself and his two dogs (Folleree and Folloeroo), he enters into the heart of a stone and comes upon the Stag of the Wood, between whose horns he sees "the Littl Shynin Man the Addom." Eusa shoots the stag and seizes the man, pulling on his outstretched arms until the man comes apart. The result of this separation is exciting to him:

> Owt uv thay 2 peaces uv the Littl Shynin Man
> the Addom thayr cum shyningnes in wayvs in
> spredin circels. Wivverin & wayverin & humin

with a hy soun. Lytin up the dark wud. Eusa seen the Littl 1 goin round & roun insyd the Big 1 and the Big 1 humin roun insyd the Littl 1. He seen thay Master Chaynjis uv the 1 Big 1. Qwik then he riten down thay Nos. uv them.

Although the dogs, speaking now in human voices, warn Eusa of the great destruction his discovery will cause, he nevertheless proceeds to give the information to Mr. Clevver, who promptly uses the "secret" against the enemy. "Thay wun the Warr," the story continues, "but the lan wuz poyzen frum it in the ayr & water as wel. Peapl din jus dy in the Warr thay kep dyin after it wuz over."

Following the devastation, a frightened Eusa takes his wife, two sons, and the dogs and tries to escape the poisoned land. On a ship on which he has taken passage, his wife is captured by the captain and his men, and, later, his sons and the dogs are led away from Eusa by the two separated halves of the Littl Shynin Man the Addom. Eusa demands that his sons be returned to him, but the little man tells him that nothing can be restored to its former state and that Eusa will now have to go through many changes, the consequences for his separating that which had been singular and whole.

Hoban eventually reveals to the reader the origins of the myth, the conflation of what little historical information is known about life before and immediately following the nuclear holocaust, and "The Legend of St. Eustace," which Goodparley will later share with and erroneously interpret for Riddley. Even without this information, the purpose of the myth makes sense. As Natalie Maynor and Richard Patteson correctly observe, "metaphysical truth may well be concealed within the webs of historical error." Indeed, such metaphysical truth is reflected in the moral principles that serve as mythic "themes"—no matter whether one believes in the strict historicity of mythic stories, for such "history" is placed at the service of revealed truth, ethical doctrine. The people of Riddley's society believe the Eusa story is true; we know that it is not. Yet we can discern in the story some of the same things they do: the sense of the Edenic world that existed prior to the fall and the irreparable damage done to that world. As is the case in the Biblical book of Genesis, pride and ambition bring about the "human condition." Riddley's people accept both the story and its moral theme, which testifies to the prestige the myth enjoys in that traditional culture.

In his review of **Riddley Walker** for *Newsweek,* Walter Clemons makes this observation:

> The downfall of "clevverness," or scientific know-
> how, has led to a revival of "1st knowing," the

intuitive mythologizing power of the primitive imagination. Handed-down tales and scraps of doggerel contain concealed truths for the hero to unravel.

I agree with his assertion that in the first quarter of the novel, we are witnessing the emergence of mythic observance in a primitive society, a feature that is common in most such social groupings. But his claim that Riddley deliberately goes out to unravel the myth's concealed truths is, in part, mistaken. In fact, prior to his departure from his group, he never once questions the facts of, or tries to interpret, the Eusa myth. In other words, he accepts the inherent truth of the story and thereby reveals the proper attitude toward the sacred document.

Indeed, it is only by chance that Riddley comes to see the possibility that the myth itself may not be fixed and inviolable—and it is this gradual revelation that, in large measure, marks the transition from myth-centered, primitive culture to modern culture in pursuit of absolute truth and, through that truth, power. Two occurrences are significant with regard to this transition: Riddley's meeting with the imprisoned Ardship of Cambry, supposedly a direct descendant of Eusa; and his subsequent alliance with the Pry Mincer, Abel Goodparley.

The Ardship (Archbishop), whose name is Lissener, descends from those who occupied ground zero (Canterbury) at the time of the nuclear blast, and, since Canterbury is the place where Eusa was said to have done his work, Lissener and his fellow citizens are regarded as the "Eusa folk." The most striking thing about the young man is that he is, as might be expected, severely deformed: " . . . he dint have no parper face," Riddley says. "It wer like it ben shapit qwik and rough out of clay. No eyes nor no hoals for eyes . . . a bit pincht out for a nose and a cut for a mouf and that wer it. Dint have a woal pair of ears. . . . Nor dint have no hair on his head." Riddley has just freed Lissener from an underground prison, where he had been placed by Goodparley. The Pry Mincer believes that the Eusa folk collectively know the secrets of Eusa (i.e., the secrets of nuclear weaponry), and he hopes that, by uniting the Eusa folk, he can learn that secret. As it turns out, then, Riddley's unwitting act of freeing the Ardship—the leader of the Eusa folk—is a treasonous act against the state for which he could be made to pay with his life. Nevertheless, he decides to proceed with Lissener to Cambry.

The most significant thing that happens as they make their way is Lissener's account of how the Eusa story concludes, an account that is not recorded in the official myth. According to Lissener, Eusa regretted the destruction brought on by his discoveries. The leaders of the devastated nation, however, try to convince him to reveal again the "clevverness" needed to make the "1 Big 1" so that they can have it before any other nation discovers the secret, and thereby be "safe." Eusa refuses on moral grounds to tell them what they want to know, and he offers to go on the road to tell people about the evils of immoderate ambition, about "what harm I done."

Angered over his refusal to yield his secrets and fearing the effects that his "sermon" is likely to produce, the leaders kill him and put his head on a pole. The head, however, continues to speak, chastising them for their immorality. Next a giant wave comes through the land where the leaders dwell (the Ram), separating it from England. As a result of these signs, the leaders are frightened and decide, as Eusa suggested, to go on the road and tell his story for moral instruction. Since Eusa is dead, they need a representative figure to stand in for him; hence, the commemorative rite of the puppet show. Nevertheless, the leaders have not given up their ambitions for nuclear superiority, and they decide that it is best to isolate the most likely source of that information— the Eusa folk themselves. Thus, for centuries the Ram has kept the people of Cambry cut off from the other citizens of England, particularly forbidding intermarriage to ensure that the group remains pure (and hence deformed), ready for the revelation they will eventually yield.

Lissener's additions to the Eusa myth turn out to be significant in a number of ways. On the most obvious level, his account provides new and disturbing information to Riddley, who is supposed to be a member of the religious elite, one of the few permitted to possess a written version of the the official myth. If Lissener is right, and Riddley never thinks to doubt him, the version of the myth Riddley knows has been deliberately left incomplete by the powers that be in order to hide their own actions and to control the people, using "connexion men" such as Riddley to further their own ambitions. Riddley further realizes that even the sacred ritual itself—the commemorative puppet show—was devised not so much for devotional as for political purposes. The Ram killed Eusa; thus, they have produced a puppet to take his place—a puppet in both the literal and figurative senses, a figure to divert the people from the government's real aims. Finally, Riddley also learns that the Ram, maintaining as it does its plans for the Eusa folk of Cambry, has not heeded Eusa's warnings and, therefore, must regard the mythical figure

as less than sacred. The deductions Riddley makes concerning the Ram's motives for action and its use of religion, in effect, to check the masses disturb him profoundly and, more important, lead him to doubt the facts of the central myth itself.

What little remains of his faith is removed later in the narrative when Goodparley, who is actively seeking the "1 Big 1" specifically and the lost "clevverness" of the past generally, relates to Riddley yet another ending to the Eusa story. Goodparley's version is directly opposed politically to Lissener's. According to the Pry Mincer, after the nuclear holocaust, Eusa was stoned by the citizens of Cambry and forced to live out his days as a wandering exile. In each of the towns to which he goes, the survivors torture him, then pass him along to the next town for similar treatment. Blinded and weak, he is eventually returned to Cambry, where he is beaten to death with iron bars "becaws it ben col iron he done Inland to death with." Moreover, Goodparley maintains that it was Eusa's own people who put his head on a pole and that the head instructed them to throw it into the sea. They did, and the head made its way to the Ram, the seat of power, and instructed the leaders of the fallen nation:

> Make a show of me for memberment and for the ansers to your askings. Make a show with han figgers put a littl woodin head of me on your finger in memberment of my real head on a poal. Keep the Eusa folk a live in memberment of the hardship they brung on. . . . When the right head of Inland fynds the right head of Eusa the anser wil come and Inland wil rise up out of what she ben brung down to.

Goodparley then reveals that he believes the time has come for England's resurgence, he himself being the "right head" that Eusa predicted would come to rule in England.

Jack Branscomb has argued that "as archetypal eater of forbidden fruit, [Eusa] wandered from city to city, mutilated, blinded, and finally killed, and so he has been passed down as the central sacramental figure of the culture." Branscomb is right to see Eusa as the central mythic figure of the primitive culture. What he overlooks in this discussion, however, is the fact that the stories of Eusa's death—whether he was killed by the Ram or by his own people—are not generally known because they are not part of the official myth. That myth, as we saw, ends with Eusa's setting forth to undergo the changes the Littl Shynin Man said must inevitably follow. The stories of Eusa's murder by different parties are, therefore, accretions to the myth that Riddley learns about merely by chance from people who have clear political ambitions.

The question to be asked at this point is this: What are we to make of the alterations and accretions introduced as the narrative progresses? Put another way, in light of the variant endings provided by Lissener and Goodparley, both of whom are obviously intent on gaining political power, what has become of the "truth" of the original myth as Riddley and his people knew it?

On the most obvious level, the answer is fairly simple. The version of the Eusa story that is codified in the "old spel," preserved in fixed form, remains the central etiological myth of the culture. The common man of the traditional society is not privy to the information that Riddley has learned and, therefore, is untouched by doubt. Hence, those people continue to conform perfectly to Eliade's descriptions of the traditional society, faithfully observing the sacred commemorative rites and believing in the truth of the unifying mysteries of Eusa.

The situation is more complicated for Riddley, however. He comes to realize that the origin of the sacred puppet show may be political rather than devotional, that the Eusa story itself may be a complete fabrication used as a means of keeping the people in check through their awe of myth (an opiate for the masses, in other words), and, most important, that the ruling powers of the country—notably Goodparley—are more concerned with history than myth, more concerned with how knowledge of the past can lead to future developments than with the lessons of the past. Indeed, what Riddley—and through him, the reader—is witnessing in these revelations is the emergence of the modern world, the modern attitude, which, as Eliade suggests, rejects the disguised truth of myth and embraces history, both as a "philosophy" and as a means toward continued progress:

> A modern man might reason as follows: I am what I am today because a certain number of things have happened to me, but those things were possible only because agriculture was discovered some eight to nine thousand years ago and because urban civilizations developed in the ancient Near East . . . because Galileo and Newton revolutionized the conception of the universe, thus opening the way to scientific discoveries and laying the groundwork for the rise of industrial civilization, because the French Revolution occurred

and the ideas of freedom, democracy, and social justice shook the Western world to its foundations after the Napoleonic wars—and so on.

> Similarly, a "primitive" could say: I am what I am today because a series of events occurred before I existed. But he would at once have to add: events that took place in *mythical times* and therefore make up a *sacred history* because the actors in the drama are Supernatural Beings.

The distinction that Eliade draws here is germane to the world we see unfolding in ***Riddley Walker.*** Hoban's vision takes on real depth and complexity when we can regard the actions of Lissener and Goodparley not merely as the schemes of petty politicians but as the symbols of progressive human endeavor—or, in this case, a re-progression of such endeavors, for better or worse. I think that we can easily extrapolate, based upon our own knowledge of humankind's anthropological progress, that the sacred myth of origin will soon lose its prestigious centrality in Riddley's world, despite his attempts to keep it alive through his performance of Punch and Judy puppet shows. Such a show—apart from its illegality, for which he expects to be punished at some point by the authorities—is too self-consciously contrived to gain a strong foothold as a sacred cultural ritual. Rather, the ruling powers are ready to cast off the primitive superstitions of the past, and their program is, by the end of the novel, fairly well defined: to regain the lost "clevverness" of the past at whatever cost and, as Hoban's ironic theme suggests, to march backward in order to move forward. "To reanimate the giants who walked before the Apocalypse—ourselves," Benjamin DeMott correctly observes, "requires nothing less than the re-creation of the instruments of a new Apocalypse." It is in this attempt at historical recreation that we see the emergence of modern humanity in ***Riddley Walker.*** It is immaterial that Goodparley is killed prior to realizing his own ambitions in this regard. The movement forward will progress nevertheless, and, indeed, even his death by means of rediscovered gunpowder ("The 1 Littl 1") points decisively toward the progressive-minded future.

In an interview with Edward Myers, Russell Hoban makes what I consider to be a surprising statement. Asked if he thinks a "mythic sense" is present in his novels, he admits that he sees such a sense but adds, "I didn't start out planning that way, but I noted its development" (Myers). Whatever the author's claims regarding intent, however, Hoban does manage to mirror subtly and evocatively the attitudes that have shaped the thinking of the Western world.

PILGERMANN (1983)

Neil Philip

SOURCE: A review of *Pilgermann*, in *The Times Educational Supplement*, No. 3480, March 11, 1983, p. 26.

"I dont have nothing only words to put down on paper. Its so hard. Some times theres mor in the emty paper nor there is when you get the writing down on it. You try to word the big things and they tern ther backs on you."

Russell Hoban's **Riddley Walker,** written in a mutilated but potent English like the stump of a severed leg that still feels the phantom limb, seems to me one of the most brilliant novelistic attempts to "word the big things" of recent years. The worn-down language becomes hypnotic; the story has the resonance of myth. Riddley, the "connexion man", expresses in his inarticulacy, in the gap between what he wants to say and the means available to say it, much that speaks deeply of our strongest desires and fears.

Hoban's new novel, **Pilgermann,** is self-consciously an extension of that book. But instead of a narrator who feels safest in silence, who tells us, "I have to stop here for a littl", it gives us a voluble narrator who never stops, but talks and talks at pace about the insights Riddley elicited slowly, tentatively. It is a text with no space for a reader; a sermon, not a connexion. Whatever lay waiting to be revealed in the empty paper has been overwritten.

If **Riddley Walker** was a religious book, **Pilgermann** is a book about religion. It is packed with quotations from sacred texts, and its heavily symbolic narrative concerns the First Crusade to Jerusalem initiated by Pope Urban II in 1095, and specifically the siege of Antioch in 1098. Pilgermann, speaking to us as a disbodied contemporary, was at that time a castrated Jew, who sets out on a pilgrimage to Jerusalem after a vision of Jesus, but revises his goal as he refines his understanding of "potentiality and actuality" and settles in Antioch with a Turk, Bembel Rudzuk, creating an infinitely extensible tile-pattern called "the Hidden Lion".

That lion has lurked in Hoban's work before: in his first novel for adults, **The Lion of Boaz-Jachin and Jachin-Boaz;** in the scriptural epigraph to **Riddley Walker.** Indeed, **Pilgermann** is largely an explicit statement of the implicit themes of Hoban's earlier work. Thus at a crucial moment Pilgermann ponders, "How to live then in this little space in which we

have a self and a name, this little space in which we are allowed to accumulate our tiny history of days, this moment that is at once the first moment and the last moment, this moment that contains our universe and such space/time as is unwound in the working of it?" The answer can be found in Hoban's children's classic **The Mouse and his Child,** in the struggle to be "self-winding", the cycle "ungoing into going and back again". But in **The Mouse and his Child** Hoban was still willing to offer a positive answer to the question of how we should live; **Pilgermann** tells us only how to die.

Hoban could not write an uninteresting book, but in **Pilgermann** he has written a ponderous, ill-digested one. Pilgermann has all the answers—"It is from the cosmic intolerable of the nothing-in-everything alternating with the everything-in-nothing that all things come"—but he leaves me cold. Riddley Walker has only questions, and he thrills me to the marrow: "Our woal life is a idear we dint think of nor we dont know what it is. What a way to live."

Philip Horne

SOURCE: A review of *Pilgermann*, in *The London Review of Books*, Vol. 5, No. 6, April 1, 1983, p. 14.

In Russell Hoban's previous, much-admired novel, **Riddley Walker,** the narrator, 'connection man' for a Kent settlement far in the future which lies beyond some obscure cataclysm, agonises in his residual English about the problem of writing. 'I dont have nothing only words to put down on paper. Its so hard. Some times theres mor in the emty paper nor there is when you get the writing down on it.' Pilgermann, Hoban's new protagonist, narrates from the ether, where he is 'waves and particles', long after his death in the Crusades at the siege of Antioch in 1098: yet this standpoint only increases his sense of the inadequacy of language, for he has even more big things to tell us than Riddley Walker. 'Precision with words is impossible,' he believes. This does not silence him; as he also says, 'I talk and I talk and words come out of me in an unending stream.'

There is a story, of sorts. The castrated Jewish hero makes a fantastic pilgrimage, full of rapes, visions and disgusting deaths, from Germany to Antioch, where he and a Moslem friend design and build a 'pattern' in order to see potentiality become actuality. Narrative line is not, however, the focus of attention here Pilgermann informs us that 'I can't tell this as a story because it isn't a story; a story is what remains when you leave out most of the action.' Where the action is, for Pilgermann and Russell Hoban, is in pseudo-philosophical consideration of 'what is called time' and 'the nature of things', couched in a self-perpetuating jargon that circles around 'the law of the allness of the everything of which each of us is a particle'. This law, not very particular, apparently licenses Pilgermann's speculative prose.

> (Yerushalayim; spinning domes of gold in the sea of the one mind that is God. Ineffable.
>
> It is the Jerusalem of the heart that must not be forgotten because in the Jerusalem of the heart is the heart of the mystery where lives the idea of the Unknowable that is God.)

The speculations alternate, until the decently-researched account of the siege of Antioch in the last fifty pages, with Russell Hoban's lurid imaginings of sex, violence and decomposition.

Answerable for much of the nonsense is the novel's inspirational self-importance, its grandly religiose version of what constitutes authorship. Russell Hoban's style (with none of the constraints of an invented language which partly anchored *Riddley Walker*) is a sustaining vehicle that transports him to a telepathic meeting of minds with the waves and particles of Pilgermann. This is a meeting to which Pilgermann himself often refers: 'By now I am only the energy of an idea; whoever is writing this down puts the name of Pilgermann to the idea, says, "What if?" and hypothesises virtualities into actualities.' The workings of the imagination, so invoked, are then taken to give an authority to Pilgermann's trans-historical eye-witness accounts of anything in history. Hieronymus Bosch (centuries after Pilgermann's death) paints a remarkable effect of light: 'I have flown beside that creature with the ladder . . . and I can testify that Bosch experienced that sky by quantum-jumping to the strange brilliance of total Now.' The torrent of random Zen wonderings—'Could the siege of Jerusalem have been painted by Vermeer?'—and of big questions and big answers—'What is the nature of things? The nature of things is that what can happen will happen'—justifies itself by an aesthetic of irresponsibility. The writer does not know what he is doing, and this makes his intuitions more valuable. 'I describe what I do not understand because I am lived by it,' Pilgermann claims at one point. A wise man says: 'Although I said those words and know them to be true I have no idea what they signify.' The same condition is ascribed to a much greater Author: 'It is my belief that God is of an artistic temperament and has therefore ehosen to let his own work be beyond his understanding.' That

'therefore' may well give us pause. The corresponding attitude for the reader is perhaps stated when Pilgermann and his friend discuss the tiled design they have built in Antioch: 'May it not be that the best way of conducting oneself with this pattern is simply to take it in without any thought and to enjoy in it the presence of the Unseen?' Such an invitation to abdicate judgment and plunge into the worldlessness of 'all-inclusive superstition' needs to be declined.

The New Yorker

SOURCE: A review of *Pilgermann,* in *The New Yorker,* Vol. 59, August 8, 1983, pp. 92-3.

"By now," says Pilgermann, twenty-nine pages into this display of high-tech pseudo mysticism, "I am only the energy of an idea; whoever is writing this down puts the name of Pilgermann to the idea, says, 'What if?' and hypothesizes virtualities into actualities." By now, the reader has probably got the hang of Pilgermann's notion of English. Whoever is writing it down also writes, under the heading "Acknowledgments" and above the initials "R. H.," that "*Riddley Walker* left me in a place where there was further action pending and this further action was waiting for the element that would precipitate it into the time and place of its own story." *Riddley Walker* hypothesized brilliantly the blasted heath of post-nuclear England and the blasted English of its neo-neolithic natives. *Pilgermann* hypothesizes badly an eleventh-century castrated Jewish pilgrim, who sets out for Jerusalem in 1096 but winds up in Antioch, where, in 1098 (during the First Crusade), he is converted (along with a lot of other unfortunates) into "waves and particles freely ranging through what is called time." In the intervening two hundred pages, he credits Jesus with "the meekness of plutonium," calls himself "a microscopic chip" and Antioch "a paradigm of history," and compares raisins to celestial bodies.

R. W. Greene

SOURCE: A review of *Pilgermann,* in *Los Angeles Times Book Review,* August 28, 1983, p. 8.

Pilgermann is an 11th-Century Jewish *castrato* who journeys to the Holy Land from Europe, winding up in Antioch where he is killed—or transformed into "waves and particles," as he puts it, during the siege of that city during the First Crusade. Along his way, he talks to animals and various unsavory characters, about what are supposed to be spiritual ideas. Author Russell Hoban's previous novel for adults, **Riddley Walker,** was much praised, but **Pilgermann** is heavy-handed pseudo-mysticism, of the sort favored by adolescents who discover Zen and science fiction at the same time. Hoban may have had some interesting or exciting conceptions—or "idea pheromones," as he calls them—when he began, but through the window of his claustrophobic and pretentious prose, they're almost impossible to discern.

Jessica Swain

SOURCE: A review of *Pilgermann,* in *Kliatt Young Adult Paperback Book Guide,* Vol. 18, No. 6, September, 1984, p. 12.

Long since transformed into "waves and particles," Pilgermann tells the story of his life as a Jew during the 11th century. After committing adultery with the wife of a Christian tax collector, Pilgermann describes how he was castrated in a pogrom and his life spared by the cuckolded husband. Christ appears to the eunch in a vision, prompting him to set out on a pilgrimage to Jerusalem. Before his demise, he comes to the realization that "Jerusalem will be wherever I am when the end comes." This complex novel blends Christian, Judaic, and Muslim tradition as it explores the nature of divine wisdom. Death, destruction, bestiality, and all forms of evil dominate a medieval world in which all humans are "castrated by mortality" and even God cannot fathom the answer to life's mystery. Hoban has created a work that is intriguing in many ways, although its difficulty and grim tone render it a marginal choice for young adults.

📖 *THE MEDUSA FREQUENCY* (1987)

Kirkus Reviews

SOURCE: A review of *The Medusa Frequency,* in *Kirkus Reviews,* Vol. LV, No. 17, September 1, 1987, p. 1250.

Spinning off from the Orpheus myth, Hoban (**Pilgermann,** 1983; **Riddley Walker,** 1982; **Turtle Diary,** 1976) offers a weird modern fable of a London writer's struggles with the quest for inspiration and for a constant, faithful, Eurydice-style love.

The narrator is twice-published yet virtually unread novelist Hermann Orff, now working for *Classic Comics* while lamenting the loss of old flame Luise

and vainly waiting for inspiration at the word processor. Desperate, Orff goes to the "Hermes Soundways" studio for electro-zap brain stimulation—with immediate results: over the next few days Orff receives periodic visits (hallucinations?) from the "eyeless and bloated" head of Orpheus ("covered with green slime and heavy with barnacles"), which retells the old myth in quirky, digressive detail. Meanwhile, despite the head's warnings that all love leads to "loss," Orff pursues a new paramour, Melanie Falsepercy. He also hops over to Holland, in search of the Vermeer portrait that's his vision of perfect womanhood. Eventually, after a small angina attack, a dear-John letter from Melanie, and increasingly opaque dialogues with "the Kraken" (a terror-symbol), Orff winds up inspired—writing a cartoon series for the backs of cereal boxes and open to a new "frequency" in women.

Thanks to tidbits of literary-world satire and *Alice in Wonderland* silliness (the Orpheus head turns into a cabbage, a grapefruit—and gets eaten), an intrepid reader may feel encouraged to press on through this difficult, allusive mesh of myths, symbols, fantasies, and themes. But, to a greater extent than in previous Hoban obstacle courses, here the imagery and illumination finally don't seem quite worth the effort.

Eric Korn

SOURCE: A review of *The Medusa Frequency,* in *The Times Literary Supplement,* No. 4405, September 4, 1987, p. 949.

Russell Hoban must sometimes grow impatient with his critical reception. He is praised generously (as he deserves) but often with a patronizing note of exasperated affection, as though he were the Clive Sinclair—the *Sir* Clive Sinclair—of the English novel, ingenious, lateral-thinking, restlessly innovative, but also the loveable, impractical English eccentric, always in the laboratory and never on the factory floor, never settling down to steady production nor getting the market penetration his ideas deserve.

Most of this is not particularly true. Hoban's ideas would not strike French, Italians or South Americans as dangerously original: nor is he any slapdash innovator: rather a painstaking, even laborious craftsman. At first sight he does seem markedly averse to repeating himself in style or content: nothing obvious unites a gently didactic parable like **The Lion of Jachin-Boaz and Boaz-Jachin** with the hip nightmare of **Kleinzeit;** the present-day liberal idyll **Turtle**

Diary with the harsh historicity of *Pilgermann* or with the indefinite post-nuclear (and almost post-articulate) future landscape of *Riddley Walker.* This is to say nothing of dozens of children's books, among them *The Mouse and his Child,* a work of great force and ambition invariably described as "a classic". But it is becoming clear that his diverse books are linked, perhaps welded, by a host of thematic and structural recurrences, almost by a pattern of obsessions.

At first sight, *The Medusa Frequency* is a new departure by virtue of not being a new departure: it does not break new ground but rather seems to plough the furrow upturned in *Kleinzeit.* It is a myth of the new technology. There's a writer called Herman Orff (Hoban does not disguise his mythopoeic intentions) who has had two near-successes and is now deeply embedded in writer's block, staring at his Apple Two that is not the apple of knowledge.

As he fixes his gaze on the monitor screen, uncomfortable messages begin to emerge. Deep in the Undermind the Kraken stirs. A mysterious invitation on yellow paper offers help for blocked writers or infertile artists. Hermes Soundways ("write orph one") provides a kind of biofeedback therapy for the uncreative, it seems; but it is actually a snare laid by Orff's rival Istvan Fallok; Orff is lumbered with a voluble ghost, the head of Orpheus dismembered by the Maenads, the head that still cried for Eurydice. It is a curse that cannot easily be wished away, manifesting in the Thames at Chelsea, as a football in the street, in the crisper compartment of his refrigerator, finally as a grapefruit which he unthinkingly consumes. (It nearly does for him.) The Head must tell his story if Orff is to be free to write; but there are infinite, hellish distractions: cryptic messages come from all directions. From Gosta Kraken, the *cineaste* whose films are spoken in Gibberish; from the ubiquitous Gom Yawncher man, "an accent so regional it used up all his articulation and left nothing over for works". Orff communes as hungrily with his monitor as Cocteau's *Orphee* did with his car radio, which also brought Underground messages, coded instructions for the Forces of the Interior.

Orpheus must have and lose a Eurydice ("Is not all art a celebration of loss?") There are plenty of Eurydices here. There is the memory of Luise von Himmelbett, the mistress he acquired from Istvan and lost. There is the Medusa of the green screen, the worm in the Apple Two, who is also the Tennysonian Kraken that dies at the end of time when it is brought to the surface, who is also, somehow, the haunting

faces of Vermeer's "Girl with the Scarf". And now there's Melanie Falsepercy, another of Fallok's ladies, the dark percyphoney. And why should such classical illusions not multiply around the unfortunate Herman, who writes captions for classic cartoons and advertising copy for Pluto Drain Magic, Hermes Foot Powder. Portents multiply, scrambled signals wait on every street corner, the Orphic song is sometimes encrypted, sometimes *en clair.*

The crisis comes, Orff makes his journey to the underworld, an unreal city much like London, specifically a hospital in the Fulham Road, gets rid of his King Charles's Head, and finds a voice, naturally at the price of the loss of Melanie and/or the Medusa: but Vermeer's girl stays with him—"Eurydice unfound and unlost". Is there irony in her "flickering and friendly" smile? Orff renounces Classic Comics, and, unblocked, is writing *The Seeker from Nexo Vollma,* a monster fantasy from the Lovecraftian deeps. The god Apollo has left him, that had loved him well.

The escape from Hell is the theme of *Kleinzeit,* where the hero is his own Persephone. What is the relationship between these refugees from Hell: Eurydice who is forever lost, Persephone who is negotiated out like a political hostage, and gets half death's kingdom from the deal? The protagonist of *Kleinzeit* was a truant from the sinister hospital where he was being treated for musical inadequacies; played his music on the Underground (no Londoner will object to the identification of the District Line with Hell) with or without the help of the Night Sister, his Eurydice.

Mythical archetypes are like adventure playgrounds in which the classically educated writer can have endless wholesome fun, but *The Medusa Frequency* reads not so much like a retackling of the themes of a *Kleinzeit* as a *rechauffe* of some of the leftovers, a pair of socks knitted from the surplus wool.

But this is a superficial response. I see, dimly, how tightly knitted are all Hoban's yarns. The broken body, the totemic animal, a whole iconostasis of images recurs. In this myth of the dismembered god, the threatening Kraken head becomes Vermeer's "Head of a Young Girl". And the girl in the picture is not just Medusa and Muse. Is she not also wounded Tammuz, the Syrian avatar of Orpheus? And Djebel Musa, the Mountain of Moses, Mount Horeb of which the dismembered Pilgermann dreams before, in that story, too, heads begin to fly (the heads of ambushed Turks, used as cannonballs by the most Christian Crusaders); and is it too far-fetched to suggest that the Medusa-Moses-Muse is also Mus, the windup mechanical Mouse who with his child is dismembered by Manny Rat, the force of necessary evil in the children's tale? Is it just coincidence that Orff turns down a film contract at the end of the story because he "had too many other things to wind up"; that Pilgermann at the end of his pilgrimage is annoyed that "Sophia and my little son . . . had come thus at the eleventh hour to interfere with the smooth and orderly winding up of my affairs"?

Vermeer's model was the servant girl Ursula Urzel, the little bear; perhaps the dead bear god that was Pilgermann's companion on the road to Jerusalem. There are even tortoises, that may be kin to the sea-turtles that William and Neaera ("to sport with Amaryllis in the shade/ Or with the tangles of Neaera's hair"—another Medusa figure) liberated from Regent's Park Zoo. The hospital, the night sister, yellow paper, the stranger who is Elijah, who is all strangers.

Are Hoban's books variations on certain obsessive themes, or are they parts of a greater whole? The key seems to lie in the detailed description (with diagrams) of the tile patterns in **Pilgermann,** the repetitive, interlocking designs that conceal figures like David's Wheel, the Willing Virgin, the Hidden Lion (perhaps the Invisible Lion of Boaz-Jachin and his child, perhaps the lion, that according to talmudic legend, castrated Noah): do all his books form a cabalistic unity which will only emerge if we look at them from the right angle?

How much of this you think is true, and if true relevant, and how much you will enjoy it may depend on how you feel about linguistic play. Since many of Hoban's protagonists are obsessed by words and their ready mutation into other words, everything contains hidden messages. This in turn means that his work is full of spoonerisms, joke names (Readham and Weap, Juan de Fulme, Luvta Dewitt), creative mishearings, anagrams, and the kind of puns that the British are so good at and so ashamed of. If on the other hand you believe that language is the real hero of every novel, the real culprit of every whodunit, you will enjoy, as I did, the tricks and tropes it gets up to here. I await his nexo vollma with interest, with awe.

Sybil Steinberg

SOURCE: A review of *The Medusa Frequency,* in *Publishers Weekly,* Vol. 232, No. 13, September 18, 1987, pp. 159-60.

Again demonstrating the versatility and creative energy exhibited in **Riddley Walker** and **Pilgermann,** in this slim novel Hoban deals with existential ques-

tions: the mystery of existence, the nature of reality, the role of art. Combining satire and fantasy, and in poetic, Joycean language mixed with the vernacular, this narrative rewards the discerning reader. Herman Orff, a failed novelist who supports himself by doing cartoons for *Classic Comics,* is accosted by the blind head of Orpheus, his progenitor, "the first of your line." Through a series of metaphysical communications that lead to an odyssey through London and Amsterdam, Orff is gradually given to understand the connection between the women in his life: his lost love Luise von Himmelbett (symbolizing Eurydice); the nubile and very available Melanie Falsepercy (symbolizing Persephone); the print of Vermeer's *Head of a Young Girl* that hangs above his desk and haunts his imagination; and the head of Medusa in a painting by the Dutch master Frans Post: all represent "femaleness." Spare and witty, full of metaphorical, mythical and mystical allusions, the narrative sings with insights. At the same time whimsical, farcical (an advertising agency is called Slithe and Tovey) and deadly serious, it brilliantly relates the tragic ancient myths to the commonplace tragedies of modern life in a violent, dislocated age.

Joanne Wilkinson

SOURCE: A review of *The Medusa Frequency,* in *Booklist,* Vol. 84, October 1, 1987, pp. 217-18.

Herman Orff spends his days writing off-color comic strips to pay the rent and spends his nights trying to write a novel. His inspiration, however, is at a low ebb, and he often finds himself sitting in front of the word processor at 3 a.m. "like a telegrapher at a lost outpost." When he receives a flyer from Hermes Soundwaves advertising a cure for writer's block, he immediately makes an appointment. A studio technician hooks Herman up to a brain wave scanner, and, after a few electronic zaps, the head of Orpheus—the original storyteller—appears to him. Herman flees the studio but not the vision; Orpheus keeps reappearing via various means, including a head of cabbage, a football, and a large Edam cheese. Author Russell Hoban has a lot of fun with this updating of classical mythology, sometimes at the reader's expense. Although this book lacks the narrative drive of his earlier **Riddley Walker,** it does echo that novel's inventive wordplay, and Hoban, unlike his narrator, continues to display unflagging imaginative flair.

Michael Dirda

SOURCE: A review of *The Medusa Frequency,* in *Book World—The Washington Post,* Vol. 17, No. 48, November 29, 1987, p. 4.

In children's literature anything is possible. Mickey may fall out of his clothes into the night kitchen, where the bakers all look like Oliver Hardy. James will go adventuring aboard a giant peach. Tom soundly beats Captain Najork at his own games of womble, muck and sneed-ball. In such worlds no one is in the least surprised by talking animals, smart-aleck computers, friendly monsters.

Such freedom to imagine absolutely anything makes for the charm of Russell Hoban's novels, no matter how serious their purpose. In *Kleinzeit,* Death hides under a hospital bed, like any hobgoblin of child-hood. In *The Lion of Boaz-Jachin and Jachin-Boaz* a mapmaker conjures up, out of airy nothingness, a lion no one can see—but which leaves its claw marks on his arms. The distorted children's rhymes of *Riddley Walker*—itself a kind of post-Armageddon *Huckleberry Finn*—foretell the hero's strange destiny. And in *The Medusa Frequency,* computers, paintings and severed heads all talk, or talk back, to the novel's hero, the frustrated writer of Classic Comics, one Herman Orff.

In all these books—about love, sickness and life's various burdens—such wonders appear with casual nonchalance. Even the most realistic of Hoban's books, *Turtle Diary,* with its plot to free sea turtles from the London Zoo, possesses a kind of Swallows-and-Amazons flavor of kids on a holiday spree. Of course, Hoban sharpened his narrative skills on children's books (which he continues to produce): Frances the Badger tales for pre-schoolers; that paean to "fooling around," *How Tom Beat Captain Najork and His Hired Sportsmen;* and *The Mouse and His Child,* as perfect a children's novel as has ever been written, a classic to rank with *Charlotte's Web* and *Tom's Midnight Garden.* Everything Hoban writes possesses this same playful seriousness, the sheer concentration, of a 5-year-old building a plane out of Legos. But Hoban's odd and affecting books actually fly.

In *The Medusa Frequency* he takes up one of the great classical myths, that of Orpheus and Eurydice, setting the action in contemporary artistic London. Virtually every character or event suggests a classical parallel. Herman Orff (note the last name) has been trying in vain to write a third novel, a successor to *Slope of Hell* and *World of Shadows;* but for the past nine years, since the departure of his beloved Luise (after an infidelity on his part), nothing has come of his efforts. So when he receives a flyer about a new computer-enchanced EEG technique that will zap his head into new places, it seems worth a try. On his way to his appointment he descends into the London underground and glimpses a leggy, attractive young woman, dressed in black:

"Her hair was brown and thick—she was altogether urban but she looked as if she might vanish behind a tree. Her eyes were remarkable: dark eyes darkly outlined, open wide so that when she looked at me there was white all round the papil. Her eyes were not like the eyes of women on Greek vases but there came the thought of a shady grove. The grove became more shadowy, became wild woodland. Her face had a sudden woodland look; as if she might just that moment have heard the baying of hounds."

Her name, he learns when they fatedly meet again at the head-zapping studio, is Melanie Falsepercy. Melanie, of course, means black; it was the true Persephone who vainly fled from Hades' hounds and who became dark queen of the underworld.

After the shock therapy, Herman experiences a kind of psychic fugue, awakening along the Thames where he discovers the eyeless, rotting head of Orpheus. He is a little taken aback, but not altogether surprised. The two discuss lost love. "In the stories they always say I turned around to look at her too soon, but that isn't how it was: I turned *away* too soon, turned away before I'd ever looked long enough, before I'd ever fully perceived her." This is Orpheus speaking, but Hoban makes clear he only voices the regret in Herman's own head. Orpheus eventually drifts away but promises to complete his story; for later installments—always comic occasions—the head pops up as a football, cabbage, and grapefruit.

Back in his workroom Herman daydreams over his reproductions of Vermeer's *Head of a Young Girl* (a painting once called the *Mona Lisa* of the North), whom he identifies with Luise/Eurydice. During the crisis of the novel Orff must make a night journey to the Netherlands—ie. the nether lands, or under-world—to find the original of the Vermeer girl. In a Hague museum he finally comes to realize that his Luise is gone forever; but in her stead he is granted a vision of the Medusa. Reversing the usual effects of the Gorgon, he stares at her and is released from his petrified state. "Behind Medusa lies Eurydice un-lost."

All this may sound like old-fashioned expressionist drama, a bit crazed, even a little corny. But it works. After all, Joyce's *Ulysses,* Eliot's *Wasteland,* Cocteau's *Orphee,* and Rilke's Orpheus poems—all patterned after familiar legends—are exciting without being Elmore Leonard thrillers. As it happens, Hoban pays homage, through pastiche or direct quotation, to all four of these accounts of spiritual desolation and recovery. When, for instance, Herman goes out searching for the Orpheus & Tower Bridge Club, the world picks up a Joycean Irish tinge:

"It was novembering hard outside; the dark air sang with the dwindle of the year, the sharpening of it to the goneness that was drawing nearer, nearer with every moment. Pinky-orange shone the electrical hibiscus street lamps; almost their light had a fragrance; the brown leaves underfoot insisted on the ghosts of dark trees standing in the place of lamps and houses; the pink-orange globes hung mingled with the swaying dark and winter branches; the winter lights and traffic, the winter walkers in the dark street all moved through the ghostly wood and went their way upon the ancient leafy track."

Very poetic, but a little of this goes a long way. So Hoban keeps varying his tone, facetiously naming a publishing company Slithe and Tovey, or enthusiastically outlining *The Seeker of Nexo Vollma,* a science fiction comic for the back of cereal boxes whose author is selling "first cereal rights." He satirizes movie people in Herman's encounter with Gosta Kraken, the avant-garde film maker who is part Bergman, part Cocteau, all pretention. And when he chooses, Hoban even writes a stripped down prose as efficient as any hard-boiled novelist's: "In the morning I came awake as I always do, like a man trapped in a car going over a cliff."

The obvious structure of *The Medusa Frequency,* apart from its extended meditations and dialogues on things amorous or eschatological, is the descent of Herman Orff into himself and his coming to terms with the loss of his beloved Luise, freeing himself to get on with his life as a writer. That kind of pattern is one every adult reader knows, and it reminds us that Hoban is, for all his myth, magic and black humor, a very serious novelist indeed. He has called himself a religious writer; and his books are less like well-crafted novels than explorations of the spirit in the face of life's crises. For instance, his early fiction—clearly autobiographical—portrays a father's alienation from his family (especially his son), love between an older man and a woman 20 years his junior, hospitalization, the prospect of death. The books, more than most, hint at the secret history of their author's soul.

"Often in my researches," says Herman, "I've come across old books of a specialist nature in which the author, usually a retired wing-commander, expresses in a modest foreword the hope that the little volume may be a *vade mecum* for the model steam engineer, coarse angler, sado-masochist or whatever. I feel that way about these pages: I hope that this little volume may be a *vade mecum* not so much for the specialist as for others like me—the general struggler and straggler, the person for whom the whole sweep of consciousness is often too much."

Who among us is not such a struggler and straggler? The sound of Hoban's works is always wistful, that of a weary pilgrim like his own Pilgermann destined never to reach Jerusalem. People who like this voice—and who find it among the most distinctive and hypnotic in fiction—will gladly read anything that bears Hoban's name. In *The Medusa Frequency,* as in **Riddley Walker** or *The Marzipan Pig,* the mundane becomes magical and even ordinary reality looks "strange and flickering and haunting."

Tom LeClair

SOURCE: A review of *The Medusa Frequency,* in *American Book Review,* Vol. 10, No. 2, May-June, 1988, p. 17.

At the end of **The Medusa Frequency,** a novelist turned *Classics Comics* writer begins doing stories for the back panels of cereal boxes, thus reviving a disused medium for narrative and initiating what I'll call post (as in Post Raisin Bran) postmodernism. In this new, "improved" product, the scale of representation is reduced for easy consumption, complex materials are processed into banal abstractions, and art literally becomes commodity packaging.

I'd like to think Hoban was mocking his novelist, but **The Medusa Frequency** is itself a cereal-box novel, a flimsy, throwaway 143-page container of cliched postmodern themes and methods.

In a letter to Hawthrone, Melville refers to a subject even larger than his mighty whale—Kraken, legendary gaint of the deep. Kraken speaks to the novelist/narrator of **The Medusa Frequency,** but novelist/author Hoban doesn't listen, doesn't attempt to represent in some analogous way the vast mystery of the creature—or any of the other mythic beings he includes in his book. Hoban's novelist is named Hermann Orff. Scurrying around London trying to make a living and trying to forget his lost lover Luise, Orff sees or thinks he sees a contemporary Hermes, listens to or hallucinates the talking head of Orpheus, reads or imagines messages from Eurydice and Medusa on his word processor, and writes all of this as *The Medusa Frequency,* a meditation on the Great Goddess and eternal female.

These larger-than-life figures still exist and can still be metaphors for postmodernity, as Barth has shown in *Chimera* and Michel Serres in his multivolume reflections on Hermes. But Hoban refuses his materials space to develop, to twine and snarl like Medusa's snakes, to make the book both a fright and a wonder, *the* postmodern achievement. With its talk of deconstruction and feminism, its self-referring jocularity and Ludlum-like title, *The Medusa Frequency* is Post packaged, not composed.

THE MOMENT UNDER THE MOMENT (1992)

Lorna Sage

SOURCE: A review of *The Moment Under the Moment,* in *The Times Literary Supplement,* No. 4645, April 10, 1992, p. 20.

Russell Hoban's occasional pieces are just that: few and far between. He's not prolific when he writes for grown-ups, indeed confesses to sometimes suffering from block—which he calls here "Blighter's Rock" in order to avoid ill-luck—and to employing various tricks, using yellow A4, for instance, never scary, truly blank white. He has always in any case flirted dangerously with the notion that invisible writing is the best. In his breakthrough book. *Riddley Walker* (1980), being able to read and write is one of the skills that nearly gets his eponymous hero killed, a doubtful blessing at best: "I don't having nothing only words to put down on paper. Its so hard. Some times theres mor in the empty paper nor there is when you get the writing down on it." And acturely, as Riddley would have put it, the dance of atoms that makes up the paper is possibly more wonderful than the characters we inscribe on it. Hoban's love of home-made orthography is only the most obvious sign that, more than most writers, he needs to kidnap the reader on to his territory. It's not easy to do this in a short story or an essay, and by conventional means, and the materials collected *The Moment Under the Moment* are probably not going to win Hoban new converts. They'll act as welcome blueprints and stopgaps and footnotes for ready-made readers, however: doodles from the oracle.

Not that he sounds pretentious exactly. He likes to see himself, I think, as a literary hunter-gatherer, a mouthpiece less by virtue of his authority than be-

cause he's still blessed/cursed at moments with the sense of strangeness children have before the world has solidified into our familiar "limited-reality consensus" around them. They are "receptors of a universal transmission", and let in horrors, visions, "palimpsest voices . . . processions, plagues, migrations, ruins, standing stone . . . ". It is entirely characteristic that in a personal piece called **"Pan Lives"**, which first appeared in *Granta,* he should wryly deplore his five-year-old son's proud acquisition of a new word for the way ink comes off a brush:

> I worry a little—and yet why should I worry?—about Ben's now having the world *flow* in his mind instead of what was there before. The ignorance that was there before was in its way a *religious* ignorance—the person was in a respectful relationship to something not fully understood, the person was respectfully offering the mind to the thing, was holding the mind open to all of the thing. Now he doesn't know any more than he did before but he has a word to call it by.

Some of the stiffness of this ("the person", etc) is perhaps explained in context by the fact that the paint-brush in question is Japanese. However, some of it reflects the double-bind of Hoban's relation to his medium—he suspects that language somehow cancels our sense of real presences, our sense of holiness in things. In fact, he's very like a devout deconstructionist turned inside out. Both detect difference rather than deference in the way words work, though for Hoban it follows that you have to enlarge the category "language" to redeem this lapse: "everything that happens is language, everything that goes on is saying something." In his children's books and novels, he cultivates his special brand of "ignorance" and makes words as thing-like as he can. Here he's doomed to write around the edges of his terrain for the most part.

The oddest pieces are those in which he sketches out apocryphal encounters between some of the mythic figures that obsess him—for example, a libretto in which Miranda and Caliban go behind the backs of Shakespeare and Prospero to invent a truly brave new world where "we two are each other". This horrid and euphoric prospect generates lines like "When Dracula's alive and well and Goldilocks is dead. . . . When there's moaning down the chimney and you dial nine nine nine, /And a voice says, SIX SIX SIX HERE, WILL IT BE YOUR PLACE OR MINE . . . ?" Lyrics that would be at home in *The Rocky Horror Show,* in fact, and a reminder that as well as crossing the frontier that divides children's fiction from adults', Hoban has broken through the *cordon sanitaire* that separates "literary fiction" from the likes of H. P. Love-craft and Stephen King. Similarly, the piece entitled **"Certain Obsessions, Certain Ideas"** has Fay Wray and Perseus comparing notes on Medusa and King Kong. He can be very funny, though it's only a sideline. He tells us about "a toy sold a few years back, a box with an on-off switch. When you switched it on a little hand came out of the box and switched it off." There are quite a few things you might have done with this; for him it suggests childhood's doom—that we grow up by switching off our early animist knowledge of the world (ignorance). He rewrites Wordsworth with a vengeance: the child is father of the failed child ("failed children . . . juiceless minds . . . poison skulls that dream in numbers and megadeaths").

The main difficulty for someone who's always finding the many in the one (the atoms in the paper) is that it's a trick that turns around on you so that you keep finding the one in the many, and so repeating yourself. Russell Hoban doesn't avoid sameness, and in a sense, I suppose, would expect to keep stumbling into it. He states his main ideas—or perhaps better, convictions—many times. The best version by far is in **"Household Tales by the Brothers Grimm"** (the introduction to a Picador edition):

> We make fiction because we *are* fiction. . . . We make stories because we are story. The fabric of our myths and folk-tales is in us from before birth. The action systems of the universe are the origin of life and stories. The patterns of blue-green algae and the numinous wings of the Great Nebula in Orion and the runic scrawl of human chromosomes are stories. . . .

This gives you a glimpse of the way that, at his best, he can bamboozle readers into awe by making meanings seem *tattooed* on your DNA. It also—that phrase about "action systems" is a giveaway—consigns him to the realms of what he calls "what-iffery", the disreputable realms of supernature. Where, indeed, he is disarmingly content to dwell, biding his moment.

Francis King

SOURCE: A review of *The Moment Under the Moment,* in *The Spectator,* Vol. 268, No. 8545, April 18, 1992, pp. 28-9.

By his own admission in his foreword to this collection of stories, essays, sketches and a libretto, Russell Hoban is constantly straining to grasp the ungraspable, to say the unsayable. A vain pursuit, as he sees it—since 'the real reality, the flickering of the seen and unseen actualities, the moment under the moment, can't be put into words.' Why then bother with words at all? Well, there are always those rare occasions when suddenly, miraculously, 'the reader finds himself in a place where the unwordable happens off the page'. This mystical view of the nature of the 'real reality' and of the writer's priest-like role as the channel through which, however fragmentarily and dimly, that 'real reality' is transmitted to the reader, now impressed and now irritated me throughout the course of this book.

The first and the most satisfactory of the stories, **'The Man with the Dagger',** is an act of homage to one of the best of Jorge Luis Borges' stories, 'The South'. In the Borges story, a Buenos Aires librarian, Dahlmann, travels to the south of Argentina, to the empty shell of a ranch which has long belonged to his family, in order to convalesce from a near-fatal illness. Provoked to a fight in the general store of the remote provincial town in which he now finds himself, he picks up the knife thrown to him by an old gaucho and leaves the store to fight the duel to which he has been challenged and to meet the possible death 'which he would have chosen or dreamt'.

In Hoban's story, the narrator, as it were Hoban himself, goes in search of Dahlmann in an attempt to solve the mystery with which Borges leaves the reader: when Dahlmann seizes that dagger, what exactly is it that he so decisively accepts? Fate? A test of his courage? The inevitability of death? And is he in fact killed or does he somehow, by some miracle, survive? Certainly, in the course of his odd quest, Hoban's 'I' is surrounded by death. In the hotel where he enquires for Dahlmann, the desk-clerk is a living skeleton; and in this same hotel he makes love to another skeleton, a prostitute called Noir. Eventually he meets Dahlmann; but the mystery remains a mystery.

The world of this story, as of the other seven, is one in which reality melts into dream, the present into the past, the animate into the inanimate. **'My Night with Leonie',** for example, is an account of how the narrator falls in love with the Sphinx on the south terrace of the Jardin des Tuileries—'Not a lovely face nor an inviting one, but so erotic in its utter propriety.' He imagines her to be a virgin; and in the course of a conversation with her, she assures him that she is. But she has lied to him, as his night-time discovery of seven Japanese tourists queuing up for her favours eventually reveals to him.

In **'Schwartz',** the inanimate object which similarly becomes animate for the narrator is a stone lion, a Sung dynasty tomb guardian in the British Museum, with a taste for Thelonius Monk. The lion, Schwartz, invisible to everyone else, accompanies his new-found friend on the tube back to his flat, where they listen to 'Blue Monk' on the hifi. Then the lion, as though he had become an embodiment of conscience, begins relentlessly to interrogate his host about a tragic and shameful incident in his past.

In **'The Colour of Love',** a story which evokes the crepuscular beauty of Venice in masterly fashion, the female narrator, a woman painter, remarks, 'If you think about it the whole thing becomes very meta-physical, but then everything does.' She is speaking of an experience of her own; but she might equally have been speaking of any of these stories.

The essays and sketches are, in general, less impressive. The best of them, written for a seminar of the Israel Association of American Studies in Tel Aviv, the theme of which was 'The American Dream', is a beautiful account, now shimmering with vaguely poetic imaginings and now etched with harshly realistic details, of Hoban's childhood in Lansdale, Pennsyl-vania. His parents were Russian Jews from the Ukraine who, after a few years of poverty and struggle, satisfactorily established themselves in the New World and so were able to create the home in which their son first heard Bach's *Art of Fugue* and Schubert's *Die Winterreise,* first read *Lord Jim* and *Darkness at Noon,* first began to walk along 'that wavering edgeline where the sea of the mystery meets the strand of the more or less known'.

The libretto, **'The History of Miranda and Caliban',** set to music for mezzosoprano and baritone by Helen Roe, is as dense and prickly as a thicket of thornbushes. Prefaced with the dubious claim that 'Shakespeare didn't invent Caliban, Caliban invented Shakespeare (and Sigmund Freud and one or two others)', it is unlikely to tempt readers to struggle far through its 39 pages.

Sadly, this collection does not always display Hoban at his strange and haunting best. But there is enough in it of the highest quality to make it worth reading.

Additional coverage of Hoban's life and career is contained in the following sources published by the Gale Group: *Contemporary Authors,* **Vols. 5-8R;** *Contemporary Authors New Revision Series,* **Vols. 23, 37, 66;** *Contemporary Literary Criticism,* **Vols. 7, 25;** *Dictionary of Literary Biography,* **Vol. 52;** *DISCovering Authors Modules,* **Novelists;** *Major Authors and Illustrators for Children and Young Adults; Major 20th-Century Writers; Something About the Author,* **Vols. 1, 40, 78.**

Carolyn Reeder
1937-

American novelist and nonfiction author.

Major works include *Shades of Gray* (1989), *Grandpa's Mountain* (1991), *Moonshiner's Son* (1993), *Across the Lines* (1997), *Captain Kate* (1999).

INTRODUCTION

A former elementary school teacher, Carolyn Reeder taught children for many years and eventually began writing books for a young audience. In such novels as *Shades of Gray* and *Moonshiner's Son*, Reeder has depicted adolescent protagonists coming of age during significant historical periods, including the Civil War, the Great Depression, and World War II. While Reeder has also coauthored several books with her husband about the Shenandoah National Park, it is her writing for children for which she is best known. Reeder is praised for the historical accuracy of her settings and for sensitive and gripping portrayals of her characters, who often endure the harsh realities of racism, war, and death. Commenting on Reeder's *Across the Lines*, *Booklist* reviewer Carolyn Phelan stated, "there are few Civil War books for children that explore the reality of war or the subtlety of race relations as sensitively as this involving novel."

BIOGRAPHICAL INFORMATION

Reeder was born to Pauline and Raymond Owens in Washington, D.C., on November 16, 1937. Growing up in Washington, she wrote for her junior high and high school newspapers even though at the time she had no serious interest in becoming a professional writer. At twelve years old, she discovered her true vocation by agreeing to teach a neighbor to read. The experience proved so rewarding that she decided to pursue a career in education. After receiving a bachelor's degree from the American University, she began teaching elementary school. Soon afterward she married Jack Reeder, and the couple had two children, David and Linda. When the children were grown, Reeder started collaborating with her husband on books about the Shenandoah National Park, a cherished getaway destination for the couple, who

enjoyed hiking together. At one point her husband's schedule prevented him from continuing with their joint writing projects, so Reeder began her solo career. After several of her works, including *Shades of Gray, Moonshiner's Son,* and *Across the Lines,* received critical acclaim, Reader ended her teaching career to devote all of her time to writing.

MAJOR WORKS

Shades of Gray, Reeder's initial work of historical fiction, focuses on Will, who as an orphan of the Civil War is forced to live with distant relatives he hardly knows. Will is at first deeply resentful of his Uncle Jed, a conscientious objector who had refused to fight in the war and who is viewed as a coward by his nephew. Will's initial anger at his uncle eventually wanes as he too experiences ridicule at the hands of several local bullies. Ultimately, Will discovers the difference between cowardice and conviction and comes to admire the courage his uncle exhibited in refusing to fight. Commenting on the story, a *Kirkus Reviews* writer noted that "a good feel for time and place makes [Will's] story memorable."

Reeder's second novel, *Grandpa's Mountain*, is set during the Great Depression. The protagonist, Carrie, is a confused young girl of eleven who arrives for a holiday at her grandfather's Blue Ridge Mountain home only to find him embroiled in a battle with the government over possession of his mountain property. Although Carrie's grandfather eventually loses his battle, she learns a great deal about the significance of fighting for your beliefs. A *Horn Book* reviewer noted that "the novel strikes many chords while exploring the relationships among family, neighbors, and strangers."

Also set in the Blue Ridge Mountains of Virginia, Reeder's next novel, *Moonshiner's Son,* centers on Tom, a young boy who helps his father manufacture illegal liquor. When a preacher intent on exposing the evils of alcohol moves to the area, Tom's life becomes increasingly complicated. Not only does he begin to doubt the morality of distilling moonshine, he also becomes involved with the preacher's daughter. The preacher further complicates this elaborate conundrum by notifying the local authorities of Tom's still. A *Kirkus Reviews* critic assessed *Moonshiner's Son* as "another excellent work from Reeder, with strong, memorable characters and a compelling plot, an unusually thoughtful and well-crafted historical novel of these mountain people."

Reeder's next work, *Across the Lines,* presents a "powerful, moving story of friendship, loss, and courage," according to a contributor in *Kirkus Reviews.* In the novel the reader finds a tale of two young friends separated by the Civil War, each fighting to discover the meaning of honor and freedom. Racial issues are treated directly: one friend, Simon, is a black slave freed by the war; the other friend, Edward, is the son of a white plantation owner. After growing up as constant companions, the boys end up fighting on opposing sides, and the story becomes a gripping tale of each boy's individual struggle to understand his circumstances.

Reeder again chose the Civil War era as the setting for her 1999 novel *Captain Kate.* A peevish twelve-year-old, Kate refuses to accept the remarriage of her mother. Her mother's current difficult pregnancy and her distant father fuel Kate's youthful anxiety. With only the aid of her inexperienced stepbrother Seth,

Kate decides to pilot the family's coal boat down a canal on a dangerous journey in search of excitement. The long journey is rife with almost constant dilemmas, through which the strong-willed Kate prevails, never admitting shortcomings on her part. During the excursion, Kate broods constantly but eventually warms to her new siblings, yet she lets no one forget the pain that exists in her young heart. Some critics believe Reeder's description of Kate's journey becomes laborious and long-winded, while others praise her accurate depiction of the time period and her meticulous attention to geographical details.

AWARDS

Reeder's first novel, *Shades of Gray,* received a number of awards, including the Scott O'Dell Historical Fiction Award, Child Study Children's Book Award, and the Notable Children's Book award from the American Library Association (ALA), all 1989, and the Jefferson Cup Award from the Virginia Library Association, Notable Children's Book for the Language Arts from the National Council of Teachers of English, and Jane Addams Children's Book Award, all in 1990. *Moonshiner's Son* also garnered the 1993 Joan G. Sugarman Children's Book Award from the Washington Independent Writers Legal and Educational Fund and was cited as the Honor Book, Hedda Seisler Mason Award, in 1995.

———————

AUTHOR COMMENTARY

Carolyn Reeder

SOURCE: "About Carolyn Reeder," http:\\reederbooks.com\info.htm. Retrieved August 20, 2000.

From the time I learned to read, I always had my nose stuck in a book. But it was many years before I discovered that *writing* can bring just as much pleasure as reading.

I never planned to be a writer, even though I worked on school newspapers from junior high all the way through college. From the summer I was twelve, and taught a neighborhood child to read—he had never learned, even though he was almost nine—I knew I'd be a teacher.

For a while, teaching and family life filled my time. But then my husband and I began to work together in the evenings, writing non-fiction books for adults while our children did their homework. (We wrote about Shenandoah National Park, our favorite place to hike and camp.)

After a few years, my husband's work allowed him little time for writing, but I had more time since our children were older and were becoming independent. So I decided to try my hand at fiction and write for young people because I knew that kids love a good story.

At first, I wrote only during school vacations, but before long, I began to write during the school year, too. Writing became more and more important to me until finally I decided to give up teaching and be a full-time author. It's wonderful to have all the time I need to research and write my historical novels and still have time to do the other things I enjoy.

When I'm not at the library or in front of a computer, I like to bicycle, hike, cross-country ski, swim, visit with friends, and see plays. And, of course, I like to read.

Carolyn Reeder

SOURCE: "Carolyn Reeder," http:\\www.children'sbookguild.org\reeder.htm. Retrieved August 20, 2000.

Until recently, my life was defined by roles and passages. First, the daughter growing up in Washington, D.C., next the student at American University, and then the longest-held roles of all: wife, mother, teacher. I'm still a wife, but I'm an out-of-work mother now that my children are grown, and I recently left my job as a reading teacher so I'd have more time to write. Today, instead of roles, I have facets—hiker, history buff, book lover, friend, theater goer, writer. . . .

Now, writing is an important part of my life—an end in itself—but my first writing was simply an outgrowth of our family's hiking experiences in Shenandoah National Park. It all began when my husband and I wrote a non-fiction adult book about the mountain people who were displaced when the park was established. We worked together on two more books about the park before I began to write fiction for children.

All of my children's books are historical novels set between 1863 and 1942, and they are read mostly by young people in grades 4-7. I'm often asked why I write historical fiction. Undoubtedly, all the times I

read through the Little House books influenced me in that direction, but part of the reason is that I enjoy the research. Children stare at me in disbelief when they hear that, but the research is my excuse to talk to people I wouldn't otherwise meet, to take excursions to places that are off the beaten track, to read in depth on fascinating subjects, and to call it "work."

TITLE COMMENTARY

SHADES OF GRAY (1989)

Diane Roback

SOURCE: A review of *Shades of Gray,* in *Publishers Weekly,* Vol. 236, No. 19, November 10, 1989, p. 61.

The Civil War has left 12-year-old Will Page an orphan, and he is sent to his mother's relatives in the country in Virginia. Prepared to hate his uncle, a "coward" who refused to fight for either side, Will slowly comes to respect the man's position. And as he fits into the hardworking farm routine, the boy discovers, to his surprise, that physical labor (which his parents' slaves used to do) can be rewarding. Will's coming-of-age story revolves around overcoming his prejudices about Yankees and Confederates. Thoughtfully told, the novel captures the hardships that followed the last war fought on U.S. soil. But Will's maturation feels too carefully mapped out, leaving the impression of didactic lessons learned; he seems less a real person than an example of error rectified. Ages 8-12.

Elizabeth M. Reardon

SOURCE: A review of *Shades of Gray,* in *School Library Journal,* Vol. 36, No. 1, January, 1990, p. 106.

Gr 5-8—Will Page, a 12-year-old orphan going to live with his aunt's family in post-Civil War Virginia, is as much a victim of the war as his recently deceased family. All of his anger over their deaths is directed at the Yankees—and at his Uncle Jed, who chooses not to fight. In this interesting psychological study of the effects of war, Will must work through his anger and grief and learn to accept his new family. It is when he finally realizes how much more courage it took for his uncle to stick to his beliefs that Will begins to heal. Reeder has drawn a fascinating character in Will, and all of the other characters are equally well constructed. While readers should enjoy the story, they may find the point a bit obvious. A very different perspective on the Civil War experience, and one that's sure to prompt questions and comment.

Nancy Vasilakis

SOURCE: A review of *Shades of Gray,* in *The Horn Book Magazine,* Vol. LXVI, No. 2, March-April, 1990, pp. 202-03.

At his mother's behest, twelve-year-old Will Page, the only member of his immediate family to survive the Civil War, is sent to live with his relatives in a backwoods cabin in the Virginia Piedmont. Far from the comfortable life he knew in town with a father who was a cavalry officer and with slaves to do all the household work, he is especially mortified at the knowledge that his uncle sat out the war, refusing to fight for the Confederate cause. Will soon discovers that, honor notwithstanding, in order to survive he must work hard alongside this quiet, uncompromising man and Aunt Emily and outgoing cousin Meg to keep themselves all fed and sheltered. Frequently, meals are made up only of whatever fish or small game they can catch, if any, and what few greens they pick. It doesn't escape Will's notice that his relatives share their meager belongings ungrudgingly, and when he sees the derision with which his uncle is treated by many of his neighbors, Will comes to understand the courage it took for the man to live by his pacifist principles during the war. The story is traditionally cast, but effective. A minor bit of action involving some local bullies whom Will eventually disarms seems somewhat of a contrivance, but the author's unforced, naturalistic prose style will engage middle-grade readers as will the novel's well-developed, amiable characters and its solid moral grounding. Unfortunately, likely readers may be put off by an unprepossessing jacket and title.

📖 *GRANDPA'S MOUNTAIN* (1991)

Katharine Bruner

SOURCE: A review of *Grandpa's Mountain,* in *School Library Journal,* Vol. 37, September, 1991, p. 259.

Gr 5-8—Historical facts surrounding the 1935 creation of Shenandoah National Park form the base on which Reeder convincingly overlays a fictional story

rich in character delineation and development. Carrie, 11, loves to spend summers at her grandparents' home in the Blue Ridge Mountains, away from hard times in the city. Everything is thrown akimbo when the government begins buying up thousands of mountain acres, evicting the occupants and burning their homes. At first Grandpa is unbelieving, then he convinces himself that, with the support of his like-minded neighbors, he can fight to win. However, many of them—poor and uneducated, some merely subsistence tenant farmers—welcome the chance to sell or be relocated near town and are furious at him for interfering. The longer Grandpa fights, the more alone he stands. While resisting change, he himself is changed, becoming as hard and intractable as the men he opposes. Carrie is torn between her respect for him and shock at his behavior. Through seemingly traitorous actions, Grandma makes it possible for him to win his personal fight against defeatism. Carrie returns to her parents' home at summer's end, strengthened by two stalwart grandparents and the way each chose to deal with crisis. This portrayal of one set of events and its consequences during the Great Depression has relevance for situations today in which the government still pits projected benefits for the many against total disruption of the few.

Sheilamae O'Hara

SOURCE: A review of *Grandpa's Mountain,* in *Booklist,* Vol. 88, No. 25, November 15, 1991, p. 625.

Gr. 4-7. Every summer, 11-year-old Carrie leaves Washington, D.C., to spend the summer with her grandparents in the Blue Ridge Mountains of Virginia. She loves her grandparents' life-style: running a country store and a lunchroom, tending their chickens and garden, and living in harmony with their neighbors and the land. When the government announces the creation of Shenandoah National Park, Carrie's grandfather is outraged and vows that he will never give up the land that the Griffins have lived on for five generations. He obstinately refuses to move even when his neighbors will not join with him to fight the condemnation proceedings. Carrie firmly believes that he will win and is devastated when they are evicted from the property. This is a slow-moving story that children may find hard to get into, but it could be a suitable read-aloud for a middle-grade teacher whose curriculum includes U.S. government. It dramatizes the human cost of eminent domain and the deep love people have for their homes as well as the wisdom of accepting what cannot be changed.

Margaret A. Bush

SOURCE: A review of *Grandpa's Mountain,* in *The Horn Book Magazine,* Vol. LXVII, No. 6, November-December, 1991, pp. 738-39.

Grandpa's mountain, where his property includes a country store and lunchroom as well as a family farm handed down through the generations, is a beautiful and troubled place. Located in Virginia's Blue Ridge Mountains, his home and many others must be sacrificed for the founding of Shenandoah National Park. The story of Grandpa's stubborn struggle to make his protest heard is told from the point of view of eleven-year-old Carrie, visiting her grandparents for the summer. Grandpa's belief in an individual's rights in a democratic system is unshakable, but his neighbors disappoint him in their reluctance to join his battle. Carolyn Reeder has given careful thought to her historical setting and the configuration of human responses to loss. Details of the Depression are a bit crudely introduced but become more interesting as Grandpa's neighbors find the state's offer of cash and resettlement in town a welcome relief from deep poverty, and the young men from the Civilian Conservation Corps camps arrive to do the unwelcome job of evicting people and demolishing homes. There are many stock characters whose familiar traits ring true. Grandmother's patience is nearly saintly, and though she is the source of wisdom for the family, she is a complex individual. Carrie's reserved mother; the nosy postmistress; the bully playing out his insecurities; and the harsh father of Carrie's friends Kate and Luanne are more stereotyped characters but contribute importantly to Carrie's eventual growth in confidence and understanding. Carrie pays a price for her loyalty to her grandfather, but the summer is her time of passage. A very special book for families in the Shenandoah region, the novel strikes many chords while exploring the relationships among family, neighbors, and strangers.

MOONSHINER'S SON (1993)

Bruce Anne Shook

SOURCE: A review of *Moonshiner's Son,* in *School Library Journal,* Vol. 39, No. 5, May, 1993, p. 128.

Gr 5-8—In the hills of Virginia during Prohibition, moonshining is an accepted way of life for 13-year-old Tom and his father, June. The boy plans to follow in this chosen career until a Bible-thumping preacher moves into the area to rid the country of the evils of liquor. As he becomes friendly with the preacher's daughter, Tom begins to wonder about the negative effects of whiskey on their customers. Conflict builds between the mountain people and the outsiders—revenuers, the preacher, and an unscrupulous bootlegger. Another stranger, a folklorist gathering material for a book, finds his way into the hearts of the native people through his interest in their crafts and tales. Tom's pa is a renowned local storyteller and the boy has inherited the talent. However, a great deal of the tension in the story lies between father and son. Tom longs for praise and approval, which the man seems incapable of giving. This is a story with a strong regional flavor. The mountaineers are portrayed as self-possessed, dignified people who have much knowledge despite their lack of book learning. The characters are well-developed individuals. The plot moves along quickly and with enough suspense to hold readers' interest. They will identify with Tom's moral dilemma and his need for parental love. A good, readable addition to historical fiction collections.

Publishers Weekly

SOURCE: A review of *Moonshiner's Son,* in *Publishers Weekly,* Vol. 240, No. 21, May 24, 1993, p. 88.

The accomplished author of **Shades of Gray** returns to the Blue Ridge Mountains for this Prohibition-era novel. Twelve-year-old Tom seems destined to become a moonshiner like his father. When a city preacher comes to the hollow with his daughter, Amy, Tom is drawn to her and feels torn: seeking Amy's approval requires rejecting moonshining. A wide cast of picturesque but sometimes sketchily developed characters personifies the struggle between old and new ways—unfortunately, many characters seem more like frames on which to hang competing concepts than like flesh-and-blood mortals. Some of the action seems forced, even melodramatic, and the epiphanies experienced by both Tom's father and Preacher Taylor are facile. Despite these limitations, the reader is drawn into the story, and Tom's concerns seem very real. Story-telling traditions are also celebrated here, and a strong sense of place and time adds resonance.

Janice Del Negro

SOURCE: A review of *Moonshiner's Son,* in *Booklist,* Vol. 89, Nos. 19 & 20, June 1, 1993, p. 1816.

Gr. 7-10. It's Prohibition, but you'd never know it by the amount of moonshine being brewed in the Virginia hills. Twelve-year-old Tom Higgins is learning the art of moonshining from his daddy and has every intention of following the family tradition. Then a new preacher convinced of the evils of drink arrives. While the locals defy the preacher, avoid the revenuers, and trade with bootleggers, Tom becomes friendly with the preacher's daughter and goes to the school run by the preacher's wife. When his good friend is injured in a fire caused by a drunken fight, Tom decides he cannot be a moonshiner after all. His confrontation with his father is violent and terrible, but it results in a new beginning. Reeder evokes the life of a proud and accomplished people, fiercely protective of their privacy and their traditions. There is action aplenty, but it's the way of life of the people who live in Bad Camp Hollow that's the real story here. Though this is a solid piece of historical fiction with likable characters and a believable premise, it may need a booktalk shove to get it off the shelf.

Elizabeth S. Watson

SOURCE: A review of *Moonshiner's Son,* in *The Horn Book Magazine,* Vol. LXIX, No. 5, September-October, 1993, p. 601.

When the preacher's temperance-minded daughter, Amy, meets the moonshiner's son, Tom, during Prohibition in Virginia's Blue Ridge Mountains, the resulting story is a struggle often humorous and sometimes tense, with unexpected conclusions. The honorbound world of the mountain folk is convincingly portrayed as their traditions and values are gradually revealed to the flatlander, Preacher Taylor. The book is like a patchwork quilt, carefully plotted in a pattern that changes Pa's profession and Tom's inheritance. Tom learns that Pa does value him and that his father's rigid high standards can be maintained despite the changes. Readers will learn as much about honesty, honor, and generosity as they will learn about this special place and time in American history.

📖 *ACROSS THE LINES* (1997)

Kirkus Reviews

SOURCE: A review of *Across the Lines,* in *Kirkus Reviews,* Vol. 65, March 1997, p. 467.

Reeder (*Shades of Gray,* 1990, etc.) returns to the era of the Civil War for this powerful, moving story of friendship, loss, and courage. In May 1864 the Union forces are massing along the Appomattox in preparation for the siege of the supposedly impregnable Petersburg, and Edward's family must flee their plantation, Riverview, to stay with a relative. In the confusion, Edward's slave and best friend, Simon, runs off to freedom. Too young to join the Union Army, he finds work doing odd jobs for the Yankees. He misses Edward, but the sight of the black Union troops, who show incredible courage in the opening battles of the siege, make him aware that there is no turning back for him. Edward misses Simon, too, and chafes at life under siege, with the constant shelling and his inability to help in the war effort. For both boys, war becomes a crucible: Simon struggles to find a place and true freedom with the Union forces; Edward watches with envy as his arrogant older brother goes off to join the Rebel forces, only to fall ill with a terrible fever that can only be brought down by doses of quinine—available behind enemy lines in the Union hospital. There are no easy answers in this clear-eyed evocation of the cruelty and dangers of a tragic war; Reeder casts problem after problem before her young protagonists, and allows them the strength and character to fend for themselves on the way to finding solutions.

Carolyn Phelan

SOURCE: A review of *Across the Lines,* in *Booklist,* Vol. 93, No. 15, April 1, 1997, p. 1331.

Gr. 4-7. Just before his family flees from the Yankees, who soon capture their Virginia plantation, Edward searches without success for his slave and lifelong companion, Simon. Hidden in the chimney, Simon waits for freedom and finds himself making his own way in a land ruled by the forces of war; Edward and his family are caught up in the siege of Petersburg. Simon and Edward struggle with issues of freedom, courage, and friendship in surroundings that are new to them and sometimes quite frightening. The point of view shifts from one boy to the other throughout the novel, ending a year after the plantation's capture when both boys return there and catch a glimpse of each other. The boys care but acknowledge that things will never be the same, speaking wordless volumes with a distant hand gesture in their secret language. The switch back and forth from one boy to another breaks the narrative flow at times, but there are few Civil War books for children that explore the reality of war or the subtlety of race relations as sensitively as this involving novel. Reeder shows great respect for her readers by presenting a many-faceted view of these complex issues, which are all too often simplified to the point of distortion by writers eager to present their own points of view. With believable characters and an eventful plot, this novel offers a memorable, convincing view of the Civil War through the eyes of Simon and Edward.

Elizabeth Bush

SOURCE: A review of *Across the Lines,* in *Bulletin of the Center for Children's Books,* Vol. 50, No. 10, June, 1997, p. 371.

No sooner do the Yankees land near Edward's Virginia plantation home than Simon, a family house slave and Edward's constant companion, claims his freedom by joining the Union side as a "contraband" camp follower. Accepting any menial work that comes his way, Simon rudely awakens to the fact that the Yankees who supposedly espouse his freedom are often outright bigots ("It struck him that Negroes who had been valuable property to their masters might be worth nothing at all to a northern general"). Meanwhile Edward, his mother, and two siblings flee to relatives in Petersburg, which quickly comes under siege by the Yankees, and Edward's disgust with his older brother Duncan's virulent militarism leads him to welcome Southern defeat, if that defeat secures peace. Ultimately the two boys function more as observers than participants in the epic events swirling around them, and their mutual regret at parting, though often reiterated, is contrived and thinly sustained. Camp scenes and battle plans may appeal to middle-grade military tacticians, however, and Civil War buffs reading their way across the many battlefields will want to add Petersburg to their list.

Harriett Fargnoli

SOURCE: A review of *Across the Lines,* in *School Library Journal,* Vol. 43, No. 6, June, 1997, p. 126.

Gr 5-9—A novel about the Civil War that takes place from May 1864, to May 1865. The story has as much introspection as action as the author shows the coming of age of two childhood companions, one black, one white. Edward (about 12), his mother, younger sister, and older brother abandon their plantation home as Union soldiers advance. They are taken in by Edward's aunt in Petersburg, a town approximately 25 miles from the Confederate capital. Edward's manservant and constant companion, Simon,

has run off to taste freedom. Told alternately in Edward and Simon's voices, the story relates both of their experiences during the war. Freedom, choice, and self-respect are constant themes as are the needs and demands of friendship. The novel gets off to a slow start but picks up each time Reeder ties the action to real events. Food and paper shortages are capably described and become more than plot devices; they provide psychological clues to Edward's growing sense of self. Historically, Petersburg was significant because of its railroad lines and munitions storage. Reeder uses the setting to focus attention on the way one family endures the hardships of war. Along the way she draws fine characters, including Aunt Charlotte, a strong, independent woman who understands war as the power of evil. A solid piece of historical fiction.

Samantha Hunt

SOURCE: A review of *Across the Lines,* in *Voice of Youth Advocates,* Vol. 20, No. 13, August, 1997, p. 188.

Twelve-year-old Edward and Simon are friends. They have always been friends, but when Union soldiers land at City Point, Virginia, Edward and his family are forced to flee to relatives in nearby Petersburg. For Simon, a slave, this is his chance to slip away from the plantation to freedom. The ensuing story of the last year of the Civil War is told alternatively from Edward's and Simon's point of view. Edward feels displaced, living in his uncle's house like a poor relation. He fears his family's presence increases the privation his aunt and cousins are already suffering. He is "counting on the war being over long before he [is] old enough to be a soldier." He cannot imagine volunteering for hardship and danger as his father has done and his brother is impatient to do; he wonders if he is a coward. Simon, on the other hand, attaches himself to the Union Army, working at a variety of jobs to earn his keep. For the first time in his life, he is alone and lonely, struggling to make his own choices and decisions. Freedom, he quickly learns, is not going to be easy; he even wonders if it will be worth the struggle. He and other liberated blacks are referred to as "contraband," and even the black Union soldiers are not treated equally with the whites. Both boys miss the friendship they once shared, but they are gradually forced to realize that not only their individual lives, but their entire world, has changed, and they will never be together again. This is not a book for the reader who wants graphic descriptions of bloody battles. The military history is minimal; even the infamous Battle of the Crater during the siege of Petersburg is sketchily drawn. The focus of this book is social history, the effect of the war, and its many hardships on the populace, both civilian and military. The author does an excellent job of presenting a large cross-section of differing perspectives through Edward and Simon: Edward's father volunteers out of personal commitment to a cause, his uncle from a somewhat reluctant sense of duty. Edward's aunt opposed secession and considers the war a tragic waste, whereas his mother, in the finest Southern tradition, thinks it glorious and honorable. Jocasta, his aunt's servant and a free black, remains with the family out of personal loyalty; the slaves from Riverview, the family's plantation, almost without exception, run away. Black, white, male, female, rich, poor, military, and civilian—all are represented here, giving the YA readers at least some notion of how varied and complex the issues and views of the day were. Recommend to YAs who have appreciated Irene Hunt's classic *Across Five Aprils* (Berkley, 1987) or Paul Fleischman's *Bull Run* (HarperCrest, 1993). This one will give them another look at the faces and hearts of this most American of wars. VOYA Codes: 4Q 3P M J (Better than most, marred only by occasional lapses, Will appeal with pushing, Middle School—defined as grades 6 to 8, and Junior High—defined as grades 7 to 9).

📖 *FOSTER'S WAR* (1998)

Kirkus Reviews

SOURCE: A review of *Foster's War,* in *Kirkus Reviews,* Vol. LXVI, January 1, 1998, p. 61.

A vivid and compelling piece of historical fiction that also serves as a telling commentary on the effects an abusive parent has on his family. By the time the US enters WW II in December 1941, Mel Simmons is already in the armed forces, driven from home by his tyrannical father. Foster, 11, his little brother, Ricky, sister Evelyn, and mother are left behind to cope not only with Mr. Simmons, who grows meaner in Mel's absence, but with the austerity of life on the home front. Home life becomes even more difficult when his best friend, Jimmy, a Japanese-American, is relocated to an internment camp, and when the family learns that Mel has been killed in action. Foster's heartbroken mother, suffering herself and witnessing

the devastation of her family, takes steps to bring them back from the brink by divulging a long-kept secret about Mr. Simmons and showing them a family album of times when they were younger. By story's end, all of them have taken the first tentative steps toward reconciliation, a moving and believable conclusion to a story of a family in conflict.

Hazel Rochman

SOURCE: A review of *Foster's War,* in *Booklist,* Vol. 94, No. 11, February 1, 1998, p. 919.

Gr. 5-8. Reeder's Civil War novel, **Shades of Gray** (1990), won the Scott O'Dell Award for historical fiction. This time the setting is the homefront in San Diego during World War II. Eleven-year-old Foster's beloved older brother, Mel, joins the army to escape their tyrannical father, who makes home a tense, fearful battleground ("Foster wondered how many kids were more afraid of their fathers than of an air raid"). Foster also misses his best friend, Jimmy, who is sent away with other "dirty Japs" to an internment camp. The racism is personalized through the friendship story, but what is most powerful is the family war: the letters home from Mel at the front, the tension when he is missing in action, the anguish of everyone (including the father) when Mel is confirmed dead. Reeder brings the war home in all its personal anger, guilt, and wrenching loss.

Publishers Weekly

SOURCE: A review of *Foster's War,* in *Publishers Weekly,* Vol. 245, No. 6, February 9, 1998, p. 96.

Foster Simmons, the 11-year-old protagonist of this ambitious historical novel, is shocked by America's entry into WWII, but he is used to war at home. While his father stops short of physical abuse, his rages and his impossibly high standards create so much friction that Foster's older brother enlisted even before Pearl Harbor, just to get away from their California home. Reeder (**Moonshiner's Son**) dexterously splices together Foster's views of the domestic battlefield with his experience of WWII, from his best friend's internment in a camp for Japanese Americans to scrap drives at school. Readers will come away with a clear grasp of the period, especially because Reeder, in describing the prejudice against Japanese Americans, unveils a bit of the dark side of the nation's patriotic fervor. The characterizations, however, are less well balanced. The children, particularly the insightful Foster, are portrayed with considerably more subtlety than the adults (e.g., countering Mr. Simmons's despotism, Mrs. Simmons shows almost saintly patience). When change comes, it is sudden and nearly total, with a tragedy inspiring an almost-overnight transformation of the Simmons into an affectionate unit. Although the tidy wrap-up undercuts the re-creation of authentic and complex family tensions, it will not dim the sharp impression of homefront America nor Foster's fresh observations of it. Ages 10-14.

Bruce Anne Shook

SOURCE: A review of *Foster's War,* in *School Library Journal,* Vol. 44, No. 3, March, 1998, p. 216.

Gr 5-7—Foster, 11, isn't sure whether it's the war with Japan he should fear more or the war in his own southern California household. To escape their father's psychological abuse, his older brother Mel has left school and enlisted in the Air Force. The three younger siblings have developed various coping strategies to escape their father's cruel and damaging behavior. The man expects perfection from his children and his wife, who attempts to placate him and be the peacemaker. Against this explosive backdrop, the family learns of the bombing of Pearl Harbor. Now they must worry about possible Japanese air raids as well as Mel's safety. Foster finds himself coping with bewildering changes, including the loss of his best friend, a Japanese-American boy relocated to an internment camp. He and an understanding elderly neighbor become friends, and this relationship helps him through some difficult times. The period details are well presented: the importance of the radio, the homefront groups mobilizing the war effort, weekly reports in *Life* magazine. However, the father is a difficult character to appreciate. Like his children, readers are expected to overcome a thorough dislike of him too quickly. To understand his background does not help to forgive him his treatment of innocents. The long-suffering mother will also be difficult for young readers to accept, but her behavior and attitudes are true to the era. A flawed effort about World War II and the war effort at home.

Susanne L. Johnson

SOURCE: A review of *Foster's War,* in *The ALAN Review,* Vol. 25, No. 3, Spring, 1998.

Foster Simmons heads up the Youth for the War effort of his fifth-grade class in San Diego during World War II, while his brother joins the army to escape an overbearing father. After the Japanese bomb Pearl Harbor, Foster's best friend, Jimmy Osaki, is forced into a Japanese internment camp. As the war escalates, Foster learns that war isn't just adults fighting battles overseas. Young people also fight through buying war bonds, collecting scrap metal and rubber, and babysitting siblings so mothers can volunteer for the Red Cross Nurses' Aide Corps. Carolyn Reeder's touching and realistic story shows the transition from the innocence of children's war games to the disturbing realities of conflict. It is a credible account of the patriotism that inspired the U.S. during WWII, and it educates younger readers about our history.

Rachelle Bilz

SOURCE: A review of *Foster's War,* in *Voice of Youth Advocates,* Vol. 21, No. 4, October, 1998, p. 277.

Eleven-year-old Foster Simmons's life is drastically altered on December 7, 1941, when his brother Mel, home on leave from the Army Air Corps, is called back to base. Foster's fifth grade class listens to FDR's declaration of war on the radio and learns the proper procedure for air-raid drills. Foster finds himself faced with new responsibilities now that his mother does volunteer work and his father works overtime at the aircraft factory. Mr. Simmons, always distant and moody, is more remote than ever. Foster's older sister Evelyn is caught up in the family's Victory Garden and six-year-old Ricky is terrified of airplanes. Not only does Foster have to baby-sit Ricky, he must also cope with the loss of his best friend Jimmy Osaki, who has been sent to a relocation camp with his family. It is Foster who is at home to sign for the telegram containing the grim news of Mel's death. When the Purple Heart medal arrives, the Simmons family feels both sorrow and pride. Reeder's novel effectively enables the reader to experience the impact of World War II on a typical middle-class family. The letters from Mel, the family gathered around the radio, the articles in *Life* magazine, the rationing of sugar and gas, the treatment of the Japanese; all these contribute to an excellent evocation of life in America during the Second World War. Written in a simple, straightforward manner, ***Foster's War*** is a good historical fiction choice for middle school students.

📖 *CAPTAIN KATE* (1999)

Shawn Brommer

SOURCE: A review of *Captain Kate,* in *School Library Journal,* Vol. 45, No. 1, January, 1999, p. 132.

Gr 4-7—A novel set during the Civil War. Kate, 12, is resentful of her new stepfather who is away fighting in the Union army and of his children, 12-year-old Seth and 9-year-old Julia. When she learns that her mother plans to rent out the family canal boat for the summer Kate decides that she will take the vessel the 184 miles down the Cumberland & Ohio Canal. Knowing that she can't possibly make the trip alone and left with no other options, she pressures her stepbrother to go along with her and they leave without her mother's knowledge. Stubborn and fiercely independent Kate adamantly designates herself captain of *The Mary Ann* and has little patience with good-natured, virtuous Seth. With quiet resolve, the boy teaches her empathy and, by the novel's end, she has newfound respect and admiration for him. During the journey, she comes to terms with her father's death and realizes that she must accept changes. Julia, Kate's mother, and her stepfather are minor characters who pale in comparison to the thoughtfully created characters of Kate and Seth. Taking place primarily on the canal, the story has plenty of action and detailed descriptions of boats and life along the waterway. Tension builds gradually and is released at exact moments. Fans of Reeder's other books, especially **Shades of Gray,** are sure to appreciate this new offering.

Carolyn Phelan

SOURCE: A review of *Captain Kate,* in *Booklist,* Vol. 95, Nos. 9 & 10, January 1, 1999, p. 857.

Gr. 6-8. Twelve-year-old Kate has never accepted her mother's remarriage, nor has she welcomed her stepbrother Seth and stepsister Julia into the family. With her stepfather fighting in the Civil War and her mother laid up with complications of pregnancy, Kate decides to take her family's coal boat down the C&O Canal with only Seth to help. On the dangerous journey, prickly Kate must confront her worst fears and the worst parts of her nature, while Seth slowly earns her respect. Though in the end, Kate begins to accept her new family, Reeder never minimizes the magnitude of the pain Kate endures, nor the pain she causes others as she makes her transition. Kate's interior change is mirrored in the canal boat trip, another dif-

ficult journey with many steps, secrets, discomforts, perils, and unexpected pleasures. The setting makes this an unusual Civil War story for young people; the characters make it a rewarding one.

Publishers Weekly

SOURCE: A review of *Captain Kate,* in *Publishers Weekly,* Vol. 246, No. 1, January 4, 1999, p. 90.

This detailed account of 19th-century travel down the C&O waterway offers a generous sprinkling of adventure starring a gutsy yet prideful heroine. Until her father's death, 12-year-old Kate had spent half of every year aboard the *Mary Ann* helping her parents haul coal from Cumberland to Washington, D.C., but now her mother, who has recently remarried, wants to rent out the family's boat for the season. Unable to bear the thought of strangers steering the *Mary Ann* (and possibly mistreating the guide mules), Kate convinces her reluctant stepbrother that they should make the trip on their own. Soon after they get underway, Kate fears she has bitten off more than she can chew by appointing herself captain, but she won't admit her error in judgment. Even after adding a second boy to the crew, she faces one crisis after another, including a dangerous run-in with Confederate soldiers. Reeder (**Shades of Gray**) balances external conflicts with Kate's mullings over her own shortcomings. Although the tedious journey may at times seem as unbearably long to readers as it does to Kate, Reeder is successful both in replicating the Civil War era and accurately tracing a canal boat's path. Students whose knowledge of waterways comes from textbook definitions will find a plethora of easy-to-digest information here Ages 8-12.

Janice M. Del Negro

SOURCE: A review of *Captain Kate,* in *Bulletin of the Center for Children's Books,* Vol. 52, No. 6, February, 1999, p. 214.

Twelve-year-old Kate's mother has remarried a year after Kate's father's death, providing Kate with an unwanted stepfather (now fighting in the Civil War), stepsister, stepbrother, and step-baby-on-the-way. Kate is in a grief-riddled fury that she takes out on everyone around her, being malicious to her twelve-year-old stepbrother, Seth, and downright mean to her nine-year-old stepsister, Julia. She is further chagrined to learn that her mother must have bedrest until the new baby is born, which effectively cancels the family's moneymaking coal trips from Cumberland, Maryland to Georgetown on the C&O Canal. Kate comes up with a mad scheme to take the family canalboat downriver with only Seth as crew, in a trip that ends up punctuated by an accumulation of nasty spats. She and Seth manage to reach Georgetown with their barge of coal, and their return home is triumphant. Kate undergoes a miraculous change of heart, her understanding stepfather (home wounded from the war) takes his place as canalboat captain, and the whole family happily plans to spend the canal season transporting coal. Reeder often tells more than she shows, and the dictionary-style explanations of locks and canalboating are a bit intrusive. As a character, Kate is strictly one-note, and her sudden transformation at the end of the novel is predictable but not credible. Readers interested in canalboat history may want to sail along; others will just breeze on by.

Additional coverage of Reeder's life and career is contained in the following sources published by the Gale Group: *Authors and Artists for Young Adults,* **Vol. 32;** *Contemporary Authors,* **Vol. 135;** *Something About the Author,* **Vols. 66, 97.**

Rosemary Wells
1943-

American author, reteller, novelist, biographer, and illustrator of picture books and fiction.

Major works include *The Fog Comes on Little Pig Feet* (1972), *Benjamin and Tulip* (1973), the "Max" series of picture books (1979), *Through the Hidden Door* (1987), *Mary on Horseback: Three Mountain Stories* (1998).

For further information on Wells's life and career, see *CLR,* Volume 16.

INTRODUCTION

Credited with being the inventor of the children's board book, Wells is a popular and versatile writer noted for the realism, perceptiveness, and humor of her picture books and young adult novels. Exploring personal relationships with a sensitive eye, she conveys recognized values with understanding and wisdom. Wells's nonsexist texts occasionally combine fantasy with reality, contain elements of slapstick, irony, and astringent wit, and often conclude with unconventional or surprise endings. Her picture books, for which she is best known, are sometimes written in verse and generally feature a variety of engaging anthropomorphic animals caught in comic predicaments and universal childhood dilemmas. Usually focusing on sibling rivalry, Wells examines such concerns as bullies, bedtime fears, and inattentive parents while also producing spoofs on more controversial topics like evolution and natural history. Several of these works, including some of her board books about Max, a charming white bunny who innocently upstages his older sister, grew out of the author's observations of her own two children. Drawn in pencil or pen and ink and washed with watercolors, Wells's uncluttered, whimsical illustrations characteristically outline deceptively simple, stumpy figures with expressive eyes and body language. Her novels, which include realistic fiction, mysteries, and psychological thrillers, explore difficult ethical choices, including premarital sex, betrayal of trust, and stealing, without offering easy answers, and often draw on incidents and details from her own youth and that of her teenage friends. Utilizing nonjudg-

mental tone, honesty, insight, and humor, Wells allows her protagonists to find their inner strength and make their own choices.

BIOGRAPHICAL INFORMATION

Wells grew up on the New Jersey coast in the post World War II era. Her mother, a former dancer in the Ballet Russe de Monte Carlo and the American Ballet, and her father, a playwright, encouraged her early artistic endeavors. From the age of two, Wells drew constantly and was determined to become an artist when she grew up. At thirteen, Wells was sent to an upscale boarding school for girls where she found the regimentation and constant supervision oppressive. After she went on a hunger strike, her parents relented and took her out of the school. Wells later finished her secondary education at Red Bank High School and then attended a small private junior college in upstate New York. After a year of college, she enrolled in the Boston Museum School where she received classic instruction in anatomy and perspective. In 1963, she married Thomas M. Wells, an architecture student. That same year, she quit school and began work in publishing as an art editor at Allyn and Bacon. Two years later, she and her husband moved to New York City where she worked in the children's book division at Macmillan Company. During her years as an art designer, she put aside pursuit of her own drawing until she made sketches to illustrate the lyrics of *The Yeoman of the Guard*, the popular Gilbert and Sullivan operetta. Upon seeing Wells's illustrations, Macmillan editor-in-chief Susan Hirschman immediately encouraged Wells to pursue her talents stating, "Sit down, Rosemary, you're a Macmillan author now."

MAJOR WORKS

Reviewers consider Wells an original writer and able illustrator whose delightful picture books capture the essence of child behavior. Wells's early successes with such picture books as *Noisy Nora* (1973) and *Benjamin and Tulip* established her reputation for creating unparalleled animal characters that evoke strong human feelings. Her reputation as an illustrator of children's books was secured when the book series for which she is most widely known—the books featuring Max and his sister Ruby—were born. Through amusingly wry drawings, Wells portrays the interactions of Max, a toddler bunny, and Ruby, his bossy older sister, as they navigate through typical sibling dilemmas. While Ruby insists she knows what is best for Max and tries to control him, Max remains undaunted and innocently outsmarts his sister, always getting the last word. Wells uses minimal but lively language and a bright palette for these books; her pictures are done in vivid primary colors on uncluttered but detailed pages. With the publication of *Max's First Word*, the first book in the "Max" series, Wells introduced a significant innovation in children's literature. Rather than following the format of the thirty-two page picture book, Wells succeeded in producing a funny, enjoyable story in only sixteen pages. Additionally, rather than utilizing a paper medium, Wells produced her story on illustration boards, a remarkable advance in creating durable books for the very young.

Interactions between siblings and friends is a theme that surfaces in several of Wells's young adult novels as well as in her picture books. Drawing upon autobiographical details, Wells has earned praise for her realistic novels in which the protagonists face important ethical choices. In *The Fog Comes on Little Pig Feet*, the protagonist, an alienated girl at boarding school, must make a pivotal decision to protect her friend or tell the truth. In such suspenseful works as *When No One Was Looking* (1980), *The Man in the Woods* (1984), and *Through the Hidden Door*, the teenage protagonists struggle with a moral dilemma that defines their entrance into maturity. Wells has also written several biographies of historical and contemporary women. One of her most acclaimed books in this genre is *Mary on Horseback: Three Mountain Stories*, a book for middle schoolers. In this work, Wells profiles the hardships and triumphs of Mary Breckinridge, a founder of the Frontier Nursing Service in the Appalachian Mountains. Admiring the range of her comic sense and her ability to create strong and endearing characters, most critics regard Wells as a multi-talented author/illustrator whose percipient probings into the human condition are both compelling and lighthearted.

AWARDS

Wells has received numerous awards for her works, including the Children's Book Showcase Award from the Children's Book Council, 1974, for *Noisy Nora*; the Irma Simonton Black Award from the Bank Street College of Education, 1975, for *Morris's Disappearing Bag: A Christmas Story*; the Edgar Allan Poe Special Award from the Mystery Writers of America, for *When No One Was Looking* in 1981 and for *Through the Hidden Door* in 1988; the Washington Irving Children's Book Choice Award from the Westchester Library Association, for *Peabody* in 1986, for *Max's Christmas* in 1988, and for *Max's Chocolate Chicken* in 1992; the Golden Sower Award, 1986, for *Peabody*; Virginia Young Readers Award, 1987, for *The Man in the Woods*; the Golden Kite Award from the Society of Children's Book Writers, 1988, for *Forest of Dreams*; the *Boston Globe-Horn Book* Award and the Parents' Choice Award from the Parents' Choice Foundation, 1989, for *Shy Charles*; the *Riverbank Review* Children's Book of Distinction Award and Notable Children's Book in the Language Arts from the National Council of Teachers of English Children's Literature Assembly, both in 1999, for *Mary on Horseback: Three Mountain Stories*. Additionally, many of Wells's books were named among the best books of the year by *School Library Journal*, received American Library Association (ALA) Notable Book citations, or won *American Bookseller* "Pick of the Lists" citations.

AUTHOR COMMENTARY

Rosemary Wells

SOURCE: "The Artist at Work: The Writer at Work," in *The Horn Book Magazine,* Vol. LXIII, No. 2, March, 1987, pp. 163-70.

My mother tells me about her grandmother. "Old Grandma," as she was always called, was born with a caul, a thin, lacy membrane that lies upon a newborn baby's face. In the nineteenth century it was considered extraordinary luck, a gift from God. I do not remember Old Grandma, but when I was young, I was shown, from time to time, examples of her painting. Old Grandma used to paint parrots in colorful oils on the corners of fringed black silk tablecloths. These tablecloths were kept folded in a mothball-filled closet by my grandmother and exhibited to me as proof that there had been artistic ability in the family; "that's where you got it from." I would tap the long-dried parrots with my fingernail until I was told not to because the acid in my fingers would crack the paint. My mother kept the caul, which had been preserved in a jar of formaldehyde for many years. Eventually, she sold it to a sailor in the 1930s for five hundred dollars.

To my knowledge I was not born with a caul but with two small lights—like tiny Italian Christmas bulbs, as I picture them—inside my brain. They are drawing and writing. I did not know about the writing light until I was long grown up. People ask all authors, "Where do you get your ideas?" The answer is, "They come to the lights like moths. Then I can see them."

I work in a spare bedroom rigged up as a studio. One side of the room has a couple of drawing boards and many shelves stacked with school trip permission slips, published and unpublished artwork, dried up ink bottles, unanswered mail, ten-year-old royalty statements, unpaid bills, antihistamines from 1975, and items which need sorting at all times, even if they have just been organized.

When I am drawing, I listen to one of four classical music stations on an old radio. I constantly change stations in quest of music written before 1810. The two dogs, West Highland white terriers, stay with me. I am restless while drawing, constantly aware of my technical limitations. I make coffee I don't drink. I call Susan Jeffers, and we gossip about our children, friends, vitamins, and so forth. I stare out the window. I think about the car-pool in one school and the Substance Abuse Committee in the other school.

Many of the stories in my books come from our two children, Victoria and Beezoo. Ruby and Max are Victoria and Beezoo. They appeared on my drawing board in the summer of 1977. Victoria was then five and Beezoo nine months. Victoria had taken it upon herself to teach her baby sister about the world and dragged her, like a sack of flour, because she was too heavy to really carry, from object to object shouting, "Table, Beezoo! say table. TA-BLE!" Beezoo did not cooperate at all and was always off in a world of her own.

Victoria tried to teach Beezoo how to get dressed—another complete failure, as Beezoo preferred to be undressed at all times. Victoria attempted to instruct vocabularyless Beezoo to share and not to take toys that didn't belong to her. This was like talking to the wind. Victoria took pride in wheeling Beezoo's stroller along the boardwalk. Beezoo had to be harnessed into it, with the zipper put on backward and pinned in four places, or she would immediately escape and crawl like a racing crab right into the ocean or the traffic or wherever danger lay.

These simple incidents from childhood are universal. The dynamics between older and younger sibling are also common to all families. What is funny is not the events but Victoria's dogged insistence on leading Beezoo in the paths of righteousness and Beezoo's complete insouciance in the face of slightly skewed authority.

I could say that I did the board books because there were no funny books around for very young children at that time, that I saw a great black hole in the marketplace. But this is not true. I did the Max and Ruby books because the characters materialized on paper in front of me, under my hand, so to speak. The characters were alive. The stories were going on all around me. I submitted them to my editor, Phyllis Fogelman, hesitantly because there had never been any books like them. Phyllis did not take them hesitantly.

Other books come from other episodes in my life, in the children's lives. Victoria, in first grade, came home the day of the Christmas concert in bitter tears. It took me three hours to get out of her what was wrong. At last the truth spilled on the damp pillow. She had selected a blouse and kilt to wear that morning. Someone in the class had noticed. "You're supposed to wear a dress to the Christmas concert, not an old kilt," little Audrey had whined, crushing Victoria. We patched up the day with conventional wisdom, but Audrey's remark struck in my mind long after it had dissolved in Victoria's. It became *Timothy Goes to School* (Dial). Audrey is still there in Victoria's eighth grade, still making trouble. It amuses Victoria and me that since *Timothy* was a successful book, we made a pretty penny on Audrey, and she and her mother will never know.

When Beezoo was in second grade, she wanted more than anything to take in her favorite stuffed animal for show and tell. She decided at the last minute against it, however, because, as she put it, "The boys would rip it up." There was *Hazel's Amazing Mother* (Dial) right in front of me. I, like all writers, take many small fragments and run them through to their logical conclusions in my mind, like a film on fast forward.

Benjamin and Tulip (Dial) was written, on the other hand, before we had any children. It is partly a story of my best friend and me wheeling our bicycles up a steep hill every day after school and being regularly ambushed by Norman Buck and his brothers who lived at the top of the hill. This happened many times. Any mother who called Mrs. Buck to complain was met with shouts of "I can't hear you," because Norman and his brothers made so much background noise. Norman did not fit well in the story, so I got rid of his brothers and changed him into Patty Lombardi, queen of the second grade at five foot six and one hundred thirty pounds, who was heard to say only two things in her career: "I'm captain" and "I'm gonna beat you up."

Once the story is there, the drawings just appear. I feel the emotion I want to show; then I let it run down my arm from my face, and it goes out the pencil. My drawings look as if they are done quickly. They are not. First they are sketched in light pencil, then nearly rubbed out, then drawn again in heavier pencil. What appears to be a confident, thick ink line is really a series of layers of tiny ink lines intensifying all day until the drawing is ready for color.

Most of my books use animals rather than children as characters. People always ask why. There are many reasons. First, I draw animals more easily and amusingly than I do children. Animals are broader in range—age, race, time, and place—than children are. They also can do things in pictures that children cannot. They can be slapstick and still real, rough and still funny, maudlin and still touching. In *Benjamin and Tulip,* Tulip falls out of a tree and mashes Benjamin in the mud. If these pictures were of children, they would be too close to violent reality for comfort, and all the humor would be lost. All of my

stories are written with deeply felt emotional content. Animals express this best most of the time for the same reason that a harpsichord expresses certain concertos better than an organ does.

At the end of a day my hand hurts. I run it under the hot tap. My glasses need strengthening. I put off the appointment with the optometrist, who keeps sending me little reminders. I hear the school bus deliver Beezoo. I jump up.

Another side of my studio is for writing. It contains a word processor which will be obsolete in three years. I slip in the discs to start it up. I am not aware of writing. I sink myself in the screen as if I were hovering over a coral reef with a snorkel mask in the warm Caribbean. I am not aware of time passing. It is a nuisance to get hungry and break my concentration. I do not feel that I get ideas. Books come up on the screen from outer space. Beezoo comes home from school. She drops her bag and opens the cookie cabinet. I do not jump up. I say, "I'll be right there, Sweetie!" Fortunately, she is a patient child who knows I love her anyway. Victoria bangs on the door two hours later. By that time I can't write anymore. I stand up with a crick in my neck and write *swim* on the calendar for the next day.

My books, all of them, have a catalyst—my editor. I do not use Phyllis Fogelman just to publish and market my work. I use her to direct me, which she does with intuitive and unfailing accuracy. The tiny bulbs in my head are all mine, but she adjusts wattage, turns them on and off sometimes, and changes the bulbs when they fizzle. Somewhere along the line I decided to give over part of my working mind to Phyllis. Her suggestions, corrections, brakes, and acceleration are crucial to a book's success. We disagree. We horse trade. We constantly joke with one another. We kid each other as only old friends can, and, like relatives, we have arguments that never vary from year to year.

"How did you get started?" is another question asked every published author. I went to art school in Boston, hoping to learn how to be an oil painter. Alas, I was stuck in a bastion of abstract expressionism, something I did not understand or like then; nor do I now, and I feel very guilty and undereducated because I don't. Abstract painting, the best of it—the work of de Kooning, Arp, Rothko—brings to my mind things I don't like to eat, fabrics that itch against the skin, divorce, paper cuts, and metallic noises. At nineteen, I married Tom Wells. This was an excellent excuse for leaving schools once and for all. Degreeless I sought employment in Boston, where at Little, Brown the waiting list for a secretary's position was ninety Wellesley and Smith names long.

Lady Luck smiled. A young art assistant left for the summer from Allyn & Bacon textbook publishers. I happened to be there the next day. I stayed for two years, never drawing but learning type and layout and how to work hard for the first time in my life. Happily, I swallowed hook, line, and sinker the myth of the day that if you got a job in publishing it was an honor to be paid seventy dollars a week. For several years I did no drawing or painting at all. I did not miss it. I was a book designer.

At last I felt I had a good skill and trade. Macmillan Children's Books offered one hundred twenty dollars a week, so I went there. My boss was Susan Hirschman, and also the art director, Ava Weiss. Dick Jackson was senior editor, and the girl at the next design desk was Susan Jeffers, fresh out of Pratt.

I took a well-worn Gilbert and Sullivan song from *The Yeoman of the Guard* (Macmillan) that I heard one day on the car radio; and, using birds as characters, I made a little dummy of it. I put it on Susan Hirschman's desk. She looked at it. Then she put it down and sang the whole thing. Several other editors were invited into her office to join choruses from *The Mikado* and *H.M.S. Pinafore*. Then, by the by, she said, "Sit down, Rosemary; you're a Macmillan author now."

There are times in one's life when a bolt from the blue just zings down without warning: telegrams saying that you have just won the lottery, calls from doctors that inform you the tests are negative, sudden and unexpected announcements from the headmaster in front of the whole applauding parent and student body that your child has won the scholarship and citizenship cup. These moments always lodge in the soul more deeply than do planned events like wedding days or the births of children. At that moment I did sit down because I had suddenly been given legitimacy of the greatest kind I knew: my name on a book and someone saying, "You're good," for the first time in six years.

I went on to publish a succession of immature books for other publishers. I worked on and off with Susan for several years, through many unpublishable trials and errors. I learned how picture books should be structured and how they should be written with brevity and originality and feeling. I learned how things had been done at Harper and Row, the size of Maurice Sendak's dummies, the jokes Tomi Ungerer

sneaked into his illustrations, hoping not to be caught out, the sensation of reading a new Else Minarik for the first time. I learned about Ursula Nordstrum and how she was the great moving force, part major general, part Florence Nightingale, in our little bailiwick of children's books. I only published a couple of books with Susan, but I still remember the hours she spent with me. Dick Jackson, at Bradbury Press, embellished the Ursula stories and spent his time and his talent with me as well.

I am glad I am not starting out now. It would be harder for me. It took me ten books to get going, ten books and five years even to learn what writing for children was about. I am glad that I got my start in this profession at a time when it would have been rightfully considered a laughable heresy to retell or reillustrate Beatrix Potter or any other book that is as perfect now as it was many years ago. I am glad I got my start in 1968 when Susan, Dick, and finally Phyllis said to me again and again, "Stop rooting around in the public domain. Write your own stuff."

This was good advice. Children's books have refried the past enough now. At the same time, in trying to keep pace with the other media, mass market books—that used to be found near the chewing gum racks in supermarkets—litter bookstore shelves, full of characters that dominate television and fill our children's heads with cotton candy values and taste.

To succeed and hold a cutting edge in our culture, children's book publishing must be fresh and intelligent. Let television follow us. Instead of resurrecting every last fairy tale and Mother Goose verse, we must encourage literary originality and let the past flower in the natural flow of time. We must imitate nothing and be true to ourselves.

Rosemary Wells

SOURCE: *Shy Charles*, in *The Horn Book Magazine*, Vol. LXVI, No. 1, January-February, 1990, pp. 28-30.

Last night I spoke on the telephone with my daughter, Victoria, who is now sixteen. She asked, "Who's up there at that convention that I know?" I mentioned several publishing people, Phyllis Fogelman and Mimi Kayden, and then I mentioned that Regina Hayes from Viking was here with Barbara Cooney.

"Barbara Cooney!" she shouted. "*The* Barbara Cooney? *Ox-Cart Man, Miss Rumphius* Barbara Cooney?"

I said, "Yes."

"Tell her I love her, Mom. Tell her she's written my all-time favorite books," instructed Victoria. Then she added, "What's she doing there?"

"She got a Boston Globe-Horn Book Honor Award this year," I answered.

There was a pause and an intake of breath. Victoria asked incredulously, "You mean Barbara Cooney came in second to *you?*"

Victoria has been my model for many characters—Ruby is probably the best known. Her latest role was the main character in **Shy Charles** (Dial). This book was written long after, rather than during, a phase. When Victoria was three or four, she spoke to only four people in the world, one of whom was a dog. Another was my mother, who delighted in showing off this little blonde dumpling. I never showed Victoria off because it was so fruitless. Every weekend there would be at least one trip to a local retailer. The florist stands out in my mind particularly; but whether it was the florist or the grocer or the lady in the bakery, each of these people would offer Victoria a little treat, which she would snatch. Then she would look away, never saying anything. Soon this produced bargaining sessions beforehand.

My mother would say, "Now what are you going to say when Mrs. Baradi gives you a flower?"

"Thank you," lisped Victoria.

"Promise?" said my mother.

"Yes."

So in we would go, and nothing would ever come out of that little mouth. The tiny hand would close on the stem of the orchid, and then the head would turn and bury itself in my mother's shoulder. Victoria turned to a pillar of salt.

One day, push came to shove and my mother laid it on the line. She said, "No thank you; no candy. Got it?"

Victoria said, "Yes."

So we went in, and the candy lady offered Victoria a chocolate bunny. The hand holding the bunny was poised midair. (It was a cheap chocolate bunny, as I remember.) Victoria really wanted it, but the moment of truth had arrived. My mother said, "It's thank you, or no bunny."

Victoria, about to snatch it, turned mute.

But the candy lady said, "Oh, the *poor* little thing." So Victoria stood her ground and won the day.

Years later, I asked her, "Why were you so intransigent? You never spoke to anyone."

She said, "I was afraid they would laugh at me."

It is a great honor to me that a small incident from my daughter's childhood and the book it became have won your greatest honor. It is not only a personal reward but a delight as well to accept this prize, because I feel strongly that our library community and the book-loving public should be united rather than separated at events and occasions important to literature. The *Boston Globe* and *Horn Book* have personified this unity for twenty-three years.

Last year the rules for this award were changed in the picture book category: the story is now given the same weight as the illustrations. This long-overdue change should be the rule of thumb in all arenas of judging picture books—whether it is a review or an award. A good picture book is written to be read aloud at least five hundred times by an intelligent adult. No matter how lush and impressive the art, if the story is overlong or boring, the book will adorn a shelf.

The books of my childhood are with me always. When I flip through them, many of these pictures now seem terribly dated, but the cadences of the words and the soul of the writer remain, like a Mozart melody. It is to be hoped, as our youngsters grow up, that they will remember the joy of early reading. I would like to think that, no matter how inundated their middle years are with commercial platitudes, deafening rock music, and movies made by and for the brain dead, they will remember books fondly and come back to them of their own accord to find humor, and poetry, and the truth.

Rosemary Wells

SOURCE: "The Well-Tempered Children's Book," in *Worlds of Childhood: The Art and Craft of Writing for Children,* edited by William Zinsser, Houghton Mifflin Company, 1990, pp. 39-62.

This is not an idly chosen title, nor is it meant to be catchy. Bach's melodies—to me the most beautiful melodies in music—emerge from a tightly constructed foundation. Some people find them cold because of their perfection. But all fine works of music, dance, painting and literature are born not from vague inspiration but—as I see it in my mind's eye—from a design as clean and spare as a house frame of New Hampshire birch. Children's picture books are a short literary form like the sonnet. The soundness of their structure is therefore crucial—more important than in longer and more leisurely forms of writing.

I want to begin with Max and Ruby. I can pinpoint exactly when Max and Ruby surfaced. Our daughter Victoria was five years old and still reverberating from the birth of Marguerite, who was by then and is still mysteriously called Beezoo. That name, Beezoo, just flew through the air one day and stuck to her like a burr. Anyway, nine months old and five years old—an age difference custom-designed to give the older child such an upper hand that the younger one doesn't have much of a chance. Fortunately, Beezoo was built like a small jet engine and had nerves of steel.

Victoria was never openly jealous because, officially being the absolute boss, there's nothing to be jealous of. She took in hand Beezoo's training. Talking, dressing, eating and going on stroller rides were Victoria's province whenever we let her, and the sessions were conducted much as they would be at Parris Island. Beezoo was hauled like a sack of flour and propped up in front of objects, her older sister repeating their names imperiously. But Beezoo would never say "table" or "chair" or "dog." She only said "da-da" and, unaccountably, "Rockefeller." She wouldn't put any clothes *on;* she would only take them off. She had to be double-buckled into a stroller, with a harness put on backwards and safety-pinned, because she was a natural Houdini. As for training Beezoo to eat politely, Victoria tried and lost that one, too.

I had written a picture book that summer. I put every ounce of love, wit and lyricism in my jittery soul into that book. It was a real loser. I had wanted to write about an old woman who digs in her heels and hangs on to her house in the face of avaricious developers who want to tear it down. It wasn't that this was a poor idea; it's just that writing *about* anything is a mistake. The only books that work are those which fly through the air—the ones you *let* happen, not *make* happen. Phyllis Fogelman, who has been my editor for eighteen years, turned it down in the nicest way she knows, which is to say she loves it but it has five terminal flaws and could I put it in a drawer for a while?

The next day I was very depressed. Rejection is borne well by strong people with healthy egos, and I don't have any of that. On my drawing table were a few pieces of illustration board left over from my previous book. Suddenly a bunny appeared on one of them. I finished his face and clothed him. I was listening to Handel and not thinking about this silly rabbit at all. Then all of what was happening downstairs—Victoria as Emily Post, the dining etiquette, the vocabulary lessons—came floating upstairs like a sonata and appeared on sixteen square-cut four-by-four boards as *Max's First Word.*

In the morning I took this sixteen-page oddity to Phyllis. (Let me say one thing about working regularly with the same editor and publisher. One reason it suits me is that when I do write something that Phyllis rejects, which mercifully almost never happens anymore, I don't get angry and take it to another editor. I write something better.) On this occasion I couldn't yet understand what had happened. I had created what was clearly a picture book, but it was only sixteen pages long and wasn't for the usual nursery school and kindergarten crew. Picture books were thirty-two pages long, some even forty. For two months I had poured my heart and soul into the manuscript about the old lady and gotten nowhere. In six hours Victoria had become Ruby and Beezoo had become Max—at a time when I was trying my best to "work" and to ignore them.

Usually Phyllis is very talkative. This time she just laughed and then stared at the book. "It's a complete innovation," she said at last. "All books for very young toddlers have one word per page and deadly dull pictures of objects. Even an eighteen-month-old can be bored by a boring book. But this is funny! And it's a real story. Go home and write three more and we'll do something that nobody has done in publishing before." What Phyllis had seen in an instant was that the essence of a good picture book can be distilled, halved in length and printed on sturdy material for children who are just learning to talk and to understand but who aren't too young to be read to.

I went home and three other books—*Max's Ride, Max's New Suit* and *Max's Toys*—all rushed onto the little square boards like tiny actors who had been waiting in the wings for their turn on the stage. Thus was born what came to be known in book circles as "board books"—books that could survive a certain amount of infant vandalizing without coming apart and, even more important, could make mothers and fathers and their babies laugh at themselves and each other and the world around them.

After that it was relatively easy, several years later, to follow the first four books with four more, because bathing, bedtime, birthdays and eating-what-you-hate hadn't been covered. More would have been redundant. Today Max and Ruby have graduated to two twenty-four-page picture books, simply because all the very young stories were used up.

I don't mean to imply that you need to have children around in order to write children's books. Beatrix Potter didn't have any children. Neither did Margaret Wise Brown, or Maurice Sendak, or many other giants of children's literature. If William Steig ever had children, they must be older than I am. Books come from absolutely everywhere. For me, they become children's books simply because that's the voice I have. You can be a superb writer and not have a voice for poetry, or for nonfiction or journalism. Children's books are a field of writing like any other, but they're not easier to do because they are for children, in the same way that making lunch for children might be easier to do.

Writing for very young children is the most difficult discipline I know. Kids will believe almost anything you tell them—provided you make it truthful. That may sound bland, but there's a catch. There really aren't many people who can do this arcane and specialized kind of writing, yet thousands of people aspire to it. This is because they love and have or are around children all day and love the literature written for them. But that's not enough. Being around adults and loving novels, for instance, doesn't make a writer out of everyone who has a flair for putting words on paper. There is a misperception that children's books are a sort of muzzy and not-quite-serious art form. They are as hard to write and edit, however, as good poetry. Like poetry, they must not have a single unneeded syllable in any line. A poem, which is a kind of chain, is as strong as its weakest rhyme or meter, whereas in a long prose work a bit of unevenness can be hidden. One false note ruins a poem. The same is true of picture book stories.

Writing well for children must be learned. There are rules. I consider myself lucky to have come into this field in the late sixties, which was the golden age of children's writing and illustration. Probably the most influential editor in the field was the late Ursula Nordstrom of Harper & Row. The books she published began a revolution in children's literature. Equally important, the editors she trained have inspired a new generation of writers and illustrators. I never met Ursula Nordstrom, but I feel that I know her well because her ideas have trickled down to me through her books and through her many disciples.

I mentioned that there are rules for writing picture books. Every time I don't go by these rules I burn the tips of my fingers.

First of all, a good picture book must ring with emotional content, so that children care about what's going on. Otherwise they will fall asleep. William Steig's *Amos and Boris* and *Sylvester and the Magic Pebble* never fail to overwhelm a reader with both worry and love. They can't be put down; they work beautifully every time. What is in them is in all of us: guilt, fear, devotion. As a writer you have little time and few pages to achieve this. The characters in a children's book must reach into the heart of the reader on page one. Emotional content is the main reason a child and a parent will go back to a book again and again.

A story for children must also be short enough to be read without giving the reader a need for sips of water between pages. I can't tell you how many times my kids used to truck out some gorgeous book with stunning pictures that took half an hour to read and how often, not without guilt, I said, "How about *Goodnight, Moon* instead?" When I conduct a workshop there's one book that is the perfect teaching book for brevity: Robert Kraus's *Whose Mouse Are You?,* which was published almost twenty years ago by Macmillan when I happened to be on the staff. José Aruego did the pictures. It has humor, plot, character, pathos and a surprise ending—and it's sixteen lines long.

Not all good picture books are funny, but I think the best ones are. Nothing is as satisfying as making somebody laugh. When somebody has been crying or is overtired or bored to tears by Wednesday afternoon's arithmetic lesson, it's gratifying to make him laugh. To place in the hands of a weary mom or dad or teacher the means to do it is to give him or her a spiritual gold coin.

All really good picture books are written to be read five hundred times. A picture book is in trouble if it's longer than eight double-spaced typewritten pages. It's also in trouble if it's bland, or if the tone is false and hysterical. It must never be cute or it will insult children. It's in trouble if it uses television characters, or if it's written by anybody with a degree in child psychology. I think the nicest thing a child has told me about my books is that he liked them because they weren't like schoolbook stories, and even if they were about mice or raccoons, they were much more real than the people in those textbooks.

Max and Ruby became books through some osmosis of events taken whole and virtually unchanged by me. *Timothy Goes to School,* however, and *Hazel's Amazing Mother* are different; they are about something deeper. They are about that happens in first and second grade. That's when our classrooms and school playgrounds turn into heated petri dishes for the determination of the school pecking order and the alleviation of huge gobs of personal tension. Timothy and Benjamin—of *Timothy Goes to School* and *Benjamin and Tulip*—are echoes of my grade school years. But more directly, Timothy comes from something that happened in our daughter Victoria's first grade class. In this case, one line was enough for the whole book to materialize.

Victoria was a careful dresser. My mother had bought her an expensive frothy dress for the lower-school Christmas concert. Victoria hated the dress and refused to be seen in it. I said, "O.K., you don't have to wear it, but you do have to conform to the school's dress code, which is no pants or denim or anything casual looking." The next morning she boarded the bus in a lace-trimmed blouse and her favorite plaid kilt, white tights and patent-leather shoes. At noon, as the girls were lining up backstage to sing for the parents a medley of twenty-eight traditional Christmas carols from Japan, another girl, Melissa, gave Victoria the word: "Nobody wears an everyday kilt to the Christmas concert!"

Of course I didn't hear about this right away. There was mostly silence until 5 P.M. Then this deteriorated into quiet sobs. Victoria is the kind of child who mentions a year later that there was a school play and she didn't get a part in it. Anyway, it was a miracle that by nine o'clock she finally sputtered out the truth, between Kleenexes: *"Nobody wears an everyday kilt to the Christmas concert!"* What a gem! Tens of thousands of hardcover copies of *Timothy Goes to School,* plus a paperback, not to mention British, French, German, Italian and Spanish editions, all trumpeting Melissa's *bon mot* to the world!

Melissa had made trouble since kindergarten. Today, in tenth grade, she's making more trouble. I could have told you then that she was destined to smoke at the age of thirteen. I've learned that kids like Melissa only get worse and more powerful. Also, they're not rolling stones—they never move away. They don't go and bother some other child in Tennessee. Anyway, when Victoria spilled the beans and this one glorious line I held her and rocked her in my arms.

"Never mind," I said. "Melissa probably didn't mean it."

"Oh, yes she did, she hates me!" Victoria said. "She never asked me to her birthday."

"You said you were just as glad, sweetie. You told me she locked Linda in the closet for three hours at the party."

"Yes, but she hates me, and today everybody heard her and everybody laughed at me."

"Maybe Melissa doesn't get enough love," I suggested.

"She has a pony," Victoria sobbed, "and ten different outfits from Saks Fifth Avenue."

"That isn't love," I said.

"Yes it is," said Victoria.

"Everyone will forget all about it after Christmas vacation," I told her.

"Then she'll say something else," Victoria answered. And of course she was right. So I didn't bother with any more discussion. I just gave her a bag of M & M's, which is a superb mood elevator because, unlike talk, it's neither cheap nor fake. That is why child psychologists shouldn't write or criticize or come near the field of children's books. They actually believe what they say.

Back to *Timothy Goes to School.*

Why are the characters raccoons and not people? They are animals because animals can do all sorts of things that kids would look overly cute doing, or overly cruel. Animals can jump out of trees and knock each other down, which of course happens to real kids, but it would take a better illustrator than I am to make such a scene palatable. Animals can also be superbly funny, where the same visual humor involving children would be slapstick. All the animals in my books, incidentally, are based on our West Highland white terrier, Angus. Born three years before our oldest daughter and resentful from her birth forward, that dog had more visible emotions than Elmer Gantry. He has been succeeded by other "westies," and each one is at least a Meryl Streep or a Laurence Olivier. Animals can live in a world that children seem to climb right into. It's a world of the past, with clothing from other times. Things aren't modern in the world of animals. Walter Gropius hasn't been born, or Arnold Schönberg, or Lee Iacocca. There are no color barriers, because animals come in all colors and no one minds. This world seems to suit my stories, and animals are easier for me to draw than people. Timothy happens to be a raccoon. He is also a boy, though Victoria is a girl, obviously. Why a boy? Because of the clothes. Boys are as sensitive about clothes as girls are, but if you make the lead characters girls in a book about a clothing fight, they come off as bitchy stereotypes. Boys come off funny and very real.

At the end of the book, after Timothy has battled the unyielding and implacable Claude until he can't stand it any longer, what happens? Well, what happened to Victoria? Nothing. She suffered until she simply outgrew Melissa and was in a different class. But years can't pass in a picture book. Things must be resolved. Fortunately, the device of *deus ex machina* is at my disposal. Almost every good writer uses it. In real life such quick fixes don't happen nearly often enough, but they must happen in children's books because the world wakes kids up in a cold sweat at 4 A.M. In fact, the world of school continues to do so even when they are forty and fifty. My worst nightmares are still those dreams in which I haven't gone to class and there's a final exam in an hour. Patty D'Amico, the bully of the kickball diamond, still lurks in my memory, and she resurrects every six months or so. So does Sue Ann Thompson, who was so beautiful that boys fell down in front of her, and Miriam Evans, valedictorian, who was so smart and so beautiful that girls, boys and teachers were her slaves.

It therefore took only a minute for me to absorb my Victoria's agony and to know how to write **Timothy Goes to School.** After that there were many occasions, like parents' night, when I wanted to go up to Melissa's mother and give her a piece of my mind. I would picture myself saying, "And what's more, it wouldn't surprise me one bit if Melissa developed a reputation for hiding in the bushes with boys in the seventh grade, and cheating on midterms in the ninth grade, and drinking beer by tenth grade"—all of which did come true, by the way. Of course I always held my tongue. But there is sweet revenge in this world after all. **Timothy** has sold steadily and well for ten years now, and Victoria is in another school—with another and bigger Melissa.

Just as there are universal emotions and predicaments common to young childhood, so there are for teenagers as well. In some ways, to be fourteen now is no different than it was for me or my mother. That part of writing for teenagers is familiar to me, and having those fragile and unstoppable joys and fears in my grasp is where I start. On the other hand, the 1980s and '90s are not like anything that has gone before. The change in what young people value and what they will become is staggering. It is the nuances of

that change that only *they* know truly, like a language. If you're not in your teens, you can only imitate the voice; you can't be there with them, because no adults are allowed. They are on a bridge, these young people. They have stepped off the shore of the land where they were safe with us. Some go early and others follow late, but sooner or later they all must walk across to the other side by themselves.

That's why they need each other's approval so desperately. This has always been so, of course—everybody has been on that bridge and, for better or worse, has made it to the other shore. But now this journey is made more perilous by the shills who are bombarding our young people with ceaseless advertising. Sex, in its most infantile forms, is the loudest and most constant commodity. Too many young people are also dressing in black and taking very dangerous substances. They are saturated with glossy images of love, death and more material things than their money can buy. Often their families have melted away like snow in the sun, if they existed at all. It's not easy for these kids to have any sense of self. What I have chosen to write about in my next book is a journey under that bridge of a solitary youngster punting his own boat.

Writing a novel is like living next door to a family that has just moved in. At first you just see the people coming and going, in and out of their house. After a while their habits become more familiar, and then one day you go in for coffee. Soon you're invited for dinner, and before you know it you're there for Thanksgiving. By then you're a part of the family, and you know where they keep the good brandy and how early they get up to let the dog out. You're stuck. If there has been a death or an illness you suffer, or if there has been a murder you wake up in the dark scared to death. Writing a novel is just like that, except that you have made all the people up. But that doesn't matter, because by the time the novel is finished you're convinced that they are alive.

At one point in my book **The Man in the Woods,** which gave me a lot of trouble, I told Phyllis, my editor, that since a great deal of the action is historically factual and involves a Civil War family in New Bedford, Massachusetts, I wanted to include old photographs of the family to illustrate the book. Phyllis told me that old photographs are the kiss of death in a teenage book and please not to do it. I was very stubborn. That summer I actually went out and scoured the antiques stores on Cape Cod for old photograph albums. I was searching for someone who looked like my character Lucy Fairchild. And I did find her—I swear I found Lucy's picture. She's a lovely, dignified woman, and obviously intelligent. I have that photograph framed. People ask who it is. I say, "That's Lucy Fairchild. She lived in New Bedford during the Civil War."

Other people's books are the greatest teachers of writers. Josephine Tey's *Miss Pym Disposes* is probably the most perfect mystery ever written. It's perfect in the sense that a Telemann oboe concerto is perfect; it's not a Mahler symphony. This book taught me that mystery stories can be splendid literature. There are no policemen in *Miss Pym Disposes*. The central character is a retired teacher who decides to visit an old classmate, a headmistress of a girls' prep school in the quiet English countryside. The girls are introduced one by one, or in groups. Their intrigues and souls are displayed gently. The life of the school, its place among other schools, its program and examinations are all explained with dry wit and unusual color. Before the reader knows it, the table is totally set—by page 100 exactly. Then, very suddenly, the sun goes in and this idyllic place becomes sinister in the light of someone's having cheated on an exam. Much depends on the results of these exams; girls' whole lives can turn on the jobs they get after school. An accidental death occurs, which only Miss Pym knows is not an accident.

There are no stolen jewels, secret formulas or packets of drugs in *Miss Pym Disposes;* only human nature at its most playful and complex. In the meantime we get a wonderful view of Josephine Tey's postwar England as it was lived by the upper middle class. The author's position is that the reader is a person with adequate education, which means, since the book is set in 1949, a positively brilliant education. This alone is enough to seduce a reader who is tired of mysteries that give every detail of a deranged massacre. Most books in this genre are also big on obligatory sex scenes, except those written by truly good writers like John le Carré and Dick Francis. Sex scenes in mystery books are like raw legs of lamb hurled into a lobster bisque.

I was so struck by the craft of *Miss Pym Disposes* that I made a chart of the plot. I used twelve different colored pens. Where were the clues hidden? Where was the structure turned from innocent to sinister? When did the sun go in? I showed the chart to Phyllis in the middle of writing **Leave Well Enough Alone,** which was my first mystery novel. She couldn't make head or tail of it. Never mind. The book went through six drafts; the next novel took four, the next one nine or ten.

Incidentally, I've intentionally emphasized my relationship with my editor. Editors are usually thanked at the end of a speech; they're seldom acknowledged as working partners. But all books need editors. When I read one that is overlong, or that has a part that's uneven or makes no sense, I don't ask what the author was doing, because I make all those mistakes myself. I do ask, "Where was the editor?" A book that is guided and preened and patted to perfection by a good editor is seamless. Before I start a novel I read John Cheever and Evan Connell. This sets the language right in my mind. When I finish, and when Phyllis has finished with it, it's the best I can do.

The next book and next family are now looming over me. I hear their voices all the time. Two nights ago I was in the Grand Union, waiting in a checkout line. There was a woman ahead of me. The cashier dragged the woman's groceries over the little screen with the dancing red light that reads the price codes on the packages. The woman asked her, "How long have you been working here, honey?" "About a year," she said. The woman put her hand on the checker's arm, pointed to the screen with the red light and said, "Those things cause cancer in mice!" That woman walked right into my next book.

The most often asked question of all authors is where their ideas come from. It's answered in a variety of ways, not the least being, "It's my job to have ideas." But that's not a good enough answer. There is a "where," and it's not in any author's head. The closest I've ever heard anyone come to it was Peter Shaffer in the play *Amadeus.* The important idea in *Amadeus* has nothing to do with whether Salieri killed Mozart or whether Mozart was a profane fool. It has to do with the fact that Mozart heard the voices of angels. He had only to sit with score paper, and the music burst out from heaven into his head and down his arm and out of his pen. Lesser mortals—like Salieri, who wrote very nice pieces that are still played by classical music stations several lifetimes after his death—might not have heard angels, but their music also came from somewhere. Salieri thought it was God over his shoulder. Perhaps he was right.

I don't hear angels' voices either, but I do know that when my ordinary conscious self is gone, stories and characters—laughing and crying and doing all kinds of things—fill not my head but my writing screen. I believe that all stories and plays and paintings and songs and dances come from a palpable but unseen space in the cosmos. Ballets and symphonies written during our lifetime were there before we were born.

According to how gifted we are, we are all given a large or small key to this treasury of wonders. I have been blessed with a small key to the world of the young. It's place where good and evil are clearly stamped. It's a place where the better part of human nature triumphs over tragedies, and where innocence rides high. It is a great pleasure to write there, because the young have what the rest of us can only envy, and that is a belief in goodness and perpetual hope.

GENERAL COMMENTARY

Donnarae MacCan and Olga Richard

SOURCE: A review of *Max's Dragon Shirt* and others, in *Wilson Library Bulletin,* Vol. 66, No. 5, January, 1992, pp. 105-07, 137.

One way to know people is to look at what they make. Another way is to look at what they admire. Picture books by Rosemary Wells have flourished over the past decade and her speeches and essays offer clues about this creative upswing. What she loves in her culture, she builds into her own illustrated stories about Max, Ruby, Morris, Nora, Benjamin, Tulip, Timothy, Fritz, etc.

She admires, for example, the tight construction of Bach's melodies. They are, she says, "as clean and spare as a house frame of New Hampshire birch" (*Worlds of Childhood: The Art and Craft of Writing for Children,* ed. by William Zinsser [Houghton Mifflin, 1990]). She admires *The Lavender Hill Mob* with Alec Guinness, who once noted that acting is the art of not taking yourself too seriously—the skill of knowing how to move about the stage without tripping over yourself. Wells puts it this way: "The only books that work are those which fly through the air—the ones you *let* happen, not *make* happen" (Zinsser). She admires Alfred Hitchcock's *The Lady Vanishes* and short stories by John Cheever and Elizabeth Bowen—all works with witty, understated, credible characters. And in the children's book field she loves such emotion-charged tales as Robert Kraus's *Whose Mouse Are You?* and William Steig's *Sylvester and the Magic Pebble.* In short, she values structural integrity, spontaneity, humor, understatement, and displays of feeling.

Wells is a writer and cartoonist, in that order. She is such a sharp observer of children and such a perfectionist when she shapes plot lines that we frequently return to her books for literary rather than visual content. But her illustrations have been gaining in importance. Her close observation of the human comedy has been gradually finding its pictorial counterpart.

We see the genesis of the much-loved Max and Ruby books in Wells's descriptions of her own offspring: "Beezoo" (when she was nine months) and Victoria (when she was at the age of five). Wells explains that the latter was senior enough to be the absolute boss:

> She took in hand Beezoo's training. Talking, dressing, eating and going on the stroller rides were Victoria's province whenever we let her, and the sessions were conducted much as they would be at Parris Island. Beezoo was hauled like a sack of flour and propped up in front of objects, her older sister repeating their names imperiously. But Beezoo would never say "table" or "chair" or "dog." She only said "da-da" and, unaccountably, "Rockefeller" (Zinsser).

The basic outlines of this scenario are repeated in *Max's First Word* (1979). Max's *only* word is "bang" despite Ruby's incessant language lessons. But when Max is presented with an apple and the words "yum yum," he glibly says, "Delicious!" This one-upmanship is the pattern in the "board" books, e.g., *Max's New Suit* (1979), *Max's Ride* (1979), *Max's Bath* (1985), *Max's Breakfast* (1985), and *Max's Birthday* (1985). Each presents the irony of the boss being outwitted by the underling. This is a subtle, topsy-turvy notion. We think it presupposes some experience in the listener, but Wells explains that her intended audience is not a narrow one. She wants "mothers and fathers and their babies [to] laugh at themselves and each other and the world around them" (Zinsser).

In *Max's Dragon Shirt* (1991), the war of wills continues. Max has a passion for a pop cult artifact (a fierce-looking "dragon shirt"), while Ruby becomes hopelessly distracted in the Girls' Better Dresses department of the store they are in. She sets out with the firm resolve to replace her brother's disheveled pants; but he slips away, locates the shirt, is rescued by police officers from the department store "crush," is treated to a three-decker cone, smears up the dragon shirt, and returns home as its triumphant owner. The ice-cream-spattered dragon has swallowed the price of the pants.

The beauty of this text is its recognizable human situation—the fixation vis-à-vis the shirt, the ability of a clever child to win favors from strangers, the tactics that defeat a domineering sister. Ruby is lovable as a tense, overly-maternal caregiver, but one who is still childish and vulnerable—easily thrown off track by the temptations of the clothes rack. She tries hard but doesn't quite make it as a surrogate parent, while Max is still in that privileged preschool phase when trespasses go unpunished.

Max's stubbornness is the result of childlike impulses, not malice. In **Max's Chocolate Chicken** (1989) his spontaneous diversions upset Ruby's rigorously organized Easter egg hunt. He begins in good faith but finds mud puddles more attractive than the tedious search. And so it goes, with Ruby constantly nagging about the rules of the game: "No eggs, no chicken, Max." Max is unimpressed and simply absconds with the prize, a delicacy that Father Rabbit will, in any case, provide for both his children.

Max's Christmas (1986) includes a nice collusion between Max and Santa:

> Guess what, Max! said Max's sister Ruby.
>
> What? said Max.
>
> It's Christmas Eve, Max, said Ruby, and you know who's coming!
>
> Who? said Max.
>
> Santa Claus is coming, that's who, said Ruby.
>
> When? said Max.

After further questions (Where? How? Why?) Max finds Ruby's replies utterly unacceptable. He sneaks downstairs, sees Santa Claus, and awakens with gifts galore plus Santa's own hat.

The style in all these books reflects Wells's belief in the need to prune wasted words. She compares picture book texts to poems and their dependence upon word choice and economy. She writes:

> Like poetry, [picture books] must not have a single unneeded syllable in any line. A poem, which is a kind of chain, is as strong as its weakest rhyme or meter, whereas in a long prose work a bit of *unevenness* can be hidden. One false note ruins a poem. The same is true of picture book stories (Zinsser).

Wells follows this rule in **Morris's Disappearing Bag** (1975, 1990). In nine terse statements she builds the background of a terrible injustice:

> It was Christmas morning. "Wow!" said Morris. Morris's brother, Victor, got a hockey outfit. Morris's sister, Rose, got a beauty kit. Morris's other sister, Betty, got a chemistry set. And Morris got a bear. All Christmas day Victor played hockey and Rose made herself beautiful and Betty mixed acids. And then Betty made herself beautiful and Victor sorted test tubes and Rose played left wing. And then Victor made himself beautiful and Betty played goalie and Rose invented a new gas.

Morris is excluded from this sharing on the grounds that he is too little. What a devastating denial of Christmas! What heartache! What inept remedies from Morris's bourgeois parents! But Providence supplies a mysterious bag—a refuge for Morris and a trick that puts all the Yuletide treasures within reach.

When adults are spoofed in a typical Wells book, the characters express remarkable inanity. Bullies attack, scorners ridicule, an inexplicable pecking order defines school culture—all without redress by "wise" elders. Wells seems to be satirizing herself, since she admits that several titles echo her own daughter's encounters with miniature terrorists, e.g., **Timothy Goes to School** (1981) and **Hazel's Amazing Mother** (1985).

Timothy is like Morris in that his initial "high" is summarily squelched. He wears a homemade sunsuit for the opening day of school and is told by Claude, "Nobody wears a sunsuit on the first day of school." After this horrible discovery, dress code violations still plague him, while the all-knowing Claude goes from glory to glory. Fortunately, Violet turns up. As in Paddy Chayefsky's memorable film *Marty,* two ordinary mortals rescue each other. Violet has suffered scorn and upstaging by Grace. The outcasts enjoy parallel problems and mutual glee.

In **Hazel's Amazing Mother,** the hero is a little darling who charms adults and incites hoodlums. Mother and daughter provide a set of dual images as Wells comments on child-parent relations. Hazel piously bestows cookies upon her doll, Eleanor, and then slyly consumes them herself. Hazel's mother bestows every advantage upon her "doll," raising a weak-kneed, dissembling brat. But the bullies are such thugs that Hazel's middle-class prissiness can be forgiven.

Human interaction is handled with such delicacy in Hazel's story that we could not ward off some disappointment with **The Little Lame Prince** (1990), a picture book based on a nineteenth-century tale by Dinah Maria Mulock Craik. We felt like Morris when deprived of the anticipated toys. We felt denied Wells's own keen observations, distilled language, and tightly constructed story lines. But she uses this text as a way to expand the treatment of her cartoon images. Over the years her work has evolved from minimal line drawings to pictures with a wider use of color and background design.

Wells is a traditional, unassuming illustrator with a more intuitive sense for words than pictures. She refers to the problem of being largely self-taught when she writes: "I am restless while drawing, constantly aware of my technical limitations" (*Children's Literature Review,* v.16, ed. by Gerard Senick and Melissa Reiff Hug [Gale Research, 1989]. The current evolution in her style is taking her from a tight, colored-in approach to the use of color against color in a more painterly manner. An overall trend is discernible that begins with the flat, decorative work in the "Max" books with solid backgrounds, to books with a few background objects (as in *Shy Charles* [1988]), to works with fully developed environments in each illustration (as in *The Little Lame Prince* and *Fritz and the Mess Fairy* [1991]). Additionally, there was a purely linear style during the early seventies.

In *Noisy Nora* (1973)—a concept book about jealousy toward a newborn—Wells uses many scratchy little lines for texture, form, and outline. The effect is tenuous, almost timid. Yet, this same mode functions effectively in *Benjamin and Tulip* (1973), where the artist's humorous intent makes all the difference. Wells creates an unabashedly nasty raccoon (it leaps on its victims from overhanging limbs), plus a nerd-like neighbor, Benjamin, and marvelous mock-violent "beating up" scenes.

Pictorial characterization is less pronounced in *Timothy Goes to School,* with illustrations following the story at a respectful distance. We glance at the wry, unobtrusive pictures briefly before getting on with the intensely felt tale.

In the "board" books, Wells uses simple means for astute psychological portraits. Tidy white rabbit-children are placed against bright, unadorned backgrounds, with an emphasis on subtle changes in facial expressions and bodily poses. When Max and Ruby are together—often struggling as Max is lifted upward by his undersized guardian—Wells produces a nice, integral joining of two chubby masses.

Ruby is still pushing and shoving the awkward toddler in *Max's Christmas.* She is both long-suffering and high-strung, acting upon the perceived needs of her impish brother. Wells does not use typical cartoon action lines but positions Max and Ruby so that

postures suggest movement. The forms are understated, but their contours are a bit jagged, a device that softens edges and adds a touch of animation. By downplaying the artwork—using clean, clear colors on minimal forms—Wells highlights character and keeps story and picture precisely in sync.

The rabbits in *Morris's Disappearing Bag* are similarly casual in treatment, and we see the same strong emphasis on body language. Morris is sulky, stationary, a babyish lump of diaper bottoms, while Father is a "superior" being: self-important, stylish, unapproachable. The enlargement of these compelling characters in a 1990 paper edition does not dampen their hilarity but does produce an odd transformation in the work as a whole. The book became an outlandish 13 1/2-by-18 inches; and since Wells's art includes large, soft areas of plain color in the first place, the addition of acres of white paper does not improve the effect. Images tend to be diluted or, at any rate, isolated from the whole. A giant edition has an element of excitement, but it seems to us less accessible, less intimate and personal.

In *Hazel's Amazing Mother,* Wells retains the same gentle mockery of the bourgeoisie but expands her treatment of background and color. In both foreground and background, hues are equally intense, and the background forms are minus contour lines. This produces an exceptional brilliance to the page, while the personalities and antics of her bizarre animal characters retain their dominance. The approach is theatrical: elegant "folks" posed and arranged in complex groupings.

Page arrangements in *Shy Charles* highlight the mice protagonists and include just enough additional objects to anchor the composition in one large mass, as well as to define the environment. Wells uses flat, opaque color and details forms with tiny patterns, favoring thin-line stripes. As in most Wells books, portraiture is the stunning feature here. The entire family resembles over-stuffed bean bags, triangular and static, but nonetheless expressive of distinct traits. Charles is recognizable in his crippling shyness. A tilt of his head or a change in his mouth is a revealing clue, as is his small, prone figure when he pretends to sleep through dance class.

Characters in *Max's Dragon Shirt* have the same motion-defying body shape, but Wells manages to move these folk along anyway. The perfume salesperson has a wicked "Gotcha!" look as she sprays her victims, and in an aerial scene shoppers circulate in a spaciously rendered mall.

Wells seems in transition from simple ornamentation to the more ambiguous texturing in *The Little Lame Prince* Flat colors shift, in this title, to color areas that are altered for surface interest and increased depth (stippled and spackled to effect that change). An example is the illustration of the prince and his nurse in a railway coach. This is a free and rhythmic arrangement (with the exception of the awkward foreground plants). A mix of fuzzy and hard edges and plain and textured surfaces produces a decorative design.

This painterly trend continues in *Fritz and the Mess Fairy.* Watercolors build form and create a transition from light to dark areas in the background. Grayed colors (mostly blues) unify the picture space while still allowing Fritz and his family to stand out as the significant images. Now and then Wells lets extraneous objects interfere, as in the dinner table scene (her stove in the background is too dominant to function as "background" material). But typically, Wells blends and arranges to produce a good synthesis.

As for the downside, Wells is not at her best when rendering actual human beings, as in *A Lion for Lewis* (1982) and *Peabody* (1983). Those works have some strong moments but not in terms of characterization. Her humans are neither expressive cartoons nor examples of sensitive traditional portraiture.

She makes a telling point when she explains that *all* her human stand-ins (her rabbits, raccoons, etc.) are modeled after the family's West Highland terriers. Her well-observed pets have been translated into a well-formulated metaphor. This mutation seems basic to her style and not merely a way of escaping racial or historical identifications. She "reads" her dogs in a unique way; she says that they have "more visible emotions than Elmer Gantry" (Zinsser).

By noticing the things that surround her and calmly extracting their meaning, she can range widely over human experience and still avoid a strident tone. "A picture book," she says: "is in trouble . . . if the tone is false or hysterical" (Zinsser). And she adds that it is also in trouble if it is bland—an unlikely problem in Wells's case. Given her diverse interests—Bach, ballet, the classic musicals of Broadway, to name but a few—she is not apt to err on the side of tameness. In a word, she usually meets her own strict standards. For young children that means lively story hours. For their older brothers and sisters it means appealing encounters with the many mysteries of human relations.

TITLE COMMENTARY

NONE OF THE ABOVE (1974)

Roger Sutton

SOURCE: "A Second Look: *None of the Above,*" in *The Horn Book Magazine,* Vol. LXIII, No. 3, May-June, 1987, pp. 368-71.

Robert Cormier's *The Chocolate War* (Pantheon) was not the only novel of despair for young adults to appear in 1974. There was William Sleator's *House of Stairs* (Dutton) and also Rosemary Wells's *None of the Above* (Dial). But where the first two are despairing on the grand scale—abstracted darkness—*None of the Above* is firmly rooted in a dreary, ordinary world, its bitterness arising from the most common details, situations, and choices faced by young adults in 1974 and today.

Wells sets the caustic tone with the first sentence: "'Marcia Mill is a big fat pill,' said Christina Van Dam in not a particularly low voice." Marcia and Chrissy are new stepsisters, Marcia's father and Chrissy's mother having remarried after their former spouses died (a rare detail, unlike the more common disposition by divorce). Cultured and smart, Chrissy's family loves to ski and read and puts exotic ingredients like tarragon and what Marcia calls "the cheese with the mold" in their salads. Marcia loves Milky Way bars, which she eats while looking at movie star magazines, and her idea of a healthy sport is bowling.

While Marcia is the protagonist, we can see why Chrissy calls her a pill. Marcia is dull and mopey, wears tight, cheap clothing, and has no intellectual interests whatsoever. Along with believing that blue cheese dressing can kill you, Marcia thinks that *The Lion in Winter* is a wildlife movie; she would rather go see *Hello, Dolly!*

There's a shared expectation between reader and author: they both know better than Marcia; she will not fulfill the conventional function of a young-adult protagonist as guide or lens. We are not expected to identify with her. We feel instead that we are looking down on Marcia, not with contempt but simply with the knowledge that we know more about her than she does. How can a reader identify with a heroine who doesn't like to read? *Heroine* is probably not the right word, for it implies more energy and will than

Marcia seems to possess. How are we supposed to feel about Marcia? Where do the author's sympathies lie? We get very few clues. Wells keeps herself out of the story, employing neither direct authorial comment nor the device of a mouthpiece in the form of a sympathetic character upon whose perceptions the reader can rely. She spares no one. Marcia's sister Sharon is blowzy and ignorant and becomes pregnant while her husband is in Vietnam. Chrissy is irritating, and her mother is given to such profundities as "'We wouldn't have disagreements if everybody agreed on the same things.'" Excepting an occasional, feeble defense of his daughters, Marcia's father is voiceless and faceless. While characters do make tentative attempts to reach one another, their motives often seem ambiguous, and their efforts are almost invariably misunderstood. All of the characters have extremely limited imaginations.

The book has much in common with today's adult fiction, in particular with short story writers like Bobbie Ann Mason and Ann Beattie: the attention to precise, tacky detail—"Marcia spent most of her money on a day-glo pink angora sweater and a Bambi pin"; disjointed, distracted conversation; a passive protagonist; the flat, ironic style. The brief first chapter of **None of the Above,** ending with Mr. Mill and Mother showing slides of their honeymoon, could stand alone as a *New Yorker* short story.

Various people have ambitions for Marcia, who herself only vaguely dreams of meeting David Cassidy or becoming a stewardess. Sharon wants Marcia to move down to her mobile home in Florida; an English teacher thinks Marcia is college prep material. So does Mother, who believes Marcia would do well at the University of Massachusetts—her own daughter is going to Yale. Carla, stepbrother John's Bohemian girlfriend, pushes Kahlil Gibran and Joseph Conrad on Marcia and takes her to foreign films. "She wished it were at least in color. Everything was twice as serious in black and white." In what is clearly as much a rivalry with Mrs. Mill as a concern for Marcia, Carla also talks her into applying to Sarah Lawrence.

Marcia tries. She moves into the College Prep track and works hard but loathes it. "This book, Marcia decided, had bored many people." The only thing Marcia genuinely enjoys is her summer job as a diner waitress, where, in a rare moment of assertion, she tells everyone her name is Kimberly. "She liked being called Kim. She enjoyed being good and being liked."

These are also the qualities that sustain Marcia in her relationship with Raymond, the school "hunk," who masks his sexual inadequacy with bragging stories and a motorcycle. While he constantly tells her she thinks too much or talks too much (neither of which could Marcia be accused of overdoing), he desperately needs her, and for Marcia, that is enough. As Marcia grows—the book takes her from her thirteenth through her eighteenth year—she gradually "notices" the emotional neediness of those around her: the way her stepmother reaches for her husband's hand; how frightened Chrissy is of boys. She notices, often acutely, but she does not know what to do with what she sees.

In the last chapter, Marcia, after an incomprehensible exam on Browning's "My Last Duchess," faces a choice. She has been accepted at both the University of Massachusetts and Sarah Lawrence, and Raymond has asked her to marry him. Which will it be? "Never, never in her whole life did she want to read a book again. Fourteen minutes to nine. Raymond would be waiting." She puts on her engagement ring, goes outside, and starts walking toward Raymond's car. She hopes he sees the diamond on her finger reflected in his headlights, but Raymond is absorbed in *Car and Driver.*

> Marcia started to run. She could already hear the voices, Mother's and even Carla's, through the floor.
>
> "Why? why? why did she do it? She could have gone to Sarah Lawrence. Anywhere! Even the University of Massachusetts wouldn't have been so bad. She had everything ahead of her."
>
> "Don't ask me. She talked to you a lot more than she talked to me. Didn't she say anything? Didn't she at least give some reason for getting married? You could talk to her. You could make sense of her."
>
> Marcia felt a tug in her stomach. The deep silent pool inside, she thought. It's nothing but a stomach full of ulcers! She ran downstairs in her imagination.
>
> "Because," she said right out to them. "Because we're in love. Isn't that enough?"
>
> The familiar pain engulfed her for a moment, but she kept on running as if it were not there at all.

The conclusion caused some confusion for reviewers, who could not decide if the ending was happy, pessimistic, or ambiguous. It was not even clear that Marcia had actually left the house. The key is found earlier in the book when Marcia makes a remark to Carla: "Through the walls, through the floor, through the roof! Sometimes I even hear things I don't hear.

Sometimes I even hear them talking when I'm miles away from the house." Marcia is running, but it is not so much an act of assertion as one of desperation, and we know she is merely exchanging one set of people's expectations for another. Life with Raymond holds no promise of satisfaction. Despite what Marcia imagines telling Carla and Mother, she doesn't love Raymond; she only knows that Raymond loves her. That quiet place inside her, a haven she seeks throughout the book, is an ulcer, and as she runs, the pain continues.

Marcia has had daydreams, fantasies, and false reassurances, but she has never been able to exert herself to any real possibilities beyond the ones presented to her. This may indicate the limits of Marcia's imagination, but even more grim, it may indicate the limits of Marcia's banal world. There are no other choices. What can we say—that she would have made an excellent waitress? And how can we say even that without becoming just another of those thundering voices?

THE *MAX* SERIES (1979-)

Trev Jones

SOURCE: A review of *Max's Bath* and others, in *School Library Journal,* Vol. 31, No. 3, March, 1985, pp. 159-60.

PreS—A four-star performance from Wells. The new titles in this board book series for youngest listeners feature Max, a toddler rabbit, and his patronizingly patient older sister Ruby. Each story portrays a typical preschool trauma resolved with humor and understanding. In the first, Ruby tries to bathe a multicolored Max (the result of jam, orange sherbet and grape juice). Each attempt produces a dirtier hare, but in the end, Max is finally clean. Ruby isn't. "Dirty," says Max, as he points at her. *Max's Bedtime* is disrupted by a beloved missing red elephant. A helpful Ruby gives him her toys, but none will do. Children will immediately spot the red tail showing under the bed, and will hold their breath until the toy is found. On *Max's Birthday,* Ruby gives him a wind-up dragon which frightens him. Ruby takes it *away,* it goes *around and around, through* Ruby's legs, etc. There's a tense moment for Ruby at the end, but all ends well as the dragon lands *on top of* Max. "Again," he says. From his expressions, every child will know that *Max's Breakfast,* a fried egg, disgusts him. But luck is with Max, and in Ruby's enthusiasm for convincing him of the egg's goodness, she eats it. "All gone," says a grinning (and all-

knowing) Max. The pages are vivid and vibrant, uncluttered but full of amusing detail. There is not a wasted stroke in these deceptively simple illustrations. Max and Ruby's expressions differ on each page, from glee (his), to exasperation (hers) to disgust (both). An engaging duo in books that are fun, funny and bound to be early childhood favorites.

Bulletin of the Center for Children's Books

SOURCE: A review of *Max's Bath,* in *Bulletin of the Center for Children's Books,* Vol. 38, No. 8, April, 1985, p. 157.

Wells does it again; like the first four books about Max (a very young rabbit) this [*Max's Bath*] is realistic, funny, beguiling, and as deft in its minimal text as in its simple and expressive pictures. Older sister Ruby, a long-suffering character, tries repeatedly to get Max clean. Since he is apt to take purple grape juice or orange sherbet into the bath, Max usually comes out as stained as when he went in. Finally Ruby puts Max in the shower; he emerges in white and fluffy state but pointing gleefully at Ruby (who's collected some of his stains) and says balefully "Dirty." His bedtime, his birthday, and his breakfast are the subject of three other new books about Max. They're equally delectable, and they should be as useful for very young children as they are appealing.

Ann A. Flowers

SOURCE: A review of *Max's Bath* and others, in *The Horn Book Magazine,* Vol. LXI, No. 4, July, 1985, pp. 446-47.

Max and his older sister Ruby, those fine stout rabbits with forceful personalities, have returned in four excellent examples of very early books. Max never utters more than one or, at most, two words; the plots or, rather, episodes—told in ten board-pages—must be considered thin, but both parents and children can enjoy endless repetition of these simple, extremely funny stories. Ruby's determined attempts to overcome Max's quiet resistance to eggs, toy dragons, going to sleep without his red elephant, and getting clean are the basis for the stories. Such great opposing forces should inevitably result, one would think, in bloody battles, but kindliness reigns supreme. In *Max's Breakfast,* Max does not care for the egg. "BAD EGG, said Max." Max hides the egg twice and himself once. Ruby, in her efforts to show Max how good it is, absently eats it herself. "ALL GONE, said Max." Another happy ending prevails in *Max's*

Bedtime when he refuses to sleep without his red rubber elephant. Ruby gives him all her stuffed animals one by one until his bed is so lumpy and bumpy he falls off and finds his elephant, leaving an exhausted Ruby asleep in his bed. "GOOD NIGHT, said Max," smiling cheerfully. In *Max's Birthday* he is extremely doubtful about a madly careening wind-up toy dragon, and in *Max's Bath* Ruby gets dirty as Max gets clean. There is no doubt that Rosemary Wells's absolute mastery of the dubious eye and the passively resisting body add immeasurably to these small sagas of everyday life. First-class stories for very young listeners.

Marilyn Carpenter

SOURCE: A review of *Max's Birthday,* in *Los Angeles Times Book Review,* December 8, 1985, p. 4.

Toddlers will relish four simple stories about a small rabbit named Max. In *Max's Bath, Max's Bedtime, Max's Birthday, Max's Breakfast* by Rosemary Wells (unpaginated; ages 18 months to 3 years), the author-illustrator demonstrates her ability to create character and humor in the briefest of tales. Max has a mind of his own, and his sister, Ruby, is always trying to guide him into a different path. But he succeeds in finding his own way and, in the process, will tickle the funny bone of even the youngest listeners. Each of these small, sturdy board books is delightful and full of fun. If your children are unacquainted with the four previous books about Max, they will also find them amusing.

School Library Journal

SOURCE: A review of *Max's Christmas,* in *School Library Journal,* Vol. 33, No. 10, October, 1986, p. 112.

PreS-Gr 2—Children won't be able to resist Max, that epitome of the small child in rabbit guise. Wells has an extraordinary talent for capturing a welter of thoughts and emotions with the placement of an eye or a turn of a smile. Here Ruby, Max's big sister, explains the ins and outs of Christmas in response to Max's adroit one-syllable questioning: Who? When? Where? How? Why? Later in bed, Max's face, reflecting that profoundly amazing logic with which children put two and two together, "didn't believe a word Ruby said." So he sneaks downstairs to wait for Santa. Soon Santa appears (a rabbit, of course), and he, too, is put through one of Max' grillings. But

Santa, veteran of generations of children, finally answers, "BECAUSE!" This is an absolutely delightful book—BECAUSE!

Bulletin of the Center for Children's Books

SOURCE: A review of *Max's Christmas,* in *Bulletin of the Center for Children's Books,* Vol. 40, No. 3, November, 1986, p. 59.

This should win new fans and delight those who are already addicted to stories about Max, the small rabbit who is cared for by his patient older sibling Ruby. What makes this series of books by Rosemary Wells so successful is the ingenious quality of the writing (and the pictures) so skillfully pruned by the author to the essentials of the story. Too, Max is the Great Success of the preschool set, appearing shy and baffled but always, at the close, surprising Ruby with a turnabout ending. Here Max has asked question after question about where (is Santa coming) and how (does Santa get down the chimney) and who (is Santa) and Ruby keeps saying "Because . . ." and, after a coup, that's Max's last word.

Marilyn Carpenter

SOURCE: A review of *Max's Christmas,* in *Los Angeles Times Book Review,* November 23, 1986, p. 12.

[C]hildren will find the questions of the chubby rabbit, Max, irresistibly funny in *Max's Christmas* by Rosemary Wells (ages 2 to 6). Max wants to know all about Santa and pesters his patient, motherly sister, Ruby, with innumerable questions. When Max stays up to see Santa, their encounter brings laughter to young listeners. Wells' skill with her pen gives the characters expressive eyes and faces. Bright colors complete the book's attractive format.

Donnarae McCann and Olga Richard

SOURCE: A review of *Max's Christmas,* in *Wilson Library Bulletin,* Vol. 61, No. 4, December, 1986, p. 49.

In *Max's Christmas* (1986), Rosemary Wells picks up on the idea of belief versus disbelief to allow young Max to be "one up" on sister, Ruby. Ruby is her usual officious self as she scrubs, dresses, and tosses Max into bed. But the ultimate insult is her reply to Max's question, "*How* [is Santa coming down our chimney into our living room]?" "BECAUSE," says Ruby. So Max sneaks downstairs, encounters Santa, and endures the same ploy when Santa says he must go to sleep "BECAUSE." It is a pleasure then to see the underdog have the last word. Ruby asks why Max is on the sofa under a lumpy looking blanket and he shouts a triumphant "BECAUSE!" as he unveils the gifts.

Wells treats the first nine illustrations with a comic flair that outranks the Santa scenes. Without the use of facial grimaces or cartoonist action lines, she simply positions Max and Ruby in such a way that we feel one is pulling or being pulled, while the other is pushing and shoving. By playing it straight in the going-to-bed sequence, Wells achieves genuinely clever characterizations, and we glimpse her talent as a designer in the colorful array of Christmas packages.

Bulletin of the Center for Children's Books

SOURCE: A review of *Max's Chocolate Chicken,* in *Bulletin of the Center for Children's Books,* Vol. 42, No. 7, March, 1989, p. 184.

3-5 yrs. It's superego vs. id all the way this Easter, with Ruby telling Max what to do and Max eating the chocolate chicken anyway. What cares he about finding the stupid eggs? A mud puddle he finds, acorns, a spoon, ants, even. ("Pull yourself together," says Ruby. "Otherwise you'll never get the chocolate chicken.") While Ruby counts her gold egg with purple stripes and her turquoise egg with silver swirls and her lavender egg with orange polka dots, Max makes ant-and-acorn pancakes in the mud. While Ruby declares herself the winner of the egg hunt, Max claims the prize and hides with it in a convenient hole under the tree. While Ruby offers to share it if he will come out, he consumes it all, tail first, head next, wings last. Thoughtfully, a benign Easter Rabbit (not unlike Max in appearance) provides a chocolate duck as well, but Max is closing in on that by the concluding picture. Bright in color and concept, this [*Max's Chocolate Chicken*] is as fresh as the spring-green grass that dominates every spread.

Trev Jones

SOURCE: A review of *Max's Chocolate Chicken,* in *School Library Journal,* Vol. 35, No. 7, March, 1989, p. 172.

PreS-Gr 1—It's cause for celebration when rabbit toddler Max and his bossy sister Ruby return to share another holiday with young readers. Max falls in love with a chocolate chicken that's been left in the bird bath by the Easter Rabbit, and he simply wants to eat it. Ruby, however, insists that they hunt for eggs, with the winner claiming it. Determined Max gets his way, but the surprise ending shows that Ruby is no loser. With her characteristic simplicity of illustration and plot, Wells once again creates an entertaining story with a beguiling main character. The illustrations, in bright jelly bean colors, reflect expression, emotion, mood, and the humor of the situations and capture the freshness of the season. An Easter treat that features two child-like hares in a tale to be enjoyed again and again.

Kirkus Reviews

SOURCE: A review of *Max's Chocolate Chicken,* in *Kirkus Reviews,* Vol. LVII, No. 5, March 1, 1989, p. 386.

Max is back, as irresistibly nonconformist as ever. "One morning somebody [it looks like the Easter Bunny, but, then, Max is a rabbit too . . .] put a chocolate chicken in the birdbath." Ruby, Max's sister, knows all the rules: whoever finds the most eggs gets the chocolate chicken. Max doesn't care about rules; he puts his basket in a mud puddle, finds a spoon, watches ants, makes ant-and-acorn pancakes, and finally takes the chocolate chicken away and eats it. Ruby doesn't know whether to be incensed or to negotiate. But not to worry—a chocolate turkey appears for her, and Max says, "I love you!" This delicious summing up of the contrast between two quintessentially different personalities is reflected in Wells' wonderfully expressive faces; despite the book's small size, cheerful colors and bold forms suit it for groups, while the text is also easy enough for beginning readers.

Mary M. Burns

SOURCE: A review of *Max's Chocolate Chicken,* in *The Horn Book Magazine,* Vol. LXV, No. 3, May-June, 1989, p. 367.

Max, the most irresistible rabbit protagonist since Peter Rabbit, seems just a tad older than in his first appearances. Consequently, Wells uses a more painterly style with more detailed definition of features to capture the change without sacrificing the charm. In his latest adventure he and his omnipresent, bossy sister Ruby compete in an egg hunting contest; the winner gets a chocolate chicken, placed in the bird bath by the Easter bunny. Easily distracted, Max finds mud, acorns, and ants as the single-minded Ruby locates the eggs and maintains a running commentary on her brother's ineptitude. Undaunted, Max wins the day by running away with the chicken to a hidden refuge. There, he consumes the prize as Ruby's commands, like a descant, hover unheeded in the air. Meanwhile, the benevolent Easter bunny places a chocolate duck in the empty birdbath, leaving succeeding events to the reader's imagination as a baffled Ruby looks at the new acquisition, and a triumphant Max nips a piece off its tail. It takes a special kind of genius to create a true picture story book, let alone one that adults never tire of reading aloud to devoted audiences. Rosemary Wells is certainly a contemporary master of the genre, for her books touch on universal feelings and celebrate the small triumphs of the underdog with humor tempered by sympathy and sensitivity strengthened by wit.

Trev Jones

SOURCE: A review of *Max's Dragon Shirt,* in *School Library Journal,* Vol. 37, No. 4, April, 1991, p. 105.

PreS-Gr2—The engaging toddler rabbit is back, clad in tattered, paint-smeared, but dearly loved old blue pants. Draconian older sister Ruby drags him to the store for new ones, but Max, insistent as ever, only has eyes for a green shirt featuring a fire-breathing dragon. When Ruby spies first one dress and then another that she loves, the two become separated, and the search that follows is a true comedy of errors. Winsome but willful Max gets his heart's desire, and once again Ruby is deflated, giving young readers and listeners the vicarious satisfaction of besting an older sibling. [*Max's Dragon Shirt*] reads well aloud, but is easy enough for beginning readers, who will soon notice that while Ruby gives her orders, Max's vocabulary is limited to one telling line repeated throughout: "Dragon shirt." Wells uses more background, more detail here than in previous "Max" stories, artfully capturing the hustle-bustle of a busy department store. Another gleeful romp with a pair of unforgettable hares.

Hannah B. Zeiger

SOURCE: A review of *Max's Dragon Shirt,* in *The Horn Book Magazine,* Vol. LXVII, No. 3, May-June, 1991, pp. 326-27.

Good news! Max is back, and Ruby is taking him shopping. She has five dollars to spend on new pants for Max to replace his "disgusting" old blue ones.

Max loves his blue pants; what he really wants is a dragon shirt. As so often happens on such expeditions, the shoppers are distracted from the task at hand. On their way to Boys' Sportswear, Ruby sees a red dress she absolutely loves. Dragging Max into the dressing room, she tries on dress after dress while Max's eyes glaze and he slumps into a doze. When he wakes, he goes out to find Ruby. Spying her yellow dress, Max follows it through one department after another, stopping on the way to pull on his dream dragon shirt. As his eyes emerge from the shirt, he is horrified to find that the yellow dress he has been following isn't Ruby. "It was a teenager. Max screamed." While Max's panic is soothed by quantities of ice cream, applied both internally and externally, a helpful saleswoman steers Ruby back into her yellow dress and takes her to reclaim Max in the ice-cream-smeared shirt—which just happens to cost five dollars. They head home with Ruby frustrated and Max radiant in his old blue pants and his dirty new dragon shirt. Rosemary Wells is, as always, a master at capturing telling expressions and human foibles. Both adults and children will recognize themselves and familiar feelings and experiences in this story for all ages.

Bulletin the Center for Children's Books

SOURCE: A review of *Max and Ruby's First Greek Myth: Pandora's Box,* in *Bulletin of the Center for Children's Books,* Vol. 47, No. 3, November, 1993, p. 106.

If Max and Ruby's first Greek myth is young listeners' first Greek myth, there may follow some confusion despite Wells' characteristically witty text and illustration. The framing story is Ruby's attempt to keep Max out of her room by posting a sign saying "No! This means you!"—which of course Max can't read, leading to his getting caught in the act of investigating Ruby's jewelry box, leading to Ruby's reading him a revisionist version of Pandora's violating her mother's injunction against opening her jewelry box. Of course Pandora does open it, releasing a slew of bugs, which are counteracted not by Hope but by an efficient spider. Pandora's mother returns to congratulate Pandora on being a good bunny and rewards her with a trip to the movies, for which they decorate themselves with a bug necklace and spider pin from the magic jewelry box. Back to Max, Ruby, and a punch line that concludes their discussion of the moral: "And what does my sign say, Max?" asks Ruby. "No!" says Max. "And who does it mean, Max?" Ruby asks. "You!" says Max. It's very funny, but it's very complicated, storywise, although Wells does a clear-cut job of distinguishing the two tales: the framing story is on white paper with plain borders around the watercolor paintings; the myth is on pale blue paper with borders of traditional Greek motifs. More than a tale within a tale, this is a spoof within a spoof, so kids will need a grounding in the myth's straightforward rendition to deconstruct this one. While fans will sit still for anything about Max and Ruby, and adults will adore the Grecian profiles of rabbits in full battle regalia (including chariot and victory wreaths), do give kids a crack at the d'Aulaires' *Book of Greek Myths* first.

Hanna B. Zeiger

SOURCE: A review of *Max and Ruby's First Greek Myth: Pandora's Box,* in *The Horn Book Magazine,* Vol. LXIX, No. 6, November-December, 1993, p. 740.

Irrepressible Max is back, and he's peeking and prying into Ruby's room with special interest in her jewelry box. When Ruby catches him, she asks if he can read the sign on her door which says "NO! This means you!" Reading the sign out loud three times doesn't seem to convince Max, so Ruby, the ever-instructive older sister, sits Max down to listen to a story about "sneaking and peeking." The story, set in ancient Greece, is about Pandora. When Pandora's mother has to leave the house, she gives her daughter instructions about having honey cake and playing but warns her not to open her magic jewelry box. After Mother leaves, Pandora can't keep her mind off the box; she tries shaking it and looking through it with X-ray vision. "I think I hear sugar lumps in there," she said. Finally, opening the box for the tiniest peek, she releases swarms of insects that buzz around her. Then Pandora hears a voice in the box, asking to be let out. A green spider emerges to spin a huge web with which she catches and eats every insect, and Pandora promises never to snoop again. With the end of the story, Ruby tries to hammer home the moral by asking Max again what her sign says. This time, Max answers, ""No!" But when Ruby asks who it means, an unrepentant Max says, "'You!'" This childlike version of the ancient tale—complete with bunnies in togas and a terraceum to play on—is certainly amusing. But Max remains the star of this adventure.

Doris Orgel

SOURCE: A review of *Max and Ruby's First Greek Myth: Pandora's Box* and *Max and Ruby's Midas,* in *The Five Owls,* Vol. 10, No. 3, January-February, 1996, p. 50.

[Thanks] to the talented Rosemary Wells, there now are Greek myths for toddlers. In the first book, *Max and Ruby's First Greek Myth: Pandora's Box* (Dial, 1993) older sister Ruby warns Max not to snoop in her jewelry box by telling him about Pandora (who's an ancient Greek bunny, of course). In the second, *Max and Ruby's Midas* (Dial, 1995), Ruby warns Max against cupcake greed by telling about insatiable Midas who turned his family into hot fudge sundaes and the like. Happily, Max is undaunted, and does not grasp the morals of these myths. Nor will very young children. But some appealing graphic detail my well linger in their memories—a sailing ship, a temple, or Pan (bunny) playing his pipes—and later on may light up the whole subject of Greek antiquity for them. Meantime parents will enjoy how cleverly Wells spoofs the preachiness with which conventional retellers have too often foisted the Midas and Pandora myths on children.

Publishers Weekly

SOURCE: A review of *Bunny Cakes,* in *Publishers Weekly,* Vol. 243, No. 48, November 25, 1996, p. 74.

It's kitchen chaos as Wells's beloved Max and Ruby become bunnies who bake [in *Bunny Cakes*]. Max and Ruby each have grand plans for Grandma's birthday cake. Max envisions an earthworm cake with caterpillar frosting and "Red-Hot Marshmallow Squirters" on top. Ruby, however, insists on an "angel surprise cake with raspberry-fluff icing." Max tries his best to help his bossy older sister but, as always, winds up making a mess. After spilling the milk or breaking the eggs, Max is repeatedly dispatched to the store with Ruby's neatly printed list of ingredients, all the while trying to figure out how to convey his own request to the grocer. Wells's (*My Very First Mother Goose*) ink-and-watercolor world is cheery as ever here, replete with a cozy, '50s-esque kitchen and friendly neighborhood market. She accurately captures the prickliness of sibling exchanges ("There's a yellow line on the floor, Max," says Ruby when Max returns with a replacement bottle of milk. "You can't step over that line"). Hapless Max maintains a happy-go-lucky demeanor in any situation, a shining example of patience and perseverance. And when it comes to the interplay between pared-down text and eventful illustrations, Wells, quite simply, takes the cake. Ages 3-7.

Martha Topol

SOURCE: A review of *Bunny Cakes,* in *School Library Journal,* Vol. 43, No. 1, January, 1997, p. 94.

PreS-Gr 1—For Grandma's birthday, Max makes an earthworm cake while Ruby decides to go all out with an "angel surprise cake with raspberry-fluff icing." Max wants to help but instead knocks the ingredients off the counter one by one. Thus, with a list from Ruby in hand, he makes repeated trips to the store. He also tries to buy Red-Hot Marshmallow Squirters for his own cake, but the grocer can't read his colorful scribbles. It's not until the fourth and final trip that silent Max discovers the power of representational drawing. In the end, Grandma is satisfyingly thrilled with both of her cakes. This deceptively simple story touches on several ideas, from birthdays and baking to making lists and shopping. More importantly, it shows two independent, self-assured youngsters accomplishing individual, age-appropriate goals. Ruby and Max have a wonderful sibling relationship; Ruby tells Max just what not to do, and Max does just what he wants and neither one gets mad. Despite the repeated mishaps, they remain undaunted and refreshingly cheerful. Vibrant ink-and-watercolor art and a clean, effective layout focus readers' attention on the action at hand and on the irresistible, busy, rabbit characters. Wells continues to speak directly to young children.

Bulletin of the Center for Children's Books

SOURCE: A review of *Bunny Cakes,* in *Bulletin of the Center for Children's Books,* Vol. 50, No. 7, March, 1997, p. 261.

Max and Ruby have their separate ideas on what would be more suitable for Grandma's birthday [in *Bunny Cakes*]: "Max made her an earthworm birthday cake," but Max's I-know-best older sister, Ruby, has decreed, "We are going to make Grandma an angel surprise cake with raspberry-fluff icing." Max's attempt to be helpful leads to a series of culinary disasters in the kitchen, and his plight worsens when he is sent to the store by Ruby and tries to expand the grocery list ("Max wanted Red-Hot Marshmallow Squirters for his earthworm cake. So he wrote 'Red-Hot Marshmallow Squirters' on the list"). In this take on written communication kidstyle, pudgy Max is at his winsome best, creating havoc in the kitchen or looking irresistibly hopeful as he passes the list with his illegible add-on to the perplexed grocer. Ruby is indomitable as only a bossy but capable sister can be. The ink-and-water-color depictions of Max's messes, Ruby's grocery lists rendered on yellow notebook paper with a black crayon, and most importantly the no-Max-allowed sign (a red circle with a slash over Max's crayoned image) that Ruby leaves on the kitchen door all add up to perfect sibling back-off fraught with good-natured, bunny-child

humor. It ends just right with—you guessed it—two cakes for Grandma, one bedecked with Red-Hot Marshmallow Squirters.

THE MAN IN THE WOODS (1985)

Susan Levine

SOURCE: A review of *The Man in the Woods,* in *Voice of Youth Advocates,* Vol. 8, No. 1, April, 1985, pp. 52-3.

Helen and her friend Pinky, both high school freshmen, witness a car accident caused by the Punk Rock Thrower. Helen follows a person she believes to be the Punk Rock Thrower in the woods but loses him. Later, the police tell her that they have arrested him but Helen isn't sure. She feels that the man in the woods may have seen her and that she is being followed by someone who wants to harm her. No one believes her, except Pinky; and the two, by delving into the town's history, discover the truth in the face of much danger.

Helen and Pinky are very well developed and interesting characters. The mystery is well plotted with the suspense building to a satisfying end. The interaction between Helen and Pinky Levy (a boy) includes lots of humor that make the story all the more appealing and original.

HAZEL'S AMAZING MOTHER (1985)

Bulletin of the Center for Children's Books

SOURCE: A review of *Hazel's Amazing Mother,* in *Bulletin of the Center for Children's Books,* Vol. 39, No. 5, January, 1986, pp. 99-100.

The power of maternal love may be exaggerated here, but the lap audience will understand that mothers are their defenders and will do extraordinary things for their young. As is true of other books by Wells, the characters are small animals in appearance; in behavior they are people. Here a youngster is sent on a pre-picnic errand, loses her way, arrives at a park where she is beset by bullies who rip her doll and dump the doll's carriage in the pond, and cries for her mother. Mother, picnic basket in hand, is caught by a strong wind, the picnic basket she's holding serving as parachute. She comes down just in time to force the bullies to tidy up their damage, and the picnic proceeds, with—a typical Wellsian touch—more food than could ever have fit in the basket. Breezy and funny, but also touching, this should appeal to children's sense of justice as well as their faith in parental omnipotence.

📖 *THROUGH THE HIDDEN DOOR* (1987)

David Gale

SOURCE: A review of *Through the Hidden Door,* in *School Library Journal,* Vol. 33, No. 4, April, 1987, p. 114.

Gr 5-9—Needing a place to hide from a group of vicious classmates, Barney Pennimen joins secretive Snowy Cobb to explore a hidden cave in which a small, unidentified bone was found. The boys find traces of a miniature village—but are not sure whether it is a model of a community or the actual remains of a 100,000-year-old civilization. Wells tells two stories here: Barney's victimization and growing strength of character, and the boys' discovery and protection of the ancient civilization. Both are suspenseful and remarkably well integrated into the novel. Obsessively private Snowy, who has emotional problems, and Barney, an intelligent boy whose past submission to peer pressure has gotten him into trouble, are both fully realized characters. These two will engage readers' interest, which will be sustained throughout by the brutal reality of Barney's school experiences and the appealing fantasy of the boys' remarkable findings. The wish fulfillment associated with that discovery will more than compensate for the minimal or non-existent scientific and historic groundings of the civilization and its unearthing (a society of six-inch humans does not fit in with evolutionary theory; the achievements of their civilization does not match cultural history; it is implausible that two boys could have the archaeological know-how to uncover the village without harming it). An absorbing school story with a twist, this one is sure to fill readers with a sense of wonder.

Bulletin of the Center for Children's Books

SOURCE: A review of *Through the Hidden Door,* in *Bulletin of the Center for Children's Books,* Vol. 40, No. 11, July, 1987, p. 220.

Like the meshed cogs of two wheels, the small but important element of fantasy and the larger one of reality together spin smoothly to create a story that has pace and suspense, strong relationships, and a

sturdy structure. That such an adventure tale should have depth and nuance and a compelling style, as well, means that this is one of the best stories Rosemary Wells has written. It is told by Barney, who is persecuted by a gang of bullies at a posh private school, and who helps a younger student keep the secret of a miniature city found in a cave. This is a story about friendship, power, ethical concepts, and courage. All that, and a page-turner, too.

Frances Bradburn

SOURCE: A review of *Through the Hidden Door,* in *Wilson Library Bulletin,* Vol. 62, No. 1, September, 1987, p. 68.

The mystery/fantasy story has always been a child-pleaser. Filled with spine-tingling adventure and mind-stimulating clues, however, the mystery/fantasy has the potential to be more than a mere pleasure source. It can be used to stimulate creativity and develop problem-solving skills.

Take, for example, Rosemary Wells's newest entry into the mystery/fantasy market, *Through the Hidden Door.* Barney Pennimen is a sixth grader at Winchester Boys' Academy who has fallen under the spell of the wrong crowd. Wanting desperately to be liked and to avoid years of torment and harassment, Pennimen helps "the untouchables" cheat on final exams, steal from a March of Dimes donation card, and put vodka in the housemaster's vaporizer. One day, however, the evil becomes more than he can bear. Faced with torturing the headmaster's collie, Barney refuses to participate and even identifies the other boys when persistently questioned by the headmaster himself. Unfortunately, he thus becomes the lightning rod for all the group's wicked ire. Friendless and terrified, Pennimen attempts to isolate himself as much as possible.

This forced isolation soon enables him to become a vital cog in Snowy Cobb's exploration of a cave in the hillside around the Academy. Once inside the cave, the boys carefully excavate a miniature ancient village whose now-extinct inhabitants obviously worshipped the deadly cobra. Day after day throughout the school year, Snowy blindfolds Barney and leads him to the secret entrance, through a maze-like tunnel, over a high ledge, down a seventy-five-second chute to an enclosed beach of white sand. It is here under this sand that the boys gradually uncover an ancient pigmy civilization—and some interesting information about courage, truth, friendship, and human nature.

It is here also that children will be able to process a great deal of information from the story to think creatively. For instance, students could take facts that they have learned about ancient civilizations to analyze which of the information Wells uses to describe the pigmy civilization could be factual and which could only be fantasy (analysis). Likewise, children could hypothesize how this ancient warm-weather civilization could have been found in a cave in Greenfield, Massachusetts (synthesis). Finally, using information from the book, they could be asked to evaluate Barney's behavior after he has been threatened by the new headmaster and the gang of untouchables. Was he wise to decide to stay at the school? Should his father have insisted upon his leaving evaluating judgment)?

This process is not an exercise destroy the readability and excitement of the book. Far from it! It is an opportunity to lead middle readers on a quest to explore the fullest potential of this and other fascinating mysteries/fantasies.

Paula J. Lacey

SOURCE: A review of *Through the Hidden Door,* in *Voice of Youth Advocates,* Vol. 10, No. 6, February, 1988, p. 284.

Wells, veteran author of suspense novels for YAs, has written a real page-turner in this story of Barney Penniman. Barney is a student at Winchester Academy who insists on staying at his school despite serious threats from five former friends and a malicious headmaster. Why does he insist on staying? After befriending Snowy Cobb, an unusual younger boy, Barney learns of Snowy's discovery of a secret cave filled with sand and Snowy's intention of finding out what is under the sand. After several days of digging, the two boys begin to uncover what appears to be a miniature ancient city. Is it the archaeological find of Snowy's dreams—a city of miniature humans? Or is it the more recent work of some mysterious person or group of people?

Throughout the story, the threats of Barney's ex-pals and the conniving of the evil headmaster force the rather unselfconfident Barney to fend for himself and make some courageous decisions. An exciting finish promises a revelation about the cave and its contents, but ends by leaving readers making their own decision. Due to the nature of the story, it's a necessary disappointment.

This is fine leisure reading with a special appeal to reluctant junior high boys. Teachers and parents will appreciate the author's ability to introduce questions of morality and good and evil into the story. It will make exciting booktalk material as well.

SHY CHARLES (1988)

Kirkus Reviews

SOURCE: A review of *Shy Charles,* in *Kirkus Reviews,* Vol. LVI, No. 13, July 1, 1988, p. 980.

Like Wells's *Noisy Nora* (1973), Charles (a dormouse) is an exemplification of a single, common characteristic. He is perfectly happy, but he prefers to be alone; he won't use the telephone, and—to his parents' embarrassment—he doesn't even say thank you. Sent to ballet, he pretends to sleep; the football coach, thinking him ill, sends him home to bed. Still, when the babysitter takes a fall, Charles rises to the emergency and summons aid, but—cheerfully holding onto his integrity—can't bring himself to respond verbally to the thanks he receives. Wells's rhymed text serves its purpose well enough, but the story's strength is in Wells's comical, vigorous illustrations, exuding common sense in the presence of normal foibles. Her dormouse faces, and Charles' round, sturdy little body, are wonderfully expressive. (*Picture book. 3-8*)

Kimberly Olson Fakih

SOURCE: A review of *Shy Charles,* in *Publishers Weekly,* Vol. 234, No. 9, August 26, 1988, p. 87.

"Charles [is as] happy as he could be," but he is so shy he won't thank Mrs. Belinski for a treat, and he refuses to play with Wanda Sue or answer the phone. "This can't go on," says Charles' father, but all attempts to nudge mousy Charles into action backfire. When Charles is enrolled in ballet class, he hides near a potted plant and pretends to be asleep. And when his father buys him a football helmet with silver wings, Charles ends up having to be carried off the field in disgrace. Then Mrs. Block, his babysitter, falls down the stairs and shy Charles efficiently handles the emergency all by himself. Wells' rhyming text is spare and clever and she shows an acute understanding of the painfully shy child. Whether Charles is anxiously peering out from underneath his helmet or eyeing the fearsome telephone, readers will find this quiet hero and his winsome smile beguiling—proof that shyness does not preclude competence. Ages 4-8.

Bulletin of the Center for Children's Books

SOURCE: A review of *Shy Charles* in *The Bulletin of the Center for Children's Books,* September 1988, pp. 21-2

5-7 yrs. Charles is a happy child whose mode of communication is minimal. He is content to accept Mrs. Belinski's chocolate surprise . . . silently. When it's time to say good-bye, Charles simply disappears into a flower bin. In ballet class, he pretends to be asleep. But when the babysitter falls down the stairs, Charles gets right on the phone, summoning the emergency service and saying everything necessary until the crisis is over. "He's a prince, a gem, a hero! / And everyone shouted, 'Thank you, Charles!' / But Charles said . . . / Zero." Like many of Wells' picture-book characters, this mouseling is quirkily endearing, with more of the humor conveyed in the illustrations than in the rhyming text. One full-page spread, for example, shows the ballet students cavorting color-fully across the floor upon which Charles lies, back to the audience, dressed in black, his tail and ears stretched stiff. Shy listeners will empathize, others will sympathize—with a smile.

📖 THE LITTLE LAME PRINCE (1990)

Bulletin of the Center for Children's Books

SOURCE: A review of *The Little Lame Prince,* in *Bulletin of the Center for Children's Books,* Vol. 44, No. 1, September, 1990, p. 19.

5-8 yrs. Rosemary Wells has benefited children's lit-erature with a versatility ranging from toddler board books to YA novels. Whether funny or serious, her style is original, and this adaptation of Dinah Craik's British classic (1874) celebrates a dramatic plot wrung free of sentimentality by twists of wildly imaginative illustration. For starters, the cast has been recast as animals, a choice that displays Wells' drafting to best advantage and that also allows her to play with visual satire—the royal family are pigs. When the plump but ailing queen dies and the king wastes away, an evilly militaristic brother of the king banishes Prince Francisco to a faraway tower. There, Francisco's fairy godmother, who always appears with the sound of popcorn, bestows on him a patched magic cape that helps him recover the suffering kingdom. Quite apart from Wells' artful abridgement of a Victorian soap opera, the narrative graphics ex-pand from self-contained domestic scenes character-istic of her past work to a larger canvas including

landscapes and complex changes of detail, expres-sion, and composition. The villains "Osvaldo, his porky wife, Isabella, and their seven wild and whiney sons" are a richly portrayed set of bad actors. The hero himself, while occasionally reminiscent of Wells' endearing Max and company, expands consid-erably on their repertoire of reactions. Ambitiously colorful, slyly funny—a real porker!

Judith Gloyer

SOURCE: A review of *The Little Lame Prince,* in *School Library Journal,* Vol. 36, No. 11, November, 1990, p. 100.

Gr 1-3—In side notes, Wells states that she hoped to adapt a favorite story of her childhood for younger children while keeping the spirit of the original. At this she is not successful. Craik's *The Little Lame Prince* more thoughtfully presents a coming-of-age story, a coming to grips with both good and evil in the world, and a realization of one's own strengths and weaknesses. Stripped of its action, this adapta-tion is more like Miss Piggy goes Anne of Green Gables. In fact, the main characters are pigs and the lady-in-waiting who drops the young prince causing his lameness is a silly goose. Taken on its own terms as a story, more parody than adaptation, it's a hoot. Wells' writing is fast paced and humorous, and she never talks down to her audience. Her good-natured illustrations are highly expressive and add additional humor to the tale. Younger children will indeed enjoy the adventure, while older children should definitely be directed to the original for its own special magic.

Sylvia S. Marantz

SOURCE: A review of *The Little Lame Prince,* in *The Five Owls,* Vol. 5, No. 2, November-December, 1990, pp. 29-30.

The fairy tale of the crippled prince, orphaned and exiled by his wicked uncle, went out of print in 1985 but still lives vividly in many memories, including that of Rosemary Wells. Here she uses the essence of the original Dina Maria Muluck Craik book to create a much shorter tale for young children that includes the magic of a cape that becomes a flying carpet and a fairy godmother. Craik's story, over a hundred pages long, has an old-fashioned, didactic flavor with, of course, many more episodes and a richer character development. The question of adaptation of "origi-nal" folk or fairy tales is a debatable one. People have been changing such stories for eons, and retelling them for a younger audience certainly has its place, especially for tales that may have limited appeal in their original form.

Although Wells's retelling is simple and easy to read, it is filled with details that stir the imagination and give texture to the basic plot. The godmother appears and vanishes to the snap of popping corn, and the names of the places and people all have a Latin flavor that establishes an exotic faraway aura, with perhaps overtones of oppressive dictators for adult readers. As in all satisfying fairy tales, good triumphs over evil, the wicked uncle who has usurped the prince's throne dies from his excesses, and the prince becomes a well-loved ruler.

But this is also a picture book, where the art tells us the story along with the words. The cover shows us the prince on his cape, half apprehensive and half delighted, flying from his wheelchair out the window. This prince is, however, a pig, which gives those with memories of the original a start. Why has Wells anthropomorphized the characters in this story? Further, when is this use of animals instead of humans in very human adventures justified? Here the depiction as pigs seems to add a dimension to the piggy qualities of the greedy uncle and his family. The use of a "silly goose" as the vain nursemaid who drops the baby prince is also appropriate.

As an illustrator, Wells has created unforgettable and appealing animal characters—Max, Peabody, Nora—to whom children relate immediately. Her simplified, abstracted creations with slightly exaggerated but convincing anatomy display definite personalities with humorous touches. In this book her full color, more-or-less transparent intense watercolors have a loose form within the varied black outline. Every page is a careful balance of words and picture. All of the characters become personalities, while the details of each scene and locale reinforce the mood and flavor of the words. The usurping uncle smokes a cigar, his wife waves a fan, the prince takes a teddy bear to bed, and in almost every scene pig-pleasing food and drink are present. Both words and pictures merit re-reading for the fun and the messages they contain.

Los Angeles Times Book Review

SOURCE: A review of *The Little Lame Prince*, in *Los Angeles Times Book Review*, November 25, 1990, p. 25.

Rosemary Wells places her unmistakably antic stamp on her very loose adaptation of Dinah Craik's classic *The Little Lame Prince* (ages 6-9). The Prince is a

pig in this version. The watercolor paintings which adorn the text herald a new, more painterly style for the popular Wells, but if her art is more finished, her images are as laugh-out-loud-funny as always and, like [Peter] Catalanotto, she remains a master of drawing animals with agreeably quirky expressions.

📖 FRITZ AND THE MESS FAIRY (1991)

Kirkus Reviews

SOURCE: A review of *Fritz and the Mess Fairy*, in *Kirkus Reviews*, Vol. LIX, No. 16, August 15, 1991, p. 1095.

The strange bedfellows that occur in creative disorder are always good for a laugh; Wells makes the device even funnier here by compounding it. Fritz, a badger, stows the mess in his room under the bed and the food he doesn't like under his seat cushion; then he makes havoc of his family's belongings as he gathers supplies for his science project. Suddenly, his experiment invokes the Mess Fairy—a winged pig who emerges like a genie from his beaker and goes on to flights of messiness that appall even Fritz. Fortunately, he figures out how to reverse his inadvertent spell, then embarks on a night-long frenzy of putting everything back to rights before fixing his family a magnificent breakfast.

This isn't Wells at her most imaginative, but she makes the most of a proven theme, capturing the subtleties of Fritz's reactions as well as the broader humor and offering a final comical turn that lightens its message. Fine for group sharing. (*Picture book. 4-8*)

Bulletin of the Center for Children's Books

SOURCE: A review of *Fritz and the Mess Fairy*, in *Bulletin of the Center for Children's Books*, Vol. 45, No. 3, November, 1991, p. 78.

Gr. K-2. One reason Rosemary Wells is popular with the readaloud audience is that she is funny; another reason is that she knows just how to time the denouement of a situation that awakens a recognition reflex in listeners. What child doesn't understand familial reaction to making messes? Having irritated the other three members of his family by being messy and using their belongings, furry Fritz is changed by the excesses of the Mess Fairy (a pig who is even more untidy than he) and resolves to clean the whole house. Very pleased with himself, he prepares separate breakfasts-in-bed for his sister and for each of his parents. Smirking with pride, he carries off a loaded tray. Children will probably enjoy the last page most, as our hero goes off, saying "It's the new Fritz," and leaving behind an incredible old-Fritz mess on every horizontal surface in the kitchen. Wells' animal characters have their usual panache and her domestic scenes, their usual cozy dishevelment—slightly more disheveled than usual, in this case.

Ruth Semrau

SOURCE: A review of *Fritz and the Mess Fairy,* in *School Library Journal,* Vol. 38, No. 1, January, 1992, p. 100.

K-Gr 2—Fritz is a walking disaster, trailing disorder wherever he steps. Under his bed lies a month's laundry, stale Halloween candy, dirty dishes, wet towels, and three library books with Popsicle stick bookmarks. When his science project goes awry, it produces an evil genie that looks like an enormous pink pig; the creature goes on to make ultimate chaos out of what parts of the house Fritz has not yet demolished. The child pulls himself together, puts the science project in reverse, and sucks the Mess Fairy back into the void from whence she came. Unfortunately, he carries his good intentions one step too far, and once again reduces the kitchen to a mess. Wells fails to make Fritz seem funny or appealing, and the story does not rise above the ordinary. Although it is not one of her best efforts, the cartoon animals—round little badgers this time-are appealingly cuddly, as always. For a more dramatic story of the child as well-meaning mischief maker, take another look at Peter Spier's *Oh, Were They Ever Happy* (Doubleday, 1978).

Robyn Sheahan

SOURCE: A review of *Fritz and the Mess Fairy,* in *Magpies,* Vol. 8, No. 1, March, 1993, p. 27.

Anthropomorphic narratives often tend to be cloying and sentimental, but with Rosemary Wells, the narrative is never in any such danger. She has a rare gift for perspicacious insight and humour, tempered with irony, and though her characters are animals, they always present realistically human foibles. Sound and witty observations on mischievous childish behaviour are made in a lovingly crafted text which serves to explore real family interaction. Quickly, though,

Wells switches in style, lapsing into a semi-magical sequence which again relates closely to the child's inventive imagination. For in this story the "Mess Fairy" arrives in the night to make the house even messier than Fritz has left it. Fritz is forced to work a scientific experiment to get rid of the fairy and makes, in the process, even a greater mess than before.

The well meaning actions of children, and their unintentionally annoying habits are cunningly conveyed. Wells never lapses into didacticism but makes her point in words and pictures which harbour many an ironic twist. Her characters are visually depicted most engagingly, portraying via facial expression, exactly the feelings of the characters. In pastel watercolours and varied layout the book is never dull or predictable. A handsomely presented volume for Wells collectors to add to their shelves.

Books for Keeps

SOURCE: A review of *Fritz and the Mess Fairy,* in *Books for Keeps,* No. 83, November, 1993, p. 10.

That my copy of this book is dog-eared already only goes to show that Rosemary Wells still has her finger well and truly on the pulse of children's deeper concerns. The panic that Fritz struggles to conquer as he inadvertently unleashes an even messier creature than himself and the horror he feels as he cowers in the corner while he views the havoc wreaked . . . is resolved—but Rosemary Wells' dry humour still leaves us with the twist in the tail that so appeals.

THE *VOYAGE TO THE BUNNY PLANET* SERIES (1992)

Lauralyn Persson

SOURCE: A review of *First Tomato, The Island Light,* and *Moss Pillows,* in *School Library Journal,* Vol. 38, No. 11, November, 1992, p. 80.

PreS-Gr 2—An unusual and charming set of books. In each, the protagonist is having a terrible day. *First Tomato* is about Claire, whose shoes fill up with snow on the way to school; in *The Island Light,* Felix throws up in art class; and Robert, in *The Moss Pillow,* visits some awful relatives who serve cold liver chili for dinner. Halfway through each book, Janet, the queen of the Bunny Planet, summons the rabbit child, saying, "'Here's the day that should have been.'" Claire's voyage to the Bunny Planet takes the form of a visit to the garden to pick the first tomato. Felix's ideal day is spent on an island, in a lighthouse with his father; Robert's is in a quiet forest. In each case, the Bunny Planet is a soothing, secure world where peace and individuality reign. Each book ends with a return to an improved reality, with the hero or heroine spotting the Bunny Planet from the real world. The illustrations are beautifully executed and perfectly scaled. Wells makes great use of contrast in mood and light, which is perfectly suited to the theme. The writing is somewhat less successful. The stories are told in rhyme, which tends towards the sing-song, and some of the musings on "the day that should have been" may appeal more to adults than to children. Still, they make a plea for catharsis via fantasy and daydeaming, something that cannot be overemphasized to today's overprogrammed children and parents.

Bulletin of the Center for Children's Books

SOURCE: A review of *First Tomato, Moss Pillows, and The Island Light,* in *Bulletin of the Center for Children's Books,* Vol. 46, No. 4, December, 1992, pp. 126-27.

Available in two formats, a small boxed set and a larger library edition series for more convenient shelving and sharing, [*First Tomato, Moss Pillows* and *The Island Light*] make good use of a magic-friend plot formula. Each rabbit-child protagonist has a terrible day (told in prose) that trips off a poetic fantasy escape: "Far beyond the moon and stars, / Twenty light-years south of Mars, / Spins the gentle Bunny Planet / And the Bunny Queen is Janet." Claire, waiting for a bus in the snow, retreats to a blissful garden and picks the perfect tomato for her mother; Felix, a victim of the flu and what he considers parental neglect, finds perfect happiness with his father in a cozy lighthouse; Robert, bullied by four obnoxious cousins, gets an idyllic forest all to himself. "Deep in a pocket of emerald moss / I lie where the leaves fall free. / My pillow is soft as milkweed / And as green as a tropical sea." Wells' poetry has a melodic ring reminiscent of Nancy Willard's, and her watercolors show characteristic whimsical pizzazz. Kids will want to hear these over and over to pick out a favorite; adults will find the experience lulling, but don't miss the sly historical note under each copyright statement.

Hanna B. Zeiger

SOURCE: A review of *First Tomato: A Voyage to the Bunny Planet,* in *The Horn Book Magazine,* Vol. LXIX, No. 1, January-February, 1993, p. 80.

Anyone experiencing a stressful, frustrating day would do well to take the advice on the back of Rosemary Wells's three new books: "Lean back in your easy chair, the Bunny Planet's waiting there." It is impossible to read the Bunny Planet books without a smile. A dreadful Sunday visit to relatives ends in a dinner of cold liver chili for Robert. Felix's bad day starts with getting sick in front of the whole art class and ends with his parents forgetting to kiss him good-night. Claire gets snow in her shoes on the way to school, endures two hours of math, and then is "the only girl not able to do a cartwheel" at playtime. But never fear—these three rabbits will each experience "the day that should have been." Their destination: "Far beyond the moon and stars, / Twenty light-years south of Mars, / Spins the gentle Bunny Planet / And the Bunny Queen is Janet." Resting on a bed of moss, spending a rainy day by a cozy fire in lighthouse, or eating soup lovingly prepared from the first tomato in the garden—each little rabbit has one lovely day, then returns home content to know the Bunny Planet is there. There are many humorous touches in both text and illustrations: the rabbits, as always, are endearing; the decoration on the hem of Queen Janet's gown forecasts the theme of each adventure; the Bunny Planet part of each story is in rhyme; and each book contains an appropriate rabbit quote by a famous person on the verso of the title page. These stories are also available in small size as a boxed set of three. If we can't travel there ourselves, we can hope that there may be more Bunny Planet books for us to enjoy.

LUCY COMES TO STAY (1994)

Publishers Weekly

SOURCE: A review of *Lucy Comes to Stay,* in *Publishers Weekly,* Vol. 241, No. 18, May 2, 1994, p. 308.

Mary Elizabeth is delighted to be given a puppy, a small scrap of a Westie called Lucy, but, as these brief vignettes eloquently illustrate, she must learn that looking after a pet is not always easy. In rapid succession Lucy manages-to chew up a new pair of shoes, cover her face in blue ink and tumble into a bubble bath. Given patience and understanding, however, she and Mary Elizabeth are soon the best of friends. Gentle, dreamy oil paintings match the quietly lyrical mood of the text, their subdued palette enlivened by dashes of light. A wispy Lucy and her angel-faced owner are the illustrations' central focus, while background details fade into a mist. This warm and simple picture book by the author of the Max and Ruby books conjures up a classic childhood experience, then imbues it with the cozy familiarity of a favorite pair of slippers. Ages 5-8.

Kirkus Reviews

SOURCE: A review of *Lucy Comes to Stay,* in *Kirkus Reviews,* Vol. LXVI, No. 12, June 15, 1994, p. 853.

Lucy, a tiny Scottish terrier, is adorable, but she has a lot to learn. Mary Elizabeth is with her at every step—curling up with the woebegone pup in her crate (Lucy isn't allowed in the child's bed); wearing old shoes after Lucy chews her new ones; bathing the pup after she tangles with a pen ("she was too blue to scold"). The outlines may be familiar, but this child and her dog are as winsomely persistent as Wells's beloved Max; readers won't be surprised when Lucy finally gets a turn in her small mistress's bed. Graham catches every bit of the story's charm and humor in freely rendered oils that echo Renoir in their deft modeling and use of light (though Mary Elizabeth has more spunk than Renoir's placid beauties). A natural for sharing aloud. (*Picture book. 4-8*)

Suzanne Hawley

SOURCE: A review of *Lucy Comes to Stay,* in *School Library Journal,* Vol. 40, No. 7, July, 1994, pp. 91-2.

K-Gr 2—Another winner from Wells. This lovely story about a child and her puppy is a universal one that will hold readers spellbound. On Lucy's first night at their house, Mary Elizabeth cleverly skirts the promise she made to her mother not to take her new pet into bed—she crawls into the cage with the tiny terrier instead. Lucy, pink-tongued and fluffy white, falls asleep on her mistress's pillow. In the next episode, readers see Lucy and Mary Elizabeth looking at the girl's "brand-new leather-laced moccasins" with abject misery. Lucy has made a meal of the laces and now the child has to wear old shoes to school. In the last scene, which takes place six months later, the mother relents and lets the pup spend the night in Mary Elizabeth's bed. Graham's marvelous illustrations contribute to the overall warmth of the text. Done in oil, they have the feeling of soft, chalk drawings. Lucy is definitely the dog of choice. A delightful addition to any collection.

📖 THE *EDWARD* SERIES (1995)

Hazel Rochman

SOURCE: A review of *Edward in Deep Water, Edward's Overwhelming Overnight,* and *Edward Unready for School,* in *Booklist,* Vol. 92, No. 1, September 1, 1995, p. 75.

Ages 2-5. Educational experts warn about "the hurried child"; Wells imagines what it's like to be one. Her amazing picture books, from *Timothy Goes to School* (1981) to *Shy Charles* (1988), always focus on the child as an individual, the one who doesn't fit in. In this set of three small books about Edward the Unready [*Edward in Deep Water, Edward's Overwhelming Overnight,* and *Edward Unready for School*], Edward is a small brown bear who is happy in his own backyard. In each book, he's pushed to do something he isn't yet ready for—start preschool, sleep overnight at a friend's house, attend a pool party. In each case, he doesn't want to go, he's miserable when he gets there, and he gets his way in the end and ends up at home, snug on his father's lap with no interruptions. Yet there are no formula solutions. Wells tells funny, touching stories. Each of the three books has its own adventure, with exciting action and individual characters. The panic and reassurance grow right out of the toddler experience. The framed ink drawings with bright watercolor paintings express how Edward sees things and what he feels. He's bewildered at the school uproar, suspicious of the hearty good cheer, overwhelmed by adults' gigantic size, cozy in his own world. His wide white eyes in his brown furry face show his fear; in the tilt of his square head, there's suspicion; in the stiffness of his heavy body, there's resistance; his smiling mouth and expansive arms show his bliss. Edward is a most determined child, quiet but unwavering in his uncertainty. One reason he gets his way is that adults are nice. They may push too hard, and they're a bit dense at times, but they do eventually get it. They love him.

Publishers Weekly

SOURCE: A review of *Edward in Deep Water, Edward's Overwhelming Overnight,* and *Edward Unready for School,* in *Publishers Weekly,* Vol. 242, No. 38, September 18, 1995, p. 131.

Featuring the wryly understated texts and drolly detailed ink-and-watercolor art of the Max and Ruby titles, these paper-over-board books introduce the late-blooming Edward the Unready. In each misadventure, the expressive-eyed bear faces a new, decidedly uncomfortable situation. At a swimming party, the lifeguard calls Edward's parents to pick him up after his water wings deflate and he is rescued from the pool's bottom. When a blizzard forces Edward to spend the night at his pal Anthony's house, Anthony's parents realize how miserable their sleepless guest is and dig out the car to take him home. And Edward's first week of playschool is so painful for him that his teacher sends for his parents, announcing, "Not everyone is ready for the same things at the same time." That, of course, encapsulates the message imparted by each of these tales, which inventively reassure kids that it is okay to be "unready." Ages 2-6.

Bulletin of the Center for Children's Books

SOURCE: A review of *Edward in Deep Water*, in *Bulletin of the Center for Children's Books*, Vol. 49, No. 3, November, 1995, p. 108.

What a relief it will be for caregiver and child to meet a protagonist who is *not* perfectly adjusted to new situations by the end of the book! Edward the Unready is the frequently distraught hero of this series, and he *is* perfectly accepted by his parents, who declare amiably after each fiasco, "Not everybody is ready for the same things at the same time." It's a commonsensical fact, but one which many competitive adults seem unable to grasp. The fact that Edward is a bear won't preclude total empathy among young listeners who have decided that (a) deep water and/or (b) school and/or (c) overnights (select one or buy all three) are just not their cup of tea—yet. Nor do the simple story lines (Edward stuck at Anthony's house during a snow storm, for instance) preclude witty lines (" 'I was not ready for overnights away from home,' said Anthony's father, 'until I was twenty-one years old!' "). And Wells' warmly patterned illustrations, literal as they are, have never precluded rich texture and expression. These are a step more complex than the Max and Ruby series but equally sly and, at the same time, telepathic.

Hanna B. Zeiger

SOURCE: A review of *Edward Unready for School*, in *The Horn Book Magazine*, Vol. LXXI, No. 6, November-December, 1995, pp. 739-41.

Another memorable character from the pen of Rosemary Wells—Edward the Unready—makes his anxious debut in three new books. In *Edward Unready for School*, Edward's parents try mightily to get their little bear to his first day of play school, but the reluctant Edward is totally uncooperative. On his arrival, the teacher's smiles and his happy fellow students make no impression. Edward sits immobile at the top of the slide or tries to hide in the wrong bathroom—much to the surprise of the little girls in his class. By Friday, the school experience is terminated by mutual consent, and Edward returns home to wait until he is more ready. At Georgina's birthday party at the town swimming pool, in *Edward in Deep Water*, Edward cannot be separated from his water wings despite an unkind whispered comment about sissies who need them. When Georgina and Ivy pop his water wings by giving him a bear hug, Edward topples into the pool and has to be rescued by the lifeguard. With assurance from his parents that "not everyone is ready for the same things at the same time," Edward asks for new water wings and wears them confidently—in the bathtub. In *Edward's Overwhelming Overnight*, an invitation to play in the snow at his friend Anthony's house is accompanied by repeated assurances that Edward's parents will come back for him soon. When it begins to snow so hard that his parents are unable to come pick him up, Edward is frozen with fear. He declines a chance to play with Anthony's train or to eat supper and cannot sleep—even in Anthony's new duck pajamas. Unable to bear his unhappiness, Anthony's parents venture out in the storm to take Edward home. Driving behind a snowplow, Anthony's father says reassuringly, "I was not ready for overnights away from home . . . until I was twenty-one years old!" With an economy of line, Rosemary Wells achieves a range of emotions in portraying Edward. His expressions vary from anxious apprehension when he contemplates some new experience to wide-eyed, smiling contentment when engaged in a familiar activity in his own home. The simple text is enhanced by the humor of the ink and watercolor art; together they work perfectly to capture this facet of childhood experience.

LASSIE, COME HOME (1995)

Kirkus Reviews

SOURCE: A review of *Lassie, Come Home*, in *Kirkus Reviews*, Vol. LXIII, No. 20, October 15, 1995, p. 1504.

Eric Knight's 1940 classic started out a short story; here Wells and Jeffers (*Waiting For The Evening Star*, 1993) bring it back to that length, enhanced with solemn, elegant artwork. The plot is evergreen in its appeal: When Joe's unemployed father reluctantly sells Lassie to the Duke of Rudling, she escapes three times and then again, even after she's been hauled from Yorkshire to Scotland. She endures dreadful abuse and privation as she travels nearly a thousand miles home. Wells tells the tale in a lean, episodic, quick-paced way, describing Joe's heartbreak and Lassie's physical trials in precise, effective phrases as she highlights the contrasts between rich and poor, kind and cruel. [Susan] Jeffers's paintings range in size from vignettes to a wordless full spread; her finely-detailed figures pose gracefully against sweeping landscapes or neat, well-kept interiors. A timeless tale, handsomely turned out and made available at last, in its essentials, to younger readers. *(Picture book. 7-9)*

Kathie Krieger Cerra

SOURCE: A review of *Lassie, Come Home,* in *The Five Owls,* Vol. 10, No. 2, November-December, 1995, pp. 35-6.

Lassie, Joe's beloved dog, is sold because Joe's father has lost his job as a coal miner in Yorkshire. After Lassie escapes and returns to Joe three times, the new owner's kennelman takes her hundreds of miles north, to Scotland. Still, Lassie returns home to the family that she loves. This familiar story, based on the 1938 short story and the 1940 novel by Eric Knight, is made accessible to younger readers and listeners in Rosemary Wells's engaging adaptation for a large-format picture book.

In this shorter version, the reader encounters principal characters that are still well developed: Joe, who yearns for the return of his dog and grapples with his emotions; Joe's parents, who struggle with poverty and honor; and Lassie herself, whose loyalty to Joe takes her over fences and mountains, through lakes and rivers and cities, into the clutches of unkind people, and into hearth and home of compassionate souls who help her on her way.

Wells preserves the original story's authenticity of time and place, and, in a flowing style, capitalizes on the dramatic events characteristic of animal stories for children. Both of these features are skillfully reflected in muted watercolor-and-ink illustrations by Susan Jeffers. Details such as a wooden table and crockery dishes, clothes hanging on the line outside, and a metal pot holder and a baking oven by the kitchen hearth serve to place the reader in the family's simple stone cottage in the village of Greenall Bridge. Jeffers has selected important events to illustrate, creating pictures that extend the reader's focus on what happens. For example, one page shows only Joe's father's overturned chair, an image that reflects his father's anger and conflict as he storms out, unable to explain to Joe why he has sold Lassie. Scenes of Lassie on her travels show her contemplating travel through a great Scottish loch surrounded by mountains, struggling in a churning river at the base of a waterfall, and lying exhausted in the driving

night rain as she is discovered by a kindly old couple. The effect of such illustrations is a heightening of the text's dramatic tension.

The carefully crafted story of this new version of *Lassie Come Home* and the spirited illustrations on every page will surely engage the hearts of young readers or listeners even if they don't have a dog of their own.

Ray Turton

SOURCE: A review of *Lassie, Come Home,* in *Magpies,* Vol. 11, No. 1, March, 1996, p. 33.

This classic story of love and determination is still capable of bringing a lump to the throat as it did those many years ago when first published.

Simplified and illustrated in an evocative manner (there are many scenes of enclosing iron bars and contrasting ones of wind-swept lonely landscapes) this book should engage a new generation of readers. The sympathetic retelling is true to the original story—we are told that Eric Knight's widow acted as consultant to the new edition. Less wordy (it is, after all, a 48 page picture book) it will hopefully entice readers who would not dream of tackling the original novel.

Recommended for middle primary to lower secondary.

Mary M. Burns

SOURCE: A review of *Lassie, Come Home,* in *The Horn Book Magazine,* Vol. LXXII, No. 2, March-April, 1996, p. 192.

Now a classic, Eric Knight's *Lassie Come-Home*—the saga of the loyal collie who surmounts incredible odds in a year-long trek from Scotland to Yorkshire in order to return to her original owner—first appeared as a short story in *The Saturday Evening Post* in 1938. Originally, Lassie was more than a dog story; it was also about love, about the tyranny of poverty, and about the power of money to control the lives of others. By returning to the essential elements of character and theme, Rosemary Wells has revitalized the narrative as one might revivify a folk legend. The text has the economy of a well-honed play script and is well matched with Susan Jeffers's handsome full-color illustrations. No one can capture a mountainous landscape better than Jeffers, as she demonstrated in *The Three Jovial Huntsmen* (Macmillan). Thus, a brilliantly composed double-page spread of Lassie standing at the edge of one of the great Scottish lochs suggests not only the wild beauty of the landscape but also the formidable impediments to the success of her journey. The retelling more closely approximates the original short story; in the novel, the motivations of the various characters Lassie encounters were expanded, and lengthy descriptions of scenery were added, which Jeffers's visual interpretations make unnecessary. With a full-page map of Lassie's journey.

THE LANGUAGE OF DOVES (1996)

Kirkus Reviews

SOURCE: A review of *The Language of Doves,* in *Kirkus Reviews,* Vol. LXIV, No. 15, August 1, 1996, p. 1159.

This story starts on a Brooklyn rooftop. Grandfather gives his granddaughter a dove, Isabella, for her birthday and tells her the story of another dove named Isabella. Grandfather was nine then, and both he and the dove were conscripted into the Italian army for the Great War. Returning to base with an important message from the front lines, Isabella was wounded by enemy fire, but struggled back to headquarters in time to save the lives of eight men. It is a story wrapped in the mists of time and memory, moody and seemingly ancient, one that [Greg] Shed's soft paintings make even dreamier. Back in Queens, when the young girl releases her dove from home, it flies straight back to the grandfather's roost. Fear not, he tells his granddaughter, learn the language of the doves and Isabella will return to you. When the grandfather dies, the doves are sold off, unbeknownst to the girl. Later, her dove appears at her window sill, bearing a message in her grandfather's spidery writing.

Wells's tale is one of remembrance, magic, and the power of love, and its melancholy air is lightened by nice touches. The best: In his youth, the grandfather would scour the woods for parasols and morelli, then launch his dove to send word of his finds to the cook at the orphanage. *(Picture book. 5-8)*

Bulletin of the Center for Children's Books

SOURCE: A review of *The Language of Doves,* in *Bulletin of the Center for Children's Books,* Vol. 50, No. 50, September, 1996, p. 36.

On a Brooklyn rooftop, an Italian grandfather gives his granddaughter Julietta a birthday dove, then tells her about growing up in an orphanage in Italy and being drafted into the army at age nine to care for the doves used to carry messages during World War I. When her grandfather dies, his doves are sold "to a pigeon breeder in Providence, Rhode Island." (Wells is somewhat poetically cavalier about the difference between doves and pigeons.) But the grief-stricken Julietta receives a dove-carried message from her grandfather: "Do not listen to a word they tell you. Having learned the language of doves, I have learned also to fly. Watch for me." The magical realism element of Julietta's bird returning with the message is credible enough, foreshadowed as it is by the grandfather's spiritual belief in the language of doves. The story teeters on the thin line between sentimentality and sentiment, but Shed's syrupy gouache illustrations (framed, full-page paintings for each double-paged spread), washed in golden light and soft around the edges, sometimes tip the balance. Although the framing device is cumbersome, the child's relationship with a beloved grandfather and the "when I was a boy in the war" aspect of the grandfather's tale may well make this story successful with older children.

Kate McClelland

SOURCE: A review of *The Language of Doves,* in *School Library Journal,* Vol. 42, No. 9, September, 1996, pp. 193-94.

Gr 1-5—A compelling book that is a story within a story, a small piece of history that may be unfamiliar to young readers, and an unusual intergenerational tale. When Julietta's grandfather gives her a homing pigeon for her birthday, she names it Isabella after a dove the elderly man had as a boy. The first Isabella was a heroic bird that carried messages for the Italian Army during World War I, was wounded, saved many lives, and was awarded a medal. Now Julietta is hoping this new Isabella will learn to fly home to her when released. To the child's disappointment, her dove always returns to her grandfather. When he dies, all the doves are sold and she is heart-broken, believing Isabella to be among them. In the end Isabella has learned to fly home to Julietta, and this time carries one last message from grandfather in his familiar spidery writing. The first-person narrative is well told. While the ending is truly affecting, it escapes being cloying or overly sentimental. The illustrations are impressionistic and painterly, executed in gouache on canvas. The artist has used a warm palette of gold, sepia, and brown. The beautiful little dove, described as the color of rain clouds, is well portrayed as a kind of richly glowing object of affectionate memory. This book will be especially appreciated where children are learning to identify history as personal story.

📖 *RACHEL FIELD'S "HITTY: HER FIRST HUNDRED YEARS"* (1999)

Ilene Cooper

SOURCE: A review of *Rachel Field's Hitty: Her First Hundred Years,* in *Booklist,* Vol. 96, No. 6, November 15, 1999, p. 638.

[*Rachel Field's Hitty*] is not just an illustrated version of the Newbery-winning *Hitty: Her First Hundred Years,* nor even an illustrated abridgement. Wells takes the story in a new direction. As she admits in the author's note, when Susan Jeffers asked her to shorten the story so Jeffers could illustrate it anew. Wells "didn't want to touch it." Warned off by both booksellers and librarians, Wells soon realized even they hadn't read the book in 30 years. Consequently, she decided to give it new life.

Librarians who do reread *Hitty* might be surprised at what they find. What readers remember, of course, is the story of a carved doll who gets lost and found all over the world. What they probably don't remember are some of the particulars: Hitty's shipwreck on a South Sea island where near-naked "savages" act "like a parcel of children." Back in America Hitty is found by black children who, along with their elders, speak a dialect that includes lots of "dis and dat" and whose white eyeballs and teeth gleam.

Hitty's political incorrectness is a topic for another piece, but suffice it to say, in the Wells and Jeffers version, it's gone. So much so that in the picture of the South Sea islanders, the men are wrapped in gleaming robes down to their toes.

Wells has abridged the first half of her text from *Hitty,* and though choppy in spots, it gives the flavor of the original and covers a good deal of ground in an abbreviated manner. Then Wells takes unexpected liberty. In the original, Hitty almost gets sent south during the Civil War. Wells brings her there and later to other new places. "Hitty's adventures tumbled suddenly into a much noisier and more diverse American landscape," Wells notes. She has indeed broadened the story, perhaps too much, with Hitty now meeting, among others, a girl in a wheelchair and Teddy Roosevelt's children.

Purists will object to the changes, but there is no doubt that Jeffers and Wells have produced a genuinely beautiful book. Jeffers is at the top of her game, offering pictures that are delightful in their detail and charming in their execution. The text, which was rewritten with the permission of Field's estate, is also winning, especially when Wells begins adding her own layers, where the writing seems most comfortable. The story continually propels readers deeper into the mix of Hitty's new and original adventures, and children will be caught in a story that's true to the original in spirit if not in details. Librarians need to know that this isn't their mothers' Hitty, but finally, that may not be a bad thing.

Clearly, bookstore patrons will be happy to find the oversize, attractive *Hitty* . . . waiting to be plucked from the shelves. Librarians, however, should ask a few questions about each "new" revival: What changes have been made to the text and the art? How does the book stack up against others in the series? And perhaps most important; would this book merit purchase if it didn't have a familiar title? Unlike Hitty, not all books need a second hundred years.

Wendy Lukehart

SOURCE: A review of *Rachel Field's Hitty: Her First Hundred Years,* in *School Library Journal,* Vol. 46, No. 1, January, 2000, pp. 113-14.

Gr 1-5—Purists may balk at this revision of the 1930 Newbery winner, but many modern readers will be charmed by this repackaged memoir of a century-old wooden doll. Many of Field's characters, destinations, and phrases remain intact, and Wells does an admirable job of matching her voice. Hitty's story still begins with a peddler's carved gift for a sea captain's daughter and concludes with the doll's anticipation of future adventures as she views an airplane. Much, however, has changed. Wells shortens the chapters, edits the wordiness, omits the black dialect, and changes the South Sea "Injuns" to "Islanders," with the overall effect of a quickened pace and heightened action. She departs completely from the original after the outbreak of the Civil War. Hitty is now mailed south of the Mason-Dixon line and encounters her first violence when the post office blows up. Jeffers's full-page gouache paintings and the smaller details carry much of the meaning, portraying with dramatic perspective the danger of a storm at sea or using architecture, flora, and fauna to create locale. The generous use of space between lines of text, the sheen of the creamy paper, and the oversized format lend luxury to the telling. Hitty is in good hands for the next 100 years.

Cathryn M. Mercier

SOURCE: A review of *Rachel Field's Hitty: Her First Hundred Years*, in *The Horn Book Magazine*, Vol. LXXVI, No. 1, January, 2000, p. 107.

Retelling, updating, and re-illustrating beloved stories of the past have long been practices essential to the development of children's literature. As writers and illustrators turn to folk- and fairy-tale traditions for source material, they simultaneously view the old stories with the fresh eyes of today's culture and bring into the present archetypal stories about the nature of being human. So why does it bother me that Rosemary Wells and Susan Jeffers have attempted to bring a well-loved and award-winning 1929 children's novel to a new generation of readers? For one thing, unlike its folkloric predecessors, *Hitty: Her First Hundred Years* is not in the public domain. But legalities aren't the issue here. For even though the copyright and permissions are all in order, it's still hard for me to see Field's book as anything other than the creation of an individual mind—and an idiosyncratic one at that.

The first time I read the story about the antique-shop doll who writes her memoirs, I found it captivating, odd, original. I had never been a child who played much with dolls, so I was surprised when I found myself engaged in Field's character. Reading the book thirty years later, I'm not at all surprised. Hitty includes the narrative elements to which I have always reacted: a strong voice and a character capable of self-reflection.

Field's first paragraph reveals these qualities as Hitty describes the weighty stillness of the antique shop and confesses that "we all have our little infirmities." The opening chapter accents Hitty's remarkable attention to detail, a necessary aspect of character if readers are to believe in her re-creation of her past. In contrast, Wells opens in the past tense: "The first words I ever heard were Phoebe Preble's. 'Look, Mamma! She's got a real face now!'" Although the chapter bears the title "I Begin My Memoirs," this alteration in Field's text displaces the reader's knowledge of Hitty's self-awareness. Hitty no longer reflects on her past from the present. Instead, she merely observes the past. The past—in tense and in subject—dominates this version and leaves the reader unprepared for Hitty's return to the present on the last page.

Some alterations, such as changing a horsehair sofa to a cracked leather sofa, are modest and serve more to update Field's language. Similarly, leaving out language that today's sensitive audience would find objectionable allows Susan Jeffers's illustrations not only to portray the shifting historical backgrounds across which Hitty traverses but also to depict what cannot now be said. For example, Wells can delete Field's word *Injuns* because Jeffers portrays clearly as American Indian those from whom Hitty and her first owner learn about lush berry patches. Although the Wells-Jeffers collaboration is an illustrated book rather than a picture book, the art both decorates and extends the text. The studied illustrations of costumes—from Phoebe's friends' party dresses to Millie Nettletree's prize-winning gown for Hitty to wear at the New York doll exhibition—bear the kind of detail Hitty herself would demand.

What bothers me about this adaptation is that Hitty loses dimensionality as a character to become merely the mechanism that transports readers through history. Wells abbreviates Field's description of farming for whale oil, adds an encounter with Abraham Lincoln and a visit to Teddy Roosevelt's White House, and imagines Hitty as inspiration to artist John Singleton Copley. As U.S. history this rendering is incomplete; as fiction, it reduces the complexity of a multilayered story with a unique narrative voice to a series of plot elements. These events do not serve to deepen one's understanding of or interaction with Hitty, who is now less actor than object acted upon. Her marvelous moments of introspective self-knowledge are gone. For example, when the embarrassed Thankful stuffs Hitty into a sofa at a birthday party, Wells prunes an entire, lengthy paragraph articulating Hitty's "daze of despair" (Field) into a scant three words: Hitty now merely feels "cramped and rejected" (Wells). As Wells trims Field's prose and adds plot and character to make the story more active, she diminishes the title character. Hitty loses her distinctive voice and her place as the story's primary subject. Better that readers return to the pleasures of Field's original Hitty.

MORRIS'S DISAPPEARING BAG (revised; 1999)

Shelley Townsend-Hudson

SOURCE: A review of *Morris's Disappearing Bag*, in *Booklist*, Vol. 96, Nos. 9 & 10, January 1 & 15, 2000, p. 938.

Ages 3-6. The classic 1975 story of the preschool rabbit who unwraps a present containing a Disappearing Bag has been reissued in a larger format and with new illustrations. Wells' bright watercolor-and-acrylic artwork adds zest and warmth to the story of the youngest rabbit, who is disappointed with the less-than-exciting stuffed bear he gets for Christmas—but delighted with an overlooked package he finds under the tree. Wells' wonderful story and artwork will captivate parents as well as children: the humorous spoof of Botticelli's *Birth of Venus* hanging on the wall is delightful, as are the characters' charming expressions and poses. A fine reissue.

Additional coverage of Wells's life and career is contained in the following sources published by the Gale Group: *Authors and Artists for Young Adults,* **Vol. 13;** *Contemporary Authors,* **Vols. 85-88;** *Contemporary Authors New Revision Series,* **Vol. 48;** *Contemporary Literary Criticism,* **Vol. 12;** *Major Authors and Illustrators for Children and Young Adults; Something About the Author Autobiography Series,* **Vol. 1;** *Something About the Author,* **Vols. 18, 69, 114.**

How to Use This Index

The main reference

> **Baum, L(yman) Frank**
> 1856-1919 .... **15**

lists all author entries in this and previous volumes of *Children's Literature Review*.

The cross-references

> See also CA 103; 108; DLB 22; JRDA;
> MAICYA; MTCW; SATA 18; TCLC 7

list all author entries in the following Gale biographical and literary sources:

AAYA = *Authors & Artists for Young Adults*
AITN = *Authors in the News*
BLC = *Black Literature Criticism*
BLCS = *Black Literature Criticism Supplement*
BW = *Black Writers*
CA = *Contemporary Authors*
CAAS = *Contemporary Authors Autobiography Series*
CABS = *Contemporary Authors Bibliographical Series*
CANR = *Contemporary Authors New Revision Series*
CAP = *Contemporary Authors Permanent Series*
CDALB = *Concise Dictionary of American Literary Biography*
CDBLB = *Concise Dictionary of British Literary Biography*
CLC = *Contemporary Literary Criticism*
CMLC = *Classical and Medieval Literature Criticism*
DA = *DISCovering Authors*
DAB = *DISCovering Authors: British*
DAC = *DISCovering Authors: Canadian*
DAM = *DISCovering Authors: Modules*
      DRAM: *Dramatists Module;* **MST:** *Most-Studied Authors Module;*
      MULT: *Multicultural Authors Module;* **NOV:** *Novelists Module;*
      POET: *Poets Module;* **POP:** *Popular Fiction and Genre Authors Module*
DC = *Drama Criticism*
DLB = *Dictionary of Literary Biography*
DLBD = *Dictionary of Literary Biography Documentary Series*
DLBY = *Dictionary of Literary Biography Yearbook*
HLC = *Hispanic Literature Criticism*
HLCS = *Hispanic Literature Criticism Supplement*
HW = *Hispanic Writers*
JRDA = *Junior DISCovering Authors*
LC = *Literature Criticism from 1400 to 1800*
MAICYA = *Major Authors and Illustrators for Children and Young Adults*
MTCW = *Major 20th-Century Writers*
NCLC = *Nineteenth-Century Literature Criticism*
NNAL = *Native North American Literature*
PC = *Poetry Criticism*
SAAS = *Something about the Author Autobiography Series*
SATA = *Something about the Author*
SSC = *Short Story Criticism*
TCLC = *Twentieth-Century Literary Criticism*
WLC = *World Literature Criticism, 1500 to the Present*
WLCS = *World Literature Criticism Supplement*
YABC = *Yesterday's Authors of Books for Children*

CLR Cumulative Author Index

Foreman, Michael 1938- **32**
See also CA 21-24R; CANR 10, 38, 68;
MAICYA; SAAS 21; SATA 2, 73

Foster, Genevieve Stump 1893-1979 .... **7**
See also CA 5-8R; 89-92; CANR 4; DLB
61; MAICYA; SATA 2; SATA-Obit 23

Fox, J. N.
See Janeczko, Paul B(ryan)

Fox, J. N.
See Janeczko, Paul B(ryan)

Fox, Mem 23
See also Fox, Merrion Frances
See also MAICYA; SATA 103

Fox, Merrion Frances 1946-
See Fox, Mem
See also CA 127; CANR 84; SATA 51

Fox, Paula 1923- **1, 44**
See also AAYA 3; CA 73-76; CANR 20,
36, 62; CLC 2, 8, 121; DLB 52; JRDA;
MAICYA; MTCW 1; SATA 17, 60, 120

Freedman, Russell (Bruce) 1929- **20**
See also AAYA 4, 24; CA 17-20R; CANR
7, 23, 46, 81; JRDA; MAICYA; SATA 16,
71

Freeman, Don 1908-1978 .... **30**
See also CA 77-80; CANR 44; MAICYA;
SATA 17

French, Fiona 1944- **37**
See also CA 29-32R; CANR 40; MAICYA;
SAAS 21; SATA 6, 75

French, Paul
See Asimov, Isaac

Fritz, Jean (Guttery) 1915- **2, 14**
See also CA 1-4R; CANR 5, 16, 37; DLB
52; INT CANR-16; JRDA; MAICYA;
SAAS 2; SATA 1, 29, 72, 119

Frost, Robert (Lee) 1874-1963 .... **67**
See also AAYA 21; CA 89-92; CANR 33;
CDALB 1917-1929; CLC 1, 3, 4, 9, 10,
13, 15, 26, 34, 44; DA; DAB; DAC; DAM
MST, POET; DA3; DLB 54; DLBD 7;
MTCW 1, 2; PC 1; SATA 14; WLC

Fujikawa, Gyo 1908-1998 .... **25**
See also CA 113; 172; CANR 46; MAI-
CYA; SAAS 16; SATA 39, 76; SATA-
Brief 30; SATA-Obit 110

Fuller, Maud
See Petersham, Maud (Sylvia Fuller)

Gaberman, Judie Angell 1937- **33**
See also AAYA 11; CA 77-80; CANR 49;
JRDA; SATA 22, 78

Gag, Wanda (Hazel) 1893-1946 .... **4**
See also CA 113; 137; DLB 22; MAICYA;
SATA 100; YABC 1

Gaines, Ernest J(ames) 1933- **62**
See also AAYA 18; AITN 1; BLC 2; BW 2,
3; CA 9-12R; CANR 6, 24, 42, 75;
CDALB 1968-1988; CLC 3, 11, 18, 86;
DAM MULT; DA3; DLB 2, 33, 152;
DLBY 80; MTCW 1, 2; SATA 86

Gal, Laszlo 1933- **61**
See also CA 161; SATA 52, 96; SATA-Brief
32

Galdone, Paul 1907(?)-1986 .... **16**
See also CA 73-76; 121; CANR 13, 76;
MAICYA; SATA 17, 66; SATA-Obit 49

Gallant, Roy A(rthur) 1924- **30**
See also CA 5-8R; CANR 4, 29, 54; CLC
17; MAICYA; SATA 4, 68, 110

Gantos, Jack 18
See also Gantos, John (Bryan), Jr.

Gantos, John (Bryan), Jr. 1951-
See Gantos, Jack
See also CA 65-68; CANR 15, 56; SATA
20, 81, 119

Gard, Janice
See Latham, Jean Lee

Gardam, Jane 1928- **12**
See also CA 49-52; CANR 2, 18, 33, 54;
CLC 43; DLB 14, 161, 231; MAICYA;
MTCW 1; SAAS 9; SATA 39, 76; SATA-
Brief 28

Garden, Nancy 1938- **51**
See also AAYA 18; CA 33-36R; CANR 13,
30, 84; JRDA; SAAS 8; SATA 12, 77, 114

Garfield, Leon 1921-1996 .... **21**
See also AAYA 8; CA 17-20R; 152; CANR
38, 41, 78; CLC 12; DLB 161; JRDA;
MAICYA; SATA 1, 32, 76; SATA-Obit 90

Garner, Alan 1934- **20**
See also AAYA 18; CA 73-76; 178; CAAE
178; CANR 15, 64; CLC 17; DAB; DAM
POP; DLB 161; MAICYA; MTCW 1, 2;
SATA 18, 69; SATA-Essay 108

Garnet, A. H.
See Slote, Alfred

Gauch, Patricia Lee 1934- **56**
See also CA 57-60; CANR 9; SAAS 21;
SATA 26, 80

Gay, Marie-Louise 1952- **27**
See also CA 135; SAAS 21; SATA 68

Gaze, Gillian
See Barklem, Jill

Gee, Maurice (Gough) 1931- **56**
See also CA 97-100; CANR 67; CLC 29;
SATA 46, 101

Geisel, Theodor Seuss 1904-1991 .... **53**
See also Dr. Seuss
See also CA 13-16R; 135; CANR 13, 32;
DA3; DLB 61; DLBY 91; MAICYA;
MTCW 1, 2; SATA 1, 28, 75, 100; SATA-
Obit 67

George, Jean Craighead 1919- **1**
See also AAYA 8; CA 5-8R; CANR 25;
CLC 35; DLB 52; JRDA; MAICYA;
SATA 2, 68

Gerrard, Roy 1935-1997 .... **23**
See also CA 110; 160; CANR 57; SATA 47,
90; SATA-Brief 45; SATA-Obit 99

Gewe, Raddory
See Gorey, Edward (St. John)

Gibbons, Gail 1944- **8**
See also CA 69-72; CANR 12; MAICYA;
SAAS 12; SATA 23, 72, 104

Giblin, James Cross 1933- **29**
See also CA 106; CANR 24; MAICYA;
SAAS 12; SATA 33, 75

Ginsburg, Mirra 45
See also CA 17-20R; CANR 11, 28, 54;
SATA 6, 92

Giovanni, Nikki 1943- **6**
See also AAYA 22; AITN 1; BLC 2; BW 2,
3; CA 29-32R; CAAS 6; CANR 18, 41,
60, 91; CDALBS; CLC 2, 4, 19, 64, 117;
DA; DAB; DAC; DAM MST, MULT,
POET; DA3; DLB 5, 41; INT CANR-18;
MAICYA; MTCW 1, 2; PC 19; SATA 24,
107; WLCS

Glenn, Mel 1943- **51**
See also AAYA 25; CA 123; CANR 49, 68;
SATA 51, 93; SATA-Brief 45

Glubok, Shirley (Astor) 1
See also CA 5-8R; CANR 4, 43; MAICYA;
SAAS 7; SATA 6, 68

Goble, Paul 1933- **21**
See also CA 93-96; CANR 16; MAICYA;
SATA 25, 69

Godden, (Margaret) Rumer 1907-1998 ... **20**
See also AAYA 6; CA 5-8R; 172; CANR 4,
27, 36, 55, 80; CLC 53; DLB 161; MAI-
CYA; SAAS 12; SATA 3, 36; SATA-Obit
109

Godfrey, Martyn 1949-
See Godfrey, Martyn N.

Godfrey, Martyn N. 1949- **57**
See also Godfrey, Martyn
See also CA 126; CANR 68; SATA 95

Goffstein, (Marilyn) Brooke 1940- **3**
See also CA 21-24R; CANR 9, 28; DLB
61; MAICYA; SATA 8, 70

Gomi, Taro 1945- **57**
See also CA 162; SATA 64, 103

Goodall, John Strickland 1908-1996 .... **25**
See also CA 33-36R; 152; MAICYA; SATA
4, 66; SATA-Obit 91

Gordon, Sheila 1927- **27**
See also CA 132; SATA 88

Gorey, Edward (St. John) 1925-2000 .... **36**
See also CA 5-8R; 187; CANR 9, 30, 78;
DLB 61; INT CANR-30; MAICYA; SATA
29, 70; SATA-Brief 27; SATA-Obit 118

Goscinny, Rene 1926-1977 .... **37**
See also CA 117; 113; SATA 47; SATA-
Brief 39

Graham, Bob 1942- **31**
See also CA 165; SATA 63, 101

Graham, Lorenz (Bell) 1902-1989 .... **10**
See also BW 1; CA 9-12R; 129; CANR 25;
DLB 76; MAICYA; SAAS 5; SATA 2, 74;
SATA-Obit 63

Grahame, Kenneth 1859-1932 .... **5**
See also CA 108; 136; CANR 80; DAB;
DA3; DLB 34, 141, 178; MAICYA;
MTCW 2; SATA 100; TCLC 64; YABC 1

Gramatky, Hardie 1907-1979 .... **22**
See also AITN 1; CA 1-4R; 85-88; CANR
3; DLB 22; MAICYA; SATA 1, 30; SATA-
Obit 23

Greenaway, Kate 1846-1901 .... **6**
See also CA 137; DLB 141; MAICYA;
SATA 100; YABC 2

Greene, Bette 1934- **2**
See also AAYA 7; CA 53-56; CANR 4; CLC
30; JRDA; MAICYA; SAAS 16; SATA 8,
102

Greene, Constance C(larke) 1924- **62**
See also AAYA 7; CA 61-64; CANR 8, 38;
JRDA; MAICYA; SAAS 11; SATA 11, 72

Greenfield, Eloise 1929- **4, 38**
See also BW 2; CA 49-52; CANR 1, 19,
43; INT CANR-19; JRDA; MAICYA;
SAAS 16; SATA 19, 61, 105

Greer, Richard
See Silverberg, Robert

Gregory, Jean
See Ure, Jean

Grewdead, Roy
See Gorey, Edward (St. John)

Grey Owl 32
See also Belaney, Archibald Stansfeld
See also DLB 92

Grifalconi, Ann 1929- **35**
See also CA 5-8R; CANR 9, 35; MAICYA;
SAAS 16; SATA 2, 66

Grimes, Nikki 1950- **42**
See also CA 77-80; CANR 60; SATA 93

Gripe, Maria (Kristina) 1923- **5**
See also CA 29-32R; CANR 17, 39; MAI-
CYA; SATA 2, 74

Grode, Redway
See Gorey, Edward (St. John)

Gruelle, John (Barton) 1880-1938
See Gruelle, Johnny
See also CA 115; 175; SATA 35; SATA-
Brief 32

Gruelle, Johnny 34
See also Gruelle, John (Barton)
See also DLB 22

Guillot, Rene 1900-1969 .... **22**
See also CA 49-52; CANR 39; SATA 7**

CLR Cumulative Nationality Index

Thomas, Ianthe **8**
Thomas, Joyce Carol **19**
Thompson, Julian F(rancis) **24**
Thompson, Kay **22**
Tobias, Tobi **4**
Tresselt, Alvin **30**
Tudor, Tasha **13**
Tunis, Edwin (Burdett) **2**
Twain, Mark **58, 60, 66**
Uchida, Yoshiko **6, 56**
Van Allsburg, Chris **5, 13**
Viorst, Judith **3**
Voigt, Cynthia **13, 48**
Waber, Bernard **55**
Walter, Mildred Pitts **15, 61**
Watson, Clyde **3**
Weiss, Harvey **4**
Wells, Rosemary **16, 69**
Wersba, Barbara **3**
White, E(lwyn) B(rooks) **1, 21**
White, Robb **3**
Whitney, Phyllis A(yame) **59**
Wibberley, Leonard (Patrick O'Connor) **3**
Wiesner, David **43**
Wiggin (Riggs), Kate Douglas (Smith) **52**
Wilder, Laura (Elizabeth) Ingalls **2**
Wilkinson, Brenda **20**
Willard, Nancy **5**
Williams, Barbara **48**
Williams, Garth (Montgomery) **57**
Williams, Jay **8**
Williams, Vera B. **9**
Williams-Garcia, Rita **36**
Willis, Connie **66**
Wisniewski, David **51**
Wojciechowska, Maia (Teresa) **1**
Wolff, Virginia Euwer **62**
Wood, Audrey **26**
Wood, Don **26**
Woodson, Jacqueline **49**
Worth, Valerie **21**
Yarbrough, Camille **29**
Yashima, Taro **4**
Yep, Laurence Michael **3, 17, 54**
Yolen, Jane (Hyatt) **4, 44**
Yorinks, Arthur **20**
Young, Ed (Tse-chun) **27**
Zelinsky, Paul O. **55**
Zim, Herbert S(pencer) **2**
Zindel, Paul **3, 45**
Zolotow, Charlotte S(hapiro) **2**

ANTIGUAN

Kincaid, Jamaica **63**

AUSTRALIAN

Baillie, Allan (Stuart) **49**
Baker, Jeannie **28**
Base, Graeme (Rowland) **22**
Brinsmead, H(esba) F(ay) **47**
Chapman, Jean **65**
Chauncy, Nan(cen Beryl Masterman) **6**
Clark, Mavis Thorpe **30**
Clarke, Judith **61**
Crew, Gary **42**
Fox, Mem **23**
Graham, Bob **31**
Hilton, Nette **25**
Jennings, Paul **40**
Kelleher, Victor (Michael Kitchener) **36**
Klein, Robin **21**
Lindsay, Norman Alfred William **8**
Marsden, John **34**
Mattingley, Christobel (Rosemary) **24**
Nix, Garth **68**
Ormerod, Jan(ette Louise) **20**
Ottley, Reginald Leslie **16**
Phipson, Joan **5**
Rodda, Emily **32**
Roughsey, Dick **41**
Rubinstein, Gillian (Margaret) **35**

Southall, Ivan (Francis) **2**
Spence, Eleanor (Rachel) **26**
Thiele, Colin (Milton) **27**
Travers, P(amela) L(yndon) **2**
Trezise, Percy (James) **41**
Wrightson, (Alice) Patricia **4, 14**

AUSTRIAN

Bemelmans, Ludwig **6**
Noestlinger, Christine **12**
Orgel, Doris **48**
Zwerger, Lisbeth **46**

BELGIAN

Herge **6**
Vincent, Gabrielle (a pseudonym) **13**

CANADIAN

Bedard, Michael **35**
Blades, Ann (Sager) **15**
Bogart, Jo Ellen **59**
Buffie, Margaret **39**
Burnford, Sheila (Philip Cochrane Every) **2**
Cameron, Eleanor (Frances) **1**
Cleaver, Elizabeth (Mrazik) **13**
Cox, Palmer **24**
Doyle, Brian **22**
Ellis, Sarah **42**
Gal, Laszlo **61**
Gay, Marie-Louise **27**
Godfrey, Martyn N. **57**
Grey Owl **32**
Haig-Brown, Roderick (Langmere) **31**
Harris, Christie (Lucy) Irwin **47**
Houston, James A(rchibald) **3**
Hudson, Jan **40**
Hughes, Monica (Ince) **9, 60**
Johnston, Julie **41**
Katz, Welwyn Winton **45**
Khalsa, Dayal Kaur **30**
Korman, Gordon (Richard) **25**
Kovalski, Maryann **34**
Kurelek, William **2**
Kushner, Donn (J.) **55**
Lee, Dennis (Beynon) **3**
Little, (Flora) Jean **4**
Lunn, Janet (Louise Swoboda) **18**
Mackay, Claire **43**
Major, Kevin (Gerald) **11**
Markoosie **23**
Matas, Carol **52**
Milne, Lorus J. **22**
Montgomery, L(ucy) M(aud) **8**
Mowat, Farley (McGill) **20**
Munsch, Robert N(orman) **19**
Oberman, Sheldon **54**
Pearson, Kit **26**
Poulin, Stephane **28**
Reid, Barbara **64**
Richler, Mordecai **17**
Roberts, Charles G(eorge) D(ouglas) **33**
Seton, Ernest (Evan) Thompson **59**
Smucker, Barbara (Claassen) **10**
Stren, Patti **5**
Taylor, Cora (Lorraine) **63**
Wallace, Ian **37**
Wynne-Jones, Tim(othy) **21, 58**
Yee, Paul (R.) **44**

CHILEAN

Krahn, Fernando **3**

CHINESE

Namioka, Lensey **48**
Young, Ed (Tse-chun) **27**

CUBAN

Ada, Alma Flor **62**

CZECH

Sasek, Miroslav **4**
Sis, Peter **45**

DANISH

Andersen, Hans Christian **6**
Bodker, Cecil **23**
Drescher, Henrik **20**
Haugaard, Erik Christian **11**
Minarik, Else Holmelund **33**
Nielsen, Kay (Rasmus) **16**

DUTCH

Biegel, Paul **27**
Bruna, Dick **7**
DeJong, Meindert **1**
Haar, Jaap ter **15**
Lionni, Leo(nard) **7**
Reiss, Johanna (de Leeuw) **19**
Schmidt, Annie M. G. **22**
Spier, Peter (Edward) **5**

ENGLISH

Adams, Richard (George) **20**
Ahlberg, Allan **18**
Ahlberg, Janet **18**
Aiken, Joan (Delano) **1, 19**
Alcock, Vivien **26**
Allan, Mabel Esther **43**
Ardizzone, Edward (Jeffrey Irving) **3**
Arundel, Honor (Morfydd) **35**
Ashley, Bernard **4**
Awdry, Wilbert Vere **23**
Baker, Jeannie **28**
Banner, Angela **24**
Barklem, Jill **31**
Base, Graeme (Rowland) **22**
Bawden, Nina (Mary Mabey) **2, 51**
Bianco, Margery (Williams) **19**
Biro, Val **28**
Blake, Quentin (Saxby) **31**
Blake, William **52**
Blyton, Enid (Mary) **31**
Bond, (Thomas) Michael **1**
Boston, L(ucy) M(aria Wood) **3**
Breinburg, Petronella **31**
Briggs, Raymond Redvers **10**
Brooke, L(eonard) Leslie **20**
Browne, Anthony (Edward Tudor) **19**
Burnett, Frances (Eliza) Hodgson **24**
Burningham, John (Mackintosh) **9**
Burton, Hester (Wood-Hill) **1**
Caldecott, Randolph (J.) **14**
Carroll, Lewis **2, 18**
Causley, Charles (Stanley) **30**
Chauncy, Nan(cen Beryl Masterman) **6**
Christopher, John **2**
Clarke, Pauline **28**
Cooper, Susan (Mary) **4, 67**
Corbett, W(illiam) J(esse) **19**
Crane, Walter **56**
Cresswell, Helen **18**
Cross, Gillian (Clare) **28**
Crossley-Holland, Kevin (John William) **47**
Cruikshank, George **63**
Dahl, Roald **1, 7, 41**
de la Mare, Walter (John) **23**
Dhondy, Farrukh **41**
Dickinson, Peter (Malcolm) **29**
Dodgson, Charles Lutwidge **2**
Doherty, Berlie **21**
Farjeon, Eleanor **34**
Farmer, Penelope (Jane) **8**
Fine, Anne **25**
Foreman, Michael **32**
French, Fiona **37**
Gardam, Jane **12**
Garfield, Leon **21**
Garner, Alan **20**

Gerrard, Roy **23**
Goble, Paul **21**
Godden, (Margaret) Rumer **20**
Godfrey, Martyn N. **57**
Goodall, John Strickland **25**
Grahame, Kenneth **5**
Greenaway, Kate **6**
Grey Owl **32**
Haig-Brown, Roderick (Langmere) **31**
Hamley, Dennis **47**
Handford, Martin (John) **22**
Harris, Rosemary (Jeanne) **30**
Hill, Eric **13**
Howker, Janni **14**
Hughes, Monica (Ince) **9, 60**
Hughes, Shirley **15**
Hughes, Ted **3**
Hutchins, Pat **20**
Jacques, Brian **21**
Jones, Diana Wynne **23**
Keeping, Charles (William James) **34**
Kelleher, Victor (Michael Kitchener) **36**
Kemp, Gene **29**
King-Smith, Dick **40**
Kipling, (Joseph) Rudyard **39, 65**
Laird, Elizabeth (Mary Risk) **65**
Lear, Edward **1**
Lewis, C(live) S(taples) **3, 27**
Lively, Penelope (Margaret) **7**
Lofting, Hugh (John) **19**
Macaulay, David (Alexander) **3, 14**
Mark, Jan(et Marjorie) **11**
Mayne, William (James Carter) **25**
McBratney, Sam **44**
McCaughrean, Geraldine **38**
McKee, David (John) **38**
McNaughton, Colin **54**
Milne, A(lan) A(lexander) **1, 26**
Mole, John **61**
Morpurgo, Michael **51**
Murphy, Jill (Frances) **39**
Naidoo, Beverley **29**
Needle, Jan **43**
Nesbit, E(dith) **3**
Nimmo, Jenny **44**
Norton, Mary **6**
Oakley, Graham **7**
Orwell, George **68**
Ottley, Reginald Leslie **16**
Owen, Gareth **31**
Oxenbury, Helen **22**
Paton Walsh, Gillian **2, 65**
Pearce, Philippa **9**
Peyton, K. M. **3**
Pienkowski, Jan (Michal) **6**
Potter, (Helen) Beatrix **1, 19**
Pratchett, Terry **64**
Pullman, Philip (Nicholas) **20; 62**
Rackham, Arthur **57**
Ransome, Arthur (Michell) **8**
Rayner, Mary **41**
Reid Banks, Lynne **24**
Rosen, Michael (Wayne) **45**
Rowling, J(oanne) K. **66**
Serraillier, Ian (Lucien) **2**
Sewell, Anna **17**
Sharp, Margery **27**
Shepard, Ernest Howard **27**
Simmonds, Posy **23**
Streatfeild, (Mary) Noel **17**
Sutcliff, Rosemary **1, 37**
Swift, Jonathan **53**
Tenniel, John **18**
Tolkien, J(ohn) R(onald) R(euel) **56**
Tomlinson, Theresa **60**
Townsend, John Rowe **2**
Travers, P(amela) L(yndon) **2**
Trease, (Robert) Geoffrey **42**
Treece, Henry **2**
Ure, Jean **34**
Walsh, Jill Paton **2, 65**
Wells, H(erbert) G(eorge) **64**

Westall, Robert (Atkinson) **13**
Wildsmith, Brian **2, 52**
Willard, Barbara (Mary) **2**
Williams, Kit **4**
Yeoman, John **46**

FILIPINO

Aruego, Jose (Espiritu) **5**

FINNISH

Jansson, Tove Marika **2**
Unnerstad, Edith (Totterman) **36**

FRENCH

Ayme, Marcel (Andre) **25**
Berna, Paul **19**
Billout, Guy (Rene) **33**
Boutet de Monvel, (Louis) M(aurice) **32**
Brunhoff, Jean de **4**
Brunhoff, Laurent de **4**
Goscinny, Rene **37**
Guillot, Rene **22**
Saint-Exupery, Antoine (Jean Baptiste Marie
  Roger) de **10**
Uderzo, Albert **37**
Ungerer, Tomi **3**

GERMAN

Baumann, Hans **35**
Benary-Isbert, Margot **12**
d'Aulaire, Edgar Parin **21**
Ende, Michael (Andreas Helmuth) **14**
Haenel, Wolfram **64**
Hartling, Peter **29**
Heine, Helme **18**
Janosch **26**
Kaestner, Erich **4**
Kruss, James **9**
Levitin, Sonia (Wolff) **53**
Rey, H(ans) A(ugusto) **5**
Rey, Margret (Elisabeth) **5**
Richter, Hans Peter **21**
Wilhelm, Hans **46**
Zimnik, Reiner **3**

GREEK

Aesop **14**
Zei, Alki **6**

HUNGARIAN

Biro, Val **28**
Gal, Laszlo **61**
Galdone, Paul **16**
Seredy, Kate **10**

INDIAN

Dhondy, Farrukh **41**
Mukerji, Dhan Gopal **10**

IRISH

Bunting, Eve **28, 56**
Colum, Padraic **36**
Dillon, Eilis **26**
O'Shea, (Catherine) Pat(ricia Shiels) **18**
Swift, Jonathan **53**

ISRAELI

Ofek, Uriel **28**
Orlev, Uri **30**
Shulevitz, Uri **5, 61**

ITALIAN

Collodi, Carlo **5**
Innocenti, Roberto **56**
Munari, Bruno **9**
Rodari, Gianni **24**
Ventura, Piero (Luigi) **16**

JAMAICAN

Berry, James **22**

JAPANESE

Anno, Mitsumasa **2, 14**
Gomi, Taro **57**
Ichikawa, Satomi **62**
Iwasaki (Matsumoto), Chihiro **18**
Kitamura, Satoshi **60**
Kuratomi, Chizuko **32**
Maruki, Toshi **19**
Mori, Kyoko **64**
Nakatani, Chiyoko **30**
Say, Allen **22**
Tejima **20**
Watanabe, Shigeo **8**
Whitney, Phyllis A(yame) **59**
Yashima, Taro **4**

KOREAN

Choi, Sook Nyul **53**

MYANMARI

Rayner, Mary **41**

NEW ZEALANDER

Allen, Pamela **44**
Cowley, (Cassia) Joy **55**
de Roo, Anne Louise **63**
Dodd, Lynley (Stuart) **62**
Duder, Tessa **43**
Gee, Maurice (Gough) **56**
Laird, Elizabeth (Mary Risk) **65**
Macdonald, Caroline **60**
Mahy, Margaret **7**
Park, (Rosina) Ruth (Lucia) **51**
Taylor, William **63**

NIGERIAN

Achebe, (Albert) Chinua(lumogu) **20**

NORTHERN IRISH

Waddell, Martin **31**

NORWEGIAN

d'Aulaire, Ingri (Mortenson Parin) **21**
Proeysen, Alf **24**

POLISH

Domanska, Janina **40**
Hautzig, Esther Rudomin **22**
Janosch **26**
Orlev, Uri **30**
Pienkowski, Jan (Michal) **6**
Shulevitz, Uri **5, 61**
Singer, Isaac Bashevis **1**
Suhl, Yuri (Menachem) **2**
Wojciechowska, Maia (Teresa) **1**

RUSSIAN

Asimov, Isaac **12**
Ginsburg, Mirra **45**
Korinetz, Yuri (Iosifovich) **4**

SCOTTISH

Baillie, Allan (Stuart) **49**
Bannerman, Helen (Brodie Cowan
  Watson) **21**
Barrie, J(ames) M(atthew) **16**
Burnford, Sheila (Philip Cochrane Every) **2**
Hunter, Mollie **25**
MacDonald, George **67**
Stevenson, Robert Louis (Balfour) **10, 11**

SOUTH AFRICAN

Daly, Nicholas **41**
Gordon, Sheila **27**

Nationality Index

CLR Cumulative Title Index

Title Index

Title Index

Boy Blue (McBratney) **44**:118
A Boy Called Slow: The True Story of Sitting Bull (Bruchac) **46**:19
The Boy from Cumeroogunga: The Story of Sir Douglas Nicholls, Aboriginal Leader (Clark) **30**:62
A Boy Had a Mother Who Bought Him a Hat (Kuskin) **4**:141
A Boy in Eirinn (Colum) **36**:22
The Boy in the Drawer (Munsch) **19**:143
A Boy of Taché (Blades) **15**:54
The Boy on the Lake (Clarke) **61**:48
The Boy Pharaoh: Tutankhamen (Streatfeild) **17**:198
Boy Scouts of America: A Handbook (Seton) **59**:81
Boy: Tales of Childhood (Dahl) **41**:33
A Boy Wants a Dinosaur (Kitamura) **60**:97
The Boy Who Could Find Anything (Nixon) **24**:137
The Boy Who Didn't Believe in Spring (Clifton) **5**:54
The Boy Who Had No Heart (Petersham and Petersham) **24**:178
The Boy Who Lived with the Bears (Bruchac) **46**:21
The Boy Who Lost His Face (Sacher) **28**:204
The Boy Who Owned the School: A Comedy of Love (Paulsen) **54**:97
The Boy Who Reversed Himself (Sleator) **29**:205
The Boy Who Sailed with Columbus (Foreman) **32**:107
The Boy Who Spoke Chimp (Yolen) **4**:268
The Boy Who Swallowed Snakes (Yep) **54**:195
The Boy Who Was Followed Home (Mahy) **7**:183
The Boy Who Wasn't There (Wilhelm) **46**:170
The Boy with the Helium Head (Naylor) **17**:57
Boy without a Name (Lively) **7**:159
The Boyfriend (Stine) **37**:115
The Boyhood of Grace Jones (Langton) **33**:113
Boys and Girls, Girls and Boys (Merriam) **14**:198
Boys at Work (Soto) **38**:207
The Boys' War: Confederate and Union Soldiers Talk about the Civil War (Murphy) **53**:108
A Boy's Will (Frost) **67**:30, 44-47, 52, 63-67, 70, 76
A Boy's Will (Haugaard) **11**:110
The Bracelet (Uchida) **56**:194
Brady (Fritz) **2**:79
Brain Wave (Anderson) **58**:9
Brainbox Sorts It Out (Noestlinger) **12**:188
The Brains of Animals and Man (Freedman) **20**:76
Brainstorm (Myers) **4**:157
Brainwashing and Other Forms of Mind Control (Hyde) **23**:162
"*Brambly Hedge Books*" (Barklem) **31**:2
The Brambly Hedge Treasury (Barklem) **31**:6
A Brand-New Uncle (Seredy) **10**:181
Brats (Kennedy) **27**:101
Brave Buffalo Fighter (Waditaka Tatanka Kisisohitika) (Fitzgerald) **1**:69
The Brave Cowboy (Anglund) **1**:19
Brave Eagle's Account of the Fetterman Fight, 21 December 1866 (Goble) **21**:129
Brave Irene (Steig) **15**:201
The Brave Little Goat of Monsieur Séguin: A Picture Story from Provence (Nakatani) **30**:156
The Brave Little Toaster: A Bedtime Story for Small Appliances (Disch) **18**:114
The Brave Little Toaster Goes to Mars (Disch) **18**:116
The Bravest Thing (Napoli) **51**:160
Bravo, Ernest and Celestine! (Vincent) **13**:216
Bravo, Tanya (Gauch) **56**:94
Bravo, Tanya (Ichikawa) **62**:139-40
Bread and Honey (Southall) **2**:149
Bread and Jam for Frances (Hoban) **3**:76

Bread—and Roses: The Struggle of American Labor, 1865-1915 (Meltzer) **13**:124
The Breadhorse (Garner) **20**:112
Breadsticks and Blessing Places (Boyd) **50**:3
The Breadwitch (Nimmo) **44**:151
Break Dancing (Haskins) **39**:51
Break for the Basket (Christopher) **33**:38
Break in the Sun (Ashley) **4**:17
Break of Dark (Westall) **13**:257
A Break with Charity: A Story about the Salem Witch Trials (Rinaldi) **46**:84
Breakaway (Yee) **44**:165
Breakfast Time, Ernest and Celestine (Vincent) **13**:219
Breaking Up (Klein) **19**:92
Breakthrough: Women in Archaeology (Williams) **48**:199
Breakthrough: Women in Politics (Williams) **48**:198
Breakthroughs in Science (Asimov) **12**:34
"*Breathing Tokens*" (Sandburg) **67**:165
Breathing Tokens (Sandburg) **67**:165
The Bremen Town Musicians (Domanska) **40**:49
The Bremen Town Musicians (Wilhelm) **46**:169
Brenda and Edward (Kovalski) **34**:114
Brendan the Navigator: A History Mystery about the Discovery of America (Fritz) **14**:114
Brer Rabbit and His Tricks (Gorey) **36**:92
Brer Rabbit: Stories from Uncle Remus (Brown) **10**:50
The Brian: Our Nervous System (Simon) **63**:163
Brian Wildsmith's 1, 2, 3s (Wildsmith) **2**:211
Brian Wildsmith's ABC (Wildsmith) **2**:208
Brian Wildsmith's Amazing World of Words (Wildsmith) **52**:201
Brian Wildsmith's Birds (Wildsmith) **2**:208
Brian Wildsmith's Circus (Wildsmith) **2**:209
Brian Wildsmith's Fishes (Wildsmith) **2**:210
Brian Wildsmith's Mother Goose: A Collection of Nursery Rhymes (Wildsmith) **2**:210
Brian Wildsmith's Puzzles (Wildsmith) **2**:211
Brian Wildsmith's The Twelve Days of Christmas (Wildsmith) **2**:212
Brian Wildsmith's Wild Animals (Wildsmith) **2**:212
Brian's Return (Paulsen) **54**:126
Brian's Winter (Paulsen) **54**:119
Brickyard Summer (Janeczko) **47**:109
The Bridge Between (St. John) **46**:99
Bridge of Friendship (Allan) **43**:26
Bridge to Terabithia (Paterson) **7**:232
Bridger: The Story of a Mountain Man (Kherdian) **24**:115
Bridges to Change: How Kids Live on a South Carolina Sea Island (Krull) **44**:109
Bridges to Cross (Janeczko) **47**:104
Bridget and William (Gardam) **12**:168
Bridie of the Wild Rose Inn (Armstrong) **66**:6-8,
A Bridle for Pegasus (Shippen) **36**:173
Bridle the Wind (Munsch) **19**:14
Briefe an Pauline (Kruss) **9**:87
Brigham Young and Me, Clarissa (Williams) **48**:196
The Bright and Morning Star (Harris) **30**:114
The Bright Design (Shippen) **36**:170
Bright Lights Blaze Out (Owen) **31**:145
Bright Morning (Bianco) **19**:57
Bright Shadow (Avi) **24**:12
Bright Shadow (Thomas) **19**:221
Bright Shark (Ballard) **60**:11
Bright Stars, Red Giants, and White Dwarfs (Berger) **32**:30
Brighty of the Grand Canyon (Henry) **4**:112
Bring to a Boil and Separate (Irwin) **40**:108
Bringing the Rain to Kapiti Plain (Aardema) **17**:6
Brinsly's Dream (Breinburg) **31**:68
British Folk Tales: New Versions (Crossley-Holland) **47**:45
The Broken Bridge (Pullman) **62**:157-9

The Broken Cord: A Family's Ongoing Struggle with Fetal Alcohol Syndrome (Dorris) **58**:78
The Broken Cord: A Father's Story (Dorris) **58**:78
Broken Days (Rinaldi) **46**:91
Broken Hearts (Stine) **37**:120
The Broken Spoke (Gorey) **36**:98
The Broken Sword (Anderson) **58**:9
Bronto's Wings (McKee) **38**:157
El Bronx Remembered: A Novella and Stories (Mohr) **22**:131
The Bronze Bow (Speare) **8**:208
The Bronze Trumpeter (Nimmo) **44**:138
Bronzeville Boys and Girls (Brooks) **27**:44-56
The Brooklyn Bridge: They Said it Couldn't Be Built (St. George) **57**:161
Brother André of Montreal (Clark) **16**:82
Brother, Can You Spare a Dime? The Great Depression, 1929-1933 (Meltzer) **13**:126
Brother Dusty-Feet (Sutcliff) **1**:184; **37**:150
Brother Eagle, Sister Sky: A Message from Chief Seattle (Jeffers) **30**:137
A Brother for Momoko (Iwasaki) **18**:153
Brother Night (Kelleher) **36**:127
Brother to the Wind (Leo and Diane Dillon) **44**:36
Brother to the Wind (Walter) **15**:207
The Brothers Grimm: Popular Folk Tales (Foreman) **32**:90
The Brothers Lionheart (Lindgren) **39**:154
Brothers of the Heart: A Story of the Old Northwest 1837-1838 (Blos) **18**:18
Brothers of the Wind (Yolen) **4**:268
Brown Angels: An Album of Pictures and Verse (Myers) **35**:204
"*The Brownie Books*" (Cox) **24**:65-83
Bruce Jenner: Decathalon Winner (Aaseng) **54**:9
Bruce of the Blue Nile (Silverberg) **59**:107
Bruderzwist (Grillparzer)
    See *Ein Bruderzwist in Habsburg*
Ein Bruderzwist im Hause Habsburg (Grillparzer)
    See *Ein Bruderzwist in Habsburg*
Brumbie Dust: A Selection of Stories (Ottley) **16**:185
Bruno Munari's ABC (Munari) **9**:125
Bruno Munari's Zoo (Munari) **9**:127
Bub, or the Very Best Thing (Babbitt) **53**:38
Bubble, Bubble (Mayer) **11**:167
Bubbles (Cummings) **48**:43
Bubbles (Greenfield) **4**:96
Bud, Not Buddy (Curtis) **68**:72, 75-76, 80-85
Buddha (Hitz) **58**:60
Buddha Stories (Hitz) **58**:63
Buddies (Park) **34**:156
Buddy's Adventures in the Blueberry Patch (Beskow) **17**:15
Budgerigar Blue (Mattingley) **24**:125
Buffalo Bill (d'Aulaire and d'Aulaire) **21**:51
The Buffalo Nickel Blues Band! (Gaberman) **33**:10
Buffalo: The American Bison Today (Patent) **19**:163
Buffalo Woman (Goble) **21**:134
Bufo: The Story of a Toad (McClung) **11**:179
Buford the Little Bighorn (Peet) **12**:198
The Bug That Laid the Golden Eggs (Selsam) **1**:160
Bugs for Dinner? The Eating Habits of Neighborhood Creatures (Epstein and Epstein) **26**:71
Bugs: Poems (Hoberman) **22**:112
Bugs Potter Live at Nickaninny (Korman) **25**:107
"*Build Soil: A Political Pastoral*" (Frost) **67**:77
Builder of the Moon (Wynne-Jones) **58**:189
Building Blocks (Voigt) **13**:235
Building Blocks of the Universe (Asimov) **12**:32
Building Construction (Berger) **32**:21
A Building on Your Street (Simon) **9**:207

Title Index

Title Index

Title Index

Title Index

Title Index